Third Edition

Walmart Locator

Directory of Stores in the United States

Roundabout Publications

Published by:

Roundabout Publications
P.O. Box 569
LaCygne, KS 66040

Phone: 913-203-7623
Internet: www.RoundaboutPublications.com

Library of Congress Control Number: 2017946424

ISBN-10: 1-885464-67-3
ISBN-13: 978-1-885464-67-5

Contents

Introduction

Walmart Locator is a directory of more than 3,850 Walmart and Walmart Supercenter stores across the United States. Following is an explanation of the layout and symbols used throughout this book.

Symbols Used In This Guide

State Maps:

A circle " ○ " is used to indicate cities and towns with a Walmart store. (Only those with a store are plotted on the map—cities and towns that do not have a store are not shown.) A solid circle " ● " indicates that fuel is available.

Store Detail Charts:

There are five columns in the chart with "icons" representing specific information for each store. The information includes:

1) " ☆ " Store Type: " ☆ " indicates Walmart and " ✪ " indicates Walmart Supercenter.

2) " ♡ " Distance from an Interstate: If 10 miles or less from an interstate exit, the number of miles is shown.

3) " 🕐 " Store hours: A " ✓ " is used to identify stores that are open 24-hours.

4) " ⛽ " Fuel Type: A " ◆ " is used for gasoline and " ❖ " for gasoline and diesel fuel.

5) " 🚫 " No Overnight Parking: A " ✓ " is used to identify stores that do not allow overnight parking.

State Maps

The *State Maps* provide a quick and easy way to locate stores and identify the availability of fuel. (Only towns with a Walmart are shown on the map.) Locations with fuel have the solid circle. Some metropolitan areas with stores in multiple cities are identified on the map in **Bold** type. See "Metro Area Charts" below for more information.

Metro Area Charts

Due to space restrictions on the map, some larger metropolitan areas are identified in **Bold** type. The associated "Area Chart" shows a complete list of the cities within that metro area. Refer to the specific city in the "Store Detail Charts" for information on each location.

Store Detail Charts

Following the *State Map* and any *Metro Area Charts* are the details for each store. The chart starts with the five columns described above. Store locations are listed alphabetically by city name within the chart. Store details include address, zip code, and phone number, followed by driving directions to the store.

Overnight Parking

Overnight parking in Walmart parking lots is popular among RVers. Walmart's official policy is to allow RVers to park overnight where they are able. Permission is granted by individual store managers, based on availability of parking space and local laws.

The overnight parking information included in this guide is used with permission from the owner of the Walmart RVing group on Yahoo. Please note that this information can and does change frequently. If you desire to park overnight in any particular location, it is highly recommended that you seek permission from the store manager. Do not rely solely on the information in this guide.

ALABAMA

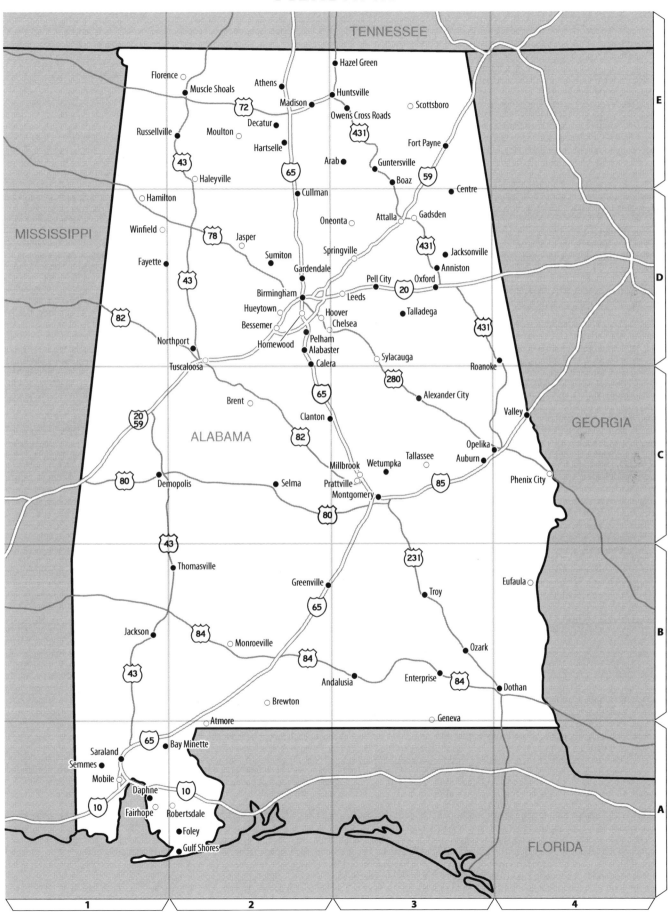

TENNESSEE

Hazel Green

Florence
Muscle Shoals
Athens
Madison
Huntsville
72
Scottsboro
Decatur
Owens Cross Roads
Russellville
Moulton
431
Fort Payne
Hartselle
43
Arab
Guntersville
Haleyville
65
Boaz
59
Centre
Hamilton
Cullman
MISSISSIPPI
Oneonta
Attalla
Gadsden
Winfield
78
Jasper
Springville
431
Jacksonville
Fayette
Sumiton
Anniston
43
Gardendale
Pell City
Oxford
Birmingham
Leeds
20
Hueytown
Hoover
Talladega
82
Bessemer
Chelsea
431
Northport
Homewood
Pelham
Alabaster
Tuscaloosa
Calera
Sylacauga
Roanoke
280
Brent
Alexander City
ALABAMA
Valley
20 59
Clanton
82
GEORGIA
Opelika
80
Millbrook
Wetumpka
Tallassee
Auburn
Demopolis
Selma
Prattville
Phenix City
Montgomery
85
80
231
43
Thomasville
Eufaula
Greenville
Troy
65
Jackson
Monroeville
Ozark
84
43
84
Enterprise
Dothan
Andalusia
84
Brewton
Geneva
Atmore
65
Bay Minette
Saraland
Semmes
Mobile
10
Daphne
10
Fairhope
Robertsdale
Foley
Gulf Shores
FLORIDA

1   2   3   4

E
D
C
B
A

☆	♡	⏰	⛽	🚫	Store Details
✪	1	✓	❖		Alabaster • 630 Colonial Promenade Pkwy, 35007 • 205-620-0360 • I-65 Exit 238 go E .3 mile on US-31 then N .6 mile on Colonial Promenade Pkwy
✪		✓	◆		Alexander City • 2643 Hwy 280, 35010 • 256-234-0316 • West end of town near jct of US-280 and SR-22
✪			❖		Andalusia • 1991 Dr M L King Jr Expy, 36420 • 334-222-6561 • East end of town near jct of US-84 and SR-100
✪	8	✓	◆		Anniston • 5560 McClellan Blvd, 36206 • 256-820-3326 • I-20 Exit 185 go N 6.2 miles on US-431 then N 1.8 miles on SR-21
✪		✓	❖		Arab • 1450 N Brindlee Mountain Pkwy, 35016 • 256-586-8168 • 1.4 miles north of town on US-231
✪	2	✓	◆		Athens • 1011 US Hwy 72 E, 35611 • 256-230-2981 • I-65 Exit 351 go W 1.2 miles on US-72
☆		✓			Atmore • 911 N Main St, 36502 • 251-368-1403 • 1 mile north of town center along SR-21
✪	1	✓			Attalla • 973 Gilbert Ferry Rd SE, 35954 • 256-538-3811 • I-59 Exit 181, west of exit
✪	1	✓	◆		Auburn • 1717 S College St, 36832 • 334-821-2493 • I-85 Exit 51 go W .9 mile on SR-147
✪	6	✓	❖		Bay Minette • 701 McMeans Ave, 36507 • 251-937-5558 • I-65 Exit 34 go SE 3.8 miles on AL-59 then S 2 miles on Bypass
✪	1	✓			Bessemer • 750 Academy Dr, 35022 • 205-424-5890 • I-20/I-59 Exit 108, southeast of exit
✪	1	✓	❖		Birmingham • 9248 Parkway E, 35206 • 205-833-7676 • I-59 Exit 134, north of exit
✪	1	✓			Birmingham • 1600 Montclair Rd, 35210 • 205-956-0416 • I-20 Exit 132, south of exit
✪	6	✓			Birmingham • 2473 Hackworth Rd, 35214 • 205-798-9721 • I-20/59 Exit 123 go N on US-78 about 6 miles
✪	1	✓			Birmingham • 5919 Trussville Crossings Pkwy, 35235 • 205-661-1957 • I-59 Exit 141, west of exit
✪		✓	❖		Boaz • 1972 US Hwy 431, 35957 • 256-593-0195 • Northeast side of town on US-431 at Butler Ave
✪					Brent • 10675 Hwy 5, 35034 • 205-926-4878 • 2.3 miles southwest of town center near jct of SR-5 and SR-25
✪					Brewton • 2578 Douglas Ave, 36426 • 251-867-4680 • 3 miles north of town center on US-31 (Douglas Ave)

☆	♡	⏰	⛽	🚫	Store Details
✪	1	✓	❖		Calera • 5100 Hwy 31, 35040 • 205-668-0831 • I-65 Exit 231, east of exit
✪		✓	❖		Centre • 1950 W Main St, 35960 • 256-927-9900 • Northwest of downtown about 2 miles on US-411/SR-25
✪		✓			Chelsea • 16077 Hwy 280, 35043 • 205-678-2222 • Northeast of town center about 1.5 miles on US-280/SR-38
✪	2	✓	◆		Clanton • 1415 7th St S, 35045 • 205-755-7574 • I-65 Exit 205 go W 2 miles on US-31
✪	1	✓			Cullman • 5601 Hwy 157, 35058 • 256-615-6667 • I-65 Exit 310 go E .6 mile on SR-157
✪	3	✓	❖		Cullman • 626 Olive St SW, 35055 • 256-739-1664 • I-65 Exit 304 go E on SR-69 about 3 miles
✪	6	✓	❖	✓	Daphne • 27520 US Hwy 98, 36526 • 251-626-0923 • I-10 Exit 35 go S on US-98 for 5.6 miles
✪	6	✓	◆		Decatur • 2800 Spring Ave SW, 35603 • 256-350-4624 • I-65 Exit 334 go W 5.8 miles on SR-67, left at Spring Ave SW
✪		✓	❖		Demopolis • 969 US Hwy 80 W, 36732 • 334-289-2385 • 1.2 miles southwest of town via US-80
✪		✓	❖		Dothan • 3300 S Oates St, 36301 • 334-702-1310 • 3.2 miles south of town center via US-231 BR (S Oates St)
✪		✓	❖		Dothan • 4310 Montgomery Hwy, 36303 • 334-793-3099 • 4.2 miles northwest of town center via US-231 BR (N Oates St) and US-231 (Montgomery Hwy)
✪		✓	◆		Enterprise • 600 Boll Weevil Cir, 36330 • 334-347-5353 • From town center, go E 1.7 miles on SR-27/88/134, then N .6 mile on US-84
✪					Eufaula • 3176 S Eufaula Ave, 36027 • 334-687-2218 • 3.7 miles south of town center via US-431
✪		✓			Fairhope • 10040 Fairhope Ave Ext, 36532 • 251-990-9006 • From town center, go E on Fairhope Ave (CR-48) 3 miles
✪		✓	◆		Fayette • 3186 Hwy 171 N, 35555 • 205-932-5277 • 3.5 miles north of town center via US-43
✪		✓			Florence • 3100 Hough Rd, 35630 • 256-767-7581 • From town center, follow US-43/US-72 E 3.7 miles, turn left (north) on SR-133 and go .5 mile to Hough Rd and turn right
✪		✓			Florence • 2701 Cloverdale Rd, 35633 • 256-712-6410 • Located 3.5 miles north of town center, north of SR-133 on Cloverdale Rd
✪		✓	◆		Foley • 2200 S McKenzie St, 36535 • 251-943-3400 • 1.6 miles south of town center via SR-59

☆	⬭	🕐	⛽	🚫	Store Details
✪	1	✓	◆		Fort Payne • 2001 Glenn Blvd SW, 35968 • 256-845-3163 • I-59 Exit 218, west of exit
✪	6	✓			Gadsden • 340 E Meighan Blvd, 35903 • 256-547-2637 • I-59 Exit 183 go W 5.3 miles on US-278/US-431
✪	1	✓	❖		Gardendale • 890 Odum Rd, 35071 • 205-631-8110 • I-65 Exit 271 go E .3 mile on Fieldstown Rd then S .3 mile on Odum Rd
☆					Geneva • 1608 W Magnolia Ave, 36340 • 334-684-3681 • Northwest of town near jct of Maple Ave (SR-52) and Magnolia Ave (SR-196)
✪	1	✓	❖		Greenville • 501 Willow Ln, 36037 • 334-382-2655 • I-65 Exit 130 go N .2 mile on SR-185, W .1 mile on Cahaba Rd, then S .2 mile
✪		✓	❖	✓	Gulf Shores • 170 E Fort Morgan Rd, 36542 • 251-968-5871 • 1.2 miles southwest of town near jct of Gulf Shores Pkwy (SR-59) and Fort Morgan Rd (SR-180)
✪		✓	◆		Guntersville • 11697 US Hwy 431, 35976 • 256-878-0685 • From town center, follow US-431 S 4.8 miles
✪					Haleyville • 42466 Hwy 195, 35565 • 205-486-9498 • 1.7 miles northeast of town center via SR-195
✪		✓			Hamilton • 1706 Military St S, 35570 • 205-921-3090 • From town center, S on US-43 for 1.5 miles
✪	4	✓	❖		Hartselle • 1201 Hwy 31 NW, 35640 • 256-773-1675 • I-65 Exit 328 go W 2.4 miles on Main St then N on US-31 about 1 mile
✪		✓	❖		Hazel Green • 14595 US 231, 35750 • 256-828-0486 • About 1 mile north of town center along US-231/US-431
✪	1	✓			Homewood • 209 Lakeshore Pkwy, 35209 • 205-945-8692 • I-65 Exit 255, west of exit
✪	4	✓			Hoover • 5335 Hwy 280, 35242 • 205-980-5156 • I-459 Exit 19 go E on US-280 3.6 miles
✪	2	✓			Hoover • 2780 John Hawkins Pkwy, 35244 • 205-733-0303 • I-459 Exit 10 go E on SR-150 1.7 miles
✪	2				Hueytown • 1007 Red Farmer Dr, 35023 • 205-744-9997 • I-20/I-59 Exit 115 go W 1 mile on Allison Bonnett Memorial Dr; turn right and continue W .2 mile on Red Farmer Dr
✪	4	✓		✓	Huntsville • 3031 Memorial Pkwy SW, 35801 • 256-536-2870 • 3.2 miles south of I-565 Exit 19 on the east side of US-231 at Drake Ave

☆	⬭	🕐	⛽	🚫	Store Details
✪	8	✓	◆		Huntsville • 11610 Memorial Pkwy SW, 35803 • 256-881-0581 • I-565 Exit 19 go S 8 miles on US-231 (S Memorial Pkwy)
✪	3	✓			Huntsville • 6140A University Dr, 35806 • 256-837-7272 • I-565 Exit 14 go N 2.2 miles on Research Park Blvd (SR-255) then W on University Dr. Westbound travelers use I-565 Exit 14B.
✪	2	✓	❖		Huntsville • 2200 Sparkman Dr NW, 35810 • 256-852-2236 • I-565 Exit 21 go W on US-72 (Sparkman Dr) 1.7 miles
✪		✓	◆		Jackson • 4206 N College Ave, 36545 • 251-247-7101 • 3 miles northeast of town center along US-43 at Industrial Bypass
✪		✓	❖		Jacksonville • 1625 Pelham Rd S, 36265 • 256-435-8100 • I-20 Exit 185 go N 6 miles on US-431 then N 8 miles SR-21
✪		✓			Jasper • 1801 Hwy 78 E, 35501 • 205-384-1100 • 2 miles east of town center on US-78 (or 30 miles west of I-65 Exit 299 via SR-69)
✪	1	✓			Leeds • 8551 Whitfield Ave, 35094 • 205-699-0701 • I-20 Exit 144A, south of exit
✪	7	✓			Madison • 8580 Highway 72 W, 35758 • 256-716-6951 • I-565 Exit 9 go N 5.4 miles on Wall Triana Hwy then W 1.5 miles on US-72
✪	1	✓	◆		Madison • 8650 Madison Blvd, 35758 • 256-461-7403 • I-565 Exit 8 go N to Madison Blvd and turn right
✪	1	✓		✓	Millbrook • 145 Kelley Blvd, 36054 • 334-285-0311 • I-65 Exit 181, east of exit
✪	1	✓			Mobile • 101 E I-65 Service Rd S, 36606 • 251-471-1105 • I-65 Exit 4 go E .2 mile on Dauphin St, S .1 mile on Springdale Bld, W .3 mile on I-65 Service Rd
✪	1	✓		✓	Mobile • 5245 Rangeline Service Rd S, 36619 • 251-666-7972 • I-10 Exit 17, west of exit
✪	10	✓			Mobile • 2500 Dawes Rd, 36695 • 251-633-6023 • I-10 exit 10 take McDonald Rd (CR-39) N 3.6 miles, Three Notch Rd W 2 miles & Dawes Rd N 3.8 miles
✪	7	✓			Mobile • 685 Schillinger Rd S, 36695 • 251-633-2211 • I-65 Exit 3 go W 6 miles on Airport Blvd then S .3 mile on Schillinger Rd
✪					Monroeville • 3371 S Alabama Ave, 36460 • 251-575-3333 • I-65 Exit 93 go W 21.6 miles on SR-12/US-84 then N 1.3 miles on SR-41
✪	1	✓	❖		Montgomery • 851 Ann St, 36107 • 334-223-7177 • I-85 Exit 3, north of exit on Ann St

☆	♡	🕐	⛽	🚫	Store Details
✪	3	✓			Montgomery • 3801 Eastern Blvd, 36116 • 334-284-4181 • I-85 Exit 6 go S on US-80 about 2.5 miles
✪	1	✓			Montgomery • 10710 Chantilly Pkwy, 36117 • 334-272-7377 • I-85 Exit 11, south of exit
✪	3	✓	❖		Montgomery • 6495 Atlanta Hwy, 36117 • 334-272-0263 • I-85 Exit 9 go N on SR-271 1.5 miles and then W .6 mile on US-80 (Atlanta Hwy)
✪		✓			Moulton • 15445 AL Hwy 24, 35650 • 256-974-1128 • 1.7 miles northeast of town center at jct of SR-24 and SR-157
✪		✓	◆		Muscle Shoals • 517 Avalon Ave, 35661 • 256-381-0987 • From jct of US-72 and US-43, go N on US-43 2.3 miles, left at Avalon Ave, .4 mile to store
✪	9	✓	◆		Northport • 5710 McFarland Blvd, 35476 • 205-333-7820 • 1.2 miles west of town center (or 9 miles northwest of I-20/59 Exit 73 via US-82)
✪		✓		✓	Oneonta • 2453 2nd Ave E, 35121 • 205-625-6474 • 2.2 miles northeast of town center via SR-75
✪	2	✓	❖		Opelika • 2900 Pepperell Pkwy, 36801 • 334-745-9333 • I-85 Exit 58 go N about 1.6 miles to US-29 and then west about .5 mile
✪		✓	❖		Owens Cross Roads • 330 Sutton Rd SE, 35763 • 256-534-4140 • 9 miles southeast of Huntsville via US-431
✪	1	✓	❖		Oxford • 92 Plaza Ln, 36203 • 256-835-4701 • I-20 Exit 185 go S on SR-21 .3 mile, left on Plaza Ln
✪		✓	◆		Ozark • 1537 S US Hwy 231, 36360 • 334-774-0272 • 1.8 miles southwest of town center near jct of US-231 and SR-249
✪	2	✓	❖		Pelham • 2181 Pelham Pkwy, 35124 • 205-987-0108 • I-65 Exit 246 go W on SR-119 .7 mile and then N .5 mile on US-31
✪	1	✓	❖		Pell City • 165 Vaughan Ln, 35125 • 205-338-5300 • I-20 Exit 158, north of exit
✪		✓			Phenix City • 3700 Hwy 431 N, 36867 • 334-291-1700 • 4 miles northwest of town center on US-431 at S Railroad St
✪	2	✓			Prattville • 1903 Cobbs Ford Rd, 36066 • 334-361-2135 • I-65 Exit 179 go W 1.7 miles on Cobbs Ford Rd
✪		✓	❖		Roanoke • 4180 Hwy 431, 36274 • 334-863-2147 • 1 mile north of town on US-431
✪	10	✓			Robertsdale • 21141 State Hwy 59, 36567 • 251-947-4424 • I-10 Exit 49 go S 7.4 miles on Baldwin Beach Express then W 2.5 miles on CR-48
✪		✓	❖		Russellville • 13675 Hwy 43, 35653 • 256-332-7382 • 1.7 miles south of town center via Madison St and US-43
✪	1	✓	❖		Saraland • 1095 Industrial Pkwy, 36571 • 251-675-8000 • I-65 Exit 13, east of exit
✪		✓			Scottsboro • 24833 John T Reid Pkwy, 35768 • 256-574-1126 • On US-72 about .5 mile north of US-72/SR-35 jct
✪		✓	◆		Selma • 1501 AL Hwy 14 E, 36703 • 334-874-7793 • 2 miles northeast of town center at US-80 and SR-14 jct
✪	8	✓	❖		Semmes • 7855 Moffett Rd, 36575 • 251-645-8224 • I-65 Exit 5B go W 8 miles on US-98
✪	2	✓			Springville • 160 Springville Station Blvd, 35146 • 205-467-6656 • I-59 Exit 156 go N .4 mile on SR-23 then W 1 mile on US-11
✪		✓	❖		Sumiton • 690 Hwy 78, 35148 • 205-648-4100 • 1 mile southeast of town center on US-78 at Bryan Rd
✪		✓			Sylacauga • 41301 US Hwy 280, 35150 • 256-245-0356 • 2.6 miles west of town center along US-280 near airport
✪		✓	❖		Talladega • 214 Haynes St, 35160 • 256-761-1681 • I-20 Exit 168 go S 12.7 miles on SR-7
✪					Tallassee • 2190 Gilmer Ave, 36078 • 334-283-6841 • 3.3 miles northwest of town center along SR-14
✪		✓	◆		Thomasville • 34301 Hwy 43, 36784 • 334-636-0219 • 1.8 miles north of town on US-43 at SR-5
✪		✓	◆		Troy • 1420 Hwy 231 S, 36081 • 334-566-8012 • 3.6 miles southeast of town center via SR-87 and US-231
✪	1	✓			Tuscaloosa • 1501 Skyland Blvd E, 35405 • 205-750-0823 • I-20/I-59 Exit 73 go S .2 mile on US-82 (McFarland Blvd) then E .3 mile on US-11 (Skyland Blvd)
✪	1	✓	◆		Valley • 3501 20th Ave, 36854 • 334-768-2118 • I-85 Exit 79 go S .8 mile on US-29
✪		✓	❖		Wetumpka • 4538 US Hwy 231, 36092 • 334-567-3066 • I-85 Exit 6 go N 11.5 miles on US-231
✪					Winfield • 2575 US Hwy 43 W, 35594 • 205-487-4359 • From town center, follow US-43 NW about 1.5 miles

ALASKA

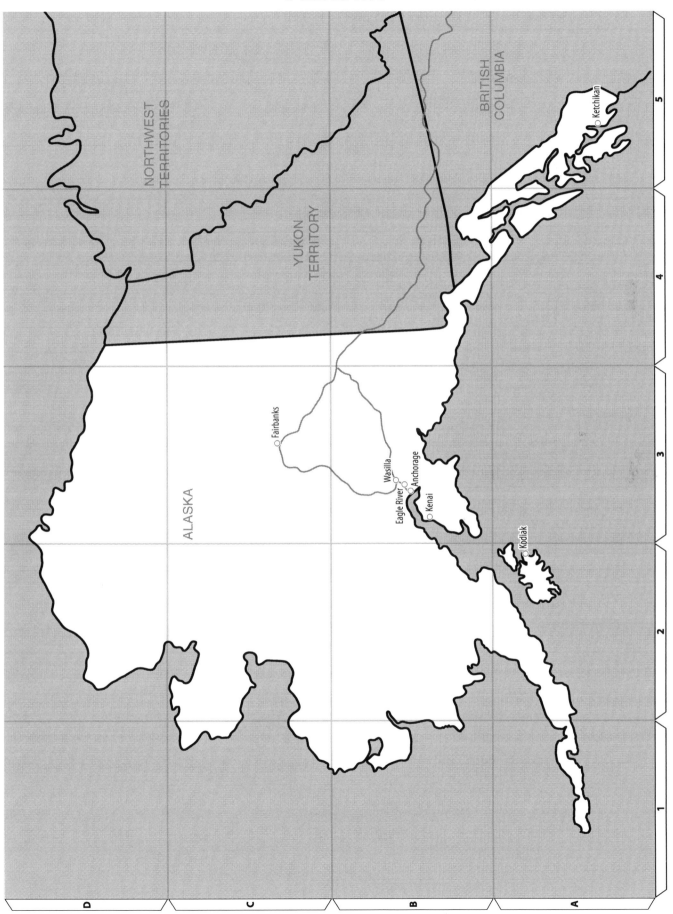

☆	◯	🕐	⛽	🚫	Store Details
✪				✓	Anchorage • 3101 A St, 99503 • 907-563-5900 • From SR-1 at Tudor Rd go W .6 mile, N on "C" St .2 mile, continue on "A" St .6 mile
✪				✓	Anchorage • 7405 Debarr Rd, 99504 • 907-339-9039 • 1/2 mile west of Seward Hwy via Dimond Blvd and Old Seward Hwy.
✪		✓		✓	Anchorage • 8900 Old Seward Hwy, 99515 • 907-344-5300 • From SR-1 at Dimond Blvd go W .2 mile then S on Old Seward Hwy .3 mile
✪		✓		✓	Eagle River • 18600 Eagle River Rd, 99577 • 907-694-9780 • From SR-1 at Eagle River Loop Rd go NE 2.6 miles
✪		✓			Fairbanks • 537 Johansen Expy, 99701 • 907-451-9900 • Jct SR-2 & SR-3 go N on SR-2 for 3.2 miles then W on Johansen Expy .3 mile
✪		✓			Kenai • 10096 Kenai Spur Hwy, 99611 • 907-395-0971 • 1 mile east of town via Kenai Spur Highway
☆					Ketchikan • 4230 Don King Rd, 99901 • 907-247-2156 • 4 miles northwest of town via SR-7 and Signot Rd
☆					Kodiak • 2911 Mill Bay Rd, 99615 • 907-481-1670 • From Abercrombie Historical Site (north of town) go S on Rezanof Dr .9 mile then SW on Mill Bay Rd .4 mile
✪		✓			Wasilla • 1350 S Seward Meridian Pkwy, 99654 • 907-376-9780 • 3.2 miles east of town center via SR-3 and Seward Meridian Pkwy

ARIZONA

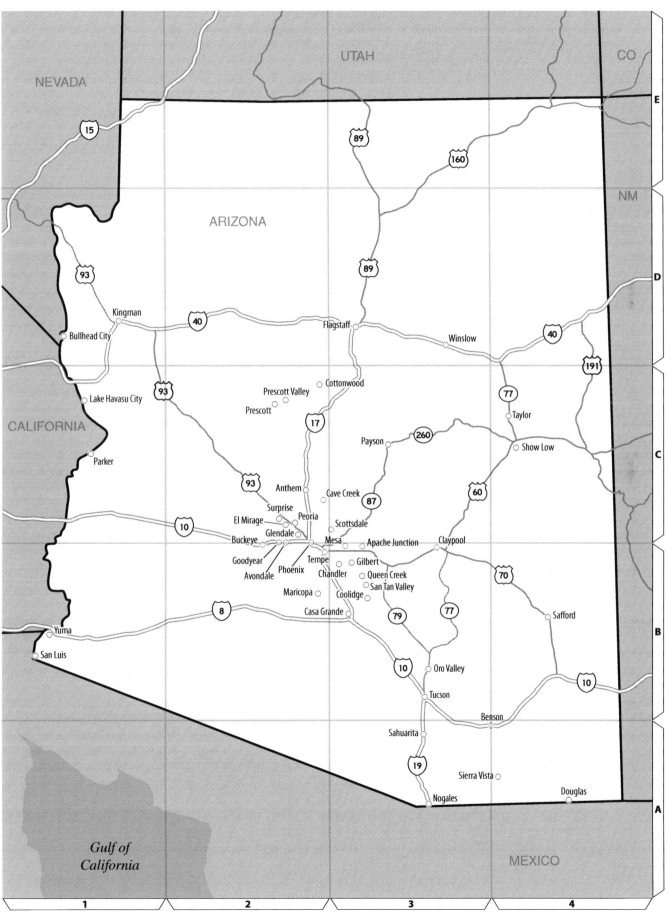

☆	♡	🕐	⛽	🚫	Store Details
✪	2	✓		✓	Anthem • 4435 W Anthem Way, 85086 • 623-551-6314 • I-17 Exit 229 go E on Anthem Way 1.4 miles
✪		✓		✓	Apache Junction • 2555 W Apache Trl, 85220 • 480-380-3800 • US-60 Exit 193 go N on Signal Butte Rd 1.9 miles then E on Apache Trl 1.4 miles
✪	1	✓			Avondale • 13055 W Rancho Santa Fe Blvd, 85323 • 623-935-4010 • I-10 Exit 129 go N on Dysart Rd .2 mile & east at W Rancho Santa Fe .1 mile
✪	2	✓		✓	Benson • 201 S Prickly Pear Ave, 85602 • 520-586-0742 • I-10 Exit 303 continue I-10 BR/SR-80 E for .9 mile & S on Prickly Pear .2 mile
✪	3	✓		✓	Buckeye • 1060 S Watson Rd, 85326 • 623-474-6728 • I-10 Exit 117 go S on Watson Rd 2.2 miles
✪		✓		✓	Bullhead City • 2840 Hwy 95, 86442 • 928-758-7222 • I-40 Exit 1 go N on SR-95 for 16.4 miles
✪	2	✓		✓	Casa Grande • 1741 E Florence Blvd, 85222 • 520-421-1200 • I-10 Exit 287 go W on SR-287/Florence Blvd 1.4 miles
✪				✓	Cave Creek • 34399 N Cave Creek Rd, 85331 • 480-296-7398 • I-17 Exit 223 go E 10 miles on Carefree Hwy then S .1 mile on Cave Creek Rd
✪				✓	Chandler • 800 W Warner Rd, 85225 • 480-786-0062 • SR-101 Loop Exit 58 go E on Warner Rd 2.3 miles
✪	9	✓		✓	Chandler • 1175 S Arizona Ave, 85248 • 480-726-0841 • I-10 Exit 161 go E on SR-202 Loop 8 miles then SR-87 N .2 mile
✪		✓			Chandler • 2750 E Germann Rd, 85249 • 480-812-2930 • SR-202 Loop Exit 44 go S on Gilbert .3 mile then W on Germann .3 mile
✪	4	✓			Chandler • 3460 W Chandler Blvd, 85226 • 480-333-2654 • I-10 Exit 160 go E 4 miles on Chandler Blvd
☆					Claypool • 100 S Ragus Rd, 85532 • 928-425-7171 • Jct US-60 & US-70 (SE of Claypool) take US-60 NW 5.5 miles then S on Ragus Rd
✪		✓			Coolidge • 1695 N Arizona Blvd, 85228 • 520-723-0945 • I-10 Exit 185 take SR-387 E 7.3 miles, SR-87 SE 7 miles & S on N Arizona Blvd .2 mile
✪		✓		✓	Cottonwood • 2003 E Rodeo Dr, 86326 • 928-634-0444 • I-17 Exit 287 take SR-260/279 NW 11.9 miles then S at Rodeo Dr .2 mile
✪		✓		✓	Douglas • 199 W 5th St, 85607 • 520-364-1281 • 1.5 miles west of town center off US-191 at 5th St

☆	♡	🕐	⛽	🚫	Store Details
✪		✓		✓	El Mirage • 12900 W Thunderbird Rd, 85335 • 623-583-1321 • SR-101 Loop Exit 11 take US-60 NW 3.3 miles, S at "A" St .1 mile & W on Thunderbird 1.3 miles
☆	1			✓	Flagstaff • 2750 S Woodlands Village Blvd, 86001 • 928-773-1117 • I-17 Exit 341 go W on McConnell Dr .2 mile, S on Beulah .2 mile & W on Woodlands Village .2 mile
✪	2	✓		✓	Flagstaff • 2601 E Huntington Dr, 86004 • 928-774-3409 • I-40 Exit 198 go W .4 mile on Butler Ave then N 1 mile on Huntington Dr
✪		✓		✓	Gilbert • 5290 S Power Rd, 85295 • 480-988-0012 • SR-202 Loop Exit 42 go S on Val Vista Dr 1.7 miles, E on Queen Creek Rd 4 miles & S on Power Rd .9 mile
✪		✓		✓	Gilbert • 2501 S Market St, 85296 • 480-224-6900 • SR-202 Loop Exit 40 go W .3 mile on Williams Field Rd then S .2 mile on Market St
✪		✓		✓	Glendale • 5605 W Northern Ave, 85301 • 623-934-6920 • SR-101 Loop Exit 8 go E on Northern Ave 4.9 miles
✪		✓		✓	Glendale • 5010 N 95th Ave, 85305 • 623-872-0058 • SR-101 Loop Exit 5 go E on Camelback Rd .4 mile & N at 95th
✪		✓		✓	Glendale • 18551 N 83rd Ave, 85308 • 623-825-1129 • SR-101 Loop Exit 15 go W on Union Hills Dr .4 mile & S on 83rd .5 mile
✪				✓	Glendale • 5845 W Bell Rd, 85308 • 602-978-8205 • SR-101 Loop Exit 14 go E on Bell Rd for 3 miles
✪	1	✓		✓	Goodyear • 1100 N Estrella Pkwy, 85338 • 623-925-9575 • I-10 Exit 126 go S on Estrella Pkwy .2 mile
✪	1	✓			Kingman • 3396 N Stockton Hill Rd, 86409 • 928-692-0555 • I-40 Exit 51 go N on Stockton Hill Rd .3 mile
✪		✓		✓	Lake Havasu City • 5695 Hwy 95 N, 86404 • 928-453-5655 • I-40 Exit 9 go S 12.4 miles on SR-95
✪		✓		✓	Maricopa • 41650 W Maricopa Casa Grande, 85238 • 520-568-0846 • 2.2 miles southeast of town center via Maricopa Casa Grande Hwy
✪		✓		✓	Mesa • 857 N Dobson Rd, 85201 • 480-962-0038 • SR-202 Loop Exit 10 go south on N Dobson Rd .3 mile
✪		✓		✓	Mesa • 1955 S Stapley Dr, 85204 • 480-892-9009 • US-60 Exit 193 go S on Stapley Dr .6 mile
✪		✓		✓	Mesa • 1606 S Signal Butte Rd, 85206 • 480-358-1122 • US-60 Exit 193 take Signal Butte Rd N for 4 miles

☆	○	⏰	⛽	🚭	Store Details
●		✓		✓	Mesa • 1710 S Greenfield Rd, 85206 • 480-892-3814 • US-60 Exit 185 go S on Greenfield Rd .3 mile
●		✓		✓	Mesa • 6131 E Southern Ave, 85206 • 480-830-3919 • US-60 Exit 186 go N on Higley Rd .5 mile & E on Southern Ave 1.2 miles
●		✓		✓	Mesa • 240 W Baseline Rd, 85210 • 480-668-9501 • US-60 Exit 179 go S on Country Club Dr .5 mile then E on Baseline Rd .2 mile
●		✓		✓	Mesa • 4505 E McKellips Rd, 85215 • 480-641-6728 • SR-202 Loop Exit 21 go south on N Higley Rd 2.1 miles & W on McKellips .9 mile
●	2	✓			Nogales • 100 W White Park Dr, 85621 • 520-281-4974 • I-19 Exit 4 go E on SR-189 for .4 mile & S on Southern Ave 1.2 miles
●		✓		✓	Oro Valley • 2150 E Tangerine Rd, 85737 • 520-544-0016 • I-10 Exit 240 go E 13 miles on Tangerine Rd
●		✓			Page • 1017 W Haul Rd, 86040 • 928-645-2622 • 2 miles southwest of town along US-89 at Haul Rd
●					Parker • 100 Riverside Dr, 85344 • 928-669-2161 • .8 miles northeast of town center via SR-95
●		✓			Payson • 300 N Beeline Hwy, 85541 • 928-474-0029 • Jct SR-188 & SR-87 take SR-87 N 16.3 miles
●		✓		✓	Peoria • 7975 W Peoria Ave, 85345 • 623-878-9907 • SR-101 Loop Exit 10 go E 1.4 miles on Peoria Ave
●		✓		✓	Peoria • 21655 N Lake Pleasant Pkwy, 85382 • 623-537-0809 • SR-101 Exit 15 go W 2.7 miles on Union Hills Dr then N 2.2 miles on 99th Ave/Lake Pleasant Rd
●	2	✓		✓	Phoenix • 1607 W Bethany Home Rd, 85015 • 602-246-1700 • I-17 Exit 204 go E on Bethany Home Rd 1.1 miles
●	2	✓			Phoenix • 6145 N 35th Ave, 85017 • 602-973-0774 • I-17 Exit 204 take Bethany Home Rd W 1.3 miles & N on 35th for .2 mile
●		✓		✓	Phoenix • 3721 E Thomas Rd, 85018 • 602-685-0555 • SR-202 Loop Exit 2 take 40th St N 1.5 miles & W on Thomas Rd .3 mile
●	1	✓		✓	Phoenix • 1825 W Bell Rd, 85023 • 602-942-4138 • I-17 Exit 212 go E on Bell Rd for .9 mile
●	3	✓			Phoenix • 5250 W Indian School Rd, 85031 • 623-845-8713 • I-10 Exit 139 take 51st Ave N 2.2 miles then W on Indian School Rd .2 mile
☆					Phoenix • 4617 E Bell Rd, 85032 • 602-482-7575 • SR-101 Loop Exit 29 take SR-51 S 2.2 miles then E on Bell Rd .3 mile
●	9				Phoenix • 4747 E Cactus Rd, 85032 • 602-404-3712 • I-17 Exit 210 go E 8.3 miles on Thunderbird Rd (which becomes Cactus Rd)
●	1	✓		✓	Phoenix • 2020 N 75th Ave, 85035 • 623-849-1030 • I-10 Exit 136 go S on 75th Ave for .8 mile
●	5	✓		✓	Phoenix • 6150 S 35th Ave, 85041 • 602-243-8506 • I-17 Exit 197 take 19th Ave S 1.6 miles, Broadway W 2 miles & 35th Ave S 1.1 miles
●	3	✓		✓	Phoenix • 7575 W Lower Buckeye Rd, 85043 • 623-907-0007 • I-10 Exit 136 go S on 75th Ave 2.8 miles then W on Buckeye Rd
●	1	✓			Phoenix • 2501 W Happy Valley Rd, 85085 • 623-780-5702 • I-17 Exit 218 go W on Happy Valley Rd .7 mile
●		✓			Prescott • 3050 N Hwy 69, 86301 • 928-445-1113 • 4 miles east of town center via SR-69
●		✓			Prescott • 1280 Gail Gardner Way, 86305 • 928-541-0071 • From town center go N 1 mile on 3rd St, .7 mile W on Whipple St, continue W .5 mile on Iron Springs Rd, then go .2 mile N on Gail Gardner Way
●		✓			Prescott Valley • 3450 Glassford Hill Rd, 86314 • 928-499-3136 • From Prescott, go E 7.6 miles on SR-69 then N .6 mile on Glassford Hill Rd
●		✓			Queen Creek • 21055 S Rittenhouse Rd, 85242 • 480-457-1158 • I-10 Exit 167 go E 16.5 miles on Riggs Rd, N 2.5 miles on Ellsworth Rd, E .2 mile on Rittenhouse Rd
●		✓			Safford • 755 S 20th Ave, 85546 • 928-428-7990 • Jct US-191 & US-70 (E of town) take US-191/70 W 11.3 miles & 20th Ave S .8 mile
●	1	✓			Sahuarita • 18680 S Nogales Hwy, 85614 • 520-625-3808 • I-10 Exit 69 go NE on I-19 BR/Nogales Hwy 1 mile
●		✓			San Luis • 1613 N Main St, 85349 • 928-722-7278 • 1 mile north of town along US-95
●		✓		✓	San Tan Valley • 1725 W Hunt Hwy, 85143 • 480-677-2149 • SR-202 Loop Exit 33 go E on Elliot Rd .4 mile, S on Ellsworth 10 miles & W on Hunt Hwy 6.4 miles
●				✓	Scottsdale • 4915 N Pima Rd, 85251 • 480-941-0333 • SR-101 Loop Exit 46 go W on Chaparrel Rd .2 mile & S on Pima Rd

☆	🛡	🕐	⛽	🚫	Store Details
✪		✓		✓	Scottsdale • 15355 N Northsight Blvd, 85260 • 480-348-5505 • SR-101 Loop Exit 39 go W on Raintree Dr .4 mile & N on Northsight Blvd .5 mile
✪		✓			Show Low • 5401 S White Mountain Rd, 85901 • 928-537-3141 • Jct US-60 & SR-77 (E of town) take US-60 W .5 mile & White Mountain Rd S 4.1 miles
✪		✓		✓	Sierra Vista • 500 N Highway 90 Bypass, 85635 • 520-458-8790 • From town center go E 2.5 miles on Fry Blvd then N .3 mile on SR-90
✪		✓			Surprise • 13770 W Bell Rd, 85374 • 623-544-2200 • SR-101 Loop Exit 11 go W on Grand Ave 6.2 miles & W on Bell Rd .3 mile
✪		✓			Surprise • 14111 N Prasada Gateway Ave, 85388 • 623-282-3208 • I-10 Exit 127 go .2 miles N on Pebble Creek Pkwy, 2.1 miles W on McDowell Rd, 10 miles N on Cotton Ln, and .2 miles E on Waddell Rd
✪	1	✓			Taylor • 715 N Main St, 85939 • 928-536-2543 • 1/2 mile north of town center on Main St/SR-77
✪	3	✓		✓	Tempe • 800 E Southern Ave, 85282 • 480-966-0264 • I-10 Exit 154 follow US-60 E 1.9 miles to Exit 174 then go N .5 mile on Rural Rd
✪	2	✓			Tempe • 1380 W Elliot Rd, 85284 • 480-345-8686 • I-10 Exit 157 go E on Elliot Rd for 1.1mile
☆	4			✓	Tucson • 455 E Wetmore Rd, 85705 • 520-292-2992 • I-10 Exit 255 go E 1.4 miles on SR-77/Miracle Mile, N 1.8 miles on SR-77/Oracle Rd, and E .7 mile on Wetmore Rd
☆	7			✓	Tucson • 7150 E Speedway Blvd, 85710 • 520-751-1882 • I-10 Exit 270 go N on Kolb Rd for 9 miles
✪	'1	✓			Tucson • 1260 E Tucson Marketplace Blvd, 85713 • 520-917-0108 • I-10 Exit 262 go N .2 miles on Park Ave then E .1 mile on Tucson Marketplace Blvd
✪	4			✓	Tucson • 3435 E Broadway Blvd, 85716 • 520-917-1655 • I-10 Exit 258 go E .3 miles on Congress St then continue straight 3.3 miles on Broadway Blvd
✪	9	✓		✓	Tucson • 2711 S Houghton Rd, 85730 • 520-918-0087 • I-10 Exit 275 go N 9 miles on Houghton Rd
✪	4	✓		✓	Tucson • 7635 N La Cholla Blvd, 85741 • 520-297-0840 • I-10 Exit 248 go E on Ina Rd 3.2 miles & S on La Chella Blvd .4 mile
✪	1	✓			Tucson • 8280 N Cortaro, 85743 • 520-744-3652 • I-10 Exit 246 go SW on Cortaro Rd for .2 mile

☆	🛡	🕐	⛽	🚫	Store Details
✪	1	✓		✓	Tucson • 1650 W Valencia Rd, 85746 • 520-573-3777 • I-19 Exit 95 go east on W Valencia Rd .7 mile
✪	2	✓		✓	Tucson • 9260 S Houghton Rd, 85747 • 520-329-6674 • I-10 Exit 275 go N 1.7 miles on Houghton Rd
✪	1				Winslow • 700 Mikes Pike St, 86047 • 928-289-4641 • I-40 Exit 253 go NE on Mikes Pike .2 mile
✪	4	✓		✓	Yuma • 2501 S Avenue B, 85364 • 928-317-2776 • I-8 Exit 2 go W on 16th St 2.5 miles then S on US-95 1.2 miles
✪	3	✓		✓	Yuma • 2900 S Pacific Ave, 85365 • 928-344-0992 • I-8 Exit 2 go E on 16th St .5 mile then S on Pacific Ave 1.6 miles
✪	3	✓		✓	Yuma • 8151 E 32nd St, 85365 • 928-344-5974 • I-8 Exit 3 go S on SR-280 for 1.4 miles then W on 32nd St .9 mile

ARKANSAS

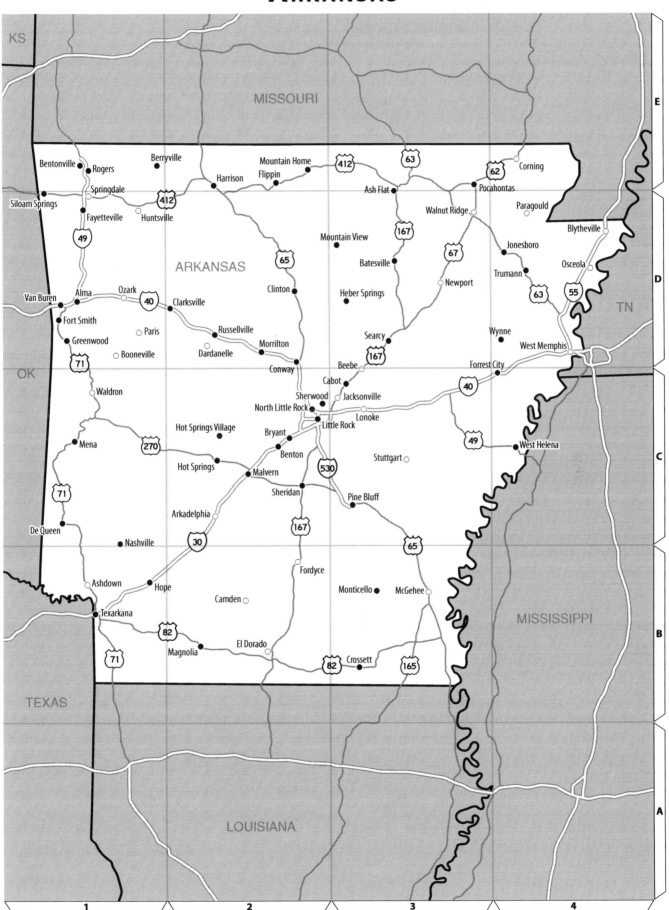

KS

MISSOURI

E

Bentonville • Rogers
Berryville

Mountain Home
Flippin

412
63
62 • Corning

Harrison

Springdale

412

Ash Flat

Pocahontas

Paragould

Siloam Springs

Fayetteville • Huntsville

Walnut Ridge

Blytheville

49

Mountain View

167

Jonesboro

ARKANSAS

65

Batesville

67

Osceola

D

Newport

Van Buren • Alma • Ozark
40 • Clarksville

Clinton

Heber Springs

Trumann

63

55

TN

Fort Smith

Paris

Russellville

Searcy

Wynne

Greenwood

Dardanelle

Morrilton

167

West Memphis

OK

Booneville

Conway

Beebe

Forrest City

Waldron

Cabot

40

Sherwood • Jacksonville

Hot Springs Village

North Little Rock

Lonoke

Bryant

Little Rock

49 • West Helena

C

Mena

270

Benton

Stuttgart

Hot Springs

Malvern

530

71

Sheridan

Pine Bluff

Arkadelphia

30

167

65

De Queen

Nashville

Fordyce

Ashdown • Hope

Camden

Monticello • McGehee

Texarkana

MISSISSIPPI

82

B

71

Magnolia

El Dorado

82 • Crossett

165

TEXAS

LOUISIANA

A

☆	🛡	🕐	⛽	🚫	Store Details
✪	1	✓	❖		Alma • 367 W Cherry St, 72921 • 479-632-4585 • I-40 Exit 13 take US-71 S .5 mile then W on US-64
✪	2	✓			Arkadelphia • 109 WP Malone Dr, 71923 • 870-246-2459 • I-30 Exit 73 take SR-8 W .3 mile then Malone Dr N 1.4 miles
✪		✓	❖		Ash Flat • 219 Hwy 412, 72513 • 870-994-7520 • Jct SR-56 & US-167 (south of town) take US-167 N 1.7 miles then US-412/62 NW .6 mile
✪		✓			Ashdown • 297 Hwy 32 Bypass, 71822 • 870-898-5126 • I-30 Exit 223B go N on US-59/71 for 14.6 miles then E on SR-32 Bypass
✪		✓	◆		Batesville • 3150 Harrison St, 72501 • 870-793-9004 • Jct SR-14 & US-167 (south of town) take US-167 N 2.6 miles then E on SR-69 for 1.7 miles
✪		✓			Beebe • 2003 W Center St, 72012 • 501-882-1017 • US-64 Exit 28, east of exit
✪	1	✓	◆		Benton • 17309 I-30, 72015 • 501-860-6135 • I-30 Exit 118 take the W Service Rd .5 mile
✪	3	✓	❖		Bentonville • 406 S Walton Blvd, 72712 • 479-273-0060 • I-49 Exit 86 go W 1.9 miles on 14th St then N .9 mile on Walton Blvd
✪		✓	◆		Berryville • 1000 W Trimble Ave, 72616 • 870-423-4636 • Jct SR-143 & US-62 (west of town) go E on US-62 for 2.2 miles
✪	1	✓			Blytheville • 3700 E Highway 18, 72315 • 870-763-0440 • I-55 Exit 67, east of exit
✪		✓			Booneville • 1400 E Main St, 72927 • 479-675-3688 • About 1 mile east of town center on Main St
✪	1	✓	❖		Bryant • 400 Bryant Ave, 72022 • 501-847-2857 • I-30 Exit 123 go W on Commerce .1 mile, N on Main St .1 mile & W on Bryant
✪		✓	◆		Cabot • 304 S Rockwood Dr, 72023 • 501-941-5200 • US-167/67 Exit 19 take SR-89 W .4 mile then S on Rockwood .2 mile
✪		✓			Camden • 950 California Ave, 71701 • 870-836-8000 • 1 mile south of town center via US-79
✪	1	✓	❖		Clarksville • 1230 E Market St, 72830 • 479-754-2046 • I-40 Exit 58 take SR-103 S .2 mile then E on Market St
✪		✓	❖		Clinton • 1966 Hwy 65 S, 72031 • 501-745-2498 • Jct SR-9 & US-65 (south of town) take US-65 N 2.8 miles
✪	1	✓	❖		Conway • 1155 Hwy 65 N, 72032 • 501-329-0023 • I-40 Exit 125 take US-65 BR south .2 mile
✪	5	✓	❖		Conway • 3900 Dave Ward Dr, 72034 • 501-328-9570 • I-40 Exit 129 take SR-286 W 4.3 miles
☆					Corning • 1900 W Main St, 72422 • 870-857-6914 • Jct US-62 & US-67 (in town) go W on US-67/Main St .5 mile
✪		✓	❖		Crossett • 910 Unity Rd, 71635 • 870-364-2165 • Jct US-425 & US-82 (east of town) take US-82 W 6.8 miles
✪	9	✓			Dardanelle • 1172 N State Hwy 7, 72834 • 479-229-2502 • I-40 Exit 81 take SR-7 S 8.3 miles
✪		✓	❖		De Queen • 926 E Collin Raye Dr, 71832 • 870-642-2794 • Jct US-371 & US-59/71 (southeast of town) take US-59/71 W 12.7 miles
✪		✓			El Dorado • 2730 N West Ave, 71730 • 870-862-2128 • Jct SR-7 & US-167 BR (northeast of town) follow US-167 BR for 1.5 miles
✪	3	✓	❖	✓	Fayetteville • 3919 N Mall Ave, 72703 • 479-443-7679 • I-49 Exit 67 go NE 1.7 miles on Fulbright Expy/US-71-BUS then W .4 mile on Joyce Blvd
✪	1	✓	◆		Fayetteville • 2875 W 6th St, 72704 • 479-582-0428 • I-49 Exit 62 go W on US-62 for .5 mile
✪		✓	❖		Flippin • 168 Walmart Dr, 72634 • 870-453-2211 • West of town center, .5 mile south of US-62/SR-178 jct
☆					Fordyce • 1123 N Hwy 79, 71742 • 870-352-5167 • Jct US-167 & US-79 (north of town) take US-79 N .4 mile
✪	1	✓	◆		Forrest City • 205 Deadrick Rd, 72335 • 870-633-0021 • I-40 Exit 241 go S on Washington St .6 mile then W on Deadrick
✪	1	✓	◆		Fort Smith • 2425 Zero St, 72901 • 479-646-6382 • I-49 Exit 11 go W on SR-255 for .8 mile
✪	2	✓			Fort Smith • 8301 Rogers Ave, 72903 • 479-484-5205 • I-49 Exit 8 (southbound use Exit 8A) take Rogers Ave SE for 1.9 miles
✪	1	✓	❖		Fort Smith • 2100 N 62nd St, 72904 • 479-785-5964 • I-49 Exit 5, east of exit
✪	9	✓	❖		Greenwood • 551 Liberty Dr, 72936 • 479-996-8500 • I-540 Exit 12 go SE 9 miles on US-71
✪		✓	◆		Harrison • 1417 Hwy 65 N, 72601 • 870-365-8400 • Jct SR-43 & US-62/65 (northwest of town) go NW on US-62/65 for .8 mile
✪		✓	◆		Heber Springs • 1500 Hwy 25B N, 72543 • 501-362-8188 • Jct SR-337 & SR-25 (south of town) follow SR-25 N 4.1 miles

☆	🛡	🕐	⛽	🚭	Store Details
✪	1	✓	❖		Hope • 2400 N Hervey St, 71801 • 870-777-5500 • I-30 Exit 30 go S on US-278 for .3 mile
✪		✓	❖	✓	Hot Springs • 1601 Albert Pike Blvd, 71913 • 501-624-2498 • US-270 Exit 1 go E on US-270 BR for 1.2 miles
✪		✓	❖	✓	Hot Springs • 4019 Central Ave, 71913 • 501-623-7605 • US-270 Exit 5 go S on Central Ave .7 mile
✪		✓	❖		Hot Springs Village • 3604 N Hwy 7, 71909 • 501-318-0185 • Jct US-270 & SR-227 (northwest of town) go N on SR-227 for 5.6 miles, NE on Glazypeau Rd 7.9 miles & N on SR-7
✪		✓			Huntsville • 157 Gary Hatfield Way, 72740 • 479-738-2001 • About 3 miles northeast of town along US-412
✪		✓			Jacksonville • 2000 John Harden Dr, 72076 • 501-985-8731 • At US-67/167 Exit 11 on John Harden Dr, 1.8 miles north of town center
✪		✓	◆		Jonesboro • 1815 E Highland Dr, 72401 • 870-931-5001 • From US-63 Exit 42 go N on Caraway Rd .9 mile & W on Highland .4 mile
✪		✓			Jonesboro • 1911 W Parker Rd, 72404 • 870-972-6350 • From US-63 Exit 45 go W on Parker Rd 1.8 miles
✪	1	✓			Little Rock • 2700 S Shackleford Rd, 72205 • 501-223-0604 • I-430 Exit 5 go S .4 mile
✪	1	✓		✓	Little Rock • 8801 Baseline Rd, 72209 • 501-565-0274 • I-30 Exit 130 go E on Baseline Rd .2 mile
✪	2	✓			Little Rock • 700 S Bowman Rd, 72211 • 501-859-8703 • I-430 Exit 5 go N .5 mile on Shackleford Rd then W .8 mile on Kanis Rd and N .2 mile on Bowmand Rd
✪	6	✓	❖		Little Rock • 19301 Cantrell Rd, 72223 • 501-868-4659 • I-430 Exit 9 go W on Cantrell Rd 5.9 miles
✪	1	✓			Lonoke • 322 Brownsville Loop, 72086 • 501-676-3191 • I-40 Exit 175, north of exit
✪		✓	❖		Magnolia • 60 Hwy 79 N, 71753 • 870-234-7800 • Jct US-82 & US-79 (southeast of town) go N on US-79 for 1.5 miles
✪	1	✓	❖		Malvern • 1910 Martin Luther King Blvd, 72104 • 501-337-9485 • I-30 Exit 98 take US-270 BR east .7 mile
☆					McGehee • 1001 Hwy 65 S, 71654 • 870-222-4184 • Jct SR-278 & US-65 (south of town) take US-65 S .5 mile
✪		✓	◆		Mena • 600 Hwy 71 N, 71953 • 479-394-0025 • Jct US-270 & US-71 take US-71 S 5.1 miles

☆	🛡	🕐	⛽	🚭	Store Details
✪		✓	◆		Monticello • 427 Hwy 425 N, 71655 • 870-367-0409 • Jct SR-35 & US-425 (north of town) take US-425 S 1.1 miles
✪	1	✓	◆		Morrilton • 1621 N Business 9, 72110 • 501-354-0290 • I-40 Exit 108 take SR-9 N .2 mile
✪		✓	❖		Mountain Home • 65 Walmart Dr, 72653 • 870-492-9299 • From Hopper Bypass (northeast of town) go SW on US-62 for 2.3 miles
✪		✓	❖		Mountain View • 409 Sylamore Ave, 72560 • 870-269-4395 • Jct SR-14 & SR-5 (north of town) take SR-14/5/9 S 5.1 miles
✪		✓	❖		Nashville • 1710 S 4th St, 71852 • 870-845-1881 • Jct US-278 & SR-27 BR go W on E Russell St for .7 mile
✪					Newport • 1211 Hwy 367 N, 72112 • 870-523-2500 • US-67 Exit 83 go W .7 mile on Stegall Rd then N .6 mile on SR-367
✪	3	✓	❖		North Little Rock • 12001 Maumelle Blvd, 72113 • 501-851-6102 • I-430 exit 12 take Maumelle Blvd (SR-100) W 2.6 miles
✪	1	✓	❖		North Little Rock • 4450 E McCain Blvd, 72117 • 501-945-2700 • I-40 Exit 156 go N on Springfield Dr .8 mile & E on McCain Blvd .2 mile
✪	2				Osceola • 2720 W Keiser Ave, 72370 • 870-563-3251 • I-55 Exit 48 go E for 2 miles on SR-140
☆	3				Ozark • 1516 N 18th St, 72949 • 479-667-2143 • I-40 Exit 37 take SR-219 W .4 mile, SR-96 SW 1.8 miles & SR-23 W
✪		✓			Paragould • 2802 W Kings Hwy, 72450 • 870-236-9707 • Jct SR-168 & US-412 (west of town) take US-412 E 7.2 miles
☆					Paris • 1501 E Walnut St, 72855 • 479-963-2152 • Jct SR-109 & Airport Rd (east of town) go W on SR-109 for 1.6 miles
✪	1	✓	❖		Pine Bluff • 5501 S Olive St, 71603 • 870-534-7054 • I-530 Exit 43 go S on Olive St .1 mile
✪		✓	◆		Pocahontas • 1415 Hwy 67 S, 72455 • 870-892-7703 • Jct US-63 & US-67 (south of town) go N on US-67 for 16 miles
✪	2	✓	◆	✓	Rogers • 2110 W Walnut St, 72756 • 479-636-3222 • I-49 Exit 85 go E on Walnut St 1.9 miles
✪	1	✓	❖		Rogers • 4208 Pleasant Crossing Blvd, 72758 • 479-621-9769 • I-49 Exit 81 go E on Pleasant Grove .3 mile then S .2 mile on Pleasant Crossing Blvd
✪	1	✓	❖		Russellville • 2409 E Main St, 72802 • 479-967-9777 • I-40 Exit 84 go S on SR-331 for .4 mile & W on Main St .6 mile

☆	♡	⏰	⛽	🚫⛽	Store Details
✪		✓	◆		Searcy • 3509 E Race Ave, 72143 • 501-268-2207 • US-67/167 Exit 46 go W on Race Ave .3 mile
✪		✓	❖		Sheridan • 1308 S Rock St, 72150 • 870-942-7171 • I-530 Exit 10 go S on US-167 for 20.8 miles
✪	5	✓	❖		Sherwood • 9053 Hwy 107, 72120 • 501-833-0972 • I-40 Exit 153A go N 4.8 miles on SR-107/John F. Kennedy Blvd
✪		✓	❖		Siloam Springs • 2901 Hwy 412 E, 72761 • 479-524-5101 • I-49 Exit 72 go W on US-412 for 18.8 miles
✪	3	✓		✓	Springdale • 2004 S Pleasant St, 72764 • 479-751-4817 • I-49 Exit 72 go E on US-412 for 2.3 miles then S on Pleasant St .5 mile
✪	1	✓			Springdale • 4870 Elm Springs Rd, 72762 • 479-306-7025 • I-49 Exit 72, west of exit
✪		✓			Stuttgart • 406 E 22nd St, 72160 • 870-673-3349 • 1.5 miles south of town center via US-79 BR (Main St) and SR-130 (22nd St)
✪	2	✓	❖		Texarkana • 133 Arkansas Blvd, 71854 • 870-772-1501 • I-30 Exit 1 go S .7 mile on Jefferson Ave then W .6 mile on Arkansas Blvd
✪		✓	❖		Trumann • 512 Industrial Park Dr, 72472 • 870-483-6491 • From US-63 Exit 29 take SR-69 E .4 mile, Pecan Grove Rd N .7 mile, SR-212 E & Industrial Dr N .2 mile
✪	1	✓	◆		Van Buren • 2214 Fayetteville Rd, 72956 • 479-474-2314 • I-40 Exit 5 take SR-59 N .3 mile
☆					Waldron • 1359 W 2nd St, 72958 • 479-637-2169 • Jct SR-23 & US-71 (north of town) go S on US-71/71 BYP 8.2 miles & E on 2nd St
☆					Walnut Ridge • 1600 W Main St, 72476 • 870-886-6605 • Jct SR-25 & US-412 (west of town) take US-412 E 7.7 miles
✪		✓	◆	✓	West Helena • 602 Sheila Dr, 72390 • 870-572-2442 • 1 mile northwest of town at jct of Quarles Ln and Sheila Dr
✪	1	✓			West Memphis • 798 W Service Rd, 72301 • 870-732-0175 • I-40 Exit 276 take the Service Rd W .1 mile
✪		✓	❖		Wynne • 800 Hwy 64 E, 72396 • 870-238-8129 • Jct SR-1 & US-64 (north of town) go W on US-64 for 9.9 miles

CALIFORNIA

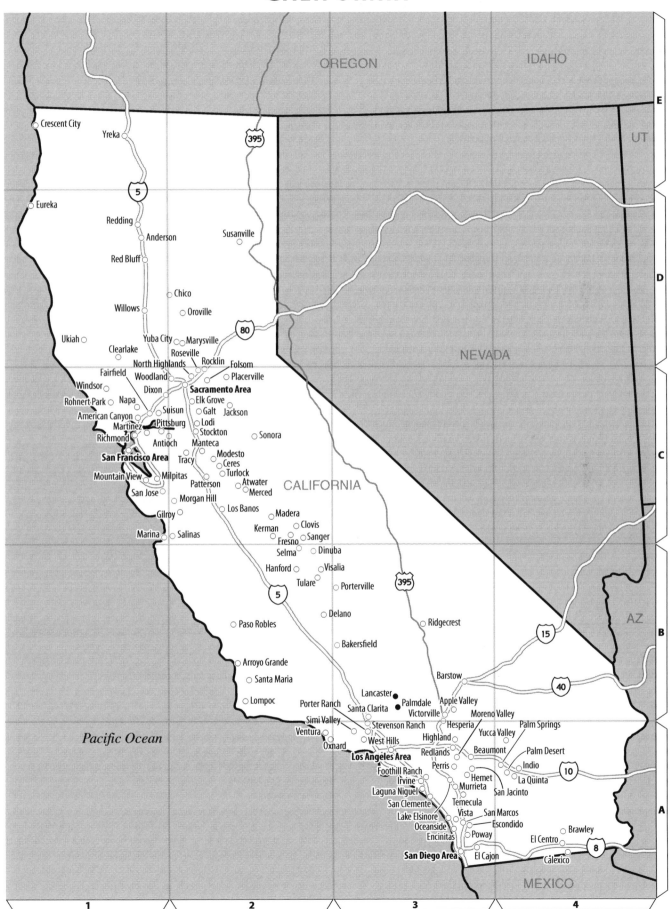

OREGON

IDAHO

UT

NEVADA

CALIFORNIA

AZ

Pacific Ocean

MEXICO

Crescent City
Yreka
Eureka
Redding
Anderson
Red Bluff
Susanville
Chico
Willows
Oroville
Ukiah
Clearlake
Yuba City
Marysville
Roseville
North Highlands
Rocklin
Folsom
Fairfield
Woodland
Placerville
Windsor
Dixon
Sacramento Area
Rohnert Park
Napa
Elk Grove
American Canyon
Suisun
Galt
Jackson
Martinez
Pittsburg
Lodi
Richmond
Stockton
Sonora
Antioch
Manteca
San Francisco Area
Tracy
Modesto
Ceres
Mountain View
Milpitas
Turlock
San Jose
Patterson
Atwater
Merced
Morgan Hill
Gilroy
Los Banos
Madera
Marina
Salinas
Kerman
Clovis
Sanger
Fresno
Selma
Dinuba
Hanford
Visalia
Tulare
Porterville
Paso Robles
Delano
Ridgecrest
Bakersfield
Arroyo Grande
Santa Maria
Barstow
Lompoc
Lancaster
Palmdale
Apple Valley
Porter Ranch
Santa Clarita
Victorville
Moreno Valley
Simi Valley
Stevenson Ranch
Hesperia
Palm Springs
Ventura
Yucca Valley
Oxnard
West Hills
Highland
Beaumont
Palm Desert
Los Angeles Area
Redlands
Indio
Foothill Ranch
Perris
La Quinta
Irvine
Hemet
Laguna Niguel
Murrieta
San Jacinto
San Clemente
Temecula
Lake Elsinore
Vista
San Marcos
Oceanside
Escondido
Encinitas
Poway
Brawley
San Diego Area
El Cajon
El Centro
Calexico

Los Angeles Metro Area

Anaheim • Baldwin Park • Brea • Buena Park • Burbank • Cerritos • Chino • City of Industry • Colton • Corona • Covina • Downey • Duarte • Fontana • Garden Grove • Glendora • Huntington Beach • La Habra • Lakewood • Long Beach • Los Angeles • Norwalk • Ontario • Orange • Panorama City • Paramount • Pico Rivera • Pomona • Rancho Cucamonga • Rialto • Riverside • Rosemead • San Bernardino • Santa Ana • Santa Fe Springs • South Gate • Torrance • Upland • West Covina • Westminster

Sacramento Metro Area

Antelope • Citrus Heights • Orangevale • Rancho Cordova • Sacramento • West Sacramento

San Diego Metro Area

Chula Vista • La Mesa • National City • San Diego • Santee

San Francisco Metro Area

Fremont • Livermore • Oakland • Pleasanton • San Leandro • Union City

☆	◯	◷	⛽	🚭	Store Details
✪	5	✓		✓	American Canyon • 7011 Main St, 94503 • 707-557-4393 • I-80 Exit 33 take SR-37 W 2 miles to Exit 19, SR-29 N 2.9 miles & E at Napa Jct Rd
✪	1	✓		✓	Anaheim • 440 N Euclid St, 92801 • 714-491-0744 • I-5 Exit 112, just east of exit
✪	4	✓		✓	Anaheim • 88 E Orangethorpe Ave, 92801 • 714-447-6751 • I-5 Exit 114 go E on SR-91 for 2.7 miles; N .4 miles on Harbor Blvd; E .3 mile on Orangethorpe Ave
✪	1	✓			Anderson • 5000 Rhonda Rd, 96007 • 530-378-0244 • I-5 Exit 667 (southbound travelers) go W .1 mile on Deschutes Rd, S .2 mile on SR-273, and W 500 feet on Rhonda Rd; Northbound travelers use Exit 667 and turn left onto Rhonda Rd at end of off-ramp.
✪	5			✓	Antelope • 7901 Watt Ave, 95843 • 916-332-3173 • I-80 Exit 98 go W 2.8 miles on Elkhorn Blvd; N 1.9 miles on Watt Ave; W .2 mile on Elverta Rd; S .1 mile on Scotland Dr
☆				✓	Antioch • 4893 Lone Tree Way, 94531 • 925-755-0900 • I-680 Exit 53 take SR-4 E 15 miles, SE on Lone Tree Way 4 miles
☆	6				Apple Valley • 20251 Hwy 18, 92307 • 760-946-2030 • I-15 Exit 154 go S on Stoddard Wells Rd 1.4 miles & E on SR-18 for 4 miles

☆	◯	◷	⛽	🚭	Store Details
☆				✓	Arroyo Grande • 1168 W Branch St, 93420 • 805-474-0800 • From US-101 at SR-227 exit, go E .1 mile then N 1 mile on Branch St
✪					Atwater • 800 Commerce Ave, 95301 • 209-676-3087 • West of SR-99 at Exit 195
✪					Bakersfield • 2601 Fashion Pl, 93306 • 661-873-7120 • From SR-99 Exit 26A take SR-178 E 4.4 miles, S at Mt Vernon Ave, E on Mall View Rd .3 mile & S on Fashion Pl .2 mile
✪					Bakersfield • 6225 Colony St, 93307 • 661-398-7297 • 6 miles south of town center, .2 mile east of SR-99 at Panama Ln (Exit 20)
✪		✓			Bakersfield • 8400 Rosedale Hwy, 93312 • 661-588-2097 • SR-99 Exit 26 go W 2.9 miles on SR-58; northbound travelers use Exit 26A
✪		✓		✓	Bakersfield • 5075 Gosford Rd, 93313 • 661-282-3099 • I-5 Exit 244 take SR-119 E for 7.3 miles, then N on Gosford for 2.8 miles
✪	1	✓		✓	Baldwin Park • 3250 Big Dalton Ave, 91706 • 626-814-2235 • I-10 Exit 32B take Garvy Ave S .3 mile & Big Dalton Ave W .3 mile
☆	1				Barstow • 621 Montara Rd, 92311 • 760-252-5000 • I-40 Exit 1 (Main St/Montara Rd) go S on Montara Rd .2 mile
✪	1	✓			Beaumont • 1540 E 2nd St, 92223 • 951-845-1529 • I-10 Exit 96 go S .2 mile on Highland Springs Ave then W .2 mile on 2nd St
✪		✓			Brawley • 250 Wildcat Dr, 92227 • 760-351-0186 • I-8 Exit 114 go N 3.5 miles on Imperial Ave then continue N 10 miles on SR-86
☆				✓	Brea • 2595 E Imperial Hwy, 92821 • 714-529-0596 • I-5 Exit 115 take SR-91 W 6.3 miles, SR-57 N 4.4 miles & SR-90 for 1 mile
☆	2			✓	Buena Park • 8450 La Palma Ave, 90620 • 714-484-8668 • I-5 Exit 113 go W on La Palma Ave 1.6 miles
✪	1	✓		✓	Burbank • 1301 N Victory Pl, 91502 • 747-261-7243 • I-5 Exit 146B go W .2 mile on Burbank Blvd then N .4 mile on Victory Pl
✪	7	✓			Calexico • 2540 Rockwood Ave, 92231 • 760-768-5013 • I-8 Exit 118 take SR-111 S 5.7 miles, E on Cole Blvd .2 mile & N on Rockwood Ave .2 mile
☆				✓	Ceres • 1670 Mitchell Rd, 95307 • 209-541-0253 • SR-99 Exit 220 go NE on Mitchell Rd 2.4 miles

☆	⛨	🕐	⛽	🚭	Store Details
✪	4			✓	Cerritos • 12701 Towne Center Dr, 90703 • 562-924-1468 • I-5 Exit 117 go W 3.1 miles on Artesia Blvd, S .2 mile on Bloomfield Ave, E .1 mile on Towne Center Dr
☆				✓	Chico • 2044 Forest Ave, 95928 • 530-899-8760 • SR-99 Exit 384 go E on 29th St .3 mile then S on Forest Ave .3 mile
✪		✓			Chino • 3943 Grand Ave, 91710 • 909-628-8916 • From Chino Valley Fwy (SR-71) at Grand Ave go E .4 mile
☆	1			✓	Chula Vista • 75 N Broadway, 91910 • 619-691-7945 • I-5 Exit 8B go E .4 mile on "E" St then N .5 mile on Broadway
☆	2			✓	Chula Vista • 1150 Broadway, 91911 • 619-591-4910 • I-5 Exit 7 take "L" St E .5 mile & Broadway S .6 mile
✪	5			✓	Chula Vista • 1360 Eastlake Pkwy, 91915 • 619-421-3140 • I-805 Exit 4 go E 4.8 miles on Olympic Pkwy then N .2 mile on Eastlake Pkwy
✪	3	✓		✓	Citrus Heights • 7010 Auburn Blvd, 95621 • 916-729-8077 • I-80 Exit 98 go E on Greenback Ln for .9 mile then N on Auburn Blvd 1.7 miles
✪	7	✓			City Of Industry • 17150 Gale Ave, 91745 • 626-854-1166 • I-605 Exit 19 take SR-60 E 6.6 miles, N on Aszusa .3 mile then W on Gale Ave
☆					Clearlake • 15960 Dam Rd, 95422 • 707-994-6881 • Jct SR-20 & SR-53 (E of town) take SR-53 S 6 miles then E on Dam Rd
✪				✓	Clovis • 1185 Herndon Ave, 93611 • 559-321-0067 • SR-168 Exit 7, east of exit
☆				✓	Clovis • 323 W Shaw Ave, 93612 • 559-297-4176 • SR-99 Exit 133 take SR-180 E 3.9 miles, SR-168 NE 4.2 miles & E on Shaw Ave 1 mile
✪	1	✓			Colton • 1120 S Mount Vernon Ave, 92324 • 909-783-0497 • I-215 Exit 39 go N on Mt Vernon Ave .3 mile
✪	3	✓		✓	Corona • 479 N McKinley St, 92879 • 951-270-0707 • I-5 Exit 96 take SR-91 E 1.8 miles then McKinley St N .3 mile
✪	1	✓		✓	Corona • 1290 E Ontario Ave, 92881 • 951-278-0924 • I-15 Exit 93, west of exit .3 mile
✪	3			✓	Covina • 1275 N Azusa Ave, 91722 • 626-339-4161 • I-10 Exit 36 go N on Azusa Ave 2.2 miles
✪		✓		✓	Crescent City • 900 E Washington Blvd, 95531 • 707-464-1198 • US-101 Exit 791, west of exit
✪		✓			Delano • 530 Woollomes Ave, 93215 • 661-370-4061 • SR-99 Exit 54, west of exit

☆	⛨	🕐	⛽	🚭	Store Details
✪		✓		✓	Dinuba • 770 W El Monte Way, 93618 • 559-591-0380 • From SR-99 Exit 115 go E on Mountain View Ave 5.2 miles then continue on El Monte Way 5.5 miles
✪	1	✓			Dixon • 235 E Dorset Dr, 95620 • 707-693-6505 • I-80 Exit 66 take SR-113 S .4 mile
✪	1	✓		✓	Downey • 9001 Apollo Way, 90242 • 562-803-3507 • I-105 Exit 17 go N on Bellflower Blvd .6 mile then left on Apollo Way
☆	1			✓	Duarte • 1600 Mountain Ave, 91010 • 626-359-7708 • I-210 Exit 35 go S on Mountain Ave .1 mile
☆	1			✓	El Cajon • 605 Fletcher Pkwy, 92020 • 619-440-2009 • I-8 Exit 17 go N on Johnson Ave .4 mile then E on Fletcher
✪	1	✓		✓	El Cajon • 13487 Camino Canada, 92021 • 619-561-0828 • I-8 Exit 22, south of exit .3 mile
✪	1	✓			El Centro • 2150 N Waterman Ave, 92243 • 760-337-1600 • I-8 Exit 114 go N on Bradshaw Rd .3 mile & W on Waterman .1 mile
☆	5			✓	Elk Grove • 10075 Bruceville Rd, 95757 • 916-585-7344 • I-5 Exit 506 go E 3.8 miles on Elk Grove Blvd then S 1.2 miles on Bruceville Rd
☆				✓	Elk Grove • 8465 Elk Grove Blvd, 95758 • 916-684-7100 • SR-99 Exit 286 go W on Elk Grove Blvd .4 mile
✪	2			✓	Encinitas • 1550 Leucadia Blvd, 92024 • 760-704-0243 • I-5 Exit 43 go E 1.7 miles on Leucadia Blvd
☆	3				Escondido • 1330 E Grand Ave, 92027 • 760-871-6622 • I-15 Exit 31 go E 2.5 miles on Valley Pkwy, 2nd Ave, and Grand Ave to Harding St and turn left
☆		✓		✓	Eureka • 3300 Broadway Bayshore Mall, 95501 • 707-832-5269 • 2.4 miles southwest of town center via US-101
✪	2			✓	Fairfield • 2701 N Texas St, 94533 • 707-428-4792 • I-80 Exit 47 go E .8 mile on Air Base Pkwy then N .3 mile on Texas St. Westbound travelers use Exit 47A
✪		✓		✓	Folsom • 1018 Riley St, 95630 • 916-983-1090 • I-80 Exit 98 go E on Greenback Ln 9.3 miles then continue on Riley St .8 mile
☆	4			✓	Fontana • 17251 Foothill Blvd, 92335 • 909-355-6922 • I-10 Exit 64 take Sierra Ave N 2.7 miles then E on Foothill Blvd .4 mile
✪	6			✓	Foothill Ranch • 26502 Towne Centre Dr, 92610 • 949-588-7923 • I-5 Exit 94 go E on Alton Pkwy for 5.4 miles

☆	◯	⏰	⛽	🚳	Store Details
☆	1				Fremont • 40580 Albrae St, 94538 • 510-440-8060 • I-880 Exit 16 go W on Stevenson Blvd then S on Albrae St .2 mile
☆	1			✓	Fremont • 44009 Osgood Rd, 94539 • 510-651-3301 • I-680 Exit 14 go W on Auto Mall Pkwy .3 mile then S on Osgood Rd .1 mile
✪				✓	Fresno • 1804 E Ashlan Ave, 93726 • 559-470-6967 • SR-41 Exit 131 go W .3 mile on Ashlan Ave
☆				✓	Fresno • 7065 N Ingram Ave, 93650 • 559-431-0107 • SR-99 Exit 142 go E on Herndon Ave 6.5 miles then N on Ingram Ave .1 mile
☆					Fresno • 3680 W Shaw Ave, 93711 • 559-277-8191 • SR-99 Exit 140 W on Shaw Ave 1.5 miles
✪		✓			Fresno • 5125 E Kings Canyon Rd, 93727 • 559-252-9457 • SR-99 Exit 133 take SR-180 E 5.2 miles, go S 1.1 miles on Peach Ave, then go W on Kings Canyon Rd
✪				✓	Galt • 10470 Twin Cities Rd, 95632 • 209-744-1938 • SR-99 Exit 277 go E .3 mile on Twin Cities Rd
✪				✓	Garden Grove • 11822 Gilbert St, 92841 • 714-591-1300 • I-5 Exit 112 go S 2.3 miles on Euclid St; W 1.5 mile on Katella Ave; S .8 mile on Gilbert St
✪		✓		✓	Gilroy • 7150 Camino Arroyo, 95020 • 408-848-8161 • US-101 Exit 356 take SR-152 E .4 mile then N at Camino Arroyo
☆	1			✓	Glendora • 1950 Auto Centre Dr, 91740 • 909-592-4866 • I-210 Exit 44 go S on Lone Hill Ave .2 mile & E on Auto Centre Dr .1 mile
✪		✓			Hanford • 250 S 12th Ave, 93230 • 559-583-6292 • SR-99 Exit 101 go W on SR-198 for 15.1 miles then N on 12th Ave .2 mile
✪		✓		✓	Hemet • 1231 S Sanderson Ave, 92545 • 951-766-1164 • I-215 Exit 15 take SR-74 E 11.1 miles then S on Sanderson Ave 1.5 miles
✪	1	✓			Hesperia • 13401 Main St, 92345 • 760-948-4851 • I-5 Exit 143, .5 mile east of exit
✪	5				Highland • 4210 Highland Ave, 92346 • 909-425-8846 • I-10 Exit 77 go N 3 miles on SR-210; E .3 mile on Base Line Rd; N 1 mile on Boulder Ave
☆	3			✓	Huntington Beach • 8230 Talbert Ave, 92646 • 714-841-5390 • I-405 Exit 15 go W on Warner Ave 1.5 miles, S on Beach Blvd 1 mile & E on Talbert Ave .2 mile
✪	1				Indio • 82491 Avenue 42, 92203 • 760-262-8004 • I-10 Exit 142, north of exit

☆	◯	⏰	⛽	🚳	Store Details
✪	3			✓	Irvine • 16555 Von Karman Ave, 92606 • 949-623-7467 • I-405 Exit 7 go N 1.6 miles on Jamboree Rd then W .5 mile on Barranca Pkwy
✪	1			✓	Irvine • 71 Technology Dr, 92618 • 949-242-6587 • I-5 Exit 94, east of exit
☆					Jackson • 10355 Wicklow Way, 95642 • 209-223-5384 • Jct SR-124 & SR-88 (W of town) take SR-88 NE 8 miles then S on Wicklow Way .2 mile
✪		✓		✓	Kerman • 14061 W Whitesbridge Ave, 93630 • 559-846-1200 • 1.5 miles northeast of town center on SR-180
✪	5	✓		✓	La Habra • 1340 S Beach Blvd, 90631 • 562-694-2707 • I-5 Exit 117 go E on Artesia Blvd .8 mile & NE on Beach Blvd 3.4 miles
✪		✓			La Habra • 1000 E Imperial Hwy, 90631 • 714-869-0530 • SR-57 (Orange Fwy) Exit 9 go W 3 miles on SR-90/Imperial Hwy
☆	2			✓	La Mesa • 5500 Grossmont Center Dr, 91942 • 619-337-3655 • I-8 Exit 12 go NE on Fletcher Pkwy 1.3 miles & S on Grossmont Center Dr .2 mile
✪	6	✓		✓	La Quinta • 79295 Hwy 111, 92253 • 760-564-3313 • I-10 Exit 137 go S on Washington St 4.3 miles then E on SR-111 for 1 mile
☆	4			✓	Laguna Niguel • 27470 Alicia Pkwy, 92677 • 949-360-0758 • I-5 Exit 88 go W 1.9 miles on Oso Pkwy, continue .9 miles on Pacific Park Dr, then S .4 mile on Alicia Pkwy
☆	1				Lake Elsinore • 31700 Grape St, 92532 • 951-245-5990 • I-15 Exit 73 go E on Diamond Dr/Railroad Canyon Rd for .2 mile then S on Grape St .4 mile
✪	5	✓		✓	Lakewood • 2770 Carson St, 90712 • 562-429-6239 • I-605 Exit 3, go W 4.3 miles on Carson St
✪		✓	◆	✓	Lancaster • 1731 E Avenue J, 93535 • 661-945-7848 • SR-114 Exit 44 go E 3.3 miles on Avenue I, S 1 mile on 10th St, E .8 mile on Avenue J
✪		✓			Lancaster • 44665 Valley Central Way, 93536 • 661-940-8744 • SR-14 Exit 44 go W .3 mile on Avenue I then S on Valley Central Way for .6 mile
☆	2			✓	Livermore • 2700 Las Positas Rd, 94551 • 925-455-0215 • I-580 Exit 47 go S on 1st St .4 mile & W at Las Positas Rd 1.5 miles
☆	6			✓	Lodi • 2350 W Kettleman Ln, 95242 • 209-368-6696 • I-5 Exit 485 go E on SR-12 for 5.1 miles
☆				✓	Lompoc • 701 W Central Ave, 93436 • 805-735-9088 • Jct SR-246 & SR-1 (N of town) go S on SR-1 for 1.2 miles then W on Central Ave .5 mile

☆	◯	🕐	⛽	🚫76	Store Details
⚫				✓	Long Beach • 3705 E South St, 90805 • 424-296-6525 • From Artesia Fwy Exit 15 go S 1.1 miles on Lakewood Blvd then W .3 mile on South St
⚫	1	✓		✓	Long Beach • 7250 E Carson St, 90808 • 562-425-5113 • I-605 Exit 3 go W on Carson St for .3 mile
⚫	5	✓			Los Banos • 1575 W Pacheco Blvd, 93635 • 209-826-9655 • I-5 Exit 403A go E on SR-152 for 4.9 miles
☆					Madera • 1977 W Cleveland Ave, 93637 • 559-675-9212 • SR-99 Exit 155 go W on Cleveland Ave for .2 mile
⚫	6	✓		✓	Manteca • 1205 S Main St, 95337 • 209-824-2000 • I-5 Exit 451 go E 4.8 miles on SR-120 then N .4 mile on Main St
⚫				✓	Marina • 150 Beach Rd, 93933 • 831-883-9138 • SR-1 Exit 410 go E on Reservation Rd for .3 mile, continue on Beach Rd for .1 mile
☆	3			✓	Martinez • 1021 Arnold Dr, 94553 • 925-313-5716 • I-680 Exit 53 take SR-4 W for 2 miles, N on Morello Ave for .1 mile & W on Arnold Dr for .5 mile
⚫		✓		✓	Marysville • 1131 N Beale Rd, 95901 • 530-634-9751 • SR-99/70 Exit 18 go W on Lindenhurst Ave 1.2 miles then N on Beale Rd for .2 mile
☆					Merced • 3055 Loughborough Dr, 95348 • 209-384-1275 • SR-99 Exit 188 take SR-59 N for .8 mile, E on Olive Ave for .3 mile & S on Loughborough
⚫	2	✓		✓	Milpitas • 301 Ranch Dr, 95035 • 408-934-0304 • I-880 Exit 10 go W .2 mile on Dixon Landing Rd then S 1.8 miles on McCarthy Blvd and turn left onto Ranch Dr
☆				✓	Modesto • 2225 Plaza Pkwy, 95350 • 209-524-4733 • SR-99 Exit 229 go NE on Briggsmore Ave for .3 mile, NW on Prescott for .1 mile & W on Plaza Pkwy for .2 mile
⚫		✓		✓	Modesto • 3848 McHenry Ave, 95350 • 209-342-0949 • 3.4 miles north of town center via SR-108 (McHenry Ave)
⚫		✓			Moreno Valley • 12721 Moreno Beach Dr, 92555 • 951-242-1185 • From SR-60 Exit 65 go S on Moreno Beach Dr for .1 mile
⚫				✓	Morgan Hill • 170 Cochrane Plaza, 95037 • 408-779-8172 • From US-101 Exit 367 go SW .2 mile
☆	7			✓	Mountain View • 600 Showers Dr, 94040 • 650-917-0796 • I-280 Exit 19 take SR-85 N 3.6 miles, NW on SR-82 for 3 miles & N on Showers Dr for .1 mile
☆	1			✓	Murrieta • 41200 Murrieta Hot Springs Rd, 92562 • 951-696-7135 • I-15 Exit 64 go W on Murrieta Springs Rd for .2 mile

☆	◯	🕐	⛽	🚫76	Store Details
⚫				✓	Napa • 681 Lincoln Ave, 94558 • 707-224-8797 • 1 mile north of town center on Lincoln Ave
⚫	1			✓	National City • 1200 Highland Ave, 91950 • 619-336-0395 • I-8 Exit 10 go W on Plaza Blvd for .8 mile & S on Highland Ave for .1 mile
⚫	1			✓	North Highlands • 4675 Watt Ave, 95660 • 916-621-1454 • I-80 Exit 94A go N .4 mile on Watt Ave and turn left onto Orange Grove Ave; westbound travelers use I-80-BUS Exit 14B
☆	1			✓	Norwalk • 11729 Imperial Hwy, 90650 • 562-929-6766 • I-5 Exit 122 go W on Imperial Hwy for .2 mile
⚫	2	✓		✓	Oceanside • 2100 Vista Way, 92054 • 760-966-0026 • I-5 Exit 51 take SR-78 E for .5 mile, N on jefferson St for .2 mile & W on Vista Way for .4 mile
⚫	4	✓		✓	Oceanside • 3405 Marron Rd, 92056 • 760-730-1371 • I-5 Exit 51 take SR-78 E for 3.1 miles, S on College Blvd for .3 mile & W on Marron Rd for .3 mile
⚫	6	✓		✓	Oceanside • 705 College Blvd, 92057 • 760-631-0434 • I-5 Exit 54A go E 6 miles on SR-76
⚫	1			✓	Ontario • 1333 N Mountain Ave, 91762 • 909-321-3165 • 1/2 mile south of I-10 Exit 50
☆				✓	Orange • 2300 N Tustin St, 92865 • 714-998-4473 • From SR-91 take SR-55 S for .7 mile then Exit 17 go S on Tustin for .6 mile
⚫	7	✓		✓	Orangevale • 8961 Greenback Ln, 95662 • 916-989-5800 • I-80 Exit 98 go E 6.2 miles on Greenback Ln
☆				✓	Oroville • 355 Oro Dam Blvd E, 95965 • 530-534-1082 • From SR-70 (S of town) take Exit 46 & go E on Oroville Dam Blvd for .1 mile
☆				✓	Oxnard • 2701 Saviers Rd, 93033 • 805-200-5224 • 1.5 miles south of town center along Saviers Rd at Channel Islands Blvd
⚫				✓	Oxnard • 2001 N Rose Ave, 93036 • 805-981-4884 • US-101 Exit 61 go S on Rose Ave for .4 mile
⚫	1	✓		✓	Palm Desert • 34500 Monterey Ave, 92211 • 760-328-4375 • I-10 Exit 131 go S on Monterey Ave for .6 mile
⚫	4	✓		✓	Palm Springs • 5601 E Ramon Rd, 92264 • 760-322-3906 • I-10 Exit 126 go S on Date Palm Dr 2.2 miles & W on Ramon Rd 1.7 miles
⚫		✓			Palmdale • 40130 10th St W, 93551 • 661-267-6496 • From SR-14 (SW of town) take Exit 37 W on Rancho Vista Blvd for .3 mile then N on 10th St for .7 mile

☆	♡	🕐	⛽	🚌	Store Details
✪		✓	✦		Palmdale • 37140 47th St E, 93552 • 661-533-0248 • From SR-14 (S of town) take Exit 30 Pearlblossom NE 3.6 miles then 47th St N 1 mile
☆	2			✓	Panorama City • 8333 Van Nuys Blvd, 91402 • 818-830-0350 • I-405 Exit 68 go E on Roscoe Blvd 1.4 miles & N at Van Nuys Blvd
✪	1			✓	Paramount • 14501 Lakewood Blvd, 90723 • 562-531-8240 • I-105 Exit 16 go S on Lakewood Blvd for .8 mile
☆				✓	Paso Robles • 180 Niblick Rd, 93446 • 805-238-1212 • From US-101 take Spring St Exit, go S on Spring St for .2 mile & W on Niblick Rd for .5 mile
✪	2			✓	Patterson • 1030 Sperry Ave, 95363 • 209-895-4407 • I-5 Exit 343 go E 2 miles on Sperry Ave
✪	1			✓	Perris • 1800 N Perris Blvd, 92571 • 951-940-0440 • I-215 Exit 19 go E .4 mile on Nuevo Rd then N .4 mile on Perris Blvd
✪	2			✓	Pico Rivera • 8500 Washington Blvd, 90660 • 562-801-2413 • I-605 Exit 13 go W on Washington Blvd 1.6 miles
☆				✓	Pittsburg • 2203 Loveridge Rd, 94565 • 925-427-2022 • I-680 Exit 53 take SR-4 E for 12.1 miles to Exit 24 then S on Loveridge Rd for .5 mile
☆				✓	Placerville • 4300 Missouri Flat Rd, 95667 • 530-621-2917 • From US-50 Exit 44A take Missouri Flat Rd SE .5 mile
☆	2			✓	Pleasanton • 4501 Rosewood Dr, 94588 • 925-734-8744 • I-580 Exit 47 go S on Santa Rita Rd .6 mile then W on Rosewood Dr .7 mile
☆	5				Pomona • 80 Rio Rancho Rd, 91766 • 909-620-4602 • I-210 Exit 45 take SR-71 S 4 miles to Exit 13 then SW on Rio Rancho Rd .4 mile
✪	7				Porter Ranch • 19821 Rinaldi St, 91326 • 818-832-0643 • From I-405 at SR-118 go W on SR-118 for 5.4 miles, N on Tampa Ave .1 mile & W on Rinaldi St .6 mile
☆					Porterville • 1250 W Henderson Ave, 93257 • 559-783-8195 • SR-99 Exit 76 go W on SR-190 for 15.3 miles, N on SR-65 for 1.9 miles & W on Henderson .4 mile
✪	5	✓		✓	Poway • 13425 Community Rd, 92064 • 858-486-1882 • I-15 Exit 22 go SE on Camino Del Norte/Twin Peaks Rd 3 miles then S on Community Rd 1.3 miles
✪				✓	Rancho Cordova • 10655 Folsom Blvd, 95670 • 916-361-0296 • SR-99 Exit 298 take US-50 E 11.1 miles, at Exit 17 go N on Zinfandel Dr for .5 mile & W on Folsom Blvd .1 mile

☆	♡	🕐	⛽	🚌	Store Details
☆	1				Rancho Cucamonga • 12549 Foothill Blvd, 91739 • 909-899-1441 • I-15 Exit 112 go E on SR-66 for .4 mile & N on Foothill Blvd
☆	1				Red Bluff • 1025 S Main St, 96080 • 530-529-5540 • I-5 Exit 647 go NW on S Main St .4 mile
✪	1	✓		✓	Redding • 1515 Dana Dr, 96003 • 530-221-2800 • I-5 Exit 678 go N on Hilltop Dr .2 mile & E on Dana Dr .8 mile
☆	1			✓	Redlands • 2050 W Redlands Blvd, 92373 • 909-798-9114 • I-10 Exit 75 go S at California St .2 mile & E on Redlands Blvd .2 mile
☆	1				Rialto • 1610 S Riverside Ave, 92376 • 909-820-9912 • I-10 Exit 68 take Riverside Ave N .3 mile
☆	1			✓	Richmond • 1400 Hilltop Mall Rd, 94806 • 510-669-1342 • I-80 Exit 19B go W .4 mile on Hilltop Dr
☆					Ridgecrest • 911 S China Lake Blvd, 93555 • 760-371-4974 • From US-395 (SW of town) go NE on China Lake Blvd 4.5 miles
☆	9			✓	Riverside • 5200 Van Buren Blvd, 92503 • 951-689-4595 • I-15 Exit 96 take SR-91 E 6.6 miles, Van Buren Blvd NW 1.8 miles then W on Audrey St
✪	1	✓		✓	Riverside • 6250 Valley Springs Pkwy, 92507 • 951-653-4849 • I-215 Exit 28 go E .2 mile on Eucalyptus Ave then N .5 mile on Valley Springs Pkwy
✪	1			✓	Rocklin • 5454 Crossings Dr, 95677 • 916-783-8281 • I-80 Exit 109, south of exit
☆				✓	Rohnert Park • 4625 Redwood Dr, 94928 • 707-586-3717 • Jct SR-116 & US-101 take US-101 N 1.9 miles, exit toward Golf Course Dr to Redwood Dr NW .3 mile
✪	2			✓	Rosemead • 1827 Walnut Grove Blvd, 91770 • 626-307-1531 • I-10 Exit 26A go S 1.5 miles on Walnut Grove Ave
✪	2			✓	Roseville • 1400 Lead Hill Blvd, 95661 • 916-724-0012 • I-80 Exit 103 go E 1 mile on Douglas Blvd, N .3 mile on Rocky Ridge Dr, W .2 mile on Lead Hill Blvd; eastbound travelers use Exit 103B
✪	3	✓		✓	Roseville • 900 Pleasant Grove Blvd, 95678 • 916-786-6768 • I-80 Exit 106 take SR-65 NW 2.4 miles then S on Pleasant Grove Blvd .3 mile
✪	3			✓	Sacramento • 3460 El Camino Ave, 95821 • 916-977-0201 • I-80 Exit 94 go S on Watt Ave 2.4 miles & W on El Camino .1 mile
✪					Sacramento • 6051 Florin Rd, 95823 • 916-427-9719 • SR-99 Exit 293A go E .6 mile on Florin Rd

☆	🛡	🕐	⛽	🚫	Store Details
☆	1			✓	Sacramento • 3661 Truxel Rd, 95834 • 916-928-9668 • I-80 Exit 88 N on Truxel Rd for .5 mile
✪	1	✓		✓	Sacramento • 5821 Antelope Rd, 95842 • 916-729-6162 • I-10 Exit 100 go SW on Antelope Rd 1 mile
✪	9				Sacramento • 8915 Gerber Rd, 95829 • 916-897-5020 • I-5 Exit 513 go E 4.7 miles on Florin Rd then S 1.1 miles on Stockton Blvd and E 2.7 miles on Gerber Rd
✪		✓		✓	Salinas • 1800 N Main St, 93906 • 831-751-0231 • From US-101 at Boronda Rd, go east .5 mile
✪		✓		✓	Salinas • 1375 N Davis Rd, 93907 • 831-998-9080 • US-101 Exit 330 go W .2 mile on Laurel Dr then N .6 mile on Davis Rd
☆	1			✓	San Bernardino • 4001 Hallmark Pkwy, 92407 • 909-880-4038 • I-215 Exit 48, west of exit
☆	2			✓	San Clemente • 951 Avenida Pico, 92673 • 949-498-6669 • I-5 Exit 76 go NE on Avenida 1.8 miles
☆	1			✓	San Diego • 4840 Shawline St, 92111 • 858-268-2885 • I-805 Exit 22 take Clairmont Mesa Blvd E .2 mile & Shawline St S .2 mile
✪	3			✓	San Diego • 3412 College Ave, 92115 • 619-858-0071 • I-8 Exit 10 go S on College Ave 3 miles
☆	1			✓	San Diego • 3382 Murphy Canyon Rd, 92123 • 858-571-6094 • I-15 Exit 8 take Aero Dr W .3 mile & Murphy Canyon Rd S .3 mile
☆	1			✓	San Diego • 710 Dennery Rd, 92154 • 619-428-4000 • I-805 Exit 2 take Palm Ave E .3 mile then Dennery Rd S .4 mile
✪	1			✓	San Diego • 575 Saturn Blvd, 92154 • 619-205-6140 • I-5 Exit 5A, west of exit
✪		✓			San Jacinto • 1861 S San Jacinto Ave, 92583 • 951-487-1492 • I-215 Exit 15 take SR-74 E 13.9 miles then San Jacinto Ave N 1.4 miles
✪				✓	San Jose • 5095 Almaden Expy, 95118 • 408-600-3072 • 7 miles south of town center off SR-85 at Almaden Expy
✪	1			✓	San Jose • 777 Story Rd, 95122 • 408-885-1142 • From I-280 at 10th St, go S .3 mile on 10th St then E .6 mile on Keyes St/Story Rd
☆	1			✓	San Leandro • 1919 Davis St, 94577 • 510-569-0200 • I-880 take the Davis St Exit & go W for .3 mile
✪	1				San Leandro • 15555 Hesperian Blvd, 94579 • 510-351-0108 • I-880 Exit 30. Southbound travelers turn left on Lewelling Blvd then left again at Hesperian Blvd. Northbound travelers turn right on Hesperian Blvd.

☆	🛡	🕐	⛽	🚫	Store Details
☆	2			✓	San Marcos • 732 Center Dr, 92069 • 760-233-8009 • I-15 Exit 32 take US-78 W 1.2 miles, Nordahl Rd N .1 mile then W on Montiel/Center Dr .4 mile
✪					Sanger • 2761 Jensen Ave, 93657 • 559-875-4268 • SR-99 Exit 130 go 11 miles E on Jensen Ave
✪	5	✓		✓	Santa Ana • 3600 W McFadden Ave, 92704 • 714-775-1804 • From I-5 at SR-22/Garden Grove Fwy, go W 2.6 miles to Harbor Blvd then S 2.2 miles to McFaden Ave and go E .2 mile
✪		✓			Santa Clarita • 26471 Carl Boyer Dr, 91350 • 661-259-0863 • SR-14 Exit 5 go N on Golden Valley Rd 2.6 miles, W on Center Pointe Pkwy & N on Boyer Dr .2 mile
✪	2			✓	Santa Clarita • 27931 Kelly Johnson Pkwy, 91355 • 661-294-5211 • I-5 Exit 172 go E 1.5 miles on Newhall Ranch Rd then N .1 mile on Rye Canyon Point Dr
✪	4	✓		✓	Santa Fe Springs • 13310 Telegraph Rd, 90670 • 562-946-6343 • I-5 Exit 120 take Bloomfield Ave N 2.6 miles & Telegraph Rd E .9 mile
☆				✓	Santa Maria • 2220 S Bradley Rd, 93455 • 805-349-7885 • Jct SR-166 & US-101 (N of town) take US-101 S 5 miles, W on Betteravia Rd .2 mile & S on Bradley Rd .3 mile
☆	10			✓	Santee • 170 Town Center Pkwy, 92071 • 619-449-7900 • I-15 Exit 11 take SR-52 E 7.7 miles, N on Mission Gorge Rd 1.4 miles, W on Cuyamaca St .3 mile & S at Town Center Pkwy .2 mile
✪		✓			Selma • 3400 Floral Ave, 93662 • 559-891-7190 • 1.5 miles west of town center off SR-99 at Floral Ave
☆					Simi Valley • 255 Cochran St, 93065 • 805-581-1666 • From SR-118 Exit 23 (Ronald Reagan Fwy/Simi Valley Fwy) go S .2 mile on 1st St then W .7 mile on Cochran St
☆				✓	Simi Valley • 2801 E Cochran St, 93065 • 805-416-5272 • SR-118 Exit 25 go S .2 mile on Sycamore Dr then E .1 mile on Cochran St
☆					Sonora • 1101 Sanguinetti Rd, 95370 • 209-533-2617 • 1.4 miles southeast of town center near jct of SR-108 and Mono Way
✪	1	✓		✓	South Gate • 4651 Firestone Blvd, 90280 • 323-282-4800 • I-710 Exit 13 go W 1 mile on Firestone Blvd
☆	1			✓	Stevenson Ranch • 25450 The Old Rd, 91381 • 661-253-1911 • I-5 Exit 167 take Pico Canyon Rd W .3 mile
✪	5	✓		✓	Stockton • 3223 E Hammer Ln, 95212 • 209-473-2796 • I-5 Exit 478 go E on Hammer Lane 4.7 miles

☆	♡	⏲	⛽	🚐	Store Details
●	1	✓			Stockton • 10355 Trinity Pkwy, 95219 • 209-235-0558 • I-5 Exit 481 go W .2 mile on 8 Mile Rd then S .4 mile on Trinity Pkwy
●	6	✓		✓	Suisun • 350 Walters Rd, 94585 • 707-639-4980 • I-80 Exit 44A go SE .3 mile on Chadbourne Rd then E 5.3 miles on SR-12 and N .2 mile on Walters Rd; eastbound travels can use I-80 Exit 43 to SR-12
☆					Susanville • 2900 Main St, 96130 • 530-251-2000 • Jct SR-44 & SR-36 (W of town) take SR-36 E for 6.8 miles
●	3	✓		✓	Temecula • 32225 Temecula Pkwy, 92592 • 951-506-7613 • I-15 Exit 58 go E 2.8 miles on Temecula Pkwy
☆	1			✓	Torrance • 19503 Normandie Ave, 90501 • 310-782-6022 • I-405 Exit 38 go S on Normandie for .5 mile
☆	4			✓	Torrance • 22015 Hawthorne Blvd, 90503 • 310-750-0179 • I-405 Exit 42A go S 4 miles on SR-107
●	1	✓		✓	Tracy • 3010 W Grant Line Rd, 95304 • 209-836-5786 • I-205 Exit 6, west of exit
☆					Tulare • 1110 E Prosperity Ave, 93274 • 559-684-1300 • SR-99 Exit 88 go E on Prosperity Ave for .2 mile
☆				✓	Turlock • 2111 Fulkerth Rd, 95380 • 209-634-8543 • SR-99 Exit 214 go E on Fulkerth Rd for .3 mile
☆				✓	Ukiah • 1155 Airport Park Blvd, 95482 • 707-468-0258 • Jct US-101 & SR-222 (S of town) go W on SR-222 for .3 mile then S on Airport Park Blvd .1 mile
☆	1			✓	Union City • 30600 Dyer St, 94587 • 510-475-5915 • I-880 Exit 23 go W on Alvarado Rd .4 mile & N on Dyer St .5 mile
☆	2				Upland • 1540 W Foothill Blvd, 91786 • 909-920-4021 • I-210 Exit 52 go E on Base Line Rd for .8 mile, S on Benson Ave 1 mile & E on Foothill Blvd
●	2			✓	Vacaville • 1501 Helen Power Dr, 95687 • 707-451-0166 • I-80 Exit 55 Eastbound: Follow Nut Tree Pkwy/Sharpe Rd E for .5 mile then Helen Power Dr .3 mile. I-80 Exit 55 Westbound: Turn right onto Monte Vista Ave .4 mile; right on Nut Tree Rd .5 mile; right onto Burton Dr .3 mile; right onto Helen Power Dr .1 mile.
☆				✓	Ventura • 1739 S Victoria Ave, 93003 • 805-665-5560 • US-101 Exit 54, north of exit
●	4	✓		✓	Victorville • 12234 Palmdale Rd, 92392 • 760-493-3047 • I-15 Exit 150 go W 4 miles on SR-18/Palmdale Rd
●	1	✓		✓	Victorville • 11896 Amargosa Rd, 92395 • 760-951-5005 • I-15 Exit 147 go W .1 mile on Bear Valley Rd then S .3 mile on Amargosa Rd
●		✓			Visalia • 3750 S Mooney Blvd, 93277 • 559-802-4429 • 4 miles southwest of town center at corner of Mooney Blvd and Caldwell Ave
☆					Visalia • 1819 E Noble Ave, 93292 • 559-636-2302 • SR-99 Exit 96 take SR-198 E 7.6 miles to Exit 107B then E on Noble Ave .2 mile
●	10	✓		✓	Vista • 1800 University Dr, 92083 • 760-945-7995 • I-5 Exit 51B take SR-78 E for 9 miles, N .2 mile on Sycamore Ave and W .2 mile on University Dr
●	1			✓	West Covina • 2753 E Eastland Center Dr, 91791 • 626-332-4608 • I-10 Exit 37A, north of exit
☆				✓	West Hills • 6433 Fallbrook Ave, 91307 • 818-719-8602 • US-101 Exit 27C merge onto Ventura Blvd .6 mile then N on Fallbrook Ave 1.5 miles
●	1	✓		✓	West Sacramento • 755 Riverpoint Dr, 95605 • 919-373-2200 • I-80 Exit 83 go E .2 mile on Reed Ave then S .2 mile
☆	3			✓	Westminster • 13331 Beach Blvd, 92683 • 714-799-0020 • I-405 Exit 16 merge onto Beach Blvd 2.8 miles
●	1	✓			Willows • 470 N Airport Rd, 95988 • 530-934-2054 • I-5 Exit 603, west of exit
☆				✓	Windsor • 6650 Hembree Ln, 95492 • 707-836-7200 • From US-101 (S of town) E on Shiloh Rd then N on Hambree Lane .3 mile
☆	1			✓	Woodland • 1720 E Main St, 95776 • 530-668-1060 • I-5 Exit 536, east of I-5
●	1	✓			Yreka • 1906 Fort Jones Rd, 96097 • 530-842-7330 • I-5 Exit 773 take SR-3 W for .3 mile
●		✓			Yuba City • 1150 Harter Rd, 95993 • 530-751-0130 • Jct SR-20 & SR-70 (E of town) go W on SR-20 for 3.6 miles & N on Harter Rd
●		✓			Yucca Valley • 58501 Twentynine Palms Hwy, 92284 • 760-365-7750 • 2.8 miles east of town along SR-62

COLORADO

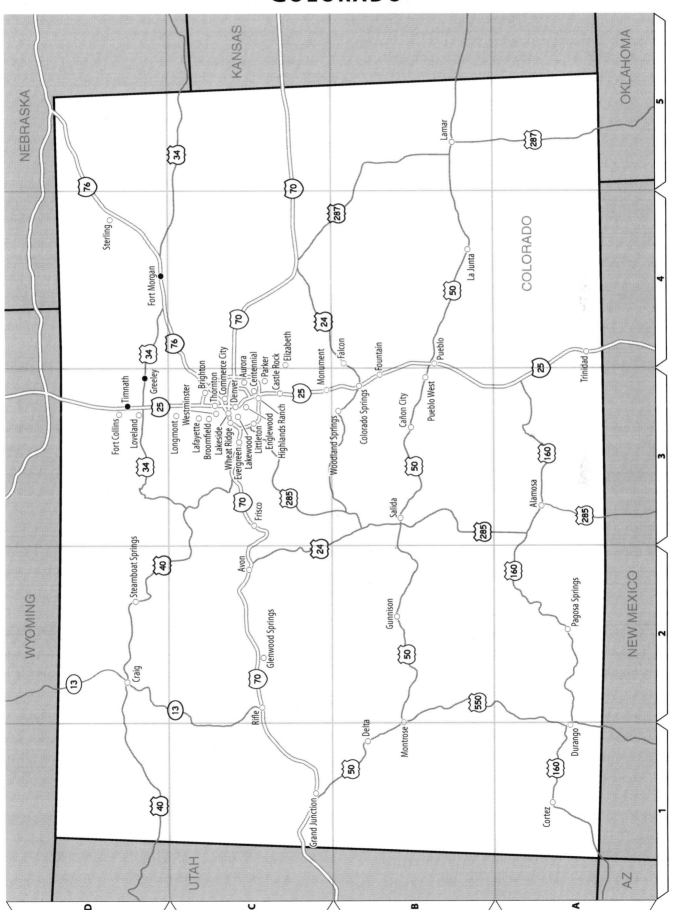

☆	○	◷	⛽	🚫	Store Details
✪		✓			Alamosa • 3333 Clark St, 81101 • 719-589-9071 • Northwest of downtown, follow US-160 NW 2 miles to Mariposa, N to Clark St.
✪	1	✓			Aurora • 3301 Tower Rd, 80011 • 720-374-0278 • I-70 Exit 286 go N on Tower Rd for .4 mile
✪	1				Aurora • 14000 E Exposition Ave, 80012 • 303-368-1115 • I-225 Exit 8 take Alameda Ave E .1 mile, Abilene St S .5 mile & Exposition E .1 mile
✪	5	✓		✓	Aurora • 5650 S Chambers Rd, 80015 • 303-693-0302 • I-225 Exit 4 go S on Parker Rd 4.5 miles then NE on Chambers Rd .3 mile
✪	10	✓			Aurora • 6101 S Aurora Pkwy, 80016 • 303-617-1261 • I-70 Exit 289 take SR-470 S 6.6 miles to Exit 13 then E on Quincy .3 mile, S on Gun Club 1.5 miles & SE on Aurora Pkwy 1.1 miles
✪	1	✓			Avon • 171 Yoder Ave, 81620 • 970-949-6442 • I-70 Exit 168 follow William J. Post Blvd SW .6 mile then go E .2 mile on Yoder Ave
✪	4	✓			Brighton • 60 W Bromley Ln, 80601 • 303-659-1560 • I-76 Exit 22 go W on Bromley Ln 3.8 miles
✪	6	✓		✓	Brighton • 7101 E 128th St, 80602 • 303-209-4339 • I-25 Exit 225 go E 3.5 miles on 136th Ave, S 1 mile on Holly St, E .9 mile on 128th Ave
✪	3	✓		✓	Broomfield • 4651 W 121st Ave, 80020 • 303-217-9374 • I-25 Exit 223 go W 3 miles on 120th Ave
✪		✓		✓	Broomfield • 500 Summit Blvd, 80021 • 303-466-3928 • I-25 Exit 217 take US-36 W 10.3 miles, W at Flatiron Cir 1 mile, continue on Coalton .3 mile, S at Tyler Dr to Summit Blvd .3 mile
✪		✓			Canon City • 3105 E Hwy 50, 81212 • 719-275-2375 • Jct SR-115 & US-50 (E of town) take US-50 W 8.6 miles
✪	1	✓		✓	Castle Rock • 133 Sam Walton Ln, 80104 • 303-688-8200 • I-25 Exit 184 go E on Founders Pkwy .4 mile then S on Front St .3 mile
✪	2	✓			Centennial • 10900 E Briarwood Ave, 80112 • 303-706-0071 • I-25 Exit 197 go E on Arapahoe Rd 1.2 miles & S at Joliet St .1 mile
✪	1	✓		✓	Colorado Springs • 707 S 8th St, 80905 • 719-633-0736 • I-25 Exit 141 go W on Cimarron St for .3 mile then S on 8th St .5 mile
✪	5	✓		✓	Colorado Springs • 3201 E Platte Ave, 80909 • 719-578-9164 • I-25 Exit 143 go E on Uintah St 2 miles, S on Union Blvd .9 mile & E on Platte Ave 1.4 miles

☆	○	◷	⛽	🚫	Store Details
✪	8	✓			Colorado Springs • 1575 Space Center Dr, 80915 • 719-597-7414 • I-25 Exit 139 take US-24 E 6.6 miles, continue on Powers Blvd .8 mile
✪	7	✓		✓	Colorado Springs • 5550 E Woodmen Rd, 80920 • 719-531-6471 • I-25 Exit 151 go E on Briargate Pkwy 3.6 miles, S on Powers Blvd 2.4 miles & W on Woodmen Rd .3 mile
✪	2	✓			Colorado Springs • 8250 Razorback Rd, 80920 • 719-593-2300 • I-25 Exit 151 merge onto Briargate Pkwy for .5 mile then S on SR-83 for 1 mile & E at Razorback Rd
✪	1	✓		✓	Commerce City • 5990 Dahlia St, 80022 • 303-287-0600 • I-270 Exit 2B take Vasquez Blvd N .5 mile then E on 60th Ave
✪		✓			Cortez • 1835 E Main St, 81321 • 970-565-6138 • 1.3 miles east of town center on US-160
✪		✓			Craig • 2000 W Victory Way, 81625 • 970-824-0340 • 1 mile west of town center on US-40
✪		✓			Delta • 37 Stafford Ln, 81416 • 970-874-1585 • 1.5 miles east of town, south of SR-92 and Stafford Ln jct
✪		✓		✓	Denver • 2770 W Evans Ave, 80219 • 303-222-7043 • US-85 at Evans Ave go W for 1.6 miles
✪	1	✓		✓	Denver • 7800 Smith Rd, 80207 • 720-941-0411 • I-70 Exit 278 go S on Quebec St .3 mile then E at Smith Rd .4 mile
✪	3	✓		✓	Denver • 9400 E Hampden Ave, 80231 • 720-748-1000 • I-25 Exit 201 go E on Hampden Ave 2.2 miles
✪		✓			Durango • 1155 S Camino Del Rio, 81303 • 970-259-8755 • Approximately 2 miles south of Durango on US-160 • US-550 (Camino Del Rio)
✪		✓			Elizabeth • 2100 Legacy Cir, 80107 • 303-646-2599 • 1.4 miles west of town center via SR-86
✪	5	✓			Englewood • 601 Englewood Pkwy, 80110 • 303-789-7201 • I-25 Exit 207B go S on US-85 for 3.4 miles, E on Dartmouth Ave .3 mile & S on Elati St .4 mile
✪	1	✓			Evergreen • 952 Swede Gulch Rd, 80401 • 303-526-1649 • Westbound I-70 travelers use Exit 252 to Swede Gulch Rd, turn left. Eastbound I-70 travelers use Exit 251, turn right and follow US-40 to Swede Gulch Rd.
✪		✓			Falcon • 11550 Meridian Market View, 80831 • 719-522-2910 • I-25 Exit 149 go E 11 miles on Woodmen Rd

☆	♡	🕐	⛽	🚭	Store Details
⊙	3	✓		✓	Fort Collins • 1250 E Magnolia St, 80524 • 970-493-3048 • I-25 Exit 269B go W on Mulberry St 2.8 miles then N at 12th St .2 mile
⊙	5	✓		✓	Fort Collins • 4625 S Mason St, 80525 • 970-372-3477 • I-25 Exit 265 go W 4.6 miles on Harmony Rd
⊙	1	✓	❖		Fort Morgan • 1300 Barlow Rd, 80701 • 970-542-2272 • I-76 Exit 82 go N on Barlow Rd for .2 mile
⊙	3	✓			Fountain • 6510 S Hwy 85/87, 80817 • 719-391-1700 • I-25 Exit 132 go E on SR-16 for .5 mile & N on US-85/87 for 1.7 miles
⊙	1				Fountain • 4425 Venetucci Blvd, 80906 • 719-313-4378 • I-25 Exit 135, west of exit
☆	1			✓	Frisco • 840 Summit Blvd, 80443 • 970-668-3959 • I-70 Exit 203, S on Summit Blvd.
☆	3			✓	Glenwood Springs • 3010 Blake Ave, 81601 • 970-945-5336 • I-70 Exit 116, N on Laurel St, E on 6th St, S on SR-82/Grand Ave/S Glen Ave, E on 29th, S on Blake Ave. Store is about 2.5 miles south of exit.
⊙	7	✓			Grand Junction • 2881 N Ave, 81501 • 970-241-6061 • I-70 Exit 37 take I-70 BR W 6 miles then N at 28th Rd .1 mile & E on Grand Ave .1 mile
⊙	3	✓			Grand Junction • 2545 Rimrock Ave, 81505 • 970-248-0031 • I-70 Exit 28 go S on 24 Rd 1.6 miles, SE on I-70 BR 1.3 miles & S on Rimrock Rd .1 mile
⊙		✓	❖		Greeley • 3103 S 23rd Ave, 80631 • 970-330-1452 • I-25 Exit 257A take US-34 E 14.8 miles then S on 23rd Ave .4 mile
⊙		✓		✓	Greeley • 920 47th Ave, 80634 • 970-353-4231 • I-25 Exit 257A take US-34 E 5.7 miles, US-34 BR E 7.2 miles & N at 47th Ave
☆				✓	Gunnison • 900 N Main St, 81230 • 970-641-1733 • .5 mile north of town center on SR-135 (Main St)
⊙	3	✓		✓	Highlands Ranch • 6675 Business Center Dr, 80130 • 303-683-3641 • I-25 Exit 194 take SR-470 W 2.1 miles, S on Quebec St .3 mile & W on Business Center Dr .3 mile
⊙		✓			La Junta • 6 Conley Rd, 81050 • 719-384-5951 • Jct SR-71 & US-50 (NW of town) take US-50 E 7.8 miles then S on Conley Rd .1 mile
⊙	7	✓		✓	Lafayette • 745 US Hwy 287, 80026 • 303-666-0340 • I-25 Exit 229 take SR-7 W 6.4 miles then N at 107th St .3 mile
⊙	1	✓		✓	Lakeside • 5957 W 44th Ave, 80212 • 303-222-4455 • I-70 Exit 270 go S .5 mile on Harlan St then E .1 mile on 44th Ave
⊙	4	✓		✓	Lakewood • 7455 W Colfax Ave, 80214 • 303-274-5211 • I-25 Exit 210A take Colfax Ave W 3.4 miles
⊙	5	✓		✓	Lakewood • 440 Wadsworth Blvd, 80226 • 303-205-0754 • I-25 Exit 209B merge onto SR-6 W 3.9 miles then S on Wadsworth Blvd .5 mile
⊙		✓			Lamar • 1432 E Olive St, 81052 • 719-336-0530 • Jct US-287 & US-50 (NW of town) follow US-50 E 7.9 miles
⊙	10	✓			Littleton • 7700 W Quincy Ave, 80123 • 303-971-0321 • I-25 Exit 201 take US-285 W 8.8 miles then S on Wadsworth Blvd 1 mile & W on Quincy
⊙	8	✓			Littleton • 13420 W Coal Mine Ave, 80127 • 303-979-2064 • I-70 Exit 260 go S on SR-470 7 miles then E on Bowles Ave .4 mile & S on Coal Mine Ave .1 mile
⊙	7	✓		✓	Longmont • 2514 Main St, 80504 • 303-774-7513 • I-25 Exit 243 go W on SR-66 for 6.5 miles then N on Main St
⊙	4	✓		✓	Longmont • 2285 E Ken Pratt Blvd, 80504 • 303-678-0803 • I-25 Exit 240 go W 3.5 miles on SR-119
⊙	3	✓		✓	Loveland • 1325 Denver Ave, 80537 • 970-669-3640 • I-25 Exit 267B follow US-34 W 2.8 miles then S on Denver Ave
⊙	8	✓			Loveland • 250 W 65th St, 80538 • 970-667-3331 • I-25 Exit 257B take US-34 W 4.2 miles then US-287 N 3.6 miles
⊙		✓			Montrose • 16750 S Townsend Ave, 81401 • 970-249-7544 • Jct US-550 & Chipeta Rd (S of town) go N on US-550 for 1 mile
⊙	3	✓			Monument • 16218 Jackson Creek Pkwy, 80132 • 719-484-0912 • I-25 Exit 158 go E on Baptist Rd then N on Struthers Rd 1.6 miles, E on Higby Rd & S at Jackson Creek Pkwy .8 mile
⊙		✓		✓	Pagosa Springs • 211 Aspen Village Dr, 81147 • 970-731-9001 • About 3.5 miles west of town center off US-160
⊙	8	✓			Parker • 11101 S Parker Rd, 80134 • 303-805-0029 • I-25 Exit 194 go E on E-470 (tollway) 5 miles then S on Parker Rd 3 miles
⊙	4	✓		✓	Pueblo • 4080 W Northern Ave, 81005 • 719-561-8495 • I-25 Exit 94 take SR-45 W 2.7 miles, Surfwood Ln W .6 mile & SR-78 N .5 mile
⊙	1	✓		✓	Pueblo • 4200 Dillon Dr, 81008 • 719-545-6404 • I-25 Exit 101 go E on SR-47 for .4 mile & N on Dillon Dr .3 mile

☆	◯	🕐	⛽	🚫	Store Details
✪	9	✓			Pueblo West • 78 N McCulloch Blvd, 81007 • 719-647-9861 • I-25 Exit 100B take 29th St W .3 mile, Elizabeth St N .7 mile, US-50 W 7.2 miles & N on McCulloch .7 mile
✪	1	✓			Rifle • 1000 Airport Rd, 81650 • 970-625-5367 • I-70 Exit 90 take SR-13 S .2 mile & Airport Rd E .4 mile
✪					Salida • 7865 W US Hwy 50, 81201 • 719-539-3566 • 2 miles west of town center on US-50, north side of highway
☆				✓	Steamboat Springs • 1805 Central Park Dr, 80477 • 970-879-8115 • 2 miles southeast of town center off US-40 at Mount Werner Rd
✪	4	✓			Sterling • 1510 W Main St, 80751 • 970-522-0600 • I-76 Exit 125, W 2 miles on US-6, S .2 mile on 4th St, W 1 mile on Main St
✪	2	✓		✓	Thornton • 9901 Grant St, 80229 • 303-451-1003 • I-25 Exit 221 take 104th Ave E .5 mile & Grant St S .7 mile
✪	1	✓	❖	✓	Timnath • 4500 Weitzel St, 80547 • 970-484-0328 • I-25 Exit 265, east of exit
✪	1	✓			Trinidad • 2921 Toupal Dr, 81082 • 719-846-4477 • I-25 Exit 11 go W to CR-69.1 then N .3 mile
✪	2	✓		✓	Westminster • 7155 Sheridan Blvd, 80003 • 303-487-1412 • I-70 Exit 1B go N 2 miles on Sheridan Blvd
✪	5	✓		✓	Westminster • 9499 Sheridan Blvd, 80031 • 303-427-4882 • I-25 Exit 220 go SW on Thornton Pkwy for 1.2 miles, continue W on 92nd Ave 2.5 miles then N on Sheridan Blvd .5 mile
✪	2	✓		✓	Westminster • 200 W 136th Ave, 80234 • 720-929-1758 • I-25 Exit 225 go W on 136th Ave for 1.8 miles
☆	1			✓	Wheat Ridge • 3600 Youngfield St, 80033 • 303-420-0640 • I-70 Exit 264 go N on Youngfield St for .3 mile
✪		✓		✓	Woodland Park • 19600 E US Hwy 24, 80863 • 719-687-1065 • 1.7 miles southeast of town along US-24

CONNECTICUT

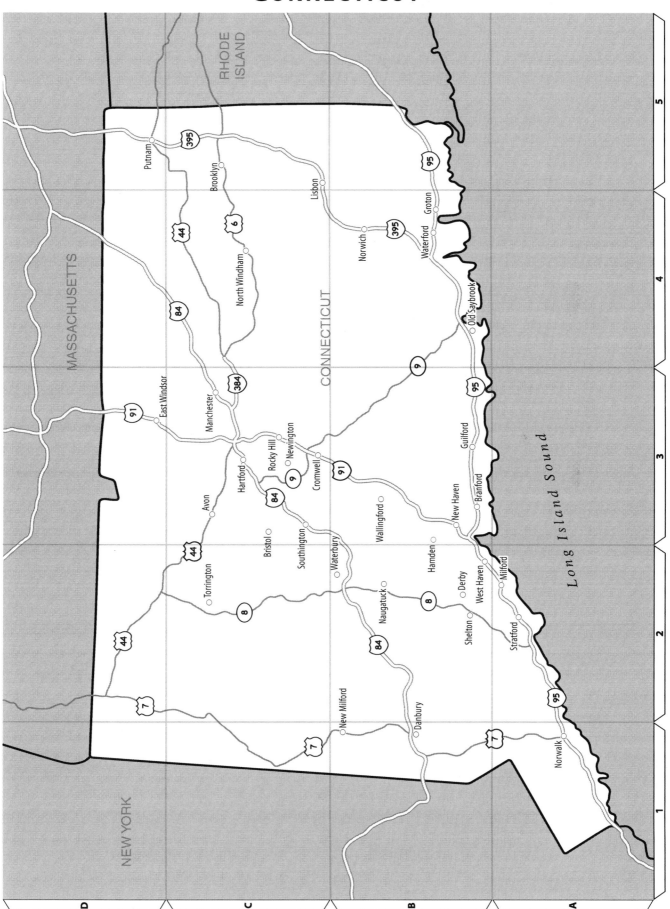

☆	♡	🕐	⛽	🚫	Store Details
☆				✓	Avon • 255 W Main St, 06001 • 860-409-0404 • Jct US-44 & US-202 (E of town) take US-44 W for 1.2 miles
☆	2				Branford • 120 Commercial Pkwy, 06405 • 203-488-4106 • I-95 Exit 54 go S .2 mile on Cedar St, W .8 mile on US-1 (Main St), N .3 mile on Commercial Pkwy
☆	6			✓	Bristol • 1400 Farmington Ave, 06010 • 860-585-1700 • I-84 Exit 33 take SR-72 W 2.1 miles, SR-177 N 2 miles & US-6 S 1 mile
✪	3	✓		✓	Brooklyn • 450 Providence Rd, 06234 • 860-412-5137 • I-395 Exit 37 go W 2.2 miles on US-6.
☆	1				Cromwell • 161 Berlin Rd, 06416 • 860-635-0458 • I-91 Exit 21 go W on Berlin Rd for .3 mile
☆	1				Danbury • 67 Newtown Rd, 06810 • 203-791-1929 • I-84 Exit 8 go S on New-town Rd .7 mile
☆					Derby • 656 New Haven Ave, 06418 • 203-736-2660 • Jct SR-8 & SR-34 (W of town) follow SR-34 E for 2.2 miles
☆	1			✓	East Windsor • 69 Prospect Hill Rd, 06088 • 860-292-1235 • I-91 Exit 44 take US-5 N for .7 mile
☆	1				Groton • 150 Gold Star Hwy, 06340 • 860-448-2022 • I-95 Exit 86 go NE on Gold Star Hwy .7 mile
☆	1				Guilford • 900 Boston Post Rd, 06437 • 203-458-1252 • I-95 Exit 59 go S on Goose Ln .2 mile then US-1 SE .8 mile
☆	6				Hamden • 2300 Dixwell Ave, 06514 • 203-230-0285 • I-91 Exit 10 take US-40 N 3.1 miles then follow SR-10 S 2.5 miles
☆	1				Hartford • 495 Flatbush Ave, 06106 • 860-953-0040 • Eastbound I-84 travelers use Exit 44 and go S .3 mile on Pros-pect Ave; continue S .2 mile on New Park Ave then go E .2 mile on Flatbush Ave. Westbound I-84 travelers use Exit 45; store entrance is across the street from the end of exit ramp.
✪	1	✓			Lisbon • 180 River Rd, 06351 • 860-376-3254 • I-395 Exit 84 go S on River Rd .3 mile
✪	2	✓		✓	Manchester • 420 Buckland Hills Dr, 06042 • 860-644-5100 • Eastbound travelers use I-84 Exit 62 and go N .4 mile on Buckland St then E on Buckland Hills Dr 1 mile; westbound travelers use I-84 Exit 62 and go E 1.2 miles from end of exit ramp
☆	1				Milford • 1365 Boston Post Rd, 06460 • 203-301-0559 • I-95 Exit 39B take Boston Post Rd (US-1) N for .3 mile
✪	7	✓			Naugatuck • 1100 New Haven Rd, 06770 • 203-729-9100 • I-84 Exit 19 take SR-8 S for 4.7 miles to Exit 26/SR-63 SE for 1.8 miles
✪	1	✓			New Haven • 315 Foxon Blvd, 06513 • 203-467-7509 • I-91 Exit 8 go E on SR-80 for .6 mile
☆					New Milford • 164 Danbury Rd, 06776 • 860-350-4823 • I-84 Exit 7 take US-7 NW for 10.1 miles
☆	5				Newington • 3164 Berlin Tpke, 06111 • 860-667-7657 • I-91 Exit 22N merge onto US-9 N 2.2 miles to Exit 21, Berlin Tpk/US-5 N 2.6 miles
✪		✓			North Windham • 474 Boston Post Rd, 06256 • 860-456-4399 • Jct US-6 & SR-66 (SW of town) follow SR-66/Boston Post Rd for 1.3 miles
☆	5				Norwalk • 650 Main Ave, 06851 • 203-846-4514 • I-95 Exit 15 follow US-7 W 4.3 miles
☆	1				Norwalk • 680 Connecticut Ave, 06854 • 203-854-5236 • I-95 Exit 13 follow US-1 N .6 miles
☆	1				Norwich • 220 Salem Tpke, 06360 • 860-889-7745 • I-395 Exit 80 (northbound travelers use Exit 80W) go W on Salem Tpk .4 mile
☆	2				Old Saybrook • 665 Boston Post Rd, 06475 • 860-388-0584 • I-95-exit 68 take US-1 S for 1.6 miles
✪	1	✓			Putnam • 625 School St, 06260 • 860-928-3999 • I-395 Exit 97, west of exit
☆	1				Rocky Hill • 80 Town Line Rd, 06067 • 860-563-4355 • I-91 Exit 24 take SR-99 W for .2 mile then S on Town Line Rd .2 mile
☆					Shelton • 465 Bridgeport Ave, 06484 • 203-929-1110 • From SR-8 Exit 12 go W on Old Stratford Rd .3 mile then N on Bridgeport Ave 1.1 miles
☆	1			✓	Southington • 235 Queen St, 06489 • 860-621-9540 • I-84 Exit 32 go S on Queen St .8 mile
☆	2				Stratford • 150 Barnum Ave Cutoff, 06614 • 203-502-7631 • I-95 Exit 34 follow US-1 S for 1.3 miles
☆					Torrington • 970 Torringford St, 06790 • 860-496-8653 • From SR-8 Exit 44 go NE on US-202 for 1.9 miles then S on Torringford St .1 mile
✪	5	✓			Wallingford • 844 N Colony Rd, 06492 • 203-269-6622 • I-690 Exit 10 take SR-15 S for 3.7 miles to Exit 66/US-5 S for 1 mile
☆	3				Waterbury • 910 Wolcott St, 06705 • 203-759-1000 • I-64 Exit 25 take E Main St .8 miles, N on Southmayd .6 mile & N on SR-69 for 1 mile
✪	1	✓			Waterford • 155 Waterford Pkwy N, 06385 • 860-447-3646 • I-95 Exit 81 go W on Cross Rd .1 mile to Waterford Pkwy N for .3 mile
☆	1				West Haven • 515 Saw Mill Rd, 06516 • 203-931-2081 • I-95 Exit 42 go S on Sawmill Rd .1 mile

DELAWARE

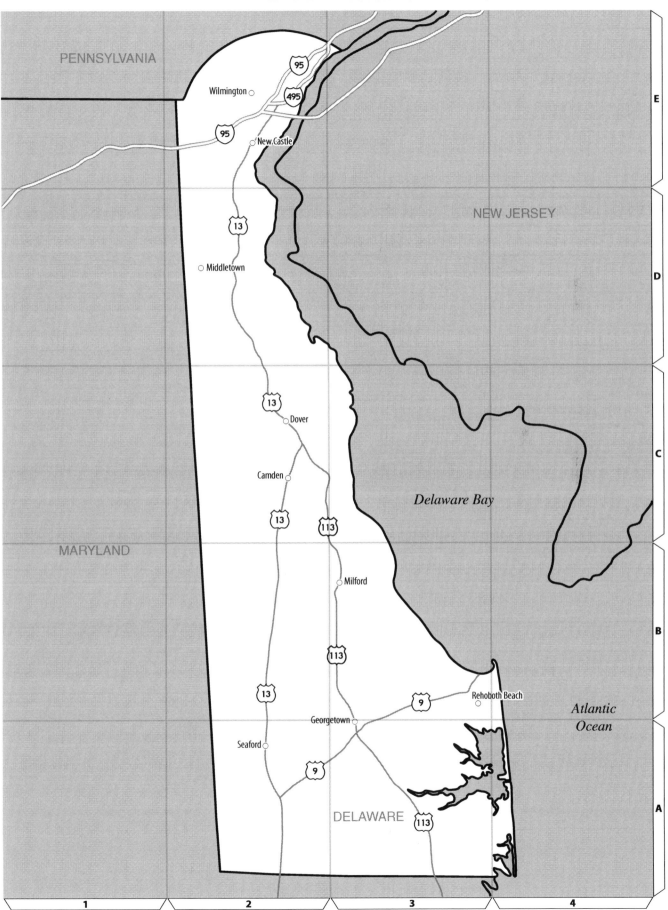

☆	⬭	🕐	⛽	🚳	Store Details
✪		✓			Camden • 263 Walmart Dr, 19934 • 302-698-9170 • 1 mile south of town along US-13
✪		✓		✓	Dover • 36 Jerome Dr, 19901 • 302-674-2159 • 5 miles north of town center along US-13
✪		✓			Georgetown • 4 College Park Ln, 19947 • 302-854-9454 • 1.7 miles northwest of town center near jct of US-113 and Bedford St
✪		✓			Middletown • 705 Middletown Warwick Rd, 19709 • 302-449-1254 • 1 mile west of town center via SR-299 and US-301
✪		✓		✓	Milford • 939 N Dupont Hwy, 19963 • 302-422-2854 • Jct SR-14 & US-13 go S on Dupont Hwy for .5 mile
☆	4				New Castle • 117 Wilton Blvd, 19720 • 302-324-0900 • I-95 Exit 3 go SE 2.2 miles on SR-273 (Christiana Rd), S on Appleby Rd .7 mile & E on Wilton Blvd .8 mile
☆				✓	Rehoboth Beach • 18922 Rehoboth Mall Blvd, 19971 • 302-644-8014 • 3 miles west of town along SR-1
✪		✓			Seaford • 22899 Sussex Hwy, 19973 • 302-628-1668 • 2 miles northeast of town center along US-13
☆	3			✓	Wilmington • 1251 Centerville Rd, 19808 • 302-683-9312 • I-95 Exit 5 take SR-141 N 1.5 miles to Exit 5, merge onto Centerville Rd N for .6 mile

FLORIDA

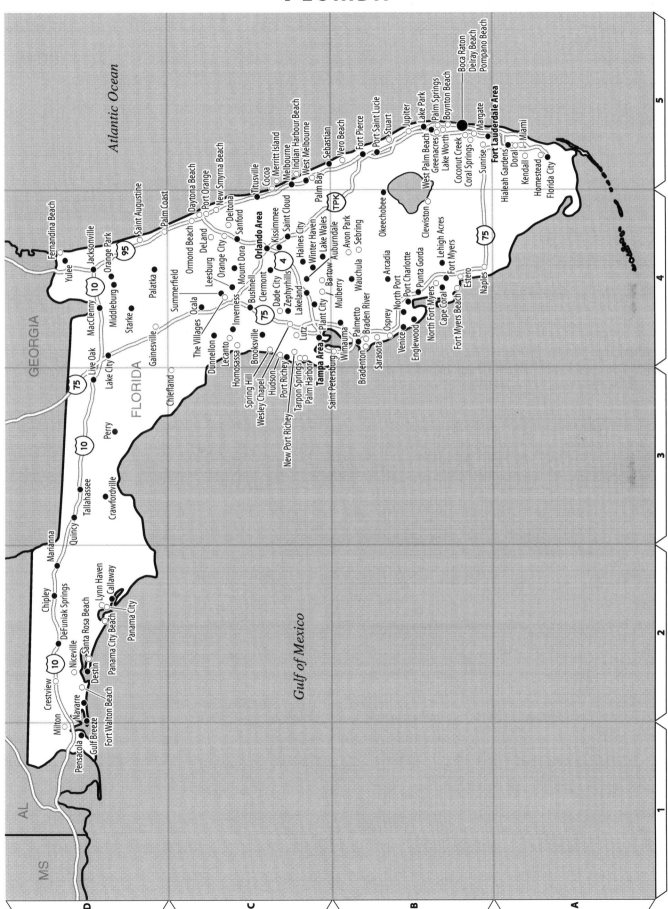

Atlantic Ocean

GEORGIA

FLORIDA

Gulf of Mexico

AL

MS

Fernandina Beach
Yulee
Jacksonville
Orange Park
Saint Augustine
Palm Coast
Ormond Beach
Daytona Beach
Port Orange
New Smyrna Beach
Titusville
Cocoa
Merritt Island
Melbourne
Indian Harbour Beach
West Melbourne
Palm Bay
Sebastian
Vero Beach
Fort Pierce
Port Saint Lucie
Stuart
Jupiter
Lake Park
Palm Springs
West Palm Beach
Greenacres
Lake Worth
Boynton Beach
Coconut Creek
Coral Springs
Sunrise
Margate
Fort Lauderdale Area
Hialeah Gardens
Doral
Miami
Kendall
Homestead
Florida City
Boca Raton
Delray Beach
Pompano Beach

Deltona
Sanford
DeLand
Orange City
Mount Dora
Leesburg
Orlando Area
Kissimmee
Saint Cloud
Haines City
Winter Haven
Lake Wales
Auburndale
Avon Park
Sebring
Okeechobee
Clewiston
Lehigh Acres
Arcadia
Port Charlotte
Punta Gorda
Fort Myers
Estero
Naples

Summerfield
Ocala
Palatka
Middleburg
Starke
MacClenny
Live Oak
Lake City
Gainesville
The Villages
Dunnellon
Lecanto
Homosassa
Chiefland
Spring Hill
Wesley Chapel
Hudson
New Port Richey
Tarpon Springs
Palm Harbor
Saint Petersburg
Tampa Area
Wimauma
Bradenton
Palmetto
Braden River
Sarasota
Osprey
Venice
Englewood
North Fort Myers
Cape Coral
Fort Myers Beach
North Port

Brooksville
Bushnell
Dade City
Zephyrhills
Lakeland
Plant City
Lutz
Mulberry
Wauchula
Clermont
Bartow

Marianna
Quincy
Tallahassee
Crawfordville
Perry
Chipley
DeFuniak Springs
Lynn Haven
Callaway
Panama City
Panama City Beach
Santa Rosa Beach
Niceville
Destin
Fort Walton Beach
Crestview
Milton
Navarre
Gulf Breeze
Pensacola

95
10
75
4
75
TPK
10

Orlando Metro Area

Altamonte Springs • Apopka • Casselberry • Ocoee • Orlando • Oviedo

Fort Lauderdale Metro Area

Cooper City • Davie • Fort Lauderdale • Hallandale Beach • Hialeah • Hollywood • Lauderdale Lakes • Miami Gardens • Miramar • North Lauderdale • North Miami Beach • Pembroke Pines

Tampa Metro Area

Brandon • Clearwater • Gibstonton • Largo • Oldsmar • Pinellas Park • Seffner • Tampa

☆	🛡	🕐	⛽	🚫	Store Details
☆	4				Altamonte Springs • 200 S State Rd 434, 32714 • 407-774-9966 • I-4 Exit 90 go W on SR-414 for 2.1 miles then SR-434 N 1 mile
✪	7	✓		✓	Apopka • 1700 S Orange Blossom Trl, 32703 • 407-889-8668 • I-4 Exit 90 go W on SR-414 for 4.9 miles & N on Orange Blosm Trl 1.8 miles
✪		✓	❖		Arcadia • 2725 SE Hwy 70, 34266 • 863-993-1677 • Jct US-17 & SR-70 go E on SR-70 for .4 mile
✪		✓	❖		Auburndale • 2120 US Hwy 92 W, 33823 • 863-967-1164 • I-4 Exit 41 take SR-570 (toll) S for 7.1 miles to Exit 17/US-92 E for 3.5 miles
✪		✓		✓	Avon Park • 1041 US Hwy 27 N, 33825 • 863-453-4177 • 1 mile north of town via US-27/US-98
✪		✓			Bartow • 1050 E Van Fleet Dr, 33830 • 863-533-5400 • Northwest of town at jct US-17 & US-98
✪	6			✓	Boca Raton • 22100 S State Rd 7, 33428 • 561-226-3157 • I-95 Exit 44 go W 5.3 miles on Palmetto Park Rd
✪	3	✓		✓	Boynton Beach • 3625 S Federal Hwy, 33435 • 561-600-3088 • I-95 Exit 56 go E .8 mile on 15th Ave then S 1.6 miles on Federal Hwy
✪	3	✓			Boynton Beach • 3200 Old Boynton Rd, 33436 • 561-742-0718 • I-95 Exit 59 go W on Gateway Blvd 1.3 miles, S on Congress Ave 1 mile & W on Old Boynton Rd .2 mile
✪	5	✓		✓	Braden River • 2911 53rd Ave E, 34203 • 941-753-6751 • I-75 Exit 217 merge onto SR-70 W 4.5 miles
✪	1	✓			Bradenton • 5810 Ranch Lake Blvd, 34202 • 941-799-5538 • I-75 Exit 217, east of exit
✪	1	✓			Bradenton • 6225 E State Rd 64, 34208 • 941-708-2800 • I-75 Exit 220 go W on SR-64 for 1 mile

☆	🛡	🕐	⛽	🚫	Store Details
✪		✓		✓	Bradenton • 5315 Cortez Rd W, 34210 • 941-798-9341 • I-75 Exit 217 take SR-70 W for 8 miles, 26th St N 1 mile & Cortez Rd W 1.7 miles
✪	5	✓			Brandon • 11110 Causeway Blvd, 33511 • 813-661-4426 • I-75 Exit 254 take US-301 NW 2.5 miles then E on Causeway Blvd 1.7 miles
✪	6	✓	❖		Brandon • 1208 E Brandon Blvd, 33511 • 813-651-9040 • I-75 Exit 257 go E on SR-60 for 5.8 miles
☆	6			✓	Brandon • 949 E Bloomingdale Ave, 33511 • 813-681-8136 • I-75 Exit 254 take US-301 S .9 mile then E on Bloomingdale Ave 4.2 miles
✪		✓	❖		Brooksville • 7305 Broad St, 34601 • 352-796-5996 • Jct US-98 & SR-50 (SE of town) go W on SR-50 for 2.3 miles then S on US-41 for .3 mile
✪		✓			Brooksville • 13300 Cortez Blvd, 34613 • 352-597-3807 • From SR-589 (toll) Exit 46 take SR-50 W for 2 miles
✪	1	✓	❖		Bushnell • 2163 W C 48, 33513 • 352-793-1300 • I-75 Exit 314 go E on CR-48 for .3 mile
✪		✓	◆		Callaway • 725 N Tyndall Pkwy, 32404 • 850-785-6011 • Jct SR-22 & US-98 go N on US-98 for 1 mile
✪	10	✓	❖	✓	Cape Coral • 1619 Del Prado Blvd S, 33990 • 239-772-9220 • I-75 Exit 136 take SR-884 W 7.6 miles, continue W on Veterans Pkwy 1.4 miles then N on Del Prado for 1 mile
✪	6	✓		✓	Casselberry • 1239 State Hwy 436, 32707 • 407-679-0377 • I-4 Exit 92 go SE on SR-436 for 5.2 miles
✪		✓			Chiefland • 2201 N Young Blvd, 32626 • 352-493-0758 • Jct US-129 & US-27 go NW on US-27/19/98 for 1.1 miles
✪	1	✓	◆	✓	Chipley • 1621 Main St, 32428 • 850-638-2243 • I-10 Exit 120 merge onto SR-77 N .5 mile
✪		✓		✓	Clearwater • 23106 US Hwy 19 N, 33765 • 727-724-7777 • I-275 Exit 30 go W 4.4 miles on SR-686 then N 6.2 miles on US-19
✪		✓	❖	✓	Clermont • 1450 Johns Lake Rd, 34711 • 352-243-6151 • Jct US-50 & US-27 take US-27 S 1.6 miles & E on Johns Lake Rd 1.6 miles
✪		✓		✓	Clermont • 550 US Hwy 27, 34714 • 352-536-2746 • Jct CR-561 & US-27 (NE of Lake Minneola) take US-27 S .4 mile
✪		✓		✓	Clewiston • 1005 W Sugarland Hwy, 33440 • 863-983-4844 • Jct SR-80 & US-27 (S of Lake Oceechobee) go E on US-27 for 8.2 miles
✪	6	✓			Cocoa • 2700 Clearlake Rd, 32922 • 321-639-1610 • I-95 Exit 201 take SR-520 E 2.4 miles & SR-501 N 2.7 miles

☆	◯	⏱	⛽	🚭	Store Details
●	5	✓		✓	Coconut Creek • 5571 W Hillsboro Blvd, 33073 • 954-426-6101 • I-95 Exit 42B go W 5 miles on Hillsboro Blvd
●	3	✓		✓	Cooper City • 4700 S Flamingo Rd, 33330 • 954-680-7810 • I-75 Exit 13A go E 2.5 miles on SR-818/Griffin Rd then S .1 mile on Flamingo Rd
●	6	✓		✓	Coral Springs • 3801 Turtle Creek Dr, 33067 • 954-341-4505 • I-95 Exit 39 take SR-834 W 5 miles then N at Turle Creek Dr .3 mile
●	10	✓		✓	Coral Springs • 6001 Coral Ridge Dr, 33076 • 954-757-0331 • I-95 Exit 41 go W on 10th St 2 miles, continue on SR-869 (toll) for 7.5 miles to Exit 10/Coral Ridge Dr N .4 mile
●		✓	❖		Crawfordville • 35 Mike Stewart Dr, 32327 • 850-926-1560 • 16 miles south of Tallahassee via US-319
●	1	✓			Crestview • 3351 S Ferdon Blvd, 32536 • 850-682-8001 • I-10 Exit 56 merge onto Ferdon Blvd N .1 mile
☆	10				Dade City • 12650 US Hwy 301, 33525 • 352-567-1551 • I-75 Exit 285 take SR-52 E 5.6 miles, Clinton Ave SE 3.1 miles & US-301 N .9 mile
●	6	✓		✓	Davie • 4301 S University Dr, 33328 • 954-331-3612 • I-95 Exit 23 go W 5.5 miles on Griffin Rd
●	4	✓		✓	Daytona Beach • 1101 Beville Rd, 32119 • 386-760-7880 • I-95 Exit 206 take SR-200 E 3.1 miles
●	2	✓	◆		DeFuniak Springs • 1226 Freeport Rd, 32435 • 850-892-3138 • I-10 Exit 85 merge onto US-331 S 1.2 miles
●		✓		✓	DeLand • 1699 N Woodland Blvd, 32720 • 386-734-4420 • Jct SR-472 & US-17 (S of town) take US-17 N 6.2 miles
☆	3		❖	✓	Delray Beach • 16205 Military Trl, 33484 • 561-495-8127 • I-95 Exit 51 go W on Linton Blvd 2 miles & S on Military Trl .1 mile
●	9	✓		✓	Deltona • 101 Howland Blvd, 32738 • 407-328-8052 • I-4 Exit 114 go SE on Howland Blvd 9 miles
●		✓	◆	✓	Destin • 15017 Emerald Coast Pkwy, 32541 • 850-650-0341 • Jct US-331 & US-98 (E of town) take US-98 W 16.5 miles
●	9	✓		✓	Doral • 8651 NW 13th Ter, 33126 • 305-470-4510 • I-95 Exit 3A take SR-836 W 8 miles, exit at NW 12th W .1 mile, Galloway Rd N .1 mile & 13th Ter E .2 mile
●		✓	❖	✓	Dunnellon • 11012 N Williams St, 34432 • 352-489-4210 • Jct SR-40 & US-41 (N of town) take US-41 S 3.3 miles

☆	◯	⏱	⛽	🚭	Store Details
●		✓	◆	✓	Englewood • 2931 S McCall Rd, 34224 • 941-475-9220 • I-75 Exit 191 merge onto River Rd SW 12.2 miles, Pine St S 1.6 miles & McCall Rd E .6 mile
●	4	✓		✓	Estero • 19975 S Tamiami Trail, 33928 • 239-590-9501 • I-75 Exit 123 go W 2 miles on Corkscrew Rd then N 1.5 miles on US-41/Tamiami Trail
☆					Fernandina Beach • 1385 Amelia Plaza, 32034 • 904-261-5306 • Jct Fletcher & Atlantic Avenues (NE of town) go W on Atlantic 1.1 miles & N on 15th St .7 mile
●		✓	◆	✓	Florida City • 33501 S Dixie Hwy, 33034 • 305-242-4447 • Florida's Tpk (toll) Exit 1 take US-1 N .2 mile
●	1				Fort Lauderdale • 2500 W Broward Blvd, 33312 • 954-453-6538 • I-95 Exit 27, west of exit
●	6	✓		✓	Fort Myers • 14821 Ben C Pratt • 6 Mile Cypress Pkwy, 33912 • 239-437-1880 • I-75 Exit 131 go W on Daniels Pkwy 2.6 miles & S on Pratt Pkwy 2.9 miles
●	1	✓	❖		Fort Myers • 4770 Colonial Blvd, 33966 • 239-274-2920 • I-75 Exit 136 go W on Colonial Blvd .7 mile
●		✓		✓	Fort Myers Beach • 17105 San Carlos Blvd, 33931 • 239-340-7074 • I-75 Exit 131 go W 5.6 miles on Daniels Pkwy/ Cypress Lake Dr then SW 5.7 miles on Summerlin Rd and turn left .2 mile on SR-865/San Carlos Blvd
●	2	✓	◆		Fort Pierce • 5100 Okeechobee Rd, 34947 • 772-468-0880 • I-95 Exit 129 merge onto SR-70 E 1.3 miles
●		✓		✓	Fort Walton Beach • 748 Beal Pkwy NW, 32547 • 850-862-0700 • Jct SR-188 & SR-189 go S on SR-189 for .6 mile
●	1	✓	❖	✓	Gainesville • 2900 SW 42nd St, 32608 • 352-371-3171 • I-75 Exit 384 go E .2 mile on SR-24; left .3 mile on Southwest 40 Blvd; right .4 mile on 42nd St
●	7	✓			Gainesville • 1800 NE 12th Ave, 32641 • 352-372-3191 • I-75 Exit 382 go N 5.6 miles on SR-331 then continue N .9 mile on SR-24 and go E .2 mile on 12th Ave
●	7	✓			Gainesville • 5700 NW 23rd St, 32653 • 352-378-0619 • I-75 Exit 390 go E 4.5 miles on 39th Ave then N 1.9 miles on 34th St
●	1	✓	❖	✓	Gibsonton • 9205 Gibsonton Dr, 33534 • 813-672-0739 • I-75 Exit 250 merge onto Gibsonton Dr W .5 mile
●	5	✓			Greenacres • 6294 Forest Hill Blvd, 33415 • 561-966-3101 • I-95 Exit 66 take SR-882/Forest Hill Blvd W 4.7 miles

★	⛨	🕐	⛽	🚫	Store Details
★		✓	❖		Gulf Breeze • 3767 Gulf Breeze Pkwy, 32563 • 850-934-0362 • I-10 Exit 22 take SR-821 (toll) S 11 miles then US-98 E .1 mile
★	8	✓	◆	✓	Haines City • 36205 US Hwy 27, 33844 • 863-422-7537 • I-4 Exit 55 take US-27 S 7.4 miles
★	3	✓		✓	Hallandale Beach • 2551 E Hallandale Beach Blvd, 33009 • 954-455-4700 • I-95 Exit 18 take SR-858 E 2.8 miles
★	6	✓	❖		Hialeah • 5851 NW 177th St, 33015 • 305-558-6069 • I-95 Exit 12 take SR-826 W 5.1 miles then SR-823 S .7 mile & W on 177th St
★		✓	◆		Hialeah Gardens • 9300 NW 77th Ave, 33016 • 305-819-0672 • I-95 Exit 3 take SR-836 W 7.4 miles then SR-826 N 5 miles
★	3	✓			Hollywood • 301 State Road 7, 33023 • 754-260-6713 • I-95 Exit 20 go W on Hollywood Blvd 2.6 miles then S .2 mile on State Road 7
★		✓		✓	Homestead • 13600 SW 288th St, 33033 • 305-910-2965 • Ronald Reagan Tpk Exit 5 go E .4 mile on 288th St/Biscayne Dr
★		✓			Homosassa • 6885 S Suncoast Blvd, 34446 • 352-628-4161 • 3 miles northeast of town along US-19
★		✓			Hudson • 12610 US Hwy 19, 34667 • 727-861-0040 • I-75 Exit 25 go W 23.5 miles on SR-52 then north .5 mile on US-19
☆	8			✓	Indian Harbour Beach • 1001 E Eau Gallie Blvd, 32937 • 321-777-5504 • I-95 Exit 183 take SR-318 E 7.4 miles
★		✓	❖		Inverness • 2461 E Gulf To Lake Hwy, 34453 • 352-637-2300 • I-75 Exit 329 follow SR-44 W 17 miles
★	1	✓	❖	✓	Jacksonville • 6830 Normandy Blvd, 32205 • 904-786-0390 • I-295 Exit 19 merge onto Normandy Blvd E 1 mile
★	1	✓	❖	✓	Jacksonville • 4250 Phillips Hwy, 32207 • 904-737-7007 • I-95 Exit 347 go W on Emerson Rd .3 mile then US-1 N .2 mile
★	1	✓			Jacksonville • 6767 103rd St, 32210 • 904-772-0011 • I-295 Exit 16 go E on 103rd St .5 mile
★		✓	❖		Jacksonville • 8808 Beach Blvd, 32216 • 904-642-4999 • Jct SR-115 & US-90 take US-90 W 1.2 miles
★	1	✓			Jacksonville • 12100 Lem Turner Rd, 32218 • 904-764-2855 • I-295 Exit 32 merge onto SR-115 S .4 mile
★	1	✓			Jacksonville • 13227 City Square Dr, 32218 • 904-751-5552 • I-95 Exit 363 take Duval Rd/CR-110 E .1 mile
★	1	✓		✓	Jacksonville • 10991 San Jose Blvd, 32223 • 904-260-4402 • I-295 Exit 5 merge onto San Jose Blvd S .4 mile
★	10	✓			Jacksonville • 13490 Beach Blvd, 32224 • 904-223-0772 • I-95 Exit 344 take SR-202 E 7 miles then Hodges Blvd N 2.6 miles
★		✓	❖		Jacksonville • 11900 Atlantic Blvd, 32225 • 904-641-8088 • SR-9A at Atlantic Blvd Exit, go E 2.1 miles
★		✓			Jacksonville • 9890 Hutchinson Park Dr, 32225 • 904-721-4941 • I-95 Exit 362A go S on SR-9A for 11.5 miles then W on Monument Rd
★	1	✓			Jacksonville • 10251 Shops Ln, 32258 • 904-288-8211 • I-95 Exit 339, east of exit
★	2	✓		✓	Jupiter • 2144 W Indiantown Rd, 33458 • 561-746-6422 • I-95 Exit 87A take SR-706 E for 1.7 miles
★		✓		✓	Kendall • 15885 SW 88th St, 33196 • 305-383-3611 • Florida's Tpk (toll) Exit 20 go W on 88th St 4 miles
★	10	✓	❖	✓	Kissimmee • 1471 E Osceola Pkwy, 34744 • 407-870-2277 • I-4 Exit 65 go E on Osceola Pkwy (toll) 9.4 miles
★	4	✓	❖	✓	Kissimmee • 3250 Vineland Rd, 34746 • 407-397-1125 • I-4 Exit 67 follow SR-536 E 2.4 miles then S on SR-535 1.1 miles
★	9	✓		✓	Kissimmee • 4444 W Vine St, 34746 • 407-397-7000 • I-4 Exit 64 follow US-192 E for 9 miles
★		✓	❖		Kissimmee • 904 Cypress Pkwy, 34759 • 407-870-1903 • 11 miles south of town via US-17, Pleasant Hill Rd, and Cypress Pkwy
★	6	✓	◆		Lake City • 2767 W US Hwy 90, 32055 • 386-755-2427 • I-75 Exit 427 take US-90 E 5.7 miles
★	2		❖		Lake Park • 101 N Congress Ave, 33403 • 561-842-8113 • I-95 Exit 77 go E on Northern Blvd .9 mile then S on Congress Ave 1 mile
★		✓	◆	✓	Lake Wales • 2000 State Hwy 60 E, 33898 • 863-676-9425 • Jct US-27 & SR-60 (W of town) go W on SR-60 for 1.6 miles
☆	3				Lake Worth • 4545 Hypoluxo Rd, 33463 • 561-642-6005 • I-95 Exit 60 go W on Hypoluxo Rd for 2.7 miles
★	7	✓		✓	Lakeland • 3501 S Florida Ave, 33803 • 863-644-5676 • I-4 Exit 27 take SR-570 (toll) E for 6.6 miles to Exit 7/Florida Ave N for .4 mile
★	5	✓	◆		Lakeland • 5800 US Hwy 98 N, 33809 • 863-815-4498 • I-4 Exit 32 take US-98 S 2.8 miles, continue SE on Bartow Rd 2.1 miles

☆	○	⏰	⛽	🚫	Store Details
✪	6	✓			Largo · 2677 Roosevelt Blvd, 33760 · 727-431-5917 · I-275 Exit 30 go W 2.8 miles on 118th Ave; N 2.4 miles on US-19; E .2 mile on Roosevelt Blvd
✪		✓		✓	Largo · 990 Missouri Ave N, 33770 · 727-587-7822 · US-19 at Roosevelt Blvd/SR-686 go W 3.5 miles on SR-686 then N .8 mile on Missouri Ave
✪	4			✓	Lauderdale Lakes · 3001 N State Hwy 7, 33313 · 954-733-7473 · I-95 Exit 32 take SR-870 W for 3.2 miles then S on 40th Ave 1.2 miles
✪		✓			Lecanto · 1936 N Lecanto Hwy, 34461 · 352-228-6000 · 3 miles north of town via CR-491 at CR-486
✪		✓	◆	✓	Leesburg · 2501 Citrus Blvd, 34748 · 352-326-3900 · Jct SR-44 & US-27 (S of town) go N on US-27 for 3 miles
✪	10	✓	◆	✓	Lehigh Acres · 2523 Lee Blvd, 33971 · 239-368-5700 · I-75 Exit 136 follow SR-884/CR-884 E for 9.2 miles
✪	1	✓	❖		Live Oak · 6868 US Hwy 129, 32060 · 386-330-2488 · I-10 Exit 283 go S on US-129 for .7 mile
✪	7	✓			Lutz · 1575 Land O' Lakes Blvd, 33548 · 813-949-4238 · I-75 Exit 275 go W 5.3 miles on SR-56/SR-54 then S .8 mile on US-41/SR-45
✪		✓			Lynn Haven · 2101 S Hwy 77, 32444 · 850-265-2626 · 1.4 miles south of town center via SR-77/Ohio Ave
✪	1		❖		MacClenny · 9218 S State Hwy 228, 32063 · 904-259-4760 · I-10 Exit 336 go NW on SR-228 1 mile
✪	5	✓		✓	Margate · 5555 W Atlantic Blvd, 33063 · 954-975-8682 · I-95 Exit 36 go W on Atlantic Blvd 4.4 miles
✪	2	✓	❖		Marianna · 2255 Hwy 71, 32448 · 850-526-5744 · I-10 Exit 142 merge onto SR-71 N for 1.6 miles
✪	3	✓	◆	✓	Melbourne · 1000 N Wickham Rd, 32935 · 321-242-1601 · I-95 Exit 183 go E on SR-518 for 2.3 miles & S on Wickham .4 mile
✪	1	✓	❖		Melbourne · 8500 N Wickham Rd, 32940 · 321-242-0225 · I-95 Exit 191 go W on Wickham Rd .3 mile
✪	8	✓		✓	Merritt Island · 1500 E Merritt Island Cswy, 32952 · 321-452-6058 · I-95 Exit 201 take SR-520 E for 7.6 miles
✪	3			✓	Miami · 3200 NW 79th St, 33147 · 305-913-8439 · I-95 Exit 7 go W 2.7 miles on 79th St
✪				✓	Miami · 8400 Coral Way, 33155 · 305-351-0725 · From the Palmetto Expy at 24th St/Coral Way exit, go W .9 mile
✪				✓	Miami · 9191 W Flager St, 33174 · 786-801-5704 · Ronald Reagan Tpk Exit 25 go E 2.6 miles on US-41 then N .5 mile on 92nd Ave

☆	○	⏰	⛽	🚫	Store Details
✪		✓		✓	Miami · 21151 S Dixie Hwy, 33189 · 305-964-4206 · About 20 miles southwest of downtown Miami via US-1 at 211th St
✪	4				Miami Gardens · 19501 NW 27th Ave, 33056 · 305-622-6664 · I-95 Exit 12 take SR-826 W 2.1 miles then SR-817 N 1.3 miles
✪	3	✓		✓	Miami Gardens · 17650 NW 2nd Ave, 33169 · 305-651-4661 · I-95 Exit 20 go W on Hollywood Blvd 2.7 miles & N on 70th Ave .1 mile
✪	10	✓	❖		Middleburg · 1580 Branan Field Rd, 32068 · 904-214-9411 · I-295 Exit 12 take Blanding Blvd/SR-21 S 9.2 miles then Branan Field Rd W .3 mile
✪	7	✓			Milton · 4965 Hwy 90, 32571 · 850-995-0542 · I-10 Exit 17 follow US-90 W for 6.6 miles
✪	6	✓		✓	Miramar · 1800 S University Dr, 33025 · 954-433-9300 · I-95 Exit 19 take SR-824 (Pembroke Rd) W 5.1 miles then S on University Dr
✪		✓	◆	✓	Mount Dora · 17030 US Hwy 441, 32757 · 352-735-3000 · Jct SR-46 & US-441 (E of town) take US-441 N 4.4 miles
✪		✓		✓	Mulberry · 6745 N Church Ave, 33860 · 863-701-2232 · From SR-570 (toll) Exit 7 take SR-37 S for 6.8 miles
✪	1	✓		✓	Naples · 5420 Juliet Blvd, 34109 · 239-254-8310 · I-75 Exit 111 go W on Immolake Rd
✪	7	✓		✓	Naples · 11225 Tamiami Trl N, 34110 · 239-591-4311 · I-75 Exit 116 merge onto Bonita Beach Rd SE 1.7 miles, Old US-41 S 2.8 miles & Tamiami Trl S 1.7 miles
☆	6			✓	Naples · 3451 Tamiami Trl E, 34112 · 239-793-5517 · I-75 Exit 107 take CR-896 W 4.3 miles then S on 9th St 1.6 miles
✪	8	✓		✓	Naples · 6650 Collier Blvd, 34114 · 239-417-1252 · I-75 Exit 101 go S on Collier Blvd 7.2 miles
✪	1	✓		✓	Naples · 9885 Collier Blvd, 34114 · 239-455-1131 · I-75 Exit 101 take Collier Blvd S .6 mile
✪		✓	❖	✓	Navarre · 9360 Navarre Pkwy, 32566 · 850-939-3998 · Jct SR-87 & US-98 (W of town) take US-98 E for 2.6 miles
✪		✓			New Port Richey · 8745 State Hwy 54, 34655 · 727-376-3811 · I-75 Exit 275 take SR-54 W 17.8 miles
✪	1	✓		✓	New Smyrna Beach · 3155 State Hwy 44, 32168 · 386-427-5767 · I-95 Exit 249, west of exit
✪		✓			Niceville · 1300 John Sims Pkwy E, 32578 · 850-389-3013 · I-10 Exit 56 go S 15.7 miles on SR-85 then E 1.9 miles on SR-20

☆	🛡	🕐	⛽	🚫	Store Details
✪	7	✓		✓	North Fort Myers • 545 Pine Island Rd, 33903 • 239-997-9991 • I-75 Exit 143 follow SR-78 W for 6.4 miles
✪	6	✓		✓	North Lauderdale • 7900 W McNab Rd, 33068 • 954-726-3368 • I-95 Exit 33 go W on Cypress Creek Rd 3.4 miles, continue W on McNab 1.9 miles
✪	5				North Miami Beach • 1425 NE 163rd St, 33162 • 305-949-5881 • I-95 Exit 16 go E on 203rd 1.1 miles, S on US-1 for 2.7 miles & E on 163rd .6 mile
✪		✓	❖	✓	North Port • 17000 Tamiami Trl, 34287 • 941-423-5266 • I-75 Exit 191 go SE on River Rd 5.5 miles then E on Tamiami Trl 5.4 miles
✪		✓	❖		Ocala • 4980 E Silver Springs Blvd, 34470 • 352-236-1188 • Jct US-441/301 & SR-40 go E on SR-40 for 3.1 miles
✪		✓			Ocala • 34 Bahia Ave, 34472 • 352-537-3095 • I-75 Exit 352 go E 2.7 miles on Silver Springs Blvd; S 1.1 miles on Pine Ave; E 2.2 miles on 17th St; SE 6.2 miles on Maricamp Rd to Bahia Ave
✪	3	✓			Ocala • 2600 SW 19th Avenue Rd, 34474 • 352-237-7155 • I-75 Exit 350 take SR-200 NE 1.5 miles, S on 27th Ave .5 mile & E on 19th .1 mile
✪	5	✓	❖		Ocala • 9570 SW Hwy 200, 34481 • 352-291-7512 • I-75 Exit 350 follow SR-200 SW for 4.9 miles
✪		✓		✓	Ocoee • 10500 W Colonial Dr, 34761 • 407-877-6900 • From SR-429 (toll) Exit 23 go W on Colonial Dr 1.5 miles
✪		✓	◆		Okeechobee • 2101 S Parrott Ave, 34974 • 863-763-7070 • 1.3 miles south of town center on US-98/US-441
✪		✓		✓	Oldsmar • 3801 Tampa Rd, 34677 • 813-854-3261 • Jct SR-589 & SR-580 go W on Hillsborough Rd 7.1 miles, continue W on Tampa Rd 1.7 miles
✪	1	✓			Orange City • 2400 Veterans Memorial Pkwy, 32763 • 386-775-1500 • I-4 Exit 111 go W on Saxon Blvd .7 mile then N on Veterans Memorial Pkwy .1 mile
✪	7	✓	❖		Orange Park • 1505 County Rd 220, 32003 • 904-278-1836 • I-295 Exit 10 take US-17 S 6.3 miles then W on CR-220 for .3 mile
✪	5	✓			Orange Park • 899 Blanding Blvd, 32065 • 904-272-0036 • I-295 exit 12 go S on Blanding Blvd 4.7 miles
✪	3	✓			Orlando • 3101 W Princeton St, 32808 • 321-354-2096 • I-4 Exit 85 go W 2.7 miles on SR-438
✪	4	✓	❖	✓	Orlando • 2500 S Kirkman Rd, 32811 • 407-290-6977 • I-4 Exit 75B go N 3.3 miles on Kirkman Rd

☆	🛡	🕐	⛽	🚫	Store Details
✪		✓		✓	Orlando • 11250 E Colonial Dr, 32817 • 407-281-8941 • From SR-417 (toll) Exit 34 go E on Colonial Dr 2.8 miles
✪	6	✓		✓	Orlando • 8101 S John Young Pkwy, 32819 • 407-354-5665 • I-4 Exit 72 take SR-528 (toll) E 2.9 miles to Exit 3/Young Pkwy N 2.3 miles
✪	1	✓			Orlando • 8990 Turkey Lake Rd, 32819 • 407-351-2229 • I-4 Exit 74A follow Sand Lake Rd W .3 mile then S on Turkey Lake Rd .6 mile
☆	7			✓	Orlando • 3838 S Semoran Blvd, 32822 • 407-277-4314 • I-4 Exit 82 take SR-408 (toll) E 4.3 miles then S on Semoran Blvd 2.3 miles
✪		✓		✓	Orlando • 5991 New Goldenrod Rd, 32822 • 407-382-8880 • From SR-528/Beachline Expy Exit 12 follow SR-551 N 1.7 miles
✪	3				Orlando • 5734 S Orange Blossom Trail, 32839 • 321-247-4817 • I-4 Exit 80 go S 2.3 miles on US-17
✪	1	✓		✓	Ormond Beach • 1521 W Granada Blvd, 32174 • 386-672-2104 • I-95 Exit 268 go E on Grenada Blvd .1 mile
✪	6	✓		✓	Osprey • 13140 S Tamiami Trail, 34229 • 941-918-1247 • I-75 Exit 205 follow SR-72 W 5.1 miles then S on Tamiami Trl .3 mile
✪		✓			Oviedo • 5511 Deep Lake Rd, 32765 • 407-618-5013 • SR-417 Exit 38, west of exit
✪		✓	❖		Palatka • 1024 S State Rd 19, 32177 • 386-328-6733 • Jct SR-20 & SR-19 (W of town) go S on SR-19 for .2 mile
✪	1	✓			Palm Bay • 1040 Malabar Rd SE, 32907 • 321-723-2171 • I-95 Exit 173 go W on Malabar Rd .5 mile
✪	1	✓		✓	Palm Coast • 174 Cypress Point Pkwy, 32164 • 386-446-8486 • I-95 Exit 289 go W on Palm Coast Pkwy .3 mile then S on Cypress Point Pkwy .3 mile
✪		✓		✓	Palm Harbor • 35404 US Hwy 19 N, 34684 • 727-784-8797 • I-275 Exit 47 go W 12.7 miles on Hillsborough Ave, continue 2.9 miles on Tampa Rd, turn left at Curlew Rd for 2.7 miles then go N 3.1 miles on US-19N/SR-55
✪	1	✓		✓	Palm Springs • 2765 10th Ave N, 33461 • 561-223-4357 • I-95 Exit 64 go W 1 mile on 10th Ave
✪	4	✓	❖	✓	Palmetto • 508 10th St E, 34221 • 941-723-2199 • I-75 Exit 224 go W on US-301 for 3.6 miles
✪		✓			Panama City • 513 W 23rd St, 32405 • 850-691-0716 • 2.5 miles north of town center and about 1 mile west of Panama City Mall at 23rd St and US-231

☆	♡	🕐	⛽	🚫	Store Details
✪		✓		✓	Panama City Beach • 10270 Front Beach Rd, 32407 • 850-234-1989 • 10 miles west of Panama City via US-98 and Front Beach Rd
✪		✓			Panama City Beach • 15495 Panama City Beach Pkwy, 32413 • 850-708-6968 • 14 miles west of Panama City town center along US-98
✪	2	✓		✓	Pembroke Pines • 12800 Pines Blvd, 33027 • 954-378-1542 • I-75 Exit 9A go E 1.4 miles on Pines Blvd
✪	4	✓		✓	Pembroke Pines • 151 SW 184th Ave, 33029 • 954-442-5822 • I-95 Exit 14 take SR-860 W for 2.9 miles then N on 17th Ave .7 mile & W on 19th St
✪	3	✓	❖		Pensacola • 2650 Creighton Rd, 32504 • 850-479-2101 • I-10 Exit 13 go S on SR-291 for .6 mile & E on Creighton Rd 1.8 miles
✪		✓	❖		Pensacola • 2951 S Blue Angel Pkwy, 32506 • 850-458-5550 • I-10 Exit 7 go S 2.5 miles on SR-297 to SR-173; turn right and continue S 10.2 miles
✪	4	✓			Pensacola • 4600 Mobile Hwy, 32506 • 850-455-4320 • I-110 Exit 4 go W on Fairfield Dr 3.5 miles then N on Mobile Hwy .2 mile
✪	6				Pensacola • 501 N Navy Blvd, 32507 • 850-453-6311 • I-110 Exit 4 follow SR-295 S for 6 miles
✪	2	✓	❖		Pensacola • 8970 Pensacola Blvd, 32534 • 850-484-3771 • I-10 Exit 10 go N on Pensacola Blvd 1.8 miles
✪		✓	❖		Perry • 1900 S Jefferson St, 32348 • 850-223-4179 • 1 mile south of town center on US-221
✪	1	✓	❖		Pinellas Park • 8001 US Hwy 19 N, 33781 • 727-576-1770 • I-275 Exit 28 take SR-694 W .9 mile & US-19 N .1 mile
✪	5	✓	◆	✓	Plant City • 2602 James L Redman Pkwy, 33566 • 813-752-1188 • I-4 Exit 22 go SW on Park Rd 3.7 miles & S on Redman Pkwy 1 mile
✪	2	✓	❖	✓	Pompano Beach • 2300 W Atlantic Blvd, 33069 • 954-971-7170 • I-95 Exit 36 go W on Atlantic Blvd 1.4 miles
✪	3	✓			Pompano Beach • 5001 N Federal Way, 33064 • 954-784-0220 • I-95 Exit 41 go E 1.6 miles on 10th St then S .9 mile on US-1
✪	8	✓		✓	Port Charlotte • 19100 Murdock Cir, 33948 • 941-625-2399 • I-75 Exit 179 go S on Toledo Blade Blvd 5.7 miles & SE on Tamiami Trl 1.5 miles
✪	1	✓	❖	✓	Port Charlotte • 375 Kings Hwy, 33983 • 941-625-1201 • I-75 Exit 170 go NE on Kings Hwy .2 mile
✪	1	✓		✓	Port Orange • 1590 Dunlawton Ave, 32127 • 386-756-2711 • I-95 Exit 256 go E on SR-321 for .9 mile

☆	♡	🕐	⛽	🚫	Store Details
✪		✓	❖		Port Richey • 8701 US Hwy 19, 34668 • 727-846-9504 • Jct SR-52 & US-19 (N of town) go S on US-19 for 3.6 miles
✪	10	✓		✓	Port Saint Lucie • 10855 S US Hwy 1, 34952 • 772-335-5359 • I-95 Exit 118 go E on Gatin Blvd 3.2 miles & Port Saint Lucie Blvd 5.8 miles then US-1 S .4 mile
✪	1	✓		✓	Port Saint Lucie • 1850 SW Gatlin Blvd, 34953 • 772-336-8212 • I-95 Exit 118 go E on Gatlin Blvd 1 mile
✪	1	✓	❖	✓	Port Saint Lucie • 1675 NW Saint Lucie West Blvd, 34986 • 772-873-2221 • I-95 Exit 121 go W on Saint Lucie Blvd .3 mile
✪	1	✓	❖	✓	Punta Gorda • 5001 Taylor Rd, 33950 • 941-637-3800 • I-75 exit 161 take Jones Loop Rd W .5 mile then Taylor Rd S .1 mile
✪	2	✓	❖		Quincy • 1940 Pat Thomas Pkwy, 32351 • 850-875-1661 • I-10 Exit 181 go N 1.2 miles on SR-267
✪	6	✓		✓	Saint Augustine • 2355 US Hwy 1 S, 32086 • 904-797-3309 • I-95 Exit 311 take SR-207 N 4.1 miles, SR-312 E 1 mile & US-1 S .8 mile
✪		✓	❖	✓	Saint Cloud • 4400 13th St, 34769 • 407-957-1300 • From Florida's Tpk (toll) Exit 242 take US-192 E 1.3 miles
✪	8	✓			Saint Petersburg • 10237 Bay Pines Blvd, 33708 • 727-347-1188 • I-275 Exit 25 go W 5.3 miles on 38th Ave; W on US-19-ALT for 1.9 miles; N .1 mile on 100th Way
✪	1	✓		✓	Saint Petersburg • 3501 34th St S, 33711 • 727-906-4647 • I-275 Exit 19 take 22nd Ave W .2 mile & 34th St S .8 mile
✪	2	✓		✓	Saint Petersburg • 201 34th St N, 33713 • 727-803-4961 • I-275 Exit 23B (southbound exit only) go W 1.2 miles on US-19/5th Ave then S .3 miles on 34th St; Northbound travelers use I-275 Exit 20, turn left and go N .4 mile on 31st S, W .2 mile on 5th Ave, N .4 mile on 34th St
✪	1	✓	❖	✓	Sanford • 1601 Rinehart Rd, 32771 • 407-321-1540 • I-4 Exit 101C go E .4 mile on SR-46 then S on Rinehart Rd .5 mile
✪	5	✓			Sanford • 3653 S Orlando Dr, 32773 • 407-321-1371 • I-4 Exit 98 go E 4.6 miles on Lake Mary Blvd then N .4 mile on Orlando Dr/US-17
✪				✓	Santa Rosa Beach • 6712 US Hwy 98 W, 32459 • 850-622-6237 • Located along US-98 about 3.5 miles west of town

☆	♡	🕐	⛽	🚫	Store Details
✪	1	✓		✓	Sarasota • 4381 Cattlemen Rd, 34233 • 941-379-3550 • I-75 Exit 207 go W on Bee Ridge Rd .2 mile & S on Cattlemen Rd .4 mile
✪	4	✓		✓	Sarasota • 8320 Lockwood Ridge Rd, 34243 • 941-351-6969 • I-75 Exit 213 go W on University Pkwy 3.6 miles & N at Lockwood Ridge Rd .2 mile
✪	10	✓	◆	✓	Sebastian • 2001 US Hwy 1, 32958 • 772-589-8528 • I-95 Exit 156 follow CR-512 E 3.7 miles, Roseland Rd N 4.7 miles & US-1 S .8 mile
✪		✓			Sebring • 3525 US Hwy 27 N, 33870 • 863-471-1200 • Jct US-98 & US-27 (N of town) go S on US-27/98 for 16.6 miles
☆	2			✓	Seffner • 11720 E Martin Luther King Blvd, 33584 • 813-681-6654 • I-75 Exit 160 go E on Martin Luther King Blvd 1.9 miles
✪		✓			Spring Hill • 1485 Commercial Way, 34606 • 352-686-0744 • From SR-589 (toll) Exit 46 go W 5.8 miles on SR-50 then S 5.5 miles on US-19
✪		✓	❖		Starke • 14500 US Hwy 301 S, 32091 • 904-964-3286 • Jct SR-100 & US-301 (S of town) go S on US-301 for 2 miles
✪	6	✓		✓	Stuart • 4001 SE Federal Hwy, 34997 • 772-288-4749 • I-95 Exit 101 take SR-76 NE 1 mile, Cove Rd W 3.2 miles & US-1 N 1.7 miles
✪		✓	◆		Summerfield • 17961 S US Hwy 441, 34491 • 352-307-4400 • Jct SR-42 & US-441 (S of town) take US-441 S 1.9 miles
✪	3	✓		✓	Sunrise • 12555 W Sunrise Blvd, 33323 • 954-845-0581 • I-75 Exit 19 go N .5 mile on SR-869 then E 2.1 miles on Sunrise Blvd
☆	7			✓	Sunrise • 3306 N University Dr, 33351 • 954-749-3111 • I-95 Exit 31 go W 6 miles on Oakland Park Blvd then N .1 mile on Unversity Dr
✪	1	✓			Tallahassee • 3221 N Monroe St, 32303 • 850-562-8383 • I-10 Exit 199 go N .6 mile on US-27/SR-63
✪	3	✓			Tallahassee • 4400 W Tennessee St, 32304 • 850-574-3588 • I-10 Exit 196 take SR-263 S 1.5 miles then US-90 E .7 mile
✪	8	✓	❖		Tallahassee • 3535 Apalachee Pkwy, 32311 • 850-656-2732 • I-10 Exit 209 take US-90 W 4.8 miles, US-319 S 2.3 miles & US-27 E .7 mile
✪	4	✓	❖		Tallahassee • 5500 Thomasville Rd, 32312 • 850-668-2511 • I-10 Exit 203 take SR-61 N 3.4 miles

☆	♡	🕐	⛽	🚫	Store Details
✪	4	✓			Tallahassee • 4021 Lagniappe Way, 32317 • 850-656-2151 • I-10 Exit 209A go SW 3.8 miles on Mahan Dr/SR-10
✪	2	✓		✓	Tampa • 1505 N Dale Mabry Hwy, 33607 • 813-872-6992 • I-275 Exit 41 go W on Dale Mabry Hwy 1.7 miles
✪	1	✓		✓	Tampa • 15302 N Nebraska Ave, 33613 • 813-371-6612 • I-275 Exit 53, east of exit
✪	5	✓		✓	Tampa • 4302 W Gandy Blvd, 33611 • 813-371-9444 • I-275 Exit 41A go S 4.2 miles on US-92 then W .6 mile on Gandy Blvd
✪	6	✓		✓	Tampa • 2701 E Fletcher Ave, 33612 • 813-558-0994 • I-75 Exit 270 go SW on Downs Blvd 5.3 miles then W at University Plaza St .4 mile
✪	8	✓			Tampa • 8220 N Dale Mabry Hwy, 33614 • 813-887-5175 • I-275 Exit 53 take Bearss Ave W 3.2 miles & Dale Mabry Hwy S 4.3 miles
☆	3				Tampa • 14941 N Dale Mabry Hwy, 33618 • 813-968-3544 • I-275 Exit 53 take Bearss Ave W 3 miles
✪	7	✓	❖		Tampa • 6192 Gunn Hwy, 33625 • 813-968-6477 • I-275 Exit 50 go W 3.2 miles on Busch Blvd then continue W 3.4 miles on Gunn Hwy
☆	7			✓	Tampa • 7011 W Waters Ave, 33634 • 813-881-0402 • I-275 Exit 50 go W 1.8 miles on Busch Blvd, S .6 mile on Armenia Ave, W 4.5 miles on Waters Ave
✪	5	✓		✓	Tampa • 19910 Bruce B Downs Blvd, 33647 • 813-994-6543 • I-75 Exit 275 take SR-56 E 2.1 miles & Downs Blvd S 2.2 miles
✪		✓		✓	Tarpon Springs • 41232 US Hwy 19 N, 34689 • 727-940-9289 • Located along US-19 about 1 mile east of town
✪		✓			The Villages • 4085 Wedgewood Ln, 32162 • 352-259-0128 • Jct SR-42 & US-301 (NW of town) take US-301 S 3.3 miles, CR-105 S .7 mile & E on Wedgewood Ln
✪	1	✓	◆		Titusville • 3175 Cheney Hwy, 32780 • 321-267-5825 • I-95 Exit 215 take SR-50 E .6 mile
✪	5	✓	❖		Venice • 4150 Tamiami Trl S, 34293 • 941-497-2523 • I-75 Exit 193 go S on Jacaranda Blvd 4.5 miles & E on Tamiami Trl .1 mile
✪	5	✓		✓	Vero Beach • 5555 20th St, 32966 • 772-778-6677 • I-95 Exit 147 take 20th St/SR-60 E 4.7 miles
✪		✓	❖		Wauchula • 1480 US Hwy 17 N, 33873 • 863-773-6419 • Jct SR-62 & US-17 (N of town) take US-17 S 3 miles

☆	♡	🕐	⛽	🚫	Store Details
✪	1	✓		✓	Wesley Chapel • 28500 State Route 54, 33543 • 813-262-2180 • I-75 Exit 279 go E .6 mile on SR-54/Wesley Chapel Blvd
✪	1	✓	◆		West Melbourne • 845 Palm Bay Rd NE, 32904 • 321-984-2715 • I-95 Exit 176 take Palm Bay Rd E .8 mile
✪	4	✓	❖		West Palm Beach • 4375 Belvedere Rd, 33406 • 561-242-8889 • I-95 Exit 70 merge onto Okeechobee Blvd W .9 mile, S on Congress Ave 1 mile & W on Belvedere Rd 1.5 miles
✪	1			✓	West Palm Beach • 4225 45th St, 33407 • 561-683-8300 • I-95 Exit 74 go W .8 mile on 45th St
✪	9	✓	❖	✓	West Palm Beach • 9990 Belvedere Rd, 33411 • 561-795-0017 • I-95 Exit 68 take US-98 W 8.1 miles, SR-7 N .8 mile then E on Belvedere Rd
✪	3	✓	❖		Wimauma • 4928 State Hwy 674, 33598 • 813-633-1467 • I-75 Exit 240 follow SR-674 E 3 miles
✪		✓		✓	Winter Haven • 355 Cypress Gardens Blvd, 33880 • 863-299-5527 • 2 miles southeast of town center via US-17 and Cypress Gardens Blvd (SR-540)
✪		✓	❖	✓	Winter Haven • 7450 Cypress Gardens Blvd, 33884 • 863-318-0752 • Jct SR-60 & US-27 (SE of town) take US-27 N 5.9 miles then W on Cypress Gardens Blvd 1.3 miles
✪	8	✓	❖		Yulee • 464016 State Hwy 200, 32097 • 904-261-9410 • I-95 Exit 373 take SR-200 E 7.1 miles
✪		✓	❖	✓	Zephyrhills • 7631 Gall Blvd, 33541 • 813-782-1957 • Jct SR-52 & US-301 (N of town) go S on US-301 for 4.2 miles

GEORGIA

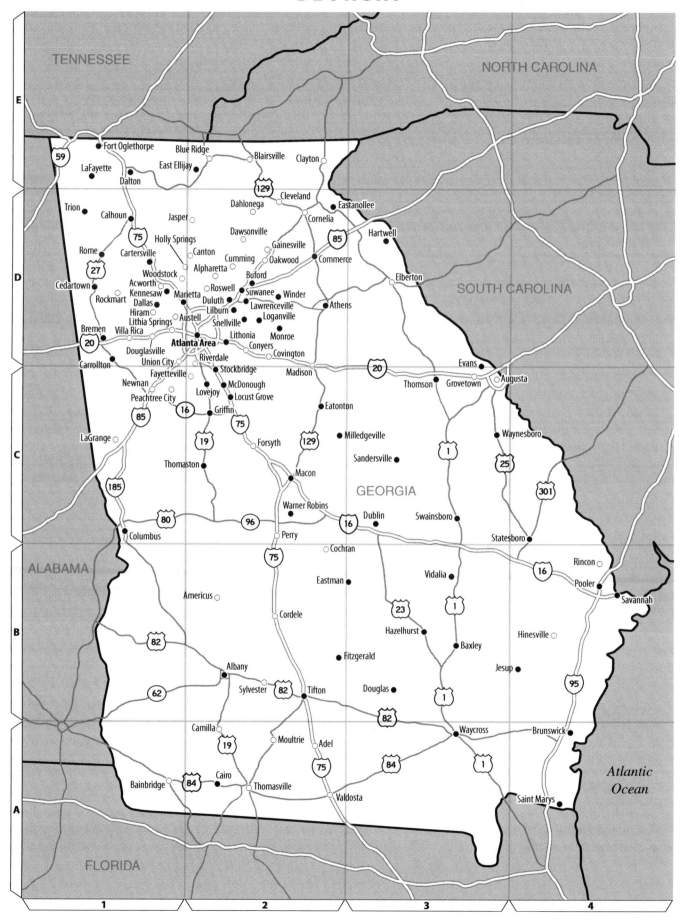

Atlanta Metro Area

Atlanta • Chamblee • College Park • Decatur • Dunwoody • East Point • Ellenwood • Morrow • Norcross • Stone Mountain • Tucker

☆	🛡	🕐	⛽	🚫	Store Details
✪	3	✓		✓	Acworth • 3826 Cobb Pkwy NW, 30101 • 770-966-1226 • I-75 Exit 278 go S .5 mile on Glade Rd, turn right and continue S 2.2 miles on Lake Acworth Dr, then turn left and go .3 mile on Kemp Rd
✪	1	✓			Adel • 351 Alabama Rd, 31620 • 229-896-9980 • I-75 Exit 39, west of exit
✪					Albany • 262 Cordele Rd, 31705 • 229-352-9332 • 5 miles east of town center off US-82 at Cordele Rd
✪		✓	❖		Albany • 2825 Ledo Rd, 31707 • 229-889-9655 • Jct US-19 & US-82 (N of town) take US-82 W 1.3 miles to Exit 7/Nottingham Way N .2 mile then W on Ledo Rd .6 mile
✪		✓			Alpharetta • 5200 Windward Pkwy, 30004 • 770-772-9033 • SR-400 (toll) Exit 11 follow Windward Pkwy W 1 mile
✪		✓			Alpharetta • 5455 Atlanta Hwy, 30004 • 770-475-4101 • From US-19/SR-400 Exit 12B follow McFarland Hwy NW 2.5 miles then Atlanta Hwy N 1.1 mile
✪		✓			Americus • 1711 E Lamar St, 31709 • 229-928-0653 • Jct US-19 & US-280 (W of town) follow US-280 E for 1.9 miles
✪		✓			Athens • 4375 Lexington Rd, 30605 • 706-355-3966 • From US-441/Athens Perimeter Exit 8 go E on US-78 for 2.8 miles
✪		✓	❖		Athens • 1911 Epps Bridge Pkwy, 30606 • 706-549-1423 • From US-441/Athens Perimeter Exit 1 go N on Epps Bridge Pkwy .7 mile
✪	2			✓	Atlanta • 835 Martin Luther King Jr Dr, 30314 • 404-460-2703 • I-20 Exit 55A go N 1 mile on Lowery Blvd then E .2 mile on Martin Luther King Jr Dr
✪	1	✓			Atlanta • 2427 Gresham Rd SE, 30316 • 404-244-3034 • I-20 Exit 63 go N on Gresham Rd .3 mile
✪	1	✓		✓	Atlanta • 1801 Howell Mill Rd NW, 30318 • 404-352-5252 • I-75 Exit 252 go S on Howell Mill Rd .2 mile
✪	1	✓		✓	Augusta • 3209 Deans Bridge Rd, 30906 • 706-792-9323 • I-520 Exit 5 go SW on Deans Bridge Rd/US-1 S .1 mile
✪	1	✓			Augusta • 260 Bobby Jones Expy, 30907 • 706-860-0170 • I-20 Exit 196B follow I-520 W for 1 mile
✪	1	✓		✓	Augusta • 3338 Wrightsboro Rd, 30909 • 706-941-5317 • I-520 Exit 2 go E .8 mile on Wrightsboro Rd

☆	🛡	🕐	⛽	🚫	Store Details
✪	7	✓			Austell • 1133 East-West Connector, 30106 • 770-863-9300 • I-20 Exit 44 go NW 1.3 miles on Thornton Rd, turn right and go N 1.8 miles on Maxham Rd, then continue N on SR-5 (Austell Rd) 2.9 miles, turn right and go E 1.1 miles on East-West Connector
✪		✓			Bainbridge • 500 E Alice St, 39819 • 229-246-2404 • Jct US-84 & US-27 (S of town) go N on US-27 BR .1 mile then W on Alice St .1 mile
✪		✓	❖		Baxley • 980 W Parker St, 31513 • 912-367-3117 • Jct US-1 & US-341 (in town) go W on US-341 for .7 mile
✪		✓			Blairsville • 2257 Hwy 515, 30512 • 706-835-2881 • 3 miles southwest of town via US-76/SR-2/SR-515
✪		✓			Blue Ridge • 97 Commerce Dr, 30513 • 706-632-9500 • US-76 at SR-5, go N .2 mile on SR-5/Blue Ridge Dr
✪	2	✓	❖		Bremen • 404 Hwy 27 N Bypass, 30110 • 770-537-5531 • I-20 Exit 11 follow US-27 N 2 miles, US-78 E 1.2 miles & N on US-27 BR .2 mile
✪	3	✓	◆		Brunswick • 150 Altama Connector, 31525 • 912-261-1616 • I-95 Exit 38 take SR-25 Spur SE for 2.3 miles then N on Altama Connector .3 mile
✪	3	✓	❖		Buford • 3250 Sardis Church Rd, 30519 • 678-546-6464 • I-85 Exit 120 go N on Hamilton Mill Rd .4 mile then NE on Sardis Church Rd 1.7 miles
✪	1	✓			Buford • 3795 Buford Dr, 30519 • 770-271-8210 • I-985 Exit 4 take Buford Dr SE .5 mile
✪		✓	❖		Cairo • 361 8th Ave NE, 39828 • 229-377-1394 • Jct SH111/93 & US-84 go E on US-84 for .2 mile
✪	2	✓	◆		Calhoun • 450 W Belmont Dr, 30701 • 706-625-4274 • I-75 Exit 312 go W on SR-53 for 1.7 miles
✪					Camilla • 165 US Hwy 19 S, 31730 • 229-336-0920 • 1 mile northeast of town center on US-19
✪	1	✓			Canton • 1550 Riverstone Pkwy, 30114 • 770-479-9891 • I-575 Exit 20 go SW on Riverstone Pkwy .1 mile
✪		✓	❖	✓	Carrollton • 1735 S Hwy 27, 30117 • 770-834-3513 • Jct SR-166 & SR-1 (S of town) go S on SR-1 for 1.1 miles
✪	2	✓	◆		Cartersville • 101 Market Place Blvd, 30121 • 770-382-0182 • I-75 Exit 290 take SR-20 W 1.8 miles
✪		✓	❖		Cedartown • 1585 Rome Hwy, 30125 • 770-748-1636 • Jct US-278 & US-27 (E of town) go NW on US-27 for 2.3 miles then S on US-27 BR .2 mile

☆	♡	🕐	⛽	🚫	Store Details
✪	3				Chamblee • 1871 Chamblee Tucker Rd, 30341 • 770-455-0422 • I-85 Exit 94 go W on Chamblee-Tucker Rd for 2.3 miles
✪	2	✓			Clayton • 1455 Hwy 441 S, 30525 • 706-782-3039 • Jct US-76 & US-441 (in town) go N on US-441 for 1.5 miles
✪		✓			Cleveland • 260 Donald E Thurman Pkwy, 30528 • 706-219-2304 • 1.5 miles south of town center via SR-11/US-129
☆				✓	Cochran • 366 Hwy 26 E, 31014 • 478-934-4919 • 1.4 miles northeast of town center along SR-26 at US-23
✪	3	✓	❖		College Park • 6149 Old National Hwy, 30349 • 770-994-9440 • I-285 Exit 62 take Old Nat'l Hwy/SR-279 S 2.4 miles
☆	1				Columbus • 4701 Buena Vista Rd, 31907 • 706-568-3222 • I-185 Exit 4 go S on Buena Vista Rd 1 mile
✪	1	✓		✓	Columbus • 2801 Airport Thruway, 31909 • 706-653-4227 • I-185 Exit 8 go E at Airport Thruwy .5 mile
✪	3	✓			Columbus • 5448 Whittlesey Blvd, 31909 • 706-322-8801 • I-185 Exit 10 take US-80 E 1 mile, US-27 S .5 mile, Adams Farm Rd S .4 mile & Whittlesey Blvd E .5 mile
✪	6	✓	❖		Columbus • 6475 Gateway Rd, 31909 • 706-563-5979 • I-185 Exit 10 follow US-80 E 5.8 miles then S on Gateway Rd
✪	1	✓	◆		Commerce • 30983 Hwy 441 S, 30529 • 706-335-7563 • I-85 Exit 149 go S on US-441 for .4 mile
✪	1	✓		✓	Conyers • 1436 Dogwood Dr SE, 30013 • 770-860-8544 • I-20 Exit 82 follow signs for SR-138 E .3 mile then E on Dogwood Dr .4 mile
✪	1	✓			Cordele • 1215 E 16th Ave, 31015 • 229-273-9270 • I-75 Exit 101 take SR-30 W .8 mile
✪		✓			Cornelia • 250 Furniture Dr, 30531 • 706-778-0353 • 2 miles north of town off US-441 at SR-15/SR-105
✪	1	✓		✓	Covington • 10300 Industrial Blvd NE, 30014 • 770-787-8030 • I-20 Exit 93, south of exit
✪	5				Covington • 4200 Salem Rd, 30016 • 678-212-3195 • I-20 Exit 84 go S 4.3 miles on SR-162
✪		✓		✓	Cumming • 1500 Market Place Blvd, 30041 • 770-889-3436 • SR-400 (toll) Exit 14 merge onto Buford Hwy .6 mile then E on Market Pl Blvd .5 mile
✪					Cumming • 2395 Peachtree Pkwy, 30041 • 770-406-5165 • US-19 Exit 13 go S 4 miles on SR-141

☆	♡	🕐	⛽	🚫	Store Details
✪		✓			Dahlonega • 270 Walmart Way, 30533 • 706-867-6912 • 1 mile northeast of town center via SR-52
✪		✓	❖		Dallas • 3615 Marietta Hwy, 30157 • 770-445-2141 • 7 miles east of town via SR-120 (or 14 miles west of I-75 Exit 263 via SR-120)
✪	1	✓	❖		Dalton • 815 Shugart Rd, 30720 • 706-281-2855 • I-75 Exit 336 E .2 mile on US-41 then S .7 mile on Shugart Rd
✪	10	✓			Dalton • 2545 E Walnut Ave, 30721 • 706-279-1905 • I-75 Exit 328 follow S Dalton Bypass 7.9 miles then NW on Airport Rd .8 mile & E on Walnut Ave .4 mile
✪		✓			Dawsonville • 156 Power Center Dr, 30534 • 706-265-8787 • 7.2 miles southeast of town center via SR-53 and SR-400, across from North Georgia Premium Outlets
✪	3			✓	Decatur • 2525 N Decatur Rd, 30033 • 404-464-4480 • I-285 Exit 39A go SW 2.4 miles on US-78 and turn left onto Medlock Rd
✪		✓			Decatur • 3580 Memorial Dr, 30032 • 404-284-0500 • I-285 Exit 41 go SW 2.2 miles on SR-154 (Cynthia McKinney Pkwy)
✪		✓	◆		Douglas • 1450 Bowens Mill Rd SE, 31533 • 912-384-4600 • From Jct US-41 & Bowens Mill Rd/SH135 (S of town) go E on Bowens Mill Rd .9 mile
✪	1	✓		✓	Douglasville • 7001 Concourse Pkwy, 30134 • 770-489-7057 • I-20 Exit 34 go N on SR-5 for .1 mile then E on Concourse Pkwy .2 mile
✪	8	✓	❖	✓	Dublin • 2423 US Hwy 80 W, 31021 • 478-272-7017 • I-16 Exit 42 take SR-338 NE 2 miles then US-80 E 5.8 miles
✪	2	✓	❖	✓	Duluth • 2635 Pleasant Hill Rd, 30096 • 770-418-0162 • I-85 Exit 103 take Steve Reynolds Blvd NW 1.4 miles & Pleasant Hill Rd NW .5 mile
✪	1				Dunwoody • 4725 Ashford Dunwoody Rd, 30338 • 770-395-0199 • I-285 Exit 29 go N on Ashford Dunwoody 1 mile
✪		✓	❖	✓	East Ellijay • 88 Highland Crossing, 30540 • 706-276-1170 • From Jct SR-382 & SR-515 (S of town) take SR-515/Zell Miller Pkwy N for 2.9 miles then E on Highland Crossing
✪	1			✓	East Point • 844 Cleveland Ave, 30344 • 404-460-6177 • I-85 Exit 76 go W .3 mile on Cleveland Ave
✪		✓	❖		Eastanollee • 3886 Hwy 17 S, 30577 • 706-886-9775 • I-85 Exit 173 go N on SR-17 for 11.9 miles then W on Veterans Memorial Way/SR-17 for 1.5 miles

☆	♡	🕐	⛽	🚭	Store Details
✪		✓	✤		Eastman • 1099 Indian Dr, 31023 • 478-374-7782 • 1.4 miles south of town at US-341/SR-87 jct
✪		✓	✤		Eatonton • 201 Walmart Dr, 31024 • 706-485-5052 • 2 miles south of town at US-129/Gray Hwy jct
☆					Elberton • 955 Elbert St, 30635 • 706-283-8660 • Jct SR-72 & SR-17 (SE of town) go N on SR-72/17 for .2 mile
✪	1				Ellenwood • 2940 Anvil Block Rd, 30294 • 404-361-6811 • I-675 Exit 7 go E .7 mile on Anvil Block Rd
✪	6	✓	✤		Evans • 4469 Washington Rd, 30809 • 706-854-9892 • I-20 Exit 194 take SR-383 N 4.2 miles then Washington Rd NW 1 mile
✪		✓			Fayetteville • 125 Pavilion Pkwy, 30214 • 770-460-0947 • From Jct SR-92 & SR-85 (in town) go N on SR-85/Glynn St 1.9 miles then W on Pavillion Pkwy .4 mile
✪		✓	✤		Fitzgerald • 120 Benjamin H Hill Dr W, 31750 • 229-423-4353 • Jct SR-125 & SR-107 (SW of town) take SR-107 E 3.4 miles
✪	1	✓			Forsyth • 180 N Lee St, 31029 • 478-994-0163 • I-75 Exit 187 go S on SR-83 .2 mile then W .2 mile on Lee St
✪	5	✓	♦		Fort Oglethorpe • 3040 Battlefield Pkwy, 30742 • 706-861-4698 • I-75 Exit 350 take Battlefield Pkwy W 4.2 miles
✪	4	✓			Gainesville • 400 Shallowford Rd NW, 30504 • 770-503-9300 • I-985 Exit 20 take SR-60 N 2.1 miles then SR-369 SW .8 mile & Shallowford Rd NW .3 mile
✪		✓	✤		Griffin • 1569 N Expressway, 30223 • 770-229-5040 • I-75 Exit 205 take SR-16 W 12.9 miles and SR-92 N .9 mile
✪	1	✓			Grovetown • 5010 Steiner Way, 30813 • 706-860-8883 • I-20 Exit 190, south of exit
✪		✓	✤		Hartwell • 1572 Anderson Hwy, 30643 • 706-376-5400 • I-85 Exit 177 follow SR-77 SE for 12.7 miles then US-29 N .1 mile
✪		✓	✤		Hazlehurst • 136 E Jarman St, 31539 • 912-375-3627 • Jct US-23 & SR-27 (S of town) go NE on SR-27 for .1 mile
✪		✓			Hinesville • 751 W Oglethorpe Hwy, 31313 • 912-369-3600 • I-95 Exit 76 take US-84/SR-38 W for 16 miles
✪		✓			Hiram • 4166 Jimmy Lee Smith Pkwy, 30141 • 770-439-1028 • I-20 Exit 36 go N on Campbellton St 1.5 miles, N on SR-92 for 10 miles & W on US-278 .2 mile
✪	1	✓		✓	Holly Springs • 2200 Holly Springs Pkwy, 30115 • 770-213-6519 • I-575 Exit 14, east of exit

☆	♡	🕐	⛽	🚭	Store Details
✪		✓			Jasper • 1100 Old Philadelphia Rd, 30143 • 706-301-5696 • From town center go W 1.7 miles on SR-53 (Church St) then N 1.1 miles on SR-5 and E .4 mile on Old Philadelphia Rd
✪		✓	♦		Jesup • 1100 N 1st St, 31545 • 912-530-6335 • 1 mile northeast of town center on US-84 (N 1st St)
✪	6	✓	✤		Kennesaw • 3105 N Cobb Pkwy NW, 30152 • 770-974-9291 • I-75 Exit 269 go W on Barrett Pkwy 1.3 miles then NW 4.7 miles on Cobb Pkwy
✪		✓	♦		La Fayette • 2625 N Hwy 27, 30728 • 706-639-4900 • Jct SR-136 & US-27 (N of town) go N on US-27 for .2 mile
✪	6	✓			Lagrange • 803 New Franklin Rd, 30240 • 706-812-0225 • I-85 Exit 18 take SR-109 W 3.4 miles then US-27/SR-1 N 1.9 miles
✪	6	✓	✤		Lawrenceville • 1400 Lawrenceville Hwy, 30044 • 770-682-1992 • I-85 Exit 107 take SR-120 E 1 mile, Sugarloaf Pkwy S 3.6 miles & Lawrenceville Hwy E .5 mile
✪	7	✓		✓	Lawrenceville • 630 Collins Hill Rd, 30045 • 770-995-0102 • I-85 Exit 107 take SR-120 E 1 mile, Sugarloaf Pkwy SE 1.4 miles, SR-316 E 4 miles & Collins Hill Rd S .3 mile
✪	5	✓	✤		Lilburn • 4004 Lawrenceville Hwy NW, 30047 • 770-921-9224 • I-85 Exit 102 take Beaver Ruin Rd SE 3.7 miles then US-29 E .5 mile
✪	1	✓		✓	Lithia Springs • 1100 Thornton Rd, 30122 • 770-819-1123 • I-20 Exit 44 merge onto Thornton Rd/SR-6 W .1 mile
✪	1	✓	✤		Lithonia • 5401 Fairington Rd, 30038 • 770-593-3540 • I-20 Exit 71, south of exit
✪	1			✓	Lithonia • 8424 Mall Pkwy, 30038 • 770-225-0428 • I-20 Exit 75, go S .2 mile on Turner Hill Rd then E .2 mile
✪	1	✓	✤		Locust Grove • 4949 Bill Gardner Pkwy, 30248 • 678-734-3395 • I-75 Exit 212, east of exit
✪		✓	✤		Loganville • 4221 Atlanta Hwy, 30052 • 770-554-7481 • Jct SR-20 & US-78 (W of town) go NW on US-78 for .5 mile
✪	8	✓	✤		Lovejoy • 11465 Tara Blvd, 30250 • 770-471-4451 • I-75 Exit 221 go W on Jonesboro Rd 5.3 miles, continue on McDonough Rd 1.9 miles then S on Tara Blvd .5
✪	1	✓	✤	✓	Macon • 6020 Harrison Rd, 31206 • 478-781-0086 • I-475 Exit 3 take US-80 E .3 mile
✪	1	✓	✤	✓	Macon • 5955 Zebulon Rd, 31210 • 478-471-9150 • I-475 Exit 9 go E on Zebulon Rd .7 mile

☆	◯	🕐	⛽	🚫	Store Details
●	2	✓		✓	Macon • 1401 Gray Hwy, 31211 • 478-745-3999 • I-16 Exit 1B go N on 2nd St .5 mile, continue on Gray Hwy .9 mile
●	1	✓			Madison • 1681 Eatonton Rd, 30650 • 706-342-9988 • I-20 Exit 114 follow US-441/Eatonton Rd N .7 mile
●	3				Marietta • 1785 Cobb Pkwy S, 30060 • 770-955-0626 • I-285 Exit 19 take Cobb Pkwy/US-41 N 2.1 miles
●	2	✓			Marietta • 210 Cobb Pkwy S, 30060 • 770-429-9029 • I-75 Exit 263 merge onto Marietta Pkwy NW .6 mile then N on Cobb Pkwy .6 mile
●	7	✓			Marietta • 3100 Johnson Ferry Rd, 30062 • 770-640-7225 • I-75 Exit 263 take SR-120 N 1.1 miles, Sewell Mill Rd NE 3.8 miles & Johnson Ferry Rd N 2.1 miles
●	8	✓			Marietta • 6520 Ernest Barrett Pkwy SW, 30064 • 770-222-6666 • I-20 Exit 44 take SR-6 NW 1.3 miles, Maxham Rd N 1.8 miles, Austell Rd N 2.9 miles, East-West Connector W 2 miles
●	1	✓	❖		Marietta • 2795 Chastain Meadows Pkwy, 30066 • 770-427-4933 • I-575 Exit 1 go E on Barrett Pkwy .2 mile then N on Chastain Meadows Pkwy .6 mile
●	1	✓	❖	✓	McDonough • 135 Willow Ln, 30253 • 678-432-2023 • I-75 Exit 218 go E on SR-20 for .4 mile & N on Willow Ln for .2 mile
●		✓	❖		Milledgeville • 2592 N Columbia St, 31061 • 478-453-0667 • From SR-22 (NW of town) continue E to Jct US-441, then N on US-441 for 1.1 miles
●		✓	❖		Monroe • 2050 W Spring St, 30655 • 770-267-4527 • I-20 Exit 98 follow SR-11 N 13.9 miles then SR-10 W 1.9 miles
●	1	✓	❖	✓	Morrow • 6065 Jonesboro Rd, 30260 • 770-968-0774 • I-75 Exit 233 take SR-54 N .8 mile
●		✓			Moultrie • 641 Veterans Pkwy S, 31788 • 229-985-3697 • Jct SR-37 & US-319 (E of town) go S on US-319 for 1.3 miles
●	1	✓			Newnan • 1025 Hwy 34 E, 30265 • 770-502-0677 • I-85 Exit 47, east of exit
●	2			✓	Norcross • 4975 Jimmy Carter Blvd, 30093 • 770-225-9882 • I-85 Exit 99 go S 1.5 miles on Jimmy Carter Blvd
●	1	✓			Oakwood • 3875 Mundy Mill Rd, 30566 • 770-535-6543 • I-985 Exit 16 take Mundy Mill Rd/SR-53 W .5 mile
●		✓		✓	Peachtree City • 2717 Hwy 54, 30269 • 770-632-6373 • I-85 Exit 61 follow SR-74 S 11 miles then E at SR-54
●	1	✓			Perry • 1009 Saint Patricks Dr, 31069 • 478-987-1444 • I-75 Exit 136 go SE on Sam Nunn Blvd .1 mile & N on St. Patricks Dr

☆	◯	🕐	⛽	🚫	Store Details
●	1	✓	◆		Pooler • 160 Pooler Pkwy, 31322 • 912-748-2677 • I-95 Exit 104 follow Pooler Pkwy W .4 mile
●	8	✓			Rincon • 434 S Columbia Ave, 31326 • 912-826-4030 • I-95 Exit 109 follow SR-21 N for 7.2 miles
●	5	✓			Riverdale • 7050 Hwy 85, 30274 • 770-994-1670 • I-75 Exit 237A follow SR-85 S 4.5 miles
●		✓			Rockmart • 1801 Nathan Dean Byp, 30153 • 678-757-8766 • 1 mile northeast of town center on US-278 (Nathan Dean Pkwy)
●		✓	❖		Rome • 825 Cartersville Hwy SE, 30161 • 706-292-0838 • Jct SR-101 & US-411 (S of town) go E on US-411 for 2.9 miles
●		✓			Rome • 2510 Redmond Cir NW, 30165 • 706-236-9595 • Jct SR-20 & SR-1 Loop (W of town) go N on SR-1 for .2 mile
●		✓		✓	Roswell • 970 Mansell Rd, 30076 • 770-993-0533 • SR-400 (toll) Exit 8 go W on Mansell Rd 1.5 miles
●	6	✓	❖		Saint Marys • 6586 GA Hwy 40 E, 31558 • 912-510-9216 • I-95 Exit 1 follow St Marys Rd E 3.3 miles, exit at Cumberland Island & take SR-40 S for 1.8 miles
●		✓	❖		Sandersville • 1308 S Harris St, 31082 • 478-552-1988 • Jct SR-68 & SR-15 (S of town) go N on SR-15 for 1 mile
●	8	✓			Savannah • 1955 E Montgomery Rd, 31406 • 912-354-0335 • I-16 Exit 164A follow SR-21 S 5.9 miles then Truman Pkwy S 1.9 miles & E on Montgomery Cross Rd .2 mile
☆					Savannah • 4725 US Hwy 80 E, 31410 • 912-898-1391 • 6 miles east of town at jct of Island Expy and US-80
●	3	✓	❖		Savannah • 6000 Ogeechee Rd, 31419 • 912-921-0882 • I-95 Exit 94 take SR-204 E 1.8 miles then US-17 S .9 mile
●	7	✓			Savannah • 14030 Abercorn St, 31419 • 912-344-9664 • I-95 Exit 94 go E 6.6 miles on SR-204/Abercorn Expy
●	10	✓	❖		Snellville • 3435 Centerville Hwy, 30039 • 770-972-7572 • I-20 Exit 75 follow SR-124 N for 9.2 miles then go W .2 mile on Annistown Rd
●		✓			Snellville • 1550 Scenic Hwy N, 30078 • 770-979-2447 • I-20 Exit 75 follow SR-124 N for 15.6 miles
●		✓	❖		Statesboro • 147 Northside Dr E, 30458 • 912-489-1910 • I-16 Exit 127 take SR-67 N 10.8 miles, N on Veterans Memorial Pkwy 2.1 miles, W on US-80 for .2 mile
●	1		❖	✓	Stockbridge • 1400 Hudson Bridge Rd, 30281 • 770-474-0123 • I-75 Exit 224 go W on Hudson Bridge Rd .3 mile

☆	⬭	🕐	⛽	🚭	Store Details
✪	1	✓	◆	✓	Stockbridge • 5600 N Henry Blvd, 30281 • 770-389-1709 • I-675 Exit 1 take SR-138 SE .6 mile
✪	4	✓		✓	Stone Mountain • 5935 Memorial Dr, 30083 • 404-260-6142 • I-285 Exit 41 go NE 3.3 miles on SR-10
✪	9	✓	❖		Stone Mountain • 1825 Rockbridge Rd, 30087 • 770-469-8660 • I-285 Exit 39B merge onto US-78 E for 8.1 miles to Exit 9, W on Park Pl Blvd .1 mile & N on Rockbridge Rd .2 mile
✪	1	✓	❖	✓	Suwanee • 3245 Lawrenceville Suwanee Rd, 30024 • 678-482-5441 • I-85 Exit 111 take SR-317 N for .6 mile
✪		✓	❖		Swainsboro • 414 S Main St, 30401 • 478-237-3318 • I-16 Exit 90 take US-1 N 10.3 miles, then US-1 BR 3.5 miles
✪					Sylvester • 1102 E Franklin St, 31791 • 229-463-6004 • 1.4 miles east of town center along US-82
✪		✓	❖		Thomaston • 855 N Church St, 30286 • 706-648-2105 • 1.6 miles north of town center via Center St and Church St
✪		✓			Thomasville • 15328 US Hwy 19 S, 31757 • 229-228-0144 • Jct US-84 & US-19 (E of town) go N on US-19 for 1.7 miles
✪	4	✓	❖		Thomson • 2205 Harrison Rd SE, 30824 • 706-595-5530 • I-20 Exit 172 follow US-78 S for 3.3 miles
✪	1	✓	❖		Tifton • 1830 US Hwy 82 W, 31793 • 229-386-0263 • I-75 Exit 62 take US-82 W .8 mile
✪		✓	❖		Trion • 13427 Hwy 27, 30753 • 706-734-2931 • 3.7 miles north of Summerville along US-27
☆	4				Tucker • 4375 Lawrenceville Hwy, 30084 • 770-939-2671 • I-285 Exit 38 merge onto Lawrenceville Hwy/US-29 N for 3.4 miles
✪	1	✓		✓	Union City • 4735 Jonesboro Rd, 30291 • 770-964-6921 • I-85 Exit 64 go W on Jonesboro Rd/SR-138 for .2 mile
✪	1	✓			Valdosta • 340 Norman Dr, 31601 • 229-249-8400 • I-75 Exit 16 go E on US-221 for .2 mile then N on Norman Dr .5 mile
✪	5	✓		✓	Valdosta • 3274 Inner Perimeter Rd, 31602 • 229-253-0312 • I-75 Exit 22 merge onto US-41 S for 3.8 miles then E on Inner Perimeter Rd .5 mile
✪		✓	◆		Vidalia • 3109 E 1st St, 30474 • 912-537-0889 • I-16 Exit 84 take SR-297 S 13.8 miles, SR-292/North St E 1.7 miles, Stockyard Rd S .2 mile & 1st St E .5 mile
✪	1	✓			Villa Rica • 600 Carrollton Villa Rica Hwy, 30180 • 770-459-6601 • I-20 Exit 24 take SR-61 S for .5 mile

☆	⬭	🕐	⛽	🚭	Store Details
✪	9	✓	❖		Warner Robins • 502 Booth Rd, 31088 • 478-918-0338 • I-75 Exit 144 go E on Russell Pkwy 7.8 miles then S on Booth Rd .5 mile
✪	5	✓			Warner Robins • 2720 Watson Blvd, 31093 • 478-953-7070 • I-75 Exit 146 follow SR-247 (Watson Blvd) E 4.1 miles
✪		✓	❖		Waycross • 2425 Memorial Dr, 31503 • 912-283-9000 • Jct State St/US-1 BR & Waring St (NW of town) go E on Waring St 1.5 miles then N on Steve St .2 mile
✪		✓	◆	✓	Waynesboro • 1500 N Liberty St, 30830 • 706-437-8380 • Jct SR-56/80 & US-25 BYP (E of town) take US-25 BYP W for 1.7 miles then N on Liberty St .1 mile
✪	3	✓	❖		Winder • 440 Atlanta Hwy NW, 30680 • 770-867-8642 • I-75 Exit 126 follow SR-211 S for 9 miles then W on US-29/Atlanta Hwy for 1.4 miles
✪	4	✓			Woodstock • 12182 Hwy 92, 30188 • 770-516-4719 • I-575 Exit 7 take SR-92 E for 3.2 miles
✪	4	✓			Woodstock • 6435 Bells Ferry Rd, 30189 • 770-926-2606 • I-575 Exit 8 go W on Towne Lake Pkwy 1.4 miles, continue on Eagle Dr 1.7 miles then N on Bells Ferry Rd .3 mile

HAWAII

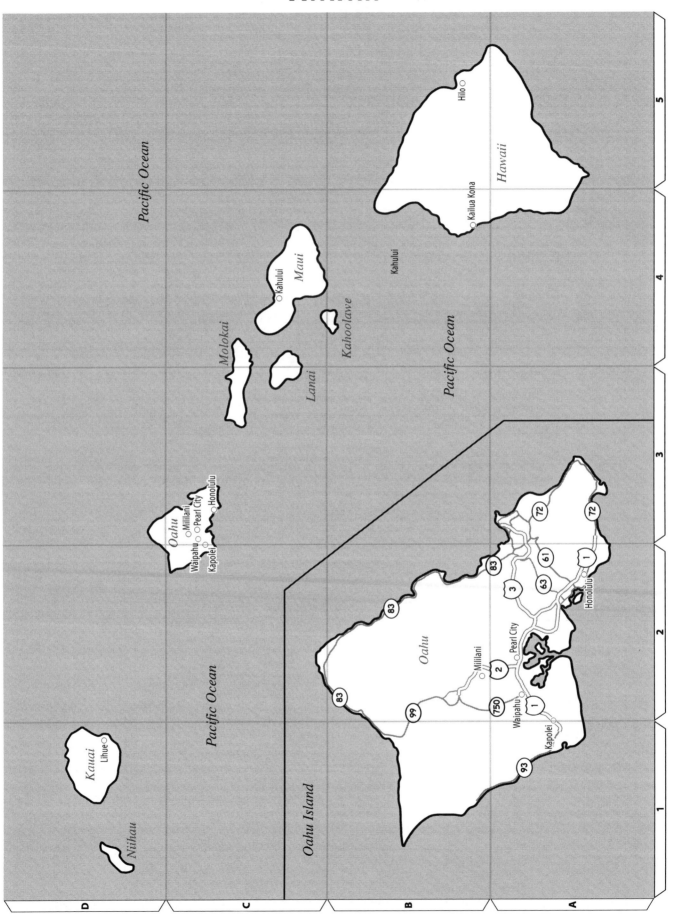

☆	◯	🕐	⛽	🚭	Store Details
☆				✓	Hilo • 325 E Makaala St, 96720 • 808-961-9115 • Jct SR-130 & SR-11 take SR-11 N 5.1 miles then E at Makaala St
☆				✓	Honolulu • 1032 Fort Street Mall, 96813 • 808-489-9836 • Downtown at corner of King St and Bethel St
☆					Honolulu • 700 Keeaumoku St, 96814 • 808-955-8441 • I-H1 Exit 22 merge onto Kinau St 1 mile then S on Keeaumoku St .5 mile
☆					Kahului • 101 Pakaula St, 96732 • 808-871-7820 • Jct SR-340 & SR-36 take SR-36 E 1.5 miles, SR-38/Dairy Rd S .6 mile & Pakaula St E .3 mile
☆				✓	Kailua Kona • 75-1015 Henry St, 96740 • 808-334-0466 • Jct Hualalai Rd & SR-11 take SR-11 N 1.3 miles then Henry St NE .1 mile
☆	✓				Kapolei • 91-600 Farrington Hwy, 96707 • 808-206-9069 • I-H1 Exit 2, south of exit
☆					Lihue • 3-3300 Kuhio Hwy, 96766 • 808-246-1599 • .5 mile north of town center on SR-56 (Kuhio Hwy)
☆					Mililani • 95-550 Lanikuhana Ave, 96789 • 808-623-6744 • I-H2 Exit 5B go SW .8 mile on Mehula Pkwy, turn left at Lanikuhana Ave .4 mile
☆					Pearl City • 1131 Kuala St, 96782 • 808-454-8785 • From I-H201 W exit onto SR-99 for 3.6 miles then N on Kuala St .2 mile
☆					Waipahu • 94-595 Kupuohi St, 96797 • 808-688-0066 • I-H1 Exit 5B merge onto SR-750 N/Kunia Rd .7 mile, E at Kupuna Loop & N on Kupuohi St .2 mile

IDAHO

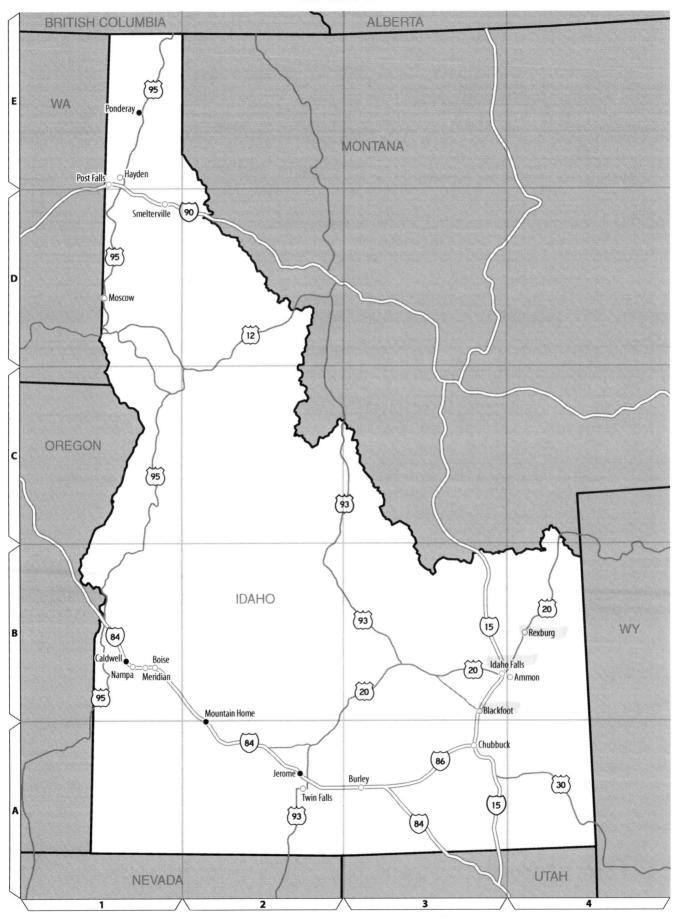

☆	🛡	🕐	⛽	🚫	Store Details
✪	6	✓			Ammon • 1201 S 25th E, 83406 • 208-522-0204 • I-15 Exit 116 go E on 33rd St 1.1 miles, N on Yellowstone Hwy 1.2 miles, E on 17th St 3 miles
✪	1	✓			Blackfoot • 565 Jensen Grove Dr, 83221 • 208-785-6937 • I-15 Exit 93 follow I-15 BR E .4 mile & N on Pkwy Dr to Jensen Grove Dr .3 mile
✪	1	✓		✓	Boise • 8300 W Overland Rd, 83709 • 208-321-9077 • I-84 Exit 50A merge onto Cole Rd .4 mile then W Overland Rd for .6 mile
✪	6	✓		✓	Boise • 7319 W State St, 83714 • 208-853-0541 • I-84 Exit 50, Cole Rd N 3.4 miles, Mt View Dr W .2 mile, Glenwood St N 1.7 miles, State St W .3 mile
✪	2	✓			Burley • 385 N Overland Ave, 83318 • 208-677-4709 • I-84 Exit 208 merge onto SR-27 S/I-84 BR E for 1.5 miles
✪	4	✓	◆		Caldwell • 5108 Cleveland Blvd, 83607 • 208-455-0066 • I-84 Exit 33A, SR-55 S .5 mile, Nampa-Cldwell Blvd W 1.5 miles, continue on Cleveland Blvd 1.4 miles
✪	1	✓			Chubbuck • 4240 Yellowstone Ave, 83202 • 208-237-5090 • I-86 Exit 61 go S on US-91 for .1 mile
✪	4	✓			Hayden • 550 W Honeysuckle Ave, 83835 • 208-209-4044 • I-90 Exit 12 go N 3.7 miles on US-95 then W .1 mile on Honeysuckle Ave
✪	1	✓			Idaho Falls • 500 S Utah Ave, 83402 • 208-528-8735 • I-15 Exit 118 take W Broadway/I-15 BR E .3 mile, then Utah Ave S .3 mile
✪	1	✓	◆		Jerome • 2680 S Lincoln Ave, 83338 • 208-324-4333 • I-84 Exit 168 take SR-79 N for .4 mile
✪	3	✓		✓	Meridian • 4051 E Fairview Ave, 83642 • 208-373-7908 • I-84 Exit 46 go N on SR-55 for 1.9 miles then E on Fairview Ave .5 mile
✪	4				Meridian • 5001 N Ten Mile Rd, 83646 • 208-982-3045 • I-84 Exit 42 go N 4 miles on Ten Mile Rd
✪	1	✓		✓	Meridian • 795 W Overland Rd, 83642 • 208-917-6902 • I-94 Exit 44 go S .2 mile on Meridian Rd then W .4 mile on Overland Rd
✪		✓			Moscow • 2470 W Pullman Rd, 83843 • 208-883-8828 • 1.8 miles west of town center along SR-8
✪	1	✓	◆		Mountain Home • 2745 American Legion Blvd, 83647 • 208-587-0601 • I-84 Exit 95 (toward Mountain Home) go S on SR-51 for .2 mile

☆	🛡	🕐	⛽	🚫	Store Details
✪	4	✓			Nampa • 2100 12th Ave Rd, 83686 • 208-467-5047 • I-84 Exit 36 go S on Franklin Blvd .9 mile, SW on 11th Ave .8 mile, S on SR-45 for 2.2 miles
✪	1	✓			Nampa • 5875 E Franklin Rd, 83687 • 208-461-6481 • I-84 Exit 38 go N on I-84 BR .5 mile then E on Franklin Rd .1 mile
✪		✓	◆		Ponderay • 476999 Hwy 95, 83852 • 208-265-8332 • From Jct US-2 & US-95 (in Sandpoint) go N on US-95 for 2.3 miles
✪	1	✓			Post Falls • 3050 E Mullan Ave, 83854 • 208-457-9866 • I-90 Exit 7 go N on SR-41 for .3 mile then W on Mullan Ave .6 mile
✪	3	✓			Post Falls • 6405 W Pointe Pkwy, 83854 • 208-777-4151 • I-90 Exit 2 go N .5 mile on Pleasant View Rd, W 1.6 miles on Seltice Way, S .3 mile on Baugh Way
☆					Rexburg • 530 N 2nd E, 83440 • 208-359-2809 • I-15 Exit 143 take SR-28/33 E for 21 miles then N on 2nd St for .6 mile
✪	1	✓			Smelterville • 583 Commerce Dr, 83868 • 208-783-0426 • I-90 Exit 48 go S on Airport Rd then W on Commerce Dr
✪	5			✓	Twin Falls • 252 Cheney Dr W, 83301 • 208-734-2136 • I-84 Exit 173 go S 3.5 miles on US-93 then W 1 mile on Pole Line Rd and S .2 mile on Washington St

ILLINOIS

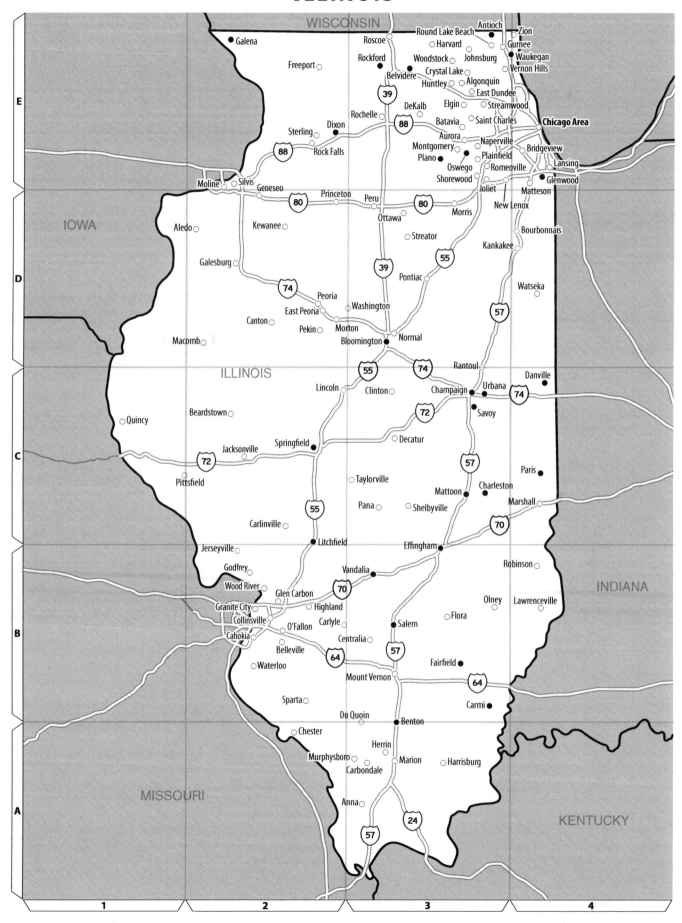

Chicago Metro Area

Addison • Bedford Park • Bloomingdale • Bolingbrook • Chicago • Cicero • Country Club Hills • Crestwood • Darien • Elk Grove Village • Evergreen Park • Forest Park • Glen Ellyn • Hodgkins • Lake Zurich • Lockport • Mount Prospect • Niles • Northlake • Orland Hills • Palatine • Rolling Meadows • Skokie • Villa Park • Wheeling

☆	◯	⏰	⛽	🚫	Store Details
✪	1	✓			Addison • 1050 N Rohlwing Rd, 60101 • 630-889-1826 • I-290 Exit 7 go S on Lake St .2 mile then E on Rohlwing Rd .1 mile
☆	8				Aledo • 1500 SE 5th St, 61231 • 309-582-5617 • Jct US-67 & SR-17 (E of town) go W on SR-17 for 7.4 miles & S on 19 Ave .1 mile
✪	6	✓		✓	Algonquin • 1410 S Randall Rd, 60102 • 847-458-5620 • From I-90 (toll) Randall Rd Exit, go N on Randall Rd 5.3 miles
✪	5	✓			Anna • 300 Leigh Ave, 62906 • 618-833-8592 • I-57 Exit 30 take SR-146 W 4.6 miles then S on Leigh St .1 mile
✪	5	✓	❖		Antioch • 475 E Hwy 173, 60002 • 847-838-2148 • I-94 (toll) Rosencrans Rd Exit (northbound access only) follow SR-173 W 5 miles
✪	2	✓		✓	Aurora • 2900 Kirk Rd, 60502 • 630-375-6207 • I-88 (toll) at Farnsworth Ave exit go N 1 mile, continue on Kirk Rd .3 mile
☆	3				Aurora • 2131 W Galena Blvd, 60506 • 630-264-1804 • I-88 (toll) Orchard Rd Exit go S on Orchard 2.2 miles & E on Galena Blvd .6 mile
☆	6				Batavia • 801 N Randall Rd, 60510 • 630-879-3970 • I-88 (toll) Orchard Rd Exit go NE on Orchard 2.6 miles & N on Randall Rd 3.3 miles
✪					Beardstown • 100 Lincoln Ave, 62618 • 217-323-1340 • 2.5 miles east of town via SR-125
☆	4				Bedford Park • 7050 S Cicero Ave, 60638 • 708-496-0230 • I-55 Exit 286 take Cicero Ave S 3.6 miles
✪	4	✓			Belleville • 2608 Green Mount Commons Dr, 62221 • 618-236-2200 • I-64 Exit 16 go S 3.7 miles on Green Mount Rd
✪	9	✓	❖		Belvidere • 2101 Gateway Center Dr, 61008 • 815-547-5447 • I-39 Exit 122 take US-20 E 8.1 miles, S at Farmington Way & W at Gateway Center Dr .3 mile
✪	1	✓	❖		Benton • 919 Giacone Dr, 62812 • 618-439-9453 • I-57 Exit 71 go E on SR-14/Main St .3 mile then S on Giacone Dr

☆	◯	⏰	⛽	🚫	Store Details
✪	4			✓	Bloomingdale • 314 W Army Trail Rd, 60108 • 630-893-5000 • I-355 Exit 29 go W 3.3 miles on Army Trail Rd
✪	1	✓	❖		Bloomington • 2225 W Market St, 61704 • 309-828-5646 • I-55/74 Exit 160 go W on Market St .8 mile
✪	1	✓		✓	Bolingbrook • 200 S Bolingbrook Dr, 60440 • 630-739-4800 • I-55 Exit 267 take Bolingbrook Dr/SR-53 N for .6 mile
✪	2	✓			Bourbonnais • 2080 N State Rt 50, 60914 • 815-937-5100 • I-57 exit 315 take SR-50 N 1.2 miles
☆	1				Bridgeview • 10260 S Harlem Ave, 60455 • 708-499-2088 • I-294 US-20 E Exit, take US-20 E .2 mile then SR-43 S .7 mile
☆	1				Cahokia • 1511 Camp Jackson Rd, 62206 • 618-332-1771 • I-255 Exit 13 go W on SR-157 for .3 mile
☆					Canton • 2071 N Main St, 61520 • 309-647-7000 • Jct SR-116 & SR-78 (N of town) take Main St/SR-78 S 7.9 miles
✪		✓			Carbondale • 1450 E Main St, 62901 • 618-457-2033 • I-57 Exit 54 merge onto SR-13 W 12.6 miles
✪		✓			Carlinville • 18600 Shipman Rd, 62626 • 217-854-4402 • I-55 Exit 60 take SR-108 W 13.5 miles then Shipman Rd/Alton Rd S .8 mile
✪				✓	Carlyle • 2591 12th St, 62231 • 618-594-2465 • 1.2 miles north of town center on US-50/SR-127
✪		✓	❖		Carmi • 1344 IL Hwy 1, 62821 • 618-382-5856 • 1.5 miles northeast of town on SR-1
☆					Centralia • 1340 W McCord St, 62801 • 618-533-1700 • I-64 Exit 61 take US-51 N 10.5 miles then W on McCord St 1.5 miles
✪	1	✓	❖		Champaign • 2610 N Prospect Ave, 61822 • 217-352-0700 • I-74 Exit 181 go N on Prospect Ave .7 mile
✪	9	✓	◆		Charleston • 2250 Lincoln Ave, 61920 • 217-345-1222 • I-57 Exit 190A take SR-16 E 8.9 miles
☆					Chester • 2206 State St, 62233 • 618-826-5041 • Jct SR-3 & SR-150 (NE of town) take SR-150 S 9.6 miles
✪	1			✓	Chicago • 8331 S Stewart Ave, 60620 • 773-358-9000 • I-94 Exit 61B (eastbound travelers): Turn right on 83rd St and go .4 miles to Holland St; turn left, then right. I-94 Exit 61B (westbound travelers): Follow State St for .6 miles; turn left on 83rd St and go .4 miles to Holland St; turn left, then right.

☆	⬭	⏱	⛽	🚫	Store Details
✪	1			✓	Chicago • 10900 S Doty Ave, 60628 • 773-344-9016 • I-94 Exit 66A, west of exit at 111th St
✪	4				Chicago • 4650 W North Ave, 60639 • 773-252-7465 • I-90/94 Exit 48B take North Ave/SR-64 W 4 miles
✪	3			✓	Chicago • 4626 W Diversey Ave, 60639 • 773-628-1880 • I-94 Exit 45B go S .6 mile on Kimball Ave and W 1.6 miles on Diversey Ave
✪	1			✓	Cicero • 3320 S Cicero Ave, 60804 • 708-735-8456 • I-55 Exit 286 go N 1 mile on SR-50/Cicero Ave
☆					Clinton • 10 Clinton Plz, 61727 • 217-935-9586 • .5 mile west of town off SR-10 at Illini Dr
✪	1	✓		✓	Collinsville • 1040 Collinsville Crossing Blvd, 62234 • 618-344-4480 • I-55/I-70 Exit 11 go S .3 mile on SR-157, turn right at Collinsville Crossing Blvd .2 mile
✪	1	✓			Country Club Hills • 4005 167th St, 60478 • 708-647-1689 • I-57 Exit 346 go E on 167th St for .5 mile
✪	2	✓			Crestwood • 4700 135th St, 60445 • 708-489-5547 • From I-294 (toll) exit onto Cicero Ave/SR-50 S 1.6 miles then E on 135th St .1 mile
✪		✓			Crystal Lake • 1205 S Hwy 31, 60014 • 815-455-4200 • 4 miles southeast of town center on SR-31 at James R Rakow Rd (south of US-14)
✪	8	✓	◆		Danville • 4101 N Vermilion St, 61834 • 217-443-9520 • I-74 Exit 215 follow SR-1 N 7.6 miles
✪	4	✓			Darien • 2189 75th St, 60561 • 630-434-0490 • I-55 Exit 271 go N on Lemont Rd 2.4 miles then E on 75th St .7 mile
✪	10	✓			Decatur • 4625 E Maryland St, 62521 • 217-864-6927 • I-72 Exit 133 take US-36 E 9.6 miles, 44th St S .2 mile & Maryland St E .1 mile
✪	1	✓			Decatur • 4224 N Prospect St, 62526 • 217-875-0016 • I-72 Exit 141 take US-51 BR S .8 mile & E on Ash Ave
✪	5	✓			Dekalb • 2300 Sycamore Rd, 60115 • 815-758-6225 • I-88 (toll) Peace Rd Exit, take Peace Rd N 3.6 miles, Barber Green Rd W .7 mile & Sycamre Rd S .2 mile
✪	1	✓	❖		Dixon • 1640 S Galena Ave, 61021 • 815-288-7770 • I-88 (toll) Dixon Exit take SR-26 N .4 mile
✪		✓			Du Quoin • 215 E Grantway St, 62832 • 618-542-8438 • I-57 Exit 71 take SR-14 W for 15.8 miles then N on US-51 for 1.8 miles
☆	2				East Dundee • 620 Dundee Ave, 60118 • 847-426-2800 • From I-90 take SR-25/Dundee Ave N 2 miles

☆	⬭	⏱	⛽	🚫	Store Details
✪	1	✓			East Peoria • 401 River Rd, 61611 • 309-694-0513 • I-74 Exit 94 take SR-40 N .1 mile then River Rd E .2 mile
✪	1	✓	❖	✓	Effingham • 1204 Avenue Of Mid America, 62401 • 217-347-5171 • I-70 Exit 160 take SR-32 N .1 mile then E at Ave of Mid-America .2 mile
✪	6	✓		✓	Elgin • 1100 S Randall Rd, 60123 • 847-468-9600 • I-90 Randall Rd Exit, go S on Randall Rd for 5.3 miles
✪	2	✓			Elk Grove Village • 801 Meacham Rd, 60007 • 847-584-7080 • I-290 Exit 4 go W on SR-53/Biesterfield Rd 1 mile then S on Meacham Rd .3 mile
✪	4				Evergreen Park • 2500 W 95th St, 60805 • 708-229-0611 • I-57 Exit 355, W on Monterey Ave/111th St 1.1 miles, N on Western Ave 2 miles & W on 95th St .2 mile
✪		✓	❖		Fairfield • 150 Commerce Dr, 62837 • 618-842-7633 • Jct US-12 & SR-22/W Main St go E on Main St 2.2 miles & N on Telser Rd .9 mile
✪		✓			Flora • 1540 N Worthey St, 62839 • 618-662-4491 • Jct US-45 & US-50 (E of town) take US-45/50 W 2.8 miles, CR-1 S .1 mile, 12th St W .5 mile & Worthey St S .4 mile
✪	1				Forest Park • 1300 Des Plaines Ave, 60130 • 708-771-2270 • I-290 Exit 21A go S on Des Plaines Ave .7 mile
✪		✓			Freeport • 2445 IL Route 26 S, 61032 • 815-232-8120 • 3 miles south of town center via SR-26
✪		✓	❖	✓	Galena • 10000 Bartel Blvd, 61036 • 815-777-0507 • 2.5 miles northwest of town center along US-20
✪	2	✓			Galesburg • 659 Knox Square Dr, 61401 • 309-344-1180 • I-74 Exit 46A go W on US-34 for 1.1 miles then Seminary St S .6 mile
☆	1				Geneseo • 125 E Bestor Dr, 61254 • 309-944-2145 • I-80 Exit 19 go N on SR-82 for .3 mile
☆	1			✓	Glen Carbon • 400 Junction Dr, 62034 • 618-692-0550 • I-270 Exit 12 go N on SR-82 for .3 mile
✪	2				Glen Ellyn • 3 S 100 State Hwy 53, 60137 • 630-545-1060 • I-355 Exit 22 go W 1.3 miles on SR-56 then S .2 mile on SR-53
☆	3		❖		Glenwood • 103 W Holbrook Rd, 60425 • 708-755-1660 • I-294/I-80 take Halsted St/SR-1 S 2.5 miles then Holbrook Rd E .3 mile
✪		✓			Godfrey • 6660 Godfrey Rd, 62035 • 618-433-3008 • 1 mile north of town via US-67

☆	⛨	🕐	⛽	🚳	Store Details
✪	3				Granite City • 379 W Pontoon Rd, 62040 • 618-451-4201 • I-270 Exit 3A take SR-3 S 2.5 miles then W onto Pontoon Rd
✪	1	✓		✓	Gurnee • 6590 Grand Ave, 60031 • 847-855-1230 • I-94 (Tri-State Tollway) at Grand Ave/SR-132 go W 1 mile
✪		✓			Harrisburg • 710 S Commercial St, 62946 • 618-252-0145 • From town center go .4 mil E on Poplar St/SR-13/SR-34 then S .6 mile on Commercial St/SR-34/US-45
✪					Harvard • 21101 McGuire Rd, 60033 • 815-943-7496 • From town center go 1 mile S on US-14 then E .3 mile on McGuire Rd
☆	7				Herrin • 1713 S Park Ave, 62948 • 618-942-7386 • I-57 Exit 59 go W on CR-2/Herron Rd 4.6 miles then S on SR-148 for 1.5 miles
✪	4	✓			Highland • 12495 IL Hwy 143, 62249 • 618-654-4596 • I-70 Exit 24 go E on SR-143 for 3.3 miles
✪	2				Hodgkins • 9450 Joliet Rd, 60525 • 708-387-2090 • I-55 Exit 279B go N 1.1 miles on US-20/US-45 (Lagrange Rd) then .2 mile E on Joliet Rd
✪		✓		✓	Huntley • 12300 Route 47, 60142 • 847-669-7126 • 1 mile south of town center via SR-47
✪	4	✓			Jacksonville • 1941 W Morton Ave, 62650 • 217-245-5146 • I-72 exit 60B go N 2.4 miles on US-67/I-72 BR then E 1.3 miles on I-72 BR
✪		✓			Jerseyville • 1316 S State St, 62052 • 618-498-7744 • Jct CR-25 & US-67 (S of town) go N on US-67 for 5.2 miles
✪		✓			Johnsburg • 3801 Running Brook Farms Blvd, 60051 • 815-344-7702 • 1.7 miles north of McHenry, Illinois, along SR-31
✪	1	✓		✓	Joliet • 2424 W Jefferson St, 60435 • 815-744-7575 • I-80 Exit 130B go N .8 mile on SR-7 then W 1 mile on US-52 (or from I-55 Exit 253 go E 2.4 miles on US-52)
✪	1	✓			Kankakee • 505 Riverstone Pkwy, 60901 • 815-802-1884 • I-57 exit 308 take US-52 N .3 mile then Riverstone Pkwy E .4 mile
✪		✓			Kewanee • 730 Tenney St, 61443 • 309-853-2020 • I-80 Exit 33 go S on SR-78 for 13.3 miles
✪		✓			Lake Zurich • 820 S Rand Rd, 60047 • 847-438-2200 • Jct Lake Cook Rd & US-12 (SE of town) go NW on US-12 for 3.3 miles
✪	1			✓	Lansing • 17625 Torrence Ave, 60438 • 708-474-6405 • I-80/I-94 Exit 161, south of exit

☆	⛨	🕐	⛽	🚳	Store Details
✪					Lawrenceville • 2610 W Haven Rd, 62439 • 618-943-7551 • .7 mile west of town center via SR-250
✪	2	✓			Lincoln • 825 Malerich Dr, 62656 • 217-735-2314 • I-55 Exit 126 take SR-10 E 1.3 miles
✪	2	✓	◆		Litchfield • 1205 W Ferdon St, 62056 • 217-324-6195 • I-55 Exit 52 take SR-16 E .9 mile, Coluimbia Blvd N .3 mile & Ferdon St E .3 mile
✪	6	✓			Lockport • 16241 S Farrell Rd, 60441 • 815-838-1027 • I-80 Exit 140 follow I-355 (toll) N 4.3 miles, W .9 mile on SR-7 (159th St), S .3 mile on Farrell Rd
✪		✓			Macomb • 1730 E Jackson St, 61455 • 309-836-3311 • Jct SR-2 & US-136 (E of town) go W on US-136 for 4.4 miles
✪	2	✓			Marion • 2802 Outer Dr, 62959 • 618-997-5618 • I-57 Exit 54B take SR-13 W 1.3 miles
✪	1	✓			Marshall • 108 Kyden Dr, 62441 • 217-826-8061 • I-70 Exit 147, south of exit
☆	1				Matteson • 21410 S Cicero Ave, 60443 • 708-503-0440 • I-57 Exit 340 go E .5 mile on US-30 (Lincoln Hwy) then S .4 mile on SR-50
✪	2	✓	◆		Mattoon • 101 Dettro Dr, 61938 • 217-234-2266 • I-57 Exit 190B merge onto SR-16 W .9 mile then S on Dettro Dr .5 mile
✪	1	✓			Moline • 3930 44th Avenue Dr, 61265 • 309-736-2270 • I-74 Exit 4B go E .5 mile on SR-5, turn right at 38th St then left 41st Ave Dr .1 mile
✪	5	✓			Montgomery • 2000 Orchard Rd, 60538 • 630-844-0292 • I-88 (toll) Orchard Rd Exit go S 4.7 miles
✪	1	✓		✓	Morris • 333 E US Hwy 6, 60450 • 815-942-6306 • I-80 Exit 112 go S .4 mile on SR-47 (Division St) then E .1 mile on US-6
✪	1	✓			Morton • 155 E Courtland St, 61550 • 309-263-7898 • I-74 Exit 102 go N on Morton Ave .3 mile then E on Courtland St
✪	4	✓			Mount Prospect • 930 Mount Prospect Plz, 60056 • 847-590-0002 • From I-294 (toll) take the Dempster Rd Exit to Rand Rd NW 3.4 miles
✪	1	✓			Mount Vernon • 110 Davidson Rd, 62864 • 618-244-7119 • I-57 Exit 95 go W on Broadway/SR-15 for .3 mile
✪		✓			Murphysboro • 6495 Country Club Rd, 62966 • 618-684-5041 • 3 miles east of town center off SR-13 at Country Club Rd

☆	⬡	🕐	⛽	🚫	Store Details
●	5	✓		✓	Naperville • 2552 W 75th St, 60564 • 630-416-1000 • I-88 at SR-59 exit, go S 3.8 miles on SR-59 then E .4 mile on 75th St
●	2	✓			New Lenox • 501 E Lincoln Hwy, 60451 • 815-215-2008 • I-80 Exit 137 go E 2 miles on US-30/Maple St
☆	1				Niles • 5630 W Touhy Ave, 60714 • 847-647-8641 • I-94 Exit 39A take W Touhy Ave .7 mile
●	5	✓			Niles • 8500 W Golf Rd, 60714 • 847-966-7904 • I-94 Exit 37A go W 1.7 miles on Dempster St; N 1 mile on Waukegan Rd; W 1.9 miles on SR-58/Golf Rd
●	3	✓			Normal • 300 Greenbriar Dr, 61761 • 309-451-1100 • I-55 Exit 167 take Veterans Pkwy/I-55 BR S 2 miles then E at Pkwy Plaza Dr
☆	1			✓	Northlake • 137 W North Ave, 60164 • 708-409-0049 • I-290 Exit 13A take Lake St/US-20 E .3 mile, Railroad Ave N .1 mile & North Ave/SR-64 E .2 mile
●	1	✓			O'Fallon • 1530 W US Hwy 50, 62269 • 618-632-9066 • I-64 Exit 14 go W on US-50 for .6 mile
●		✓			Olney • 1001 N West St, 62450 • 618-395-7317 • Jct US-50 & SR-130 (S of town) take SR-130/West St N 1.7 miles
●	4	✓			Orland Hills • 9245 159th St, 60487 • 708-349-4300 • I-80 Exit 145 take US-45 N 3.5 miles then US-6 E .5 mile
●		✓	❖		Oswego • 2300 US Hwy 34, 60543 • 630-554-3014 • Jct US-30 & US-34 (NE of town) take US-34 SW 1.3 miles
●	1	✓			Ottawa • 4041 Veterans Dr, 61350 • 815-434-0120 • I-80 Exit 90 take SR-23/Columbus St S .4 mile
☆	7				Palatine • 1555 N Rand Rd, 60074 • 847-202-9189 • I-90 & SR-53 (S of town) go N on SR-53 for 5.3 miles then W on Rand Rd for 1.1 miles
☆					Pana • 10 W 2nd St, 62557 • 217-562-5081 • Jct US-51 & SR-16 (E of town) go W on SR-16 for 5.2 miles
●		✓	◆		Paris • 15150 US Hwy 150, 61944 • 217-466-5428 • Jct US-150 & SR-1 (E of town) take US-150 W 4.8 miles
●	8	✓			Pekin • 3320 Veterans Dr, 61554 • 309-353-1123 • I-55 Exit 28 take Broadway/CR-19 W 5.5 miles & S on Veterans Dr 2.1 miles
☆	2			✓	Peoria • 3315 N University St, 61604 • 309-682-0055 • I-74 Exit 91 go N on University St 1.3 miles
●	6	✓			Peoria • 8915 N Allen Rd, 61615 • 309-693-0525 • I-74 Exit 87B take US-6 N 5.3 miles to Exit 5 then S on Allen Rd .3 mile

☆	⬡	🕐	⛽	🚫	Store Details
●	1	✓			Peru • 5307 State Rt 251, 61354 • 815-224-2396 • I-80 Exit 75, north of exit
☆	7				Pittsfield • 151 Shetland Dr, 62363 • 217-285-9621 • I-72 Exit 35 take SR-107/US-54 S 5.3 miles, Washington St W 1.2 miles & Shetland Dr N
●	6	✓			Plainfield • 12690 S Rt 59, 60585 • 815-267-3041 • I-55 Exit 263 take Weber Rd N .8 mile, Rodeo Dr W 2.6 miles, 119th St W 1.4 miles & SR-59 S 1 mile
●		✓	❖		Plano • 6800 W US Hwy 34, 60545 • 630-552-1580 • Jct SR-15 & US-34 (W of town) go W on US-34 for 1.2 miles
●	1	✓			Pontiac • 1706 W Reynolds St, 61764 • 815-844-3600 • I-55 Exit 197 go E on Reynolds St .7 mile
●	1	✓			Princeton • 2111 Claude Bailey Pkwy, 61356 • 815-875-4521 • I-80 Exit 56, south of exit
●	1	✓	❖		Quincy • 5211 Broadway St, 62305 • 217-223-9930 • I-172 Exit 14 go W on SR-104/Broadway St .6 mile
●	1	✓			Rantoul • 845 Broadmeadow Dr, 61866 • 217-892-9151 • I-57 Exit 250, east of exit
●		✓			Robinson • 1304 E Main St, 62454 • 618-546-5676 • Jct SR-33 & SR-1 (E of town) go W on SR-33 for 2.2 miles
●	2	✓			Rochelle • 311 E Route 38, 61068 • 815-562-3424 • I-39 Exit 99 take SR-38 W 1.5 miles
☆	1				Rock Falls • 1901 1st Ave, 61071 • 815-626-6800 • I-88 Exit 41 take SR-40/88 N 1 mile
●	8	✓	❖		Rockford • 3902 W Riverside Blvd, 61101 • 815-962-4071 • From I-90/39 take Riverside Blvd W 7.8 miles
●	1	✓		✓	Rockford • 7219 Walton St, 61108 • 815-399-7143 • I-90/39 Exit 63 take US-20 BR W .7 mile & Buckley Dr S for .2 mile
●	4	✓			Rockford • 3849 Northridge Dr, 61114 • 815-636-0101 • I-90/39 take Riverside Blvd W 3.6 miles, S on Forest Hills Rd .2 mile & N on Northridge .2 mile
☆	2			✓	Rolling Meadows • 1460 Golf Rd, 60008 • 847-734-0456 • I-90 (toll) exit at Arlington Heights Rd Ext go N .2 mile, NW on Algonquin Rd .8 mile & W on Golf Rd .2 mile
●	4	✓		✓	Romeoville • 420 Weber Rd, 60446 • 815-439-1666 • I-55 Exit 263 take Weber Rd S 3.3 miles
●	1	✓		✓	Roscoe • 4781 E Rockton Rd, 61073 • 815-389-4055 • I-90/39 Exit 3 go W on Rockton Rd for 1.6 miles

☆	🛡	🕐	⛽	🚫	Store Details
✪	8	✓			Round Lake Beach • 2680 N State Hwy 83, 60073 • 847-265-3687 • I-94/Tri-State Tollway at Grand Ave Exit go W 2.9 miles, then S .3 mile on US-45, then W 3.1 miles on Rollins Rd, then N 1.1 miles on SR-83
✪		✓		✓	Saint Charles • 150 Smith Rd, 60174 • 630-513-9559 • 2.6 miles east of town center along SR-64
✪	1	✓	❖		Salem • 1870 W Main St, 62881 • 618-548-4383 • I-57 Exit 116 take US-50 W .3 mile
✪	6	✓	❖		Savoy • 505 S Dunlap Ave, 61874 • 217-355-5845 • I-74 Exit 182 go S on Neil St 3.5 miles, continue S on Dunlap Ave 2.4 miles
✪		✓			Shelbyville • 2607 W Main St, 62565 • 217-774-1560 • 1.6 miles west of town center along SR-16
✪	3	✓		✓	Shorewood • 1401 State Hwy 59, 60431 • 815-609-3381 • I-55 Exit 253 take W Jefferson St/US-52 W for .6 mile & N on SR-59 for 1.8 miles
✪	6	✓			Silvis • 1601 18th St, 61282 • 309-796-3526 • I-80 exit 7 take Cleveland Rd & SR-84 W 3.6 miles, continue W .9 mile on Colona Rd, then N .9 mile on John Deere Rd
✪	2	✓		✓	Skokie • 3626 Touhy Ave, 60076 • 847-983-1409 • I-94 Exit 39B go E 1.4 miles on Touhy Ave
✪		✓			Sparta • 1410 N Market St, 62286 • 618-443-5800 • On SR-4 1 mile north of town
✪	2	✓	❖		Springfield • 2760 N Dirksen Pkwy, 62702 • 217-522-3090 • I-55 Exit 100 take SR-54 W .9 mile then N on Dirksen Pkwy .6 mile
✪	1	✓			Springfield • 1100 Lejune Dr, 62703 • 217-529-6221 • I-55/I-72 Exit 92A or I-72 Exit 97B, north of exit
✪	1	✓			Springfield • 3401 Freedom Dr, 62704 • 217-793-3310 • I-72 Exit 93 go N on SR-4 for .7 mile then W .2 mile on Lindbergh Blvd
✪		✓			Sterling • 4115 E Lincolnway, 61081 • 815-626-7200 • Jct SR-40/88 & SR-2 (S of town) follow SR-2 NE 2.8 miles
✪	7	✓			Streamwood • 850 S Barrington Rd, 60107 • 630-213-7000 • I-90 at SR-59/Sutton Rd Exit go S 1.5 miles on SR-59; east 2.5 miles on Golf Rd; S 2.2 miles on Barrington Rd
✪		✓			Streator • 2415 N Bloomington St, 61364 • 815-672-3071 • 2 miles north of town center along SR-23
✪		✓			Taylorville • 1530 W Springfield Rd, 62568 • 217-287-7219 • Jct SR-104 & SR-29 (N of town) go N on SR-29 for .5 mile

☆	🛡	🕐	⛽	🚫	Store Details
✪	2	✓	❖		Urbana • 100 S High Cross Rd, 61802 • 217-344-6148 • I-74 Exit 185 take SR-130 S .8 mile, E on US-150/University Ave 1.2 miles & S at High Cross Rd
✪	1	✓	❖		Vandalia • 201 N Mattes Ave, 62471 • 618-283-4777 • I-70 Exit 61, south of exit
☆	3			✓	Vernon Hills • 555 E Townline Rd, 60061 • 847-918-0555 • From I-94 go W on Townline Rd/SR-60 for 2.6 miles
✪		✓		✓	Villa Park • 900 S Route 83, 60181 • 630-530-2550 • 2.6 miles southeast of town center along SR-83
✪		✓			Washington • 1980 Freedom Pkwy, 61571 • 309-745-3339 • Jct SR-8 & US-24 (W of town) go NW on US-24 BR/Mc-clugage Rd .3 mile & E on Freedom Pkwy .2 mile
✪		✓			Waterloo • 961 N Market St, 62298 • 618-939-3416 • Jct SR-158 & SR-3 (N of town) go S on SR-3 for 5.7 miles then W on HH Rd & S on Market St
✪		✓			Watseka • 1790 E Walnut St, 60970 • 815-432-2200 • 2 miles east of town center along US-24/SR-1
✪	4	✓	❖		Waukegan • 3900 Fountain Square Pl, 60085 • 847-473-2193 • I-94 (toll) at Buckley Rd (SR-137) go E .6 mile then N 2.3 miles on IL-43 (Waukegan Rd) and left .2 mile
✪	4	✓		✓	Wheeling • 1455 E Lake Cook Rd, 60090 • 847-537-5090 • I-94 at Lake Cood Rd Exit, go W 3.9 miles
✪	9	✓			Wood River • 610 Wesley Dr, 62095 • 618-259-0290 • I-270 & SR-255 follow SR-255 N 8.1 miles to Exit 8 then follow SR-111 W .5 mile
✪		✓			Woodstock • 1275 Lake Ave, 60098 • 815-206-0256 • Jct Ridgefield Rd & US-14 (S of town) take US-14 N 2.8 miles & continue on Lake Ave .1 mile
✪	5	✓			Zion • 4000 Route 173, 60099 • 847-731-8172 • I-94 at SR-173 exit (westbound travelers only) turn right and go 4.7 miles on SR-173; eastbound travelers use the I-94 US-41 exit, follow US-41 .9 mile then turn left and go 3.9 miles on SR-173

INDIANA

☆					Store Details
✪	1	✓			Anderson • 2321 Charles St, 46013 • 765-642-5025 • I-69 Exit 26 take SR-9 N for 1 mile
✪	5	✓	❖		Angola • 2016 N Wayne St, 46703 • 260-665-7313 • I-69 Exit 148 go E on US-20 for 2.5 miles then N on Wayne St for 1.7 miles
✪	1	✓			Auburn • 505 Touring Dr, 46706 • 260-925-8080 • I-69 Exit 129 take SR-8 E .1 mile then S on Touring Dr .3 mile
✪	10	✓			Aurora • 100 Sycamore Estates Dr, 47001 • 812-926-4322 • I-275 Exit 21 take US-50 W for 9.8 miles
✪	5	✓	❖	✓	Avon • 9500 E US Hwy 36, 46123 • 317-209-0857 • I-465/74 Exit 13B take US-36 W for 4.6 miles
✪		✓			Bedford • 3200 John Williams Blvd, 47421 • 812-275-0335 • Jct US-50 & SR-37 go N on SR-37 for 3.2 miles & E at Williams Blvd .2 mile
✪		✓	❖		Bloomington • 3313 W State Hwy 45, 47403 • 812-337-0002 • Jct SR-46 & SR-45 (W of town) follow SR-45 S 3.6 miles
✪		✓	◆		Bluffton • 2100 N Main St, 46714 • 260-824-0296 • I-69 Exit 86 take US-224 E .2 mile, SR-116 E 10.2 miles & S on Main St 1.2 miles
✪		✓			Boonville • 1115 American Way, 47601 • 812-897-5964 • I-164 Exit 10 go E on Lynch Rd 1.8 miles then SR-62 E for 8.2 miles & N on American Way
☆	7				Brazil • 2150 E National Ave, 47834 • 812-443-0667 • I-70 Exit 23 take SR-59 N 5.1 miles then US-40 NE 1.4 miles
✪	1	✓			Brownsburg • 400 W Northfield Dr, 46112 • 317-858-0206 • I-74 Exit 66 go S on SR-267 for .2 mile
✪	5	✓			Camby • 8191 Upland Way, 46113 • 317-856-5748 • I-70 Exit 68 go SE 2.1 miles on Ameriplex Pkwy; turn right and follow SR-67 S 2.8 miles
✪	7	✓			Carmel • 2001 E 151st St, 46033 • 317-844-0096 • I-465 Exit 33 take SR-431 N 5.7 miles, US-31 N .5 mile & E at 151st St .1 mile
✪	1	✓			Clarksville • 1351 Veterans Pkwy, 47129 • 812-284-9926 • I-65 Exit 5, west of exit
☆					Clinton • 1795 E IN Hwy 163, 47842 • 765-832-3533 • I-70 Exit 7 go N on 3rd St/US-150 for 4.2 miles, SR-63 N 11.9 miles & SR-163 E .2 mile
✪		✓			Columbia City • 402 W Plaza Dr, 46725 • 260-244-4060 • I-69 Exit 109B take US-30 W 17.2 miles then N on SR-109 & W on Plaza Dr

☆					Store Details
✪	2	✓			Columbus • 2025 Merchant Mile, 47201 • 812-376-8680 • I-65 Exit 68, take SR-46 W .5 mile, Goller & Terrace Lake Blvd S 1.1 miles, Carr Hill Rd E .2 mile
✪	2	✓	❖		Columbus • 735 Whitfield Dr, 47201 • 812-372-0227 • I-65 Exit 76A take US-31 S 9 miles & 10th St W .3 mile
✪		✓			Connersville • 4200 Western Ave, 47331 • 765-827-1255 • 3 miles north of town center via SR-1
✪	2	✓			Corydon • 2363 Hwy 135 NW, 47112 • 812-738-4551 • I-64 Exit 105 take SR-135 S 1.3 miles
✪	7	✓	❖		Crawfordsville • 1835 S US Hwy 231, 47933 • 765-362-5930 • I-74 Exit 39 take SR-32 E 4.9 miles & US-231 S 2.1 miles
✪		✓	❖		Decatur • 1700 S 13th St, 46733 • 260-724-9990 • 2 miles south of town on US-27/US-33
✪	1	✓			Elkhart • 175 County Rd 6 W, 46514 • 574-266-7448 • I-80/90 (toll) Exit 92 go S on SR-19 for .7 mile & W on CR-6 for .2 mile
✪	8	✓		✓	Elkhart • 30830 Old US 20, 46514 • 574-674-2656 • I-80/I-90 Exit 83 go S 3.8 miles on Capital Ave (SR-331) then E 4.2 miles on McKinley Hwy/Old US-20
✪		✓	❖		Evansville • 335 S Red Bank Rd, 47712 • 812-424-5475 • I-164 Exit 7B take Lloyd Expy W for 9.8 miles & N on Red Bank Rd .4 mile
✪	2	✓			Evansville • 401 N Burkhardt Rd, 47715 • 812-473-1815 • I-164 Exit 7B take SR-66 W 1 mile & Burkhardt Rd W .1 mile
✪	1	✓	❖	✓	Fishers • 8300 E 96th St, 46037 • 317-578-4336 • I-69 Exit 3 go E on 96th St .5 mile
✪	2	✓	◆		Fort Wayne • 1710 Apple Glen Blvd, 46804 • 260-436-0113 • I-69 Exit 105 go E on Illinois Rd 1.2 miles & S on Apple Glen Blvd .2 mile
✪	9	✓	❖		Fort Wayne • 7502 Southtown Crossing Blvd, 46816 • 260-441-7071 • I-69 Exit 99 go E on Lower Huntington & Airport Expy 7.3 miles, E on Tillman 1.1 miles, S on Phoenix Pkwy .1 mile
✪	4	✓	❖		Fort Wayne • 10105 Lima Rd, 46818 • 260-490-6510 • I-69 Exit 116 go W 3.3 miles on Dupont Rd then S .2 mile on Lima Rd
✪	1	✓			Fort Wayne • 5311 Coldwater Rd, 46825 • 260-484-4198 • I-69 Exit 112A take Coldwater Rd E .6 mile
✪	1	✓	❖		Fort Wayne • 10420 Maysville Rd, 46835 • 260-492-5845 • I-469 Exit 25 go W on Maysville Rd .3 mile

☆	🛡	🕐	⛽	🚫	Store Details
✪		✓	❖		Frankfort • 2460 E Wabash St, 46041 • 765-654-5528 • I-65 Exit 146 take SR-47 E 1.8 miles, SR-39 N 10.8 miles & US-421 E 1.7 miles
✪	6	✓	❖		Franklin • 2125 N Morton St, 46131 • 317-736-5377 • I-65 Exit 95 take Whiteland Rd W 1.6 miles then US-31 S 3.7 miles
✪		✓			Goshen • 2304 Lincolnway E, 46526 • 574-534-4094 • I-80/90 (toll) Exit 101 follow SR-15 S for 11.7 miles then US-33 SE 3.1 miles
☆					Goshen • 4024 Elkhard Rd, 46526 • 574-875-6601 • Jct US-20 & US-33 (NW of town) go SE on US-33/Elkhart Rd for 3.2 miles
✪	10	✓			Greencastle • 1750 Indianapolis Rd, 46135 • 765-653-2481 • I-70 Exit 41 take US-231 N 7.8 miles then follow SR-240 E 1.8 miles
✪	1	✓	❖	✓	Greenfield • 1965 N State St, 46140 • 317-462-8850 • I-70 Exit 104 go S on State St .4 mile
✪	1	✓			Greensburg • 790 Greensburg Commons Ctr, 47240 • 812-663-3434 • I-74 Exit 134A take SR-3 S .1 mile & E at Freeland Rd .2 mile
✪	1	✓	❖		Greenwood • 1133 N Emerson Rd, 46143 • 317-885-9059 • I-65 Exit 101 go W on County Line Rd .3 mile then S on Emerson Rd .1 mile
✪	6	✓		✓	Greenwood • 882 S State Road 135, 46143 • 317-851-1102 • I-65 Exit 99 go W .4 mile on Main St, turn left onto Emerson Ave .5 mile and continue onto Smith Valley Rd for 4.1 miles, then go S .2 mile on SR-135
✪	1			✓	Hammond • 1100 5th Ave, 46320 • 219-473-9653 • I-90 Exit 0 (westbound exit only), north of exit
✪	1	✓		✓	Hammond • 7850 Cabela Dr, 46324 • 219-989-0258 • I-94 Exit 2, south of exit
✪					Huntington • 2800 Walmart Dr, 46750 • 260-358-8311 • I-69 Exit 86 follow US-224 W 10.4 miles
✪	1	✓	❖	✓	Indianapolis • 4650 S Emerson Ave, 46203 • 317-783-0950 • I-74/I-465 Exit 52, south of exit
✪	4	✓			Indianapolis • 7245 US Hwy 31 S, 46227 • 317-888-7906 • I-465 Exit 2B follow US-31 S 3.7 miles
✪	3	✓			Indianapolis • 10617 E Washington St, 46229 • 317-895-0065 • I-465 Exit 46 follow US-40 E 2.7 miles
✪	4	✓	❖		Indianapolis • 10735 Pendleton Pike, 46236 • 317-823-1054 • I-465 Exit 42 take US-36 E 3.9 miles
✪	7	✓			Indianapolis • 7325 N Keystone Ave, 46240 • 317-202-9720 • I-70 Exit 85B go N on Keystone Ave 6.4 miles

☆	🛡	🕐	⛽	🚫	Store Details
✪	1	✓			Indianapolis • 4545 Lafayette Rd, 46254 • 317-328-0325 • I-65 Exit 121, south of exit
✪	2	✓			Indianapolis • 3221 W 86th St, 46268 • 317-875-0273 • I-465 Exit 27 go S on Michigan Rd .8 mile then E on 86th St .3 mile
✪		✓			Jasper • 4040 N Newton St, 47546 • 812-634-1233 • 1 mile north of town center on US-231
✪	9	✓	❖		Kendallville • 2501 E North St, 46755 • 260-347-4300 • I-69 Exit 134 take US-6 W 8.9 miles
✪		✓			Kokomo • 1920 E Markland Ave, 46901 • 765-456-3550 • Jct US-33 & US-35 (E of town) go E on US-35/Markland Ave .1 mile
✪	7	✓			La Porte • 333 Boyd Blvd, 46350 • 219-325-3130 • I-80/90 (toll) follow SR-39 S 4.4 miles, SR-2 E 1.6 miles & Boyd Blvd S .2 mile
✪	1	✓			Lafayette • 4205 Commerce Dr, 47905 • 765-446-0100 • I-65 Exit 172 take SR-26 W .4 mile, Well Spring Dr S .1 mile & Commerce Dr E
✪	5	✓			Lafayette • 2347 Veterans Memorial Pkwy S, 47909 • 765-477-9379 • I-65 Exit 168 go W on SR-25/39 for 1.5 miles, continue W on "E-350-S" 2.8 miles
✪	3	✓			Lebanon • 2440 N Lebanon St, 46052 • 765-482-6070 • I-65 Exit 139 go N 2.7 miles on SR-39/Lebanon St
✪		✓	◆		Linton • 2251 E IN Hwy 54, 47441 • 812-847-2127 • From town center go E 2 miles on SR-54
✪		✓			Logansport • 240 Mall Rd, 46947 • 574-732-0221 • 2.3 miles east of town center via Market St and Mall Dr
✪		✓	◆		Madison • 567 Ivy Tech Dr, 47250 • 812-273-4993 • Jct SR-7 & SR-62 (NW of town) take SR-62 E 2.4 miles then S on Ivy Tech Dr .1 mile
✪	9	✓			Marion • 3240 S Western Ave, 46953 • 765-662-0809 • I-69 Exit 64 take SR-18 W 5 miles, Penn St & Lincoln Blvd W 1.7 miles, 30th St W 1.6 miles & Western Ave S .2 mile
✪		✓	❖	✓	Martinsville • 410 Grand Valley Blvd, 46151 • 765-342-3786 • From SR-39/SR-37 jct south of town, follow SR-37 N 2.3 miles
✪	2	✓			Merrillville • 2936 E 79th Ave, 46410 • 219-947-1309 • I-65 Exit 253 take US-30 E 1.3 miles then N at Merrillville Crossing .2 mile
✪	1	✓			Michigan City • 5780 Franklin St, 46360 • 219-879-3620 • I-94 exit 34B take US-421 N .7 mile

☆	🛡	🕐	⛽	🚭	Store Details
✪	4	✓		✓	Mishawaka • 316 Indian Ridge Blvd, 46545 • 574-243-9188 • I-80/90 (toll) Exit 77, follow Douglas Rd E 3.3 miles, Grape Rd N .2 mile & Indian Ridge Blvd E .1 mile
✪		✓			Monticello • 1088 W Broadway St, 47960 • 574-583-2063 • Jct SR-43 & US-24 (W of town) take US-24 E 5.1 miles
✪		✓	❖		Muncie • 1501 E 29th St, 47302 • 765-282-7467 • Jct SR-67 & SR-3 (S of town) go N on Old SR-3 for 1 mile then W on 29th St .2 mile
✪	7	✓			Muncie • 4801 W Clara Ln, 47304 • 765-284-7181 • I-69 Exit 41 take SR-332 E 6.4 miles, S at Morrison Rd .1 mile & W at Clara Ln .1 mile
✪	2	✓			New Albany • 2910 Grant Line Rd, 47150 • 812-944-0635 • I-64 Exit 3 take Grant Line Rd S 1.3 miles
✪	4	✓			New Castle • 3167 S State Hwy 3, 47362 • 765-529-5990 • I-70 Exit 123 follow SR-3 N 3.2 miles
✪	3	✓			Newburgh • 8599 Highpointe Dr, 47630 • 812-842-2361 • I-64 Exit 7A go E 2.3 miles on SR-66/Lloyd Expy
✪	6	✓			Noblesville • 16865 Clover Rd, 46060 • 317-773-5212 • Northbound I-69 travelers use Exit 5 and go N 4.6 miles on SR-37. Southbound I-69 travelers use Exit 10 and follow SR-238 NW for 4.6 miles then go N .7 mile on SR-37.
✪		✓			North Vernon • 2410 N State Hwy 3, 47265 • 812-346-5100 • 1.7 miles northwest of town center along SR-3
✪		✓			Paoli • 735 N Gospel St, 47454 • 812-723-4444 • Jct US-150 & SR-37 (in town) go N on SR-37 for .7 mile
✪	4	✓	❖	✓	Plainfield • 2373 E Main St, 46168 • 317-839-2261 • I-70 Exit 66 take SR-267 N 3 miles then E on Main St .5 mile
✪		✓	◆		Plymouth • 2505 N Oak Dr, 46563 • 574-935-9000 • Jct US-30 & US-31 (E of town) go W on US-30 for 3.2 miles then N on Oak Rd .1 mile
✪	3	✓			Portage • 6087 US Hwy 6, 46368 • 219-759-5900 • I-80/90 Exit 23 go S on Willowcreek Rd 2.4 miles then E on US-6 for .2 mile
✪		✓	❖		Portland • 950 W Votaw St, 47371 • 260-726-3682 • Jct US-27 & SR-67/26 (in town) go W on SR-67/26 (Votaw St) for .6 mile
✪		✓			Princeton • 2700 W Broadway St, 47670 • 812-386-6620 • I-64 Exit 25B merge onto US-41 N 14 miles then E on SR-64/65 for .5 mile
☆	8				Rensselaer • 905 S College Ave, 47978 • 219-866-0266 • I-65 Exit 205 go N on US-231 for 8 miles

☆	🛡	🕐	⛽	🚭	Store Details
✪	2	✓	❖		Richmond • 3601 E Main St, 47374 • 765-965-5387 • I-70 Exit 156A take US-40 W 1.8 miles
✪		✓			Rochester • 2395 Main St, 46975 • 574-223-9481 • 1 mile south of town center on Main St at US-31
☆					Rushville • 1850 N Main St, 46173 • 765-932-2133 • Jct US-52 & SR-3 (S of town) go N on SR-3/N Main St for 1.5 miles
☆	9				Schererville • 1555 US Hwy 41, 46375 • 219-865-6309 • I-65 Exit 253 follow US-30 W for 7.9 miles then US-41 N for .2 mile
✪	1	✓	◆		Scottsburg • 1618 W McClain Ave, 47170 • 812-752-7122 • I-65 Exit 29B take SR-56 W for .3 mile
✪	2	✓			Seymour • 1600 E Tipton St, 47274 • 812-522-8838 • I-65 Exit 50B take US-50 W 1.1 miles
✪	1	✓	❖		Shelbyville • 2500 Progress Pkwy, 46176 • 317-392-4940 • I-74 Exit 116 take SR-44 W .2 mile & Lee Blvd N .3 mile
✪		✓			South Bend • 700 W Ireland Rd, 46614 • 574-299-1284 • I-80/90 Exit 72 take US-31 S 9.5 miles, exit at US-31 BR N .6 mile & W on Ireland Rd .4 mile
✪	5	✓	❖		South Bend • 3701 Portage Rd, 46628 • 574-243-4915 • I-80/90 Exit 72 take US-31 N 1.6 miles, Breck Rd E 2.3 miles & Portage Rd S .8 mile
☆					Spencer • 823 W IN Hwy 46, 47460 • 812-829-2251 • I-70 Exit 23 take SR-59 S for 5 miles then SR-46 E for 9.6 miles
☆					Sullivan • 757 W Wolfe St, 47882 • 812-268-3381 • Jct US-41 & SR-154 (W of town) go E on SR-154/Wolfe St for .1 mile
✪		✓			Tell City • 730 US Hwy 66 E, 47586 • 812-547-8434 • Jct SR-237 & SR-66 (S of town) go N on SR-66 for 1.7 miles
✪	3	✓		✓	Terre Haute • 5555 S US Hwy 41, 47802 • 812-299-4677 • I-70 Exit 7 take US-150 E/US-41 S for 2.2 miles
✪	3	✓			Terre Haute • 2399 S State Hwy 46, 47803 • 812-872-2520 • I-70 Exit 11 go N on SR-46 for 2.1 miles
✪		✓			Valparaiso • 2400 Morthland Dr, 46383 • 219-465-2799 • I-65 Exit 253 follow US-30 E 15 miles
✪		✓			Vincennes • 650 Kimmel Rd, 47591 • 812-886-0312 • Jct US-50/150 & US-41 (E of town) take US-41 S 1.7 miles, Hart St E .3 mile & Kimmel Rd N .1 mile
✪		✓			Wabash • 1601 N Cass St, 46992 • 260-563-5536 • 2 miles northwest of town center near US-24/SR-15 jct

☆	◯	🕐	⛽	🚐	Store Details
✪		✓	❖		Warsaw • 2501 Walton Blvd, 46582 • 574-269-7811 • Jct US-30 & SR-15 (N of town) take Detroit St/SR-15 N .3 mile, Jalynn St W & Walton Blvd N .1 mile
✪		✓			Washington • 1801 S State Hwy 57, 47501 • 812-254-6681 • 2 miles south of town near the jct of US-50 and SR-57
✪	5	✓			West Lafayette • 2801 Northwestern Ave, 47906 • 765-463-0201 • I-65 Exit 175 go W on Schuyler Ave 1.3 miles, continue on US-52 W 3.1 miles, Yeager Rd S .2 mile & US-231 N
✪		✓			Winchester • 950 E Greenville Pike, 47394 • 765-584-2199 • I-70 Exit 151B take US-27 N 21.2 miles then Greenville Pike E .1 mile

IOWA

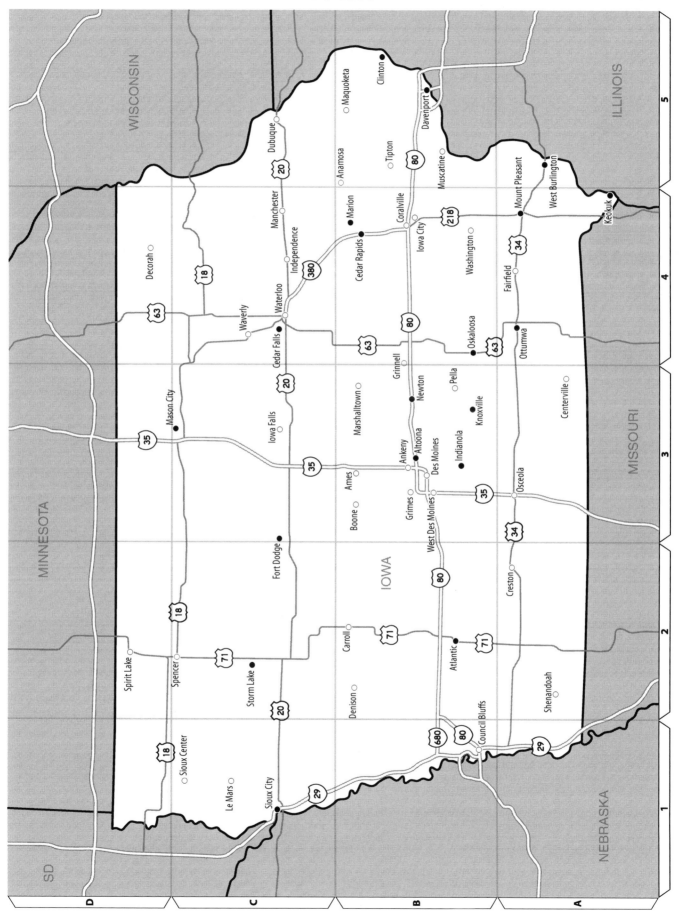

☆	⬡	🕐	⛽	🚫	Store Details
✪	2	✓	◆		Altoona • 3501 8th St SW, 50009 • 515-967-1711 • I-80 Exit 142A take US-6 W for .5 mile then S on 56th St .8 mile
☆	4				Ames • 3015 Grand Ave, 50010 • 515-233-1345 • I-35 Exit 113 go W on 13th St 2.2 miles, N on Duff Ave 1.5 miles & W on US-69
✪	3	✓			Ames • 534 S Duff Ave, 50010 • 515-956-3536 • I-35 Exit 111B take US-30 W 1.7 miles to Exit 148 then go N .8 mile on Duff Ave
✪		✓			Anamosa • 101 115th St, 52205 • 319-462-4311 • Jct US-150 & SR-64 (E of town) go SE on SR-64 for .5 mile then W on 115th St .2 mile
✪	1	✓			Ankeny • 1002 SE National Dr, 50021 • 515-963-1111 • I-35 Exit 90 take SR-160 W .4 mile, Delaware Ave N .1 mile & National Dr W .1 mile
✪	9	✓	❖		Atlantic • 1905 E 7th St, 50022 • 712-243-5214 • I-80 Exit 60 merge onto US-71 S 8.9 miles
✪				✓	Boone • 1515 SE Marshall St, 50036 • 515-432-2416 • I-35 Exit 111B go W 15.7 miles on US-30 to Marshall St
✪		✓			Carroll • 2014 Kittyhawk Rd, 51401 • 712-792-2280 • 1.6 miles northwest of town center along US-30
✪		✓	❖		Cedar Falls • 525 Brandilynn Blvd, 50613 • 319-277-6391 • US-20 Exit 225 take SR-27/58 N 1.3 miles, Viking Rd E .1 mile, Andrea Dr N & Brandilynn Blvd E .2 mile
✪	1	✓			Cedar Rapids • 2645 Blairs Ferry Rd NE, 52402 • 319-393-0444 • I-380 Exit 24 go W on Blairs Ferry Rd .2 mile
✪		✓	◆		Cedar Rapids • 3601 29th Ave SW, 52404 • 319-390-9922 • From US-30 Exit 250 go N .7 mile on Edgewood Rd then W .1 mile on 29th Ave
✪		✓			Centerville • 23148 Hwy 5, 52544 • 641-437-7181 • 1.5 miles south of town center along SR-5
✪		✓	❖		Clinton • 2715 S 25th St, 52732 • 563-243-0001 • Jct US-30 & US-61 (W of town) tke US-30 E for 17.2 miles then N on 25th St
✪	1	✓			Coralville • 2801 Commerce Dr, 52241 • 319-545-6400 • I-80 Exit 240 merge onto US-6 W .4 mile then Commerce Dr W .3 mile
✪	1	✓			Council Bluffs • 1800 N 16th St, 51501 • 712-890-3914 • I-29 Exit 55 go S to Nash Blvd, turn left and follow .8 mile; southbound travelers can use Exit 56 and go straight at end of exit ramp
✪	1	✓			Council Bluffs • 3201 Manawa Centre Dr, 51501 • 712-366-3326 • I-29/I-80 Exit 3 go S on Expy St/SR-192 for .2 mile & E at 32nd Ave .2 mile
✪		✓			Creston • 806 Laurel St, 50801 • 641-782-6954 • 1 mile southwest of town center off US-34 at Laurel St
✪	4	✓	❖		Davenport • 3101 W Kimberly Rd, 52806 • 563-445-0272 • I-280 Exit 1 take US-6 E 3.6 miles
✪	1	✓	❖		Davenport • 5811 Elmore Ave, 52807 • 563-359-0023 • I-74 Exit 1 go W on 53rd St .2 mile & N on Elmore Ave .2 mile
✪		✓			Decorah • 1798 Old Stage Rd, 52101 • 563-382-8737 • Jct US-52 & SR-9 (SW of town) go E on SR-9 for 2.6 miles then NE on Old Stage Coach Rd
✪		✓			Denison • 510 Avenue C, 51442 • 712-263-2000 • 1 mile northwest of town along US-59
✪	1	✓			Des Moines • 1001 73rd St, 50311 • 515-274-6224 • I-235 Exit 3 go N on 73rd St .1 mile
✪	5	✓			Des Moines • 5101 SE 14th St, 50320 • 515-287-7700 • I-235 Exit 8B go S 4.1 miles on US-69 (14th St)
✪		✓			Dubuque • 4200 Dodge St, 52003 • 563-582-1003 • Jct SR-32 & US-20 (W of town) go E on US-20 for .1 mile
✪		✓			Fairfield • 2701 W Burlington Ave, 52556 • 641-472-6858 • 1.5 miles west of town center on Burlington Ave
✪		✓	❖		Fort Dodge • 3036 1st Ave S, 50501 • 515-576-7400 • US-20 Exit 124 take CR-P59 N 3.5 miles, US-20 BR W 1.5 miles, 29th St N .3 mile & 1st St E .1 mile
✪	3	✓			Grimes • 2150 E 1st St, 50111 • 515-986-1783 • I-35 Exit 127 go N 2.7 miles on SR-141 then E .1 mile on 70th Ave
✪	2	✓			Grinnell • 415 Industrial Ave, 50112 • 641-236-4999 • I-80 Exit 182 take SR-146 N 1.8 miles then E on Industrial Ave
✪		✓			Independence • 302 Enterprise Dr, 50644 • 319-334-7128 • US-20 Exit 254 follow SR-150 N 2.1 miles, 8th St E .2 mile & Park Ave N .1 mile
✪		✓	◆		Indianola • 1500 N Jefferson Way, 50125 • 515-961-8955 • I-35 Exit 56 go E 11.9 miles on SR-92 then N 1.1 miles on US-69
✪	7	✓			Iowa City • 919 Highway 1 W, 52246 • 319-337-3116 • I-80 Exit 239A follow US-218 S for 5.3 miles then go E 1.1 miles on SR-1
☆					Iowa Falls • 840 S Oak St, 50126 • 641-648-5145 • I-35 Exit 142A merge onto US-20 E 15.6 miles to Exit 168 then US-65 N 3.9 miles

☆	⬭	🕐	⛽	🚫	Store Details
✪		✓	❖		Keokuk • 300 N Park Dr, 52632 • 319-524-6941 • Jct US-61 & US-218 (NW of town) follow US-218/Main St SE 1.9 miles then W at Park Ave
✪		✓	◆		Knoxville • 814 W Bell Ave, 50138 • 641-828-7584 • Jct SR-5 & SR-14 (S of town) go N on SR-14 for .2 mile & E on Bell Ave .2 mile
✪		✓			Le Mars • 1111 Holton Dr, 51031 • 712-546-4900 • Jct SR-60 & US-75 (N of town) go S on US-75 1.5 miles
✪		✓			Manchester • 1220 W Main St, 52057 • 563-927-3377 • 1 mile west of town on Main St
✪					Maquoketa • 103 E Carlisle, 52060 • 563-652-6703 • 1.4 miles south of town center at US-61 Exit 156
✪	7	✓	❖		Marion • 5491 Hwy 151, 52302 • 319-447-2395 • I-380 Exit 24 go E on SR-100/Collins Rd for 6.5 miles & S on US-151 for .5 mile
✪		✓			Marshalltown • 2802 S Center St, 50158 • 641-753-7846 • Jct US-30 & SR-14 (S of town) take SR-14 N for .6 mile
✪	5	✓	❖	✓	Mason City • 4151 4th St SW, 50401 • 641-423-6767 • I-35 Exit 194 take US-18 BR E 4.8 miles
✪		✓	❖		Mount Pleasant • 1045 N Grand Ave, 52641 • 319-385-4600 • From US-218 (N of town) take Exit 45 toward Jewel Ave .4 mile, merge on Grand Ave .9 mile
✪		✓			Muscatine • 3003 N Hwy 61, 52761 • 563-263-8312 • From town center go E .7 mile on 2nd St then continue N on Park Ave for 1.7 miles then go E .4 mile on US-61
✪	2	✓	◆		Newton • 300 Iowa Speedway Dr, 50208 • 641-791-5322 • I-80 Exit 168 go N 1.4 miles on Iowa Speedway Dr
✪	1	✓			Osceola • 2400 College Dr, 50213 • 641-342-1650 • I-35 exit 33, west of exit
✪		✓	❖		Oskaloosa • 2203 Avenue A West, 52577 • 641-673-3839 • Jct US-63 & SR-92 (in town) go W on SR-92/Ave A for 1.3 miles
✪		✓	❖		Ottumwa • 1940 Venture Dr, 52501 • 641-682-1715 • 3 miles west of town center on US-34
✪		✓			Pella • 1650 Washington St, 50219 • 641-628-9881 • 1 mile west of town center via Washington St
✪		✓			Shenandoah • 705 S Fremont St, 51601 • 712-246-4044 • 1 mile west of town center on US-59
✪		✓			Sioux Center • 255 16th St SW, 51250 • 712-722-1990 • 1 mile south of town on US-75

☆	⬭	🕐	⛽	🚫	Store Details
✪	1	✓	❖		Sioux City • 3400 Singing Hills Blvd, 51106 • 712-252-0210 • I-29 Exit 143 go E on Industrial Rd .3 mile & continue E on Singing Hills Blvd .3 mile
✪	4	✓	❖		Sioux City • 3101 Floyd Blvd, 51108 • 712-239-8901 • I-29 Exit 147A go NE on Floyd Blvd 3.3 miles
✪		✓			Spencer • 500 11th St SW, 51301 • 712-262-5001 • Jct US-18 & US-71 (S of town) go S on US-71 for .4 mile
✪		✓			Spirit Lake • 2200 17th St, 51360 • 712-336-1339 • Jct SR-9 & US-71 (N of town) go E on 17th St .2 mile
✪		✓	❖		Storm Lake • 1831 Lake Ave, 50588 • 712-732-7940 • 1.2 miles north of town on SR-71
☆					Tipton • 1126 Hwy 38 N, 52772 • 563-886-3153 • I-80 Exit 267 take SR-38 N 10.4 miles
✪		✓			Washington • 2485 Hwy 92, 52353 • 319-653-7213 • 1.5 miles east of town center via SR-92
✪	1	✓			Waterloo • 1334 Flammang Dr, 50702 • 319-232-3661 • I-380 Exit 72 go SW .8 mile on San Marnan Dr then left at Flammang Dr
✪		✓			Waverly • 2700 4th St SW, 50677 • 319-352-5260 • From US-218 Exit 198 (S of town) merge onto Easton Ave/US-218 BR N .5 mile
✪		✓	❖		West Burlington • 324 W Agency Rd, 52655 • 319-753-6526 • Jct US-34 & US-61 (in town) go S on US-61 for .3 mile & W on Agency St for 1 mile
✪	2	✓		✓	West Des Moines • 6365 Stagecoach Dr, 50266 • 515-453-2747 • I-35 Exit 70 go W on Mills Pkwy .8 mile then S on Stagecoach Dr .4 mile

KANSAS

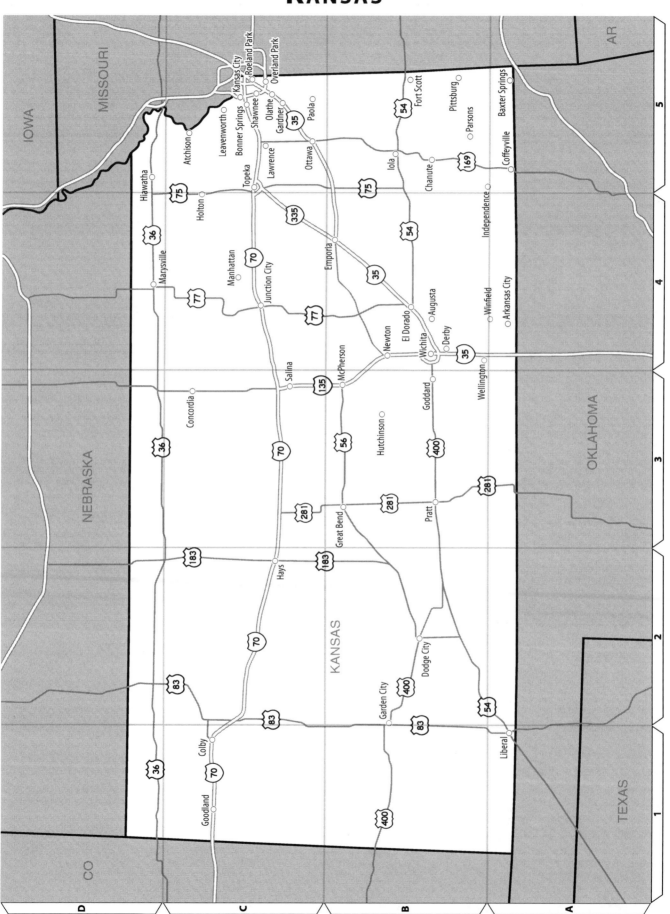

☆	⬡	🕐	⛽	🚫	Store Details
✪		✓			Arkansas City • 2701 N Summit St, 67005 • 620-442-2063 • I-35 Exit 4 take US-166 E 16 miles then Summit St N 2.5 miles
✪		✓			Atchison • 1920 US Hwy 73, 66002 • 913-367-4062 • Jct US-59 & US-73 (S of town) go S on US-73 for 4.8 miles
✪		✓			Augusta • 719 W 7th Ave, 67010 • 316-775-2254 • I-35 Exit 50 go E 13.2 miles on US-54
☆					Baxter Springs • 2970 Military Ave, 66713 • 620-856-2327 • Jct US-166 & US-69 (in town) take US-69 S 1.2 miles
✪	2	✓			Bonner Springs • 12801 Kansas Ave, 66012 • 913-441-6751 • I-70 Exit 224 take SR-7 S .9 mile then E on Kansas Ave .2 mile
✪		✓			Chanute • 2700 S Santa Fe Ave, 66720 • 620-431-3077 • From US-169 (S of town) take 35th St Exit E 1.4 miles then N on Santa Fe Ave .6 mile
✪		✓			Coffeyville • 1863 County Road 5300, 67337 • 620-251-2290 • 2.4 miles east of town on US-166
✪	1	✓			Colby • 115 W Willow St, 67701 • 785-462-8634 • I-70 Exit 54 go N on Country Club Dr .1 mile & W on CR-20 for .5 mile
✪		✓			Concordia • 140 E College Dr, 66901 • 785-243-2602 • On west side of US-81 on the south edge of town
✪	4	✓			Derby • 2020 N Nelson Dr, 67037 • 316-788-9400 • I-35 Exit 45 take SR-15 S 3.6 miles
✪		✓			Dodge City • 1905 N 14th Ave, 67801 • 620-225-3917 • Jct US-283 & US-400 (S of town) take US-400 W .8 mile & N on 14th Ave 1 mile
✪	1	✓			El Dorado • 301 S Village Rd, 67042 • 316-322-8100 • I-35 Exit 71 go E .5 mile on Central Ave/SR-254
✪	1	✓			Emporia • 2301 Industrial Rd, 66801 • 620-343-1500 • I-35 Exit 128 go N on Industrial Rd .4 mile
✪		✓			Fort Scott • 2500 S Main St, 66701 • 620-223-2867 • 2.5 miles south of town on US-69
✪		✓			Garden City • 3101 E Kansas Ave, 67846 • 620-275-0775 • 1.8 miles northeast of town center via SR-156 (Kansas Ave)
✪	1	✓		✓	Gardner • 1725 E Santa Fe St, 66030 • 913-884-8004 • I-35 Exit 210 merge onto US-56 W .2 mile then S at Cedar Niles Rd
✪	9	✓			Goddard • 18631 W Kellogg Dr, 67052 • 316-347-2092 • I-235 Exit 7B go W 8.4 miles on US-54/US-400

☆	⬡	🕐	⛽	🚫	Store Details
✪	1	✓			Goodland • 2160 Commerce Rd, 67735 • 785-899-2111 • I-70 Exit 17 go N .5 mile on Commerce Rd
✪		✓			Great Bend • 3503 10th St, 67530 • 620-792-3632 • Jct US-281 & US-56 (S of town) take US-56 W 1.2 miles
✪	1	✓			Hays • 4301 Vine St, 67601 • 785-625-0001 • I-70 Exit 159 take US-183 N .2 mile
✪		✓			Hiawatha • 701 Hopi St, 66434 • 785-742-7445 • Jct US-73 & US-36 (S of town) take US-36 W .8 mile, 12th St N .5 mile & E on Iowa St
☆					Holton • 209 Arizona Ave, 66436 • 785-364-4148 • Jct SR-16 & US-75 (W of town) go S on US-75/Arizona Ave .2 mile
✪		✓			Hutchinson • 1905 E 17th Ave, 67501 • 620-669-9090 • Jct US-50 & SR-61 (SE of town), N on SR-61/Kennedy Pkwy 3.3 miles & E on 17th Ave .3 mile
✪		✓			Independence • 121 Peter Pan Rd, 67301 • 620-331-5805 • Jct US-160 & US-75 (W of town), E on US-160/75 for 1.3 miles & N on Peter Pan Rd
✪		✓			Iola • 2200 N State St, 66749 • 620-365-6981 • 2 miles northwest of town center via US-54 and State St
✪	1	✓			Junction City • 521 E Chestnut St, 66441 • 785-238-8229 • I-70 Exit 298 go W on Chestnut St .2 mile
✪	1	✓			Kansas City • 10824 Parallel Pkwy, 66102 • 913-788-3331 • I-435 Exit 14B go W .7 mile on Parallel Pkwy
✪	5	✓			Lawrence • 3300 Iowa St, 66046 • 785-832-8600 • I-70 Exit 202 take S McDonald Dr 1.2 miles, US-59 S 3.2 miles & 33rd St E .1 mile
✪	3	✓			Lawrence • 550 Congressional Dr, 66049 • 785-841-1700 • I-70 Exit 197 (KS Tpk) go S 1.5 miles on SR-10 then E 1.3 miles on US-40 (6th St) to Congressional Dr
✪		✓			Leavenworth • 5000 10th Ave, 66048 • 913-250-0182 • I-70 Exit 224 (KS Tpk) go N 12 miles on SR-7 then W 1.5 miles on Eisenhower Rd
✪		✓			Liberal • 250 E Tucker Rd, 67901 • 620-624-0106 • Jct SR-51 & US-83 (N of town), US-83 S 6.8 miles, Kansas Ave W 1.3 miles, 15th St N 1 mile & Western Ave E .1 mile
✪	10	✓			Manhattan • 101 Bluemont Ave, 66502 • 785-776-4897 • I-70 Exit 313 follow SR-177 N 8.9 miles, US-24 E .5 mile & W at Bluemont Ave
✪		✓			Marysville • 1174 Pony Express Hwy, 66508 • 785-562-2390 • Jct US-77 & US-36 (W of town) take US-36 E 3.3 miles

☆	♡	🕐	⛽	🚫	Store Details
✪	1	✓			McPherson • 205 S Centennial Dr, 67460 • 620-241-0800 • I-135 Exit 60, west of exit
✪	1	✓			Newton • 1701 S Kansas Rd, 67114 • 316-284-0555 • I-135 Exit 30 take US-50 W .6 mile then SR-15 S .4 mile
✪	3	✓			Olathe • 395 N K-7 Hwy, 66061 • 913-764-7150 • I-35 Exit 218 go W 2.5 miles on Santa Fe St
✪	2	✓			Olathe • 13600 S Alden St, 66062 • 913-829-4404 • I-35 Exit 218 take Santa Fe St E 1.8 miles then S on Alden St
✪	1	✓			Ottawa • 2101 S Princeton St, 66067 • 785-242-9222 • I-35 Exit 183 take US-59 N .4 mile
☆	1			✓	Overland Park • 7701 Frontage Rd, 66204 • 913-648-5885 • I-35 Exit 227 go E on Frontage Rd .4 mile
✪	2	✓			Overland Park • 11701 Metcalf Ave, 66210 • 913-338-2202 • I-435 Exit 79 take Metcalf Ave S 1.3 miles
✪	8	✓		✓	Overland Park • 15700 Metcalf Ave, 66223 • 913-685-9959 • I-435 Exit 81 take US-69 S 6.3 miles, 151st St E .5 mile & Metcalf Ave S .7 mile
✪		✓			Paola • 310 Hedge Ln, 66071 • 913-294-5400 • On Baptiste Dr at US-169 about 1.3 miles east of town center
✪		✓			Parsons • 3201 N 16th St, 67357 • 620-421-0375 • Jct US-400 & US-59 (N of town) go S on US-59 for 1.4 miles
✪		✓			Pittsburg • 2710 N Broadway St, 66762 • 620-232-1593 • Jct SR-126 & US-69/160 (W of town), N on US-69/160 for 2.3 miles & S on Broadway .5 mile
✪		✓			Pratt • 2003 E 1st St, 67124 • 620-672-7548 • Jct SR-61 & US-400 (E of town) go W on US-400 for .2 mile
☆	1				Roeland Park • 5150 Roe Blvd, 66205 • 913-236-8898 • I-35 Exit 232B go E on 18th St Expy .4 mile, continue on Roe Blvd .3 mile
✪	2	✓			Salina • 2900 S 9th St, 67401 • 785-825-6800 • I-135 Exit 90 go E on Magnolia Rd .4 mile & S on 9th St .8 mile
✪	2	✓			Shawnee • 16100 W 65th St, 66217 • 913-268-3468 • I-435 Exit 6A go E .8 mile on Shawnee Mission Pkwy, N .3 mile on Maurer Rd, W .2 mile on 65th St
✪	6	✓		✓	Shawnee • 5701 Silverheel St, 66226 • 913-535-5120 • I-70 Exit 224 go S 5.4 miles on SR-7 to Johnson Dr; store is on east side of highway
✪	2	✓			Topeka • 1501 SW Wanamaker Rd, 66604 • 785-271-6444 • I-70 Exit 356 go S on Wanamaker Rd 1.1 miles (or south of I-470 Exit 1B)

☆	♡	🕐	⛽	🚫	Store Details
✪	1	✓			Topeka • 1301 SW 37th St, 66611 • 785-267-7900 • I-470 Exit 5 take Burlington Rd N .1 mile & 37th St E .6 mile
✪	5	✓			Topeka • 2600 NW Rochester Rd, 66617 • 785-357-4827 • I-70 Exit 358A take US-75 N 1.5 miles, US-24 E 3.1 miles & Rochester Rd N .2 mile
✪	1				Topeka • 2630 SE California Ave, 66605 • 785-379-2325 • I-70 Exit 364A go S 1 mile on California Ave
✪	2	✓			Wellington • 2022 E 16th St, 67152 • 620-326-2261 • I-35 Exit 19 go W on US-160 for 2 miles
✪	3	✓			Wichita • 5475 N Meridian Ave, 67204 • 316-831-9425 • I-135 exit 13 take 53rd St W 2.5 miles then N on Meridian Ave .1 mile
✪	4	✓			Wichita • 10600 W 21st St N, 67205 • 316-729-5446 • I-235 Exit 10 go NW on Zoo Blvd .8 mile & W on 21st St 3 miles
✪	3	✓			Wichita • 11411 E Kellogg Dr, 67207 • 316-683-0735 • I-35 Exit 50 take US-400/Kellogg Dr E 2.1 miles
✪	2	✓			Wichita • 6110 W Kellogg Dr, 67209 • 316-945-2800 • I-235 Exit 7B take W Kellogg Dr 1.6 miles
✪	2	✓			Wichita • 501 E Pawnee St, 67211 • 316-267-2400 • I-135 Exit 3B go W on Pawnee St 1.2 miles
✪	4	✓			Wichita • 3030 N Rock Rd, 67226 • 316-636-4482 • I-135 Exit 10 follow SR-96 E 3.5 miles then S on Rock Rd .4 mile
✪		✓			Winfield • 2202 Pike Rd, 67156 • 620-221-6233 • Jct US-160 & US-77 (W of town) take US-77/Main St S .8 mile & E at Sunnyside Ave

KENTUCKY

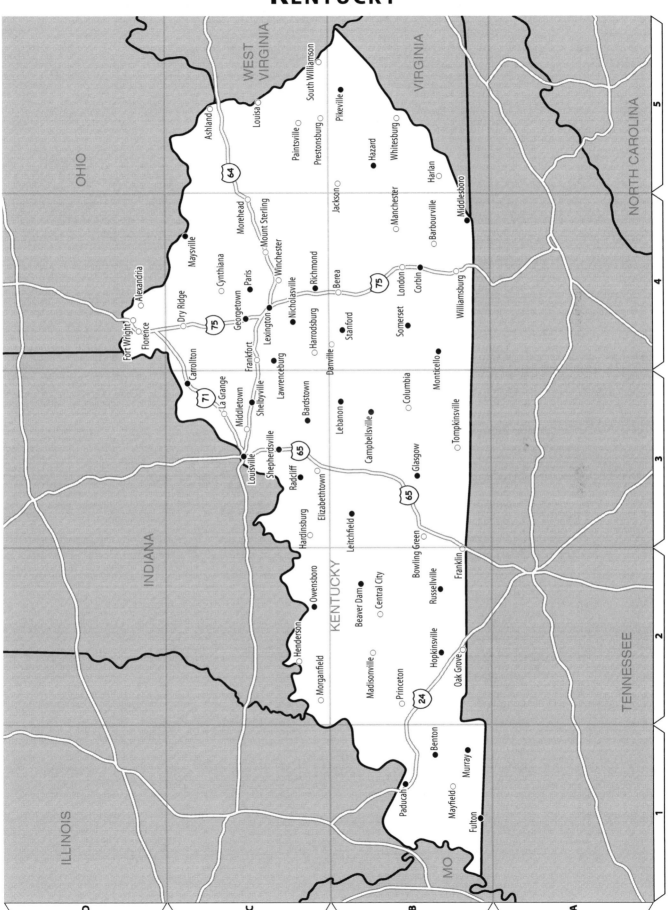

☆	🛡	🕐	⛽	🚫	Store Details
✪	6				Alexandria • 6711 Alexandria Pike, 41001 • 859-635-8800 • I-275 Exit 77 go S 3.4 miles on SR-9 then S 2 miles on US-27
✪		✓			Ashland • 351 River Hill Dr, 41101 • 606-329-0012 • I-64 Exit 181 take US-60 N 2.2 miles, follow SR-5 N 10.4 miles, then SR-1093 NE 1.7 miles
✪	5	✓			Ashland • 12504 US Hwy 60, 41102 • 606-929-9510 • I-64 Exit 181 follow US-60 E 4.2 miles
☆					Barbourville • 301 Parkway Plz, 40906 • 606-546-5454 • I-75 Exit 29 take US-24E S 18.7 miles, W on Treuhaft Blvd .2 mile & S on Hurricane Ln .3 mile
✪		✓	❖		Bardstown • 3795 E John Rowan Blvd, 40004 • 502-349-6007 • From ML Collins Blue Grass Pkwy Exit 25 take US-150/Springfield Rd N for .2 mile
✪		✓	◆		Beaver Dam • 1701 N Main St, 42320 • 270-274-9608 • From Westrn KY Pkwy Exit 75 take US-231 N 4.2 miles
✪	10	✓	◆		Benton • 310 W 5th St, 42025 • 270-527-1605 • I-24 Exit 25A merge onto Carroll Pkwy S 9.1 miles to Exit 43, then SR-348 E .5 mile
✪	1	✓			Berea • 120 Jill Dr, 40403 • 859-986-2324 • I-75 Exit 76 take SR-21 E .3 mile then S at McKinney Dr
✪	10	✓			Bowling Green • 1201 Morgantown Rd, 42101 • 270-780-9996 • I-65 Exit 20 take Natcher Pkwy N 8 miles to Exit 7, then US-231 S for 1.1 miles
✪	2	✓			Bowling Green • 150 Walton Ave, 42104 • 270-781-7903 • I-65 Exit 22 take US-231 N 1.6 miles then W on SR-880 for .4 mile
✪		✓	◆		Campbellsville • 725 Campbellsville Byp, 42718 • 270-789-0707 • From Cumberland Pkwy Exit 49 follow SR-55 N for 18.1 miles, continue on SR-210 for 1 mile
✪	2	✓	❖		Carrollton • 200 Floyd Dr, 41008 • 502-732-0645 • I-71 Exit 44 go W on SR-227 for .9 mile then N on Floyd Dr .2 mile
✪		✓			Central City • 1725 W Everely Brothers Blvd, 42330 • 270-754-4512 • From Western KY Pkwy Exit 58 take US-431 N .6 mile then US-62 W 1.8 miles
✪		✓			Columbia • 2988 Burkesville Rd, 42728 • 270-384-4745 • 3 miles southwest of town center off Cumberland Parkway Exit 46, north of exit
✪	1	✓	◆		Corbin • 60 S Stewart Rd, 40701 • 606-523-1770 • I-75 Exit 29 take US-25E S for .5 mile then Sawyers/Stewart Rd W .3 mile

☆	🛡	🕐	⛽	🚫	Store Details
✪		✓			Cynthiana • 805 US Hwy 27 S, 41031 • 859-234-3232 • I-75 Exit 126 take US-62 E 15.3 miles, continue on US-27 N for 2.8 miles
✪		✓			Danville • 100 Walton Ave, 40422 • 859-236-9572 • From Danville Bypass (S of town) continue S on US-127 for .2 mile
✪	1	✓		✓	Dry Ridge • 20 Ferguson Blvd, 41035 • 859-824-0575 • I-75 Exit 159 take SR-22 E .2 mile & S on Ferguson Blvd
✪	5	✓			Elizabethtown • 100 Walmart Dr, 42701 • 270-763-1600 • I-65 Exit 94 take US-62 W .5 mile then NW on Ring Rd 3.9 miles & N on Wal Mart Ln
✪	1	✓			Florence • 7625 Doering Dr, 41042 • 859-282-8333 • I-75 Exit 181 go W on SR-18 for .3 mile, N on Houston Rd .5 mile & W at Kiley Pl
✪	2	✓		✓	Fort Wright • 3450 Valley Plaza Pkwy, 41017 • 859-341-7900 • I-275 Exit 79 merge onto Taylor Mill Rd 1.8 miles then W at Valley Sq Dr .1 mile
✪	2	✓			Frankfort • 301 Leonardwood Rd, 40601 • 502-875-5533 • I-64 Exit 53B follow US-127 N .7 mile then S on Leonardville Rd .7 mile
✪	3	✓			Franklin • 1550 Nashville Rd, 42134 • 270-586-9281 • I-65 Exit 2 take US-31 W 2.3 miles
✪		✓	❖		Fulton • 1405 Middle Rd, 42041 • 270-472-1426 • Purchase Pkwy Exit 1 go S .3 mile on Noland Ave then W .6 mile on SR-166 (Middle Rd)
✪	1	✓	❖		Georgetown • 112 Osbourne Way, 40324 • 502-867-0547 • I-75 Exit 126 take US-62 NE .5 mile then W at Osbourne Way
✪		✓	❖		Glasgow • 2345 Happy Valley Rd, 42141 • 270-651-1136 • From Nunn Cumberland Pkwy Exit 11 follow US-31E N 2.5 miles & SR-90 NW 1.1 miles
☆					Hardinsburg • 1002 Old Hwy 60, 40143 • 270-756-6012 • Jct SR-259 & US-60 (SE of town) go W on US-60 for 1.9 miles & N on 3rd St .5 mile
☆					Harlan • 201 Walton Rd, 40831 • 606-573-2206 • 1.8 miles south of town center along US-421
✪					Harrodsburg • 591 Joseph Dr, 40330 • 859-734-5721 • From ML Collins Blue Grass Pkwy Exit 59A take US-127 S 15.9 miles & W on Joseph Dr
✪		✓	❖		Hazard • 120 Daniel Boone Plz, 41701 • 606-439-1882 • 4 miles north of town via SR-15 and SR-80

☆	♡	🕐	⛽	🚭	Store Details
✪		✓			Henderson • 1195 Barrett Blvd, 42420 • 270-826-6036 • From Audubon Pkwy Exit 1A take Pennyrile Pkwy N 3.4 miles, then US-41 N .7 mile & E on Barrett Blvd
✪	10	✓	◆		Hopkinsville • 300 Clinic Dr, 42240 • 270-886-1900 • I-24 Exit 86 take US-41 ALT N 8.9 miles then E at Clinic Dr .3 mile
☆					Jackson • 1589 Hwy 15 S, 41339 • 606-666-4907 • 1.8 miles east of town center along SR-15/SR-30
✪	1	✓			La Grange • 1015 New Moody Ln, 40031 • 502-222-4260 • I-71 Exit 22 take SR-53 E .1 mile then S at New Moody Ln .2 mile
✪	1	✓	❖		Lawrenceburg • 1000 Bypass N, 40342 • 502-839-5178 • I-64 Exit 53A merge onto US-127 S for 1 mile then E at Laurenceburg Rd
✪		✓	❖		Lebanon • 2136 Campbellsville Hwy, 40033 • 270-692-1880 • 2 miles southwest of town via US-68
✪		✓	❖		Leitchfield • 1801 Elizabethtown Rd, 42754 • 270-259-5622 • From Ford Western KY Pkwy Exit 112 take SR-224 W .7 mile & US-62 S 2.5 miles
✪		✓			Lexington • 4051 Nicholasville Rd, 40503 • 859-971-0572 • I-64 Exit 115 merge onto Newtown Pike 1.5 miles, W on New Circle Rd 9.2 miles & US-27 S 1.2 miles
✪	1	✓	❖		Lexington • 2350 Grey Lag Way Rd, 40509 • 859-263-0999 • I-75 Exit 110 take US-60 W .4 mile, Sir Barton Way S .4 mile
☆	3				Lexington • 3180 Richmond Rd, 40509 • 859-268-2001 • I-75 Exit 108 follow Man O'War Blvd W 2.5 miles then N at Richmond Rd .2 mile
✪	3	✓			Lexington • 500 W New Circle Rd, 40511 • 859-381-9370 • I-64 Exit 113 take US-68 W 1 mile & S on New Circle Rd 1.2 miles
✪	1	✓			London • 1851 Hwy 192 W, 40741 • 606-878-6119 • I-75 Exit 38 take SR-192 E .6 mile
✪		✓			Louisa • 275 Walton Dr, 41230 • 606-673-4427 • 2 miles southwest of town near US-23/SR-32 jct
✪	5	✓			Louisville • 175 Outer Loop, 40214 • 502-361-0225 • I-65 Exit 125B merge onto Snyder Fwy W 4.3 miles to Exit 6, New Cut Rd N .3 mile & Outer Loop W .2 mile
✪	3	✓			Louisville • 7100 Raggard Rd, 40216 • 502-447-4677 • I-264 Exit 5B follow SR-1934 (Cane Run Rd) S 3 miles
✪	2		❖	✓	Louisville • 2020 Bashford Manor Ln, 40218 • 502-451-6766 • I-264 Exit 16 follow US-150/31 SE .7 mile then go SW on Bashford Manor Ln for .4 mile
✪	1	✓			Louisville • 1915 S Hurstbourne Pkwy, 40220 • 502-499-1050 • I-64 Exit 15 take SR-1747/Hurstbourne Pkwy S 1 mile
✪	2	✓		✓	Louisville • 11901 Standiford Plaza Dr, 40229 • 502-968-6800 • I-265 Exit 12 take SR-61 S 1.5 miles then E on Antle Dr
✪	1	✓			Louisville • 3706 Diann Marie Rd, 40241 • 502-326-9166 • I-265 Exit 32 take SR-1447 E .3 mile & N at Chamberlain Ln .1 mile
✪	7	✓			Louisville • 10445 Dixie Hwy, 40272 • 502-935-3233 • I-264 Exit 8A go S on Dixie Hwy 6.3 miles
✪	1	✓	❖		Louisville • 7101 Cedar Springs Blvd, 40291 • 502-231-4880 • I-265 Exit 17 take US-150 N .6 mile
✪		✓			Madisonville • 1756 E Center St, 42431 • 270-821-6388 • Western KY Pkwy Exit 38B take US-41 N 8.2 miles to Exit 42, W on SR-70/85 for .3 mile
☆					Manchester • 240 Manchester Square Shpg Ctr, 40962 • 606-598-6123 • Hal Rogers Pkwy Exit 20, north of exit
✪		✓			Mayfield • 1225 Paris Rd, 42066 • 270-247-0358 • From JM Carroll Pkwy Exit 22 take SR-80 E for 1.8 miles then S on SR-121 for 1.3 miles
✪		✓	❖		Maysville • 240 Walmart Way, 41056 • 606-759-5040 • Jct US 62/68 & SR-546 (W of town) go NW on SR-546/Gov Brown Hwy for .6 mile
✪		✓	◆		Middlesboro • US Hwy 25E at Hwy 441, 40965 • 606-248-9087 • 1.5 miles northeast of town center at US25E/SR-441 jct
✪	1	✓			Middletown • 12981 Shelbyville Rd, 40243 • 502-244-2551 • I-265 Exit 27 take US-60 W .7 mile
✪		✓	❖		Monticello • 175 Walmart Plaza Dr, 42633 • 606-348-3331 • From town center go W 1.4 miles on Columbia Ave then go N 1.4 miles on SR-90
✪	1	✓			Morehead • 200 Walmart Way, 40351 • 606-784-3262 • I-64 Exit 137 take SR-32 N .6 mile
✪		✓			Morganfield • 901 US Hwy 60 E, 42437 • 270-389-1828 • From Pennyride Pkwy Exit 76 follow US-60 W for 22.7 miles
✪	1	✓			Mount Sterling • 499 Indian Mound Dr, 40353 • 859-497-9401 • I-64 Exit 110 take US-460 S .3 mile then SR-686 W .7 mile

☆	◯	◷	🛢	🚐̸	Store Details
✪		✓	◆	✓	Murray • 809 N 12th St, 42071 • 270-753-2195 • From JM Carroll Pkwy Exit 41 follow US-641 S 17.5 miles
✪		✓	❖		Nicholasville • 1024 N Main St, 40356 • 859-885-3299 • Jct US-27 & New Circle Rd (in Lexington) follow US-27 S for 7.3 miles
✪	3	✓			Oak Grove • 14800 Fort Campbell Blvd, 42262 • 270-640-4744 • I-24 Exit 86 merge onto US-41 ALT S 2.5 miles
✪		✓			Owensboro • 5031 Frederica St, 42301 • 270-685-2060 • Audubon Pkwy Exit 24A go E on US-60 BYP for 3.1 miles to Exit 4 & S on Frederica Rd .4 mile
✪		✓	❖		Owensboro • 3151 Leitchfield Rd, 42303 • 270-683-5553 • Audubon Pkwy Exit 24A go E on US-60 BYP for 7.4 miles to Exit 9, S on Leitchfld Rd .5 mile
✪	1	✓	◆		Paducah • 5130 Hinkleville Rd, 42001 • 270-444-0066 • I-24 Exit 4 follow US-60 W for .5 mile
✪	6	✓			Paducah • 3220 Irvin Cobb Dr, 42003 • 270-444-6941 • I-24 Exit 16 take US-68 N .3 mile then follow US-62/I-24 BR for 5.7 miles
✪		✓			Paintsville • 470 N Mayo Trail, 41240 • 606-789-8920 • Jct US-460 & SR-40/321 (NW of town) go S on SR-40/321 for 1 mile
✪		✓	❖		Paris • 305 Letton Dr, 40361 • 859-987-2817 • I-64 Exit 113 follow US-27 N 13.5 miles
✪		✓	❖		Pikeville • 254 Cassidy Blvd, 41501 • 606-432-6177 • Jct US-23/460 & US-119 (NE of town) go W on Cassidy Blvd .2 mile
☆					Prestonsburg • 477 Village Dr, 41653 • 606-886-6681 • 1 mile southwest of town at US-23/SR-114 jct
✪		✓			Princeton • 1500 US Hwy 62 W, 42445 • 270-365-7692 • I-24 Exit 40 follow US-62 NE for 11.7 miles
✪		✓	❖		Radcliff • 1165 Walmart Way, 40160 • 270-352-2720 • I-65 Exit 102 take SR-313 W .4 mile, SR-434 W for 9.9 miles & Dixie Hwy N 4 miles
✪	3	✓	◆		Richmond • 820 Eastern Byp, 40475 • 859-624-4330 • I-75 Exit 87 go E on SR-876/Bypass 2.8 miles
✪		✓	❖		Russellville • 120 Sam Walton Dr, 42276 • 270-726-2880 • From town center go W 1.8 miles on Hopkinsville Rd then N .4 mile on US-431
✪	1	✓	◆		Shelbyville • 500 Taylorsville Rd, 40065 • 502-633-0705 • I-64 Exit 32A take SR-55 S .3 mile

☆	◯	◷	🛢	🚐̸	Store Details
✪	1	✓	❖		Shepherdsville • 545 Conestoga Pkwy, 40165 • 502-281-5005 • I-65 Exit 117 go SW .2 mile on 4th St then right on Adam Shepherd Pkwy .2 mile and right again on Conestoga Pkwy for .4 mile
✪		✓	◆	✓	Somerset • 177 Washington Dr, 42501 • 606-679-9204 • Jct SR-80 BYP & US-27 (W of town) go S on US-27 for 2 miles & W on Washington Dr .1 mile
✪		✓			South Williamson • 28402 US Hwy 119, 41503 • 606-237-0477 • Jct SR-319 & US-119 (S of town) go N on US-119 for 1.7 miles
✪		✓	❖		Stanford • 1283 US Hwy 27 N, 40484 • 606-365-2153 • Jct US-150 BYP & US-27 go S on US-27 for 2.3 miles
✪					Tompkinsville • 1650 Edmonton Rd, 42167 • 270-487-0780 • Jct SR-678 & SR-163 (N of town) go S on SR-163 for 6.2 miles
☆					Whitesburg • 350 Whitesburg Plaza, 41858 • 606-633-0152 • Jct SR-15 & US-119 (W of town) go NE on US-119 for .7 mile & E at Whitesburg Plaza
✪	1	✓			Williamsburg • 589 W Hwy 92, 40769 • 606-549-4075 • I-75 Exit 11 go E on SR-92 for .2 mile
✪	2	✓			Winchester • 1859 Bypass Rd, 40391 • 859-744-5070 • I-64 Exit 94 follow SR-1958 S 1.7 miles

LOUISIANA

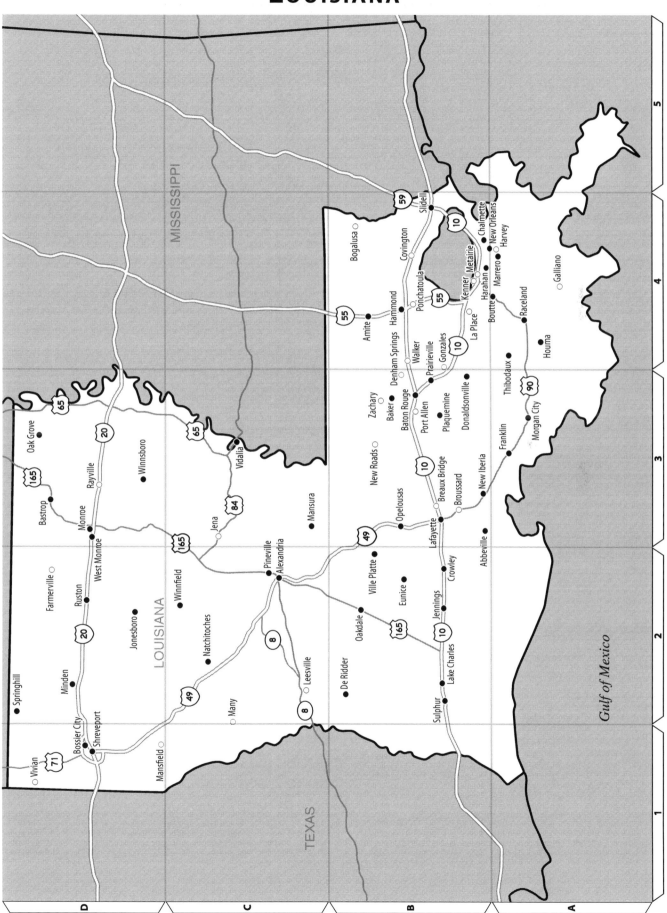

☆	🛡	🕐	⛽	🚫	Store Details
✪		✓	❖		Abbeville • 3005 Veterans Memorial Dr, 70510 • 337-893-6485 • 2.4 miles east of town center on SR-14
✪	2	✓			Alexandria • 2050 N Mall Dr, 71301 • 318-445-2300 • I-49 Exit 83, Broadway W .7 mile, Lee St N .2 mile, Memorial Dr W .6 mile & North Blvd S .2 mile
✪	4	✓	❖		Alexandria • 6225 Coliseum Blvd, 71303 • 318-448-8881 • I-49 Exit 86 go SW 1.6 miles on US-71/US-165 then W 1.8 miles on SR-28
✪	1	✓	❖		Amite • 1200 W Oak St, 70422 • 985-748-7707 • I-55 Exit 46 take SR-16 E .7 mile
✪	7	✓	❖		Baker • 14507 Plank Rd, 70714 • 225-774-2050 • I-110 Exit 6 take Plank Rd/SR-67 NE 6.8 miles
✪			❖		Bastrop • 6091 Mer Rouge Rd, 71220 • 318-281-9384 • 3 miles east of town center on US-165
✪	1	✓			Baton Rouge • 3132 College Dr, 70808 • 225-952-9022 • I-10 Exit 158 merge onto College Dr S .2 mile
✪	1	✓			Baton Rouge • 10606 N Mall Dr, 70809 • 225-291-8104 • I-10 Exit 163 merge onto SR-3246 S/Siegen Ln .3 mile & S on N Mall Dr .3 mile
✪	4				Baton Rouge • 10550 Burbank Dr, 70810 • 225-412-5054 • I-10 Exit 162A go S 3.2 miles on Bluebonnet Blvd then left on Burbank Dr
✪	4	✓	❖		Baton Rouge • 9350 Cortana Pl, 70815 • 225-923-3400 • I-12 Exit 2B take US-61 N 2.9 miles, E at Florline Blvd .1 mile & S on Cortana Pl .6 mile
✪	3	✓			Baton Rouge • 2171 O'Neal Ln, 70816 • 225-751-3505 • I-12 Exit 7 go S on O'Neal Lane 2.5 miles
✪	10	✓	❖		Baton Rouge • 10200 Sullivan Rd, 70818 • 225-262-6599 • I-110 Exit 6 take Harding Blvd/SR-408 E 8.4 miles then Sullivan Rd S 1.1 miles
✪		✓			Bogalusa • 401 Ontario Ave, 70427 • 985-732-5870 • 1 mile west of town center off SR-10
✪	2	✓	◆		Bossier City • 2536 Airline Dr, 71111 • 318-747-0173 • I-20 Exit 22 take Airline Dr N 1.7 miles (or .6 mile south of I-220 Exit 12)
✪		✓	❖		Boutte • 13001 Hwy 90, 70039 • 985-785-0855 • I-10 Exit 220 go SE on I-310 for 10.9 miles then US-90 E for 2 miles
✪	1	✓			Breaux Bridge • 1932 Rees St, 70517 • 337-332-1280 • I-10 Exit 109 take SR-328 S .5 mile
✪	10				Broussard • 123 Saint Nazaire Rd, 70518 • 337-837-8886 • I-10 Exit 103A follow Evangeline Trwy S 9.8 miles

☆	🛡	🕐	⛽	🚫	Store Details
✪	5	✓	◆		Chalmette • 8101 W Judge Perez Dr, 70043 • 504-278-2331 • I-10 Exit 236B follow SR-39 E 5 miles; Westbound travelers use Exit 236C
✪	2	✓			Covington • 880 N Hwy 190, 70433 • 985-867-8701 • I-12 Exit 63A merge onto US-190 E 1.6 miles
✪	1	✓	◆		Crowley • 729 Odd Fellows Rd, 70526 • 337-783-6387 • I-10 Exit 82 follow SR-111 S .6 mile
✪		✓			Denham Springs • 34025 State Hwy 16, 70706 • 225-271-2307 • 5 miles north of town center along SR-16
✪	2	✓			Denham Springs • 904 S Range Ave, 70726 • 225-665-0270 • I-12 Exit 10 take SR-3002/Range Ave N 1.1 miles
✪		✓	◆		Deridder • 1125 N Pine St, 70634 • 337-462-0259 • Jct SR-3226 & US-171 (N of town) take US-171 S 2.5 miles
✪	9		❖		Donaldsonville • 37000 Hwy 3089, 70346 • 225-473-6687 • I-10 Exit 177 take SR-30 W 1.1 miles, SR-3251 SW 3.8 miles & SR-75 S 3.3 miles
✪		✓	❖		Eunice • 1538 Hwy 190, 70535 • 337-457-7392 • 2 miles west of town center on US-190
✪				✓	Farmerville • 833 Sterlington Hwy, 71241 • 318-368-2535 • I-20 Exit 86 take SR-33 N 21.5 miles then SR-2 E .7 mile
☆					Franklin • 200 Northwest Blvd, 70538 • 337-828-2418 • Jct US-90 & SR-3211 (N of town) go E on SR-3211/NW Blvd 1.7 miles
✪		✓			Galliano • 16759 Hwy 3235, 70354 • 985-632-4040 • Jct US-90 & SR-1 follow SR-1 S 25.5 miles, 107th St W .5 mile & SR-3235 S .7 mile
✪	9	✓			Gonzales • 308 N Airline Hwy, 70737 • 225-647-8950 • I-10 Exit 187 merge onto US-61 N 8.7 miles
✪	1	✓	◆		Hammond • 2799 W Thomas St, 70401 • 985-345-8876 • I-55 Exit 31 take US-190 E .9 mile
✪	8	✓	❖		Harahan • 5110 Jefferson Hwy, 70123 • 504-733-4923 • I-10 Exit 226 merge onto Clearview Pkwy S 3.3 miles then SR-48/Jefferson Hwy W 4 miles
✪	1	✓			Harvey • 1501 Manhattan Blvd, 70058 • 504-366-5255 • I-10 Exit 6 merge onto Westbank Expy .1 mile then S on Manhattan Blvd .9 mile
✪		✓			Houma • 1633 Martin Luther King Jr Blvd, 70360 • 985-851-6373 • Jct US-90 & SR-24 (NW of town) take SR-24 SE 6.3 miles, SR-664 S .5 mile & SR-3040 S .1 mile

☆	◯	⏱	⛽	🚫	Store Details
✪		✓	❖		Houma • 933 Grand Caillou Rd, 70363 • 985-917-0151 • Jct US-90 & SR-182 take SR-182 S 3.2 miles, SR-3087 S 5 miles, Prospect Blvd S 1.1 miles & SR-57 W .5 mile
✪		✓			Jena • 3670 W Oak St, 71342 • 318-992-1351 • .8 mile northwest of town center on US-84
✪	1	✓	◆		Jennings • 303 E Interstate Dr, 70546 • 337-824-4838 • I-10 Exit 64, on Frontage Rd W
✪		✓	◆		Jonesboro • 184 Old Winnfield Rd, 71251 • 318-259-4149 • I-20 Exit 85 follow US-167 S 24.8 miles
✪	2	✓			Kenner • 300 W Esplanade Ave, 70065 • 504-464-1653 • I-10 Exit 221 take Loyola Dr N 1.1 miles then E on W Esplanade Ave
✪	3	✓			La Place • 1616 W Airline Hwy, 70068 • 985-652-8994 • I-10 Exit 206 take SR-3188 S 2.5 miles then E on Airline Hwy .3 mile
✪	2	✓	◆		Lafayette • 1229 NE Evangeline Trwy, 70501 • 337-232-1677 • I-10 Exit 103A go S 1.3 miles on US-167
✪	5	✓	❖		Lafayette • 3142 Ambassador Caffery Pkwy, 70506 • 337-989-4082 • I-10 Exit 100 take Ambassador Caffery Pkwy/SR-3184 S 4.7 miles
✪	7	✓	❖		Lafayette • 2428 W Pinhook Rd, 70508 • 337-231-1852 • I-10 Exit 103A take US-167 S 2.6 miles, continue on Evangeline Trwy 1.9 miles, then W on Saloom Rd 1.2 miles, and S on Pinhook Rd .7 mile
✪	2	✓	❖		Lake Charles • 2500 N Martin Luther King Hwy, 70601 • 337-436-3909 • I-10 Exit 33 take US-71 N 1.8 miles
✪	2	✓	❖		Lake Charles • 3451 Nelson Rd, 70605 • 337-477-3785 • I-210 Exit 4 go SE on Nelson Rd 1.3 miles
✪	1	✓	◆	✓	Lake Charles • 3415 Gerstner Memorial Blvd, 70607 • 337-477-7799 • I-210 Exit 8, south of exit
✪		✓			Leesville • 2204 S 5th St, 71446 • 337-238-9041 • Jct SR-10 & US-171 (S of town) go N on US-171 for 6.5 miles
✪	7	✓			Mansfield • 7292 Hwy 509, 71052 • 318-872-5711 • I-49 Exit 177 take SR-509 S 7 miles
✪		✓	❖		Mansura • 7162 Hwy 1, 71350 • 318-253-4069 • Jct SR-452/Preston St & SR-1 (N of town) go S on SR-1 for 1.4 miles
✪					Many • 25800 Highway 171, 71449 • 318-256-9207 • 2 miles northwest of town via US-171
✪	10	✓	❖		Marrero • 4810 Lapalco Blvd, 70072 • 504-341-0075 • I-10 Exit 234 (near the Superdome) follow US-90BR/Westbank Expy 8 miles to Exit 4B, then go S 1.1 miles on Barataria Blvd and W .5 mile on Promenade Blvd
✪	2				Metairie • 8912 Veterans Memorial Blvd, 70003 • 504-465-0155 • I-10 Exit 225 follow Veterans Memorial Blvd W 1.2 miles
✪	4	✓	◆		Minden • 1379 Homer Rd, 71055 • 318-371-9290 • I-20 Exit 49 take SR-531 N 3.2 miles then W at Homer Rd
✪	3	✓	❖		Monroe • 2701 Louisville Ave, 71201 • 318-324-0016 • I-20 Exit 118B take US-165 N 1.5 miles then US-165 BR/US-80 W 1 mile
✪		✓	◆		Morgan City • 973 Hwy 90 E, 70380 • 985-395-2094 • Jct SR-662 & US-90 Exit 182 (E of town) take US-90 W 5.8 miles
✪	7	✓	◆		Natchitoches • 925 Keyser Ave, 71457 • 318-352-5607 • I-49 Exit 138 take SR-6 N 3.5 miles, follow SR-6 BR 1.5 miles & E on Keyser Ave 1.3 miles
✪		✓	❖		New Iberia • 1205 E Admiral Doyle Dr, 70560 • 337-367-9333 • Jct US-90 & SR-14 (W of town) take SR-14 E 1.8 miles then S on SR-674 for 1 mile
✪	5	✓	❖		New Orleans • 4001 Behrman Pl, 70114 • 504-364-0414 • I-10 Exit 234 go E 3.3 miles on US-90-BUS to Exit 9B then go SE 1.7 miles on SR-428
✪	1				New Orleans • 4301 Chef Menteur Hwy, 70126 • 504-434-6076 • I-10 Exit 239 go W on Old Gentilly Rd, right onto Louisa St, left onto US-90; eastbound travelers use I-10 Exit 239B and go N .2 mile on Louisa St then left onto US-90
✪	3				New Orleans • 1901 Tchoupitoulas St, 70130 • 504-522-4142 • I-10 Exit 234 follow US-90-BUS E 1.2 miles to Exit 11C; merge onto Calliope St .1 mile; S .8 mile on Religious St; E on Felicity; S .1 mile on Tchoupitoulas
✪	1				New Orleans • 6000 Bullard Ave, 70128 • 504-434-6266 • I-10 Exit 245, south of exit
✪		✓			New Roads • 460 Hospital Rd, 70760 • 225-638-8609 • 2 miles west of town center on SR-1
✪			❖		Oak Grove • 705 S Constitution Ave, 71263 • 318-428-9631 • Jct SR-589 & SR-17 (S of town) go N on SR-17 for 4.5 miles
✪		✓	❖		Oakdale • 1900 Hwy 165 S, 71463 • 318-335-2502 • Jct Allen Parish Airport Rd & US-165 (S of town) go N on US-165 for 3.3 miles

☆	♡	🕐	⛽	🚫	Store Details
✪	1	✓	❖		Opelousas • 1629 Cresswell Ln Ext, 70570 • 337-942-9853 • I-49 Exit 18 follow Cresswell Ln E .4 mile
✪	5	✓	◆		Pineville • 3636 Monroe Hwy, 71360 • 318-640-6900 • I-49 Exit 84 take US-167 NE 4.1 miles then US-165 N .8 mile
✪			❖		Plaquemine • 59690 Belleview Dr, 70764 • 225-687-2550 • I-10 Exit 153 take SR-1 S 12.7 miles then SW on SR-75/Belleview Rd 1.8 miles
✪	1	✓			Ponchatoula • 1331 Hwy 51, 70454 • 985-467-8046 • I-55 Exit 26 go E .2 mile on SR-22 then N .4 mile on US-51-BUS
✪	2				Port Allen • 3255 LA Hwy 1 S, 70767 • 225-749-7455 • I-10 Exit 153 go S on SR-1 for 1.8 miles
✪	5	✓	❖	✓	Prairieville • 17585 Airline Hwy, 70769 • 225-677-7375 • I-10 Exit 166 follow Highland Rd/SR-42 E 1.6 miles then S on Airline Hwy 2.5 miles
✪			❖		Raceland • 4858 Hwy 1, 70375 • 985-532-6936 • Jct US-90 & SR-1 (S of town) go N on SR-1 for .5 mile
✪	1				Rayville • 1806 Julia St, 71269 • 318-728-6437 • I-20 Exit 138 take SR-137 N .6 mile then W at Glenda St
✪	1	✓	◆		Ruston • 1201 N Service Rd E, 71270 • 318-251-1168 • I-20 Exit 86 merge onto Woodward Ave & go W on Service Rd E .3 mile
✪	3	✓			Shreveport • 1125 Shreveport Barksdale Hwy, 71105 • 318-861-9202 • I-49 Exit 205 go E 2.2 miles on Kings Hwy then continue E .7 mile on SR-3032 (Shreveport Barksdale Hwy)
✪	4	✓	◆		Shreveport • 1645 E Bert Kouns Industrial Loop, 71105 • 318-797-5970 • I-49 Exit 199 merge onto Ind Loop/SR-526 E for 3.4 miles
✪	1			✓	Shreveport • 4701 Northport Blvd, 71107 • 318-929-3502 • I-49 Exit 215, west of exit
✪	5	✓	❖		Shreveport • 9550 Mansfield Rd, 71118 • 318-688-0538 • I-49 Exit 199 take Ind Loop/SR-526 W 3.2 miles then Mansfield Rd/US-171 S 1.2 miles
✪	1	✓	◆		Shreveport • 6235 W Port Ave, 71129 • 318-688-7700 • I-20 Exit 10 go S on Pines Rd then W on Port Ave .1 mile
✪	1	✓			Slidell • 167 Northshore Blvd, 70460 • 985-690-0123 • I-12 Exit 80 go S on Northshore Blvd .2 mile
✪	1	✓	❖		Slidell • 39142 Natchez Dr, 70461 • 985-641-8572 • I-10 Exit 266 take Gause Blvd/US-190 E .2 mile, Tyler Dr S .2 mile & Natchez Dr W
✪			❖		Springhill • 1920 S Arkansas St, 71075 • 318-539-5660 • Jct SR-2 & US-371 (S of town) go N on US-371 for 6.5 miles
✪	2	✓	◆		Sulphur • 525 N Cities Service Hwy, 70663 • 337-625-2849 • I-10 Exit 23 take SR-108 N for 1.3 miles
✪		✓	◆		Thibodaux • 410 N Canal Blvd, 70301 • 985-446-2257 • Jct SR-1 & SR-20 (N of town) go N on SR-20/Canal Blvd .4 mile
✪			❖		Vidalia • 4283 Carter St, 71373 • 318-336-8996 • Jct SR-131 & US-84/65 (W of town) go W on US-84/65 for .8 mile
✪		✓	❖		Ville Platte • 891 E Lasalle St, 70586 • 337-363-5623 • I-49 Exit 23 take US-167 N 15.2 miles
☆					Vivian • 929 S Pine St, 71082 • 318-375-4810 • Jct US-7 & SR-2 (E of town) follow SR-2 W 6.7 miles then Pine St/SR-2 S .2 mile
✪	1	✓			Walker • 28270 Walker Rd S, 70785 • 225-667-2335 • I-12 Exit 15 take Walker Rd/SR-447 S .6 mile
✪	1	✓	◆		West Monroe • 1025 Glenwood Dr, 71291 • 318-322-0127 • I-20 Exit 114 take Thomas Rd/SR-617 N .1 mile then Glenwood Dr S .8 mile
✪		✓	◆		Winnfield • 5940 Hwy 167 N, 71483 • 318-628-2194 • Jct SR-156 & US-167 (N of town) go S on US-167 for .3 mile
✪		✓	❖		Winnsboro • 3360 Front St, 71295 • 318-435-3438 • Jct SR-130 & SR-15 (N of town) go N on SR-15 .9 mile
✪	9	✓			Zachary • 5801 Main St, 70791 • 225-654-0313 • I-110 Exit 8 take SR-19 N 7.9 miles then E on Main St .5 mile

MAINE

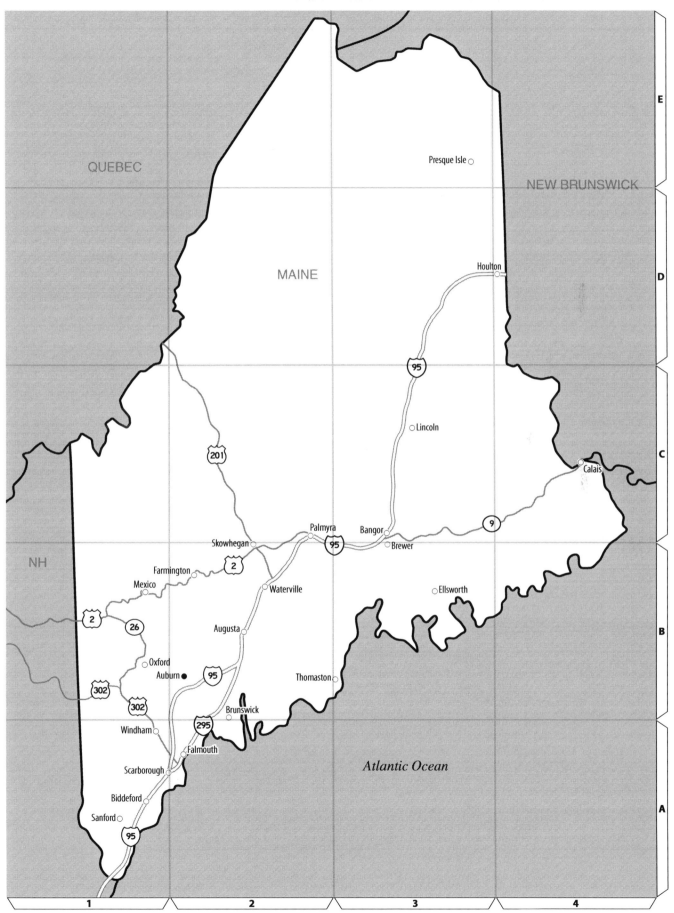

QUEBEC

NEW BRUNSWICK

Presque Isle ○

MAINE

Houlton ○

95

Lincoln ○

Calais ○

201

9

Palmyra ○
Skowhegan ○   95   Bangor ○
                      Brewer ○

Farmington ○   2
Mexico ○   Waterville ○   Ellsworth ○

NH

2
26
Augusta ○

Oxford ○
Auburn ●   95   Thomaston ○

302
302   Brunswick ○

Windham ○   295

Falmouth ○

Scarborough ○

Biddeford ○

Sanford ○

95

Atlantic Ocean

E

D

C

B

A

1   2   3   4

☆	◯	🕐	⛽	🚐	Store Details
✪		✓	◆		Auburn • 100 Mount Auburn Ave, 04210 • 207-784-0738 • 1.8 miles north of town center, west of SR-4 (Center St)
✪	1	✓			Augusta • 201 Civic Center Dr, 04330 • 207-623-8223 • I-95 Exit 112A take Civic Center Dr E .1 mile
✪	1				Bangor • 900 Stillwater Ave, 04401 • 207-947-5254 • I-95 Exit 186 go NE .8 mile on Stillwater Ave
✪	1	✓			Biddeford • 50 Boulder Way, 04005 • 207-286-9551 • I-95 Exit 32, east of exit
✪	1	✓			Brewer • 24 Walton Dr, 04412 • 207-989-5068 • I-395 Exit 1A merge onto Wilson St/US-1A W .5 mile then S at Walton Dr
✪	5	✓			Brunswick • 15 Tibbetts Dr, 04011 • 207-725-0773 • I-295 Exit 28 follow US-1 N 4.4 miles, SR-24 W .6 mile & Tibbets Dr S
✪					Calais • 379 South St, 04619 • 207-454-8178 • 1/2 mile south of town center
✪					Ellsworth • 17 Myrick St, 04605 • 207-667-6780 • 1.5 miles southeast of town center via US-1
☆	1				Falmouth • 206 US Route 1, 04105 • 207-781-3879 • I-295 Exit 10 take Bucknam Rd E .3 mile & US-1 S .5 mile
✪		✓			Farmington • 615 Wilton Rd, 04938 • 207-778-5344 • Jct SR-27/Famington Falls Rd & US-2 (S of town) take US-2 S for 2.5 miles
☆	1				Houlton • 17 Ludlow Rd, 04730 • 207-532-2181 • I-95 Exit 302 take US-1 N .2 mile then E on Ludlow Rd
☆	5				Lincoln • 250 W Broadway, 04457 • 207-794-8436 • I-95 Exit 227 go E 4 miles on Penobscot Valley Ave then N .2 mile on Broadway
✪					Mexico • 258 River Rd, 04257 • 207-364-2557 • Jct SR-142/Weld St & US-2/River Rd (SE of town) go NW on US-2 for 3.2 miles
✪		✓			Oxford • 1240 Main St, 04270 • 207-743-0882 • Jct SR-121/King St & SR-26/Main St (E of town) go N on Main St 3.1 miles
✪	2	✓			Palmyra • 1573 Main St, 04965 • 207-368-2448 • I-95 Exit 157 follow US-2 NW 1.1 miles
✪		✓			Presque Isle • 781 Main St, 04769 • 207-764-8485 • Jct SR-227/Parsons Rd & US-1/Main St (N of town) go S on Main St .2 mile
✪	8				Sanford • 1930 Main St, 04073 • 207-490-1988 • I-95 Exit 19 go W 7.2 miles on SR-109

☆	◯	🕐	⛽	🚐	Store Details
✪	2			✓	Scarborough • 500 Gallery Blvd, 04074 • 207-885-5567 • I-95 Exit 45 to Maine Mall Rd and turn left .5 mile to Gallery Blvd; turn left and follow .4 mile to store entrance
✪					Skowhegan • 60 Fairgrounds Market Pl, 04976 • 207-474-2126 • 1 mile north of town center along US-201
✪					Thomaston • 55 Thomaston Commons Way, 04861 • 207-596-0885 • From town center travel E 2.6 miles on US-1
✪	1	✓			Waterville • 80 Waterville Commons Dr, 04901 • 207-877-8774 • I-95 Exit 130 go E on SR-104 for .2 mile & S on Waterville Commons .2 mile
✪	7	✓			Windham • 30 Landing Rd, 04062 • 207-893-0603 • I-95 Exit 63 follow SR-115 W 6.6 miles, N on US-302 for .4 mile & W at Landing Rd

MARYLAND

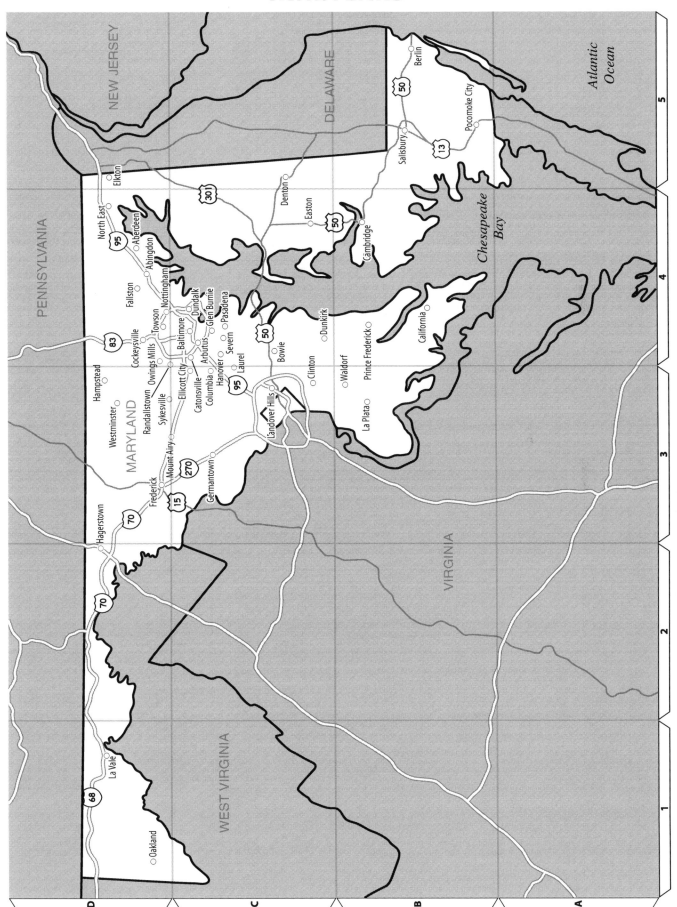

☆	🛡	🕐	⛽	🚫	Store Details
●	4	✓			Aberdeen • 645 S Philadelphia Blvd, 21001 • 410-273-9200 • I-95 Exit 85 take SR-22 E .7 mile, SR-132 E 1.6 miles & US-40 W 1.7 miles
☆	1				Abingdon • 401 Constant Friendship Blvd, 21009 • 410-569-9403 • I-95 Exit 77B take SR-24 N .8 mile then S on Tollgate Rd .1 mile
●	2	✓			Arbutus • 3601 Washington Blvd, 21227 • 410-737-7700 • I-95 Exit 50 take Caton Ave S .6 mile then right at Washington Blvd .6 mile
☆	6				Baltimore • 112 Carroll Island Rd, 21220 • 410-335-5669 • Jct I-695 & SR-702 take SR-702 S 1.5 miles, SR-150 E 3.5 miles & Carroll Island Rd E .2 mile
●	1	✓			Baltimore • 6420 Petrie Way Rd, 21237 • 410-687-4858 • I-695 Exit 35B, east of exit
●		✓		✓	Berlin • 11416 Ocean Gateway, 21811 • 410-629-0502 • From town center go N 1.3 miles on US-113 then E 3 miles on US-50
☆				✓	Bowie • 3300 Crain Hwy, 20716 • 301-805-8850 • US-50 Exit 13 merge onto US-301 S 2.4 miles
●		✓			California • 45485 Miramar Way, 20619 • 301-737-4420 • Jct SR-4 & SR-235 (in town) go S on SR-235 for 1.3 miles
●		✓		✓	Cambridge • 2775 Dorchester Sq, 21613 • 410-221-0292 • Jct SR-16 & US-50 (E of town) go W on US-50/Ocean Gateway 3.1 miles
☆	3				Catonsville • 6205 Baltimore National Pike, 21228 • 410-719-0600 • I-70 Exit 91 merge onto I-695 S 1.7 miles to Exit 15B then US-40 W .7 mile
☆	4				Clinton • 8745 Branch Ave, 20735 • 301-877-0502 • I-95/495 Exit 7A merge onto Branch Ave/SR-5 S 4 miles
●	2	✓			Cockeysville • 1 Frankel Way, 21030 • 410-628-0980 • I-83 Exit 17 go E .7 mile on Padonia Rd then N 1 mile on York Rd
☆	3				Columbia • 6405 Dobbin Rd, 21045 • 410-740-2448 • I-95 Exit 41 follow SR-175 W 2.3 miles then S at Dobbin Rd .2 mile
●		✓			Denton • 610 Legion Rd, 21629 • 410-479-0278 • 1 mile southeast of town center off SR-313 at Legion Rd
☆	3				Dundalk • 2399 N Point Blvd, 21222 • 410-284-5412 • I-95 Exit 59 take SR-150 E .8 mile then S on N Point Blvd 1.3 miles
☆					Dunkirk • 10600 Towne Center Blvd, 20754 • 410-257-2610 • I-95/495 Exit 11A follow SR-4 SE 16.6 miles then left on Town Center Blvd .1 mile

☆	🛡	🕐	⛽	🚫	Store Details
☆					Easton • 8155 Elliott Rd, 21601 • 410-819-0140 • Jct US-50 & SR-328 (E of town) go E on SR-328 for .2 mile & S on Elliott Rd .4 mile
●	6	✓			Elkton • 1000 E Pulaski Hwy, 21921 • 410-398-1070 • I-95 Exit 109 take SR-279 S 2.7 miles, SR-213 S 1.4 miles & US-40 E 1.9 miles
●	3	✓			Ellicott City • 3200 N Ridge Rd, 21043 • 410-418-5780 • I-70 Exit 87 merge onto US-29 S 1.5 miles to Exit 24 - US-40 E .6 mile & N on Ridge Rd .2 mile
●	5	✓			Fallston • 303 Fallston Blvd, 21047 • 443-686-7037 • I-95 Exit 74 go W 4.2 miles on SR-152 then N .6 mile on Belair Rd
☆	6				Frederick • 1811 Monocacy Blvd, 21701 • 301-644-2440 • I-70 Exit 53B take US-40 W 1.2 miles, US-15 N 2.4 miles, Liberty Rd E 1.1 miles & Monocacy Blvd S .8 mile
●	1	✓		✓	Frederick • 7400 Guilford Dr, 21704 • 301-631-0805 • I-70 Exit 54 go S on SR-355/Market St .8 mile then W on Guilford Dr .2 mile
●	1	✓			Germantown • 20910 Frederick Rd, 20876 • 301-515-6700 • I-270 Exit 16 go NE .6 mile on Ridge Rd then right .3 mile on Observation Dr to Shakespeare Blvd and turn left
●	1	✓			Glen Burnie • 6721 Chesapeake Center Dr, 21060 • 410-863-1280 • I-695 Exit 3B take I-895 Spur S .2 mile, SR-2 S .6 mile, SR-710 E .2 mile & S at Chesapeake Center Dr
●	2	✓			Hagerstown • 17850 Garland Groh Blvd, 21740 • 301-714-1373 • I-81 Exit 6B take US-40 W .8 mile, Centre Blvd N & Garland Groh Blvd E .7 mile
●		✓			Hampstead • 2320 N Hanover Pike, 21074 • 410-374-5344 • 2.5 miles north of town on SR-30
☆	5				Hanover • 7081 Arundel Mills Cir, 21076 • 410-579-8725 • I-95 Exit 43A take SR-100 E 3.9 miles to Exit 10A then SR-713 S .3 mile, Bass Pro Dr W & Arundel Mills Cir S .1 mile
☆					La Plata • 40 Drury Dr, 20646 • 301-392-9112 • Jct SR-225/Hawthorne Rd & US-301 (N of town) go N on US-301 .6 mile
☆	3				Landover Hills • 6210 Annapolis Rd, 20784 • 301-773-7848 • I-95/495 Exit 20 go SW 2.7 miles on Annapolis Rd
●	6	✓			Laurel • 3549 Russett Green E, 20724 • 301-604-0180 • I-95 Exit 38 take SR-32 E 3.9 miles, SR-295 S 1.9 miles, Laurel Rd W .1 mile & Russett Grn E .1 mile

☆	◯	🕐	⛽	🚫	Store Details
✪	1	✓			La Vale • 12500 Country Club Mall Rd, 21502 • 301-729-5081 • I-68 Exit 40 go S .5 mile on Vocke Rd, continue S .3 mile on SR-53/Winchester Rd
☆	1				Mount Airy • 209 E Ridgeville Blvd, 21771 • 301-829-4433 • I-70 Exit 68 merge onto SR-27 N .4 mile then W on Ridgeville Blvd .2 mile
✪	2	✓			North East • 75 North East Plz, 21901 • 410-287-2915 • I-95 Exit 100 follow SR-272 S for 1.6 miles
✪	3	✓			Nottingham • 8118 Perry Hills Ct, 21236 • 410-882-9815 • I-95 Exit 67 take SR-43 W 2.8 miles then S on Perry Hills Ct
✪		✓			Oakland • 13164 Garrett Hwy, 21550 • 301-334-8400 • On US-219 N of town
☆	2				Owings Mills • 9750 Reisterstown Rd, 21117 • 443-394-0168 • I-795 Exit 4 take Owings Mill Blvd N .7 mile & Reisterstown Rd E 1.1 miles
✪		✓			Pasadena • 8107 Governor Ritchie Hwy, 21122 • 410-689-1509 • 1.5 miles north of town along SR-2
✪		✓			Pocomoke City • 2132 Old Snow Hill Rd, 21851 • 410-957-9600 • Jct US-13/Bypass & US-13 (E of town) go N on US-13 for .9 mile then E on Old Snow Hill Rd
☆					Prince Frederick • 150 Solomons Island Rd N, 20678 • 410-535-3790 • Jct SR-231 & SR-2/SR-4 (E of town) go N on SR-2/SR-4 for .4 mile
✪	3	✓		✓	Randallstown • 8730 Liberty Rd, 21133 • 443-576-3132 • I-695 Exit 18 go W 2.2 miles on Liberty Rd
✪		✓			Salisbury • 2702 N Salisbury Blvd, 21801 • 410-860-5095 • From town center go N 4.3 miles on Salisbury Blvd
✪		✓			Salisbury • 409 N Fruitland Blvd, 21804 • 410-341-4803 • From town center go N .7 mile on Fruitland Blvd
✪	1	✓			Severn • 407 George Clauss Blvd, 21144 • 410-969-1050 • I-97 Exit 13 west side of the interstate at Quarterfield Rd
✪	9			✓	Sykesville • 6400A Ridge Rd Ste 1, 21784 • 410-549-5400 • I-70 Exit 80 go N 7.4 miles on SR-32 then E .9 mile on Liberty Rd and turn right onto Hemlock Dr
☆	2				Towson • 1238 Putty Hill Ave, 21286 • 410-494-4610 • I-695 Exit 29B merge on Loch Raven Blvd S .8 mile & W on Putty Hill Ave .9 mile
☆					Waldorf • 11930 Acton Ln, 20601 • 301-705-7070 • I-95/495 Exit 7A take SR-5 S 12.3 miles, continue S on US-301 for 1.7 miles then E on Acton Ln

☆	◯	🕐	⛽	🚫	Store Details
☆					Westminster • 280 Woodward Rd, 21157 • 410-857-8307 • Jct SR-97 & SR-140 (N of town) take SR-140 S .9 mile, Englar Rd E .2 mile & Woodward Rd S .1 mile

MASSACHUSETTS

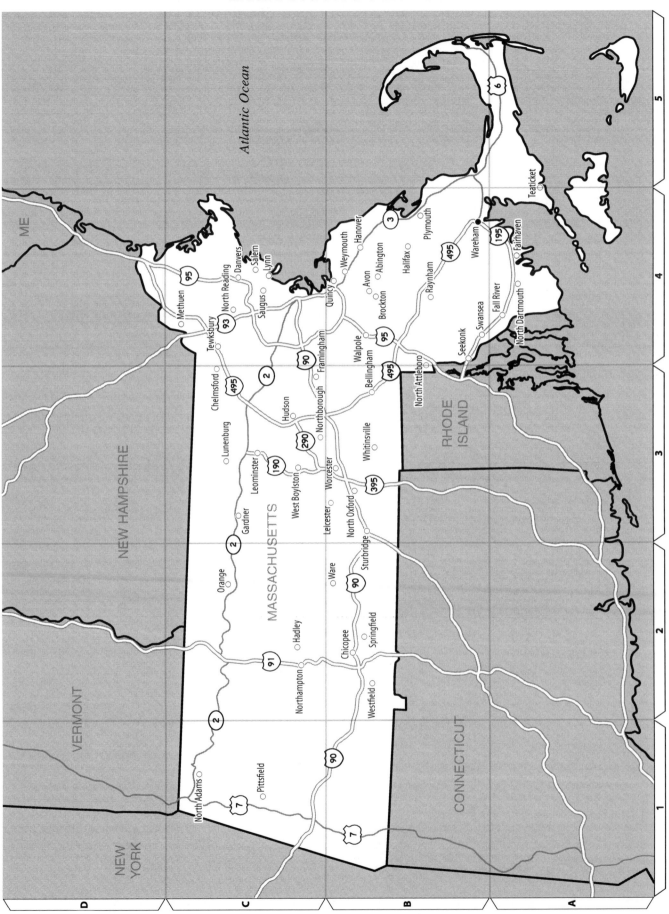

☆	◯	🕐	⛽	🚫	Store Details
☆					Abington • 777 Brockton Ave, 02351 • 781-857-2345 • SR-24 Exit 18A follow SR-27 SE 2.8 miles, continue on SR-123 for 2.6 miles
●					Avon • 30 Memorial Dr, 02322 • 508-427-9460 • SR-24 Exit 19A go E 1.6 miles on Harrison Blvd then S .3 mile on SR-28
☆	1				Bellingham • 250 Hartford Ave, 02019 • 508-966-7633 • I-495 Exit 18 take SR-126 N .1 mile
☆					Brockton • 700 Oak St, 02301 • 508-584-2333 • SR-24 Exit 18B merge onto SR-27 N .9 mile then E on Oak St .5 mile
☆	2			✓	Chelmsford • 66 Parkhurst Rd, 01824 • 978-459-1818 • I-495 Exit 33 follow SR-4 N 1.1 miles then Parkhurst Rd NE .6 mile
●	1	✓			Chicopee • 591 Memorial Dr, 01020 • 413-593-3192 • I-90 (toll) Exit 5 take Memorial Dr N .3 mile
☆	1				Danvers • 55 Brooksby Village Way, 01923 • 978-777-6977 • I-95 Exit 47A take SR-114 E .7 mile then S at Brooksby Village Dr .1 mile
☆	2			✓	Fairhaven • 42 Fairhaven Commons Way, 02719 • 508-993-8100 • I-195 Exit 18 merge onto SR-240 S 1 mile, W at Bridge St .2 mile & S at Alden Rd .1 mile
●	1			✓	Fall River • 638 Quequechan St, 02721 • 508-730-2677 • I-195 Exit 8A go S .1 mile on SR-24 ; W .2 mile on Brayton Ave; N .2 mile on Jefferson St
☆	2			✓	Framingham • 121 Worcester Rd, 01701 • 508-872-6575 • I-90 (toll) Exit 13 take SR-30 W .9 mile, S on Ring Rd .5 mile & W on Worchester Rd
●					Gardner • 677 Timpany Blvd, 01440 • 978-630-3244 • From town center go 2 miles south on SR-68
☆	5				Hadley • 337 Russell St, 01035 • 413-586-4231 • I-91 Exit 20 follow SR-9 NE 4.8 miles
☆				✓	Halifax • 295 Plymouth St, 02338 • 781-294-9339 • From SR-24 Exit 15 follow SR-104 E 7.3 miles, continue E on SR-106 3.6 miles
☆					Hanover • 1775 Washington St, 02339 • 781-826-0606 • From SR-3/SE Expy Exit 13 follow SR-53 S .4 mile
●	2				Hudson • 280 Washington St, 01749 • 978-568-3383 • I-495 Exit 25A take Hudston St E 1.6 miles then S at Washington St .3 mile
●		✓			Leicester • 20 Soojian Dr, 01524 • 508-892-9461 • 1.6 miles west of town center along SR-9 (Main St)
●	1	✓		✓	Leominster • 11 Jungle Rd, 01453 • 978-466-1313 • I-190 Exit 7 go W .2 mile on SR-117 then S .2 mile on Jungle Rd
☆					Lunenburg • 301 Massachusetts Ave, 01462 • 978-582-6000 • From SR-2 Exit 32 take SR-13 N 4.1 miles then W at SR-2A/Massachusetts Ave .1 mile
☆	7			✓	Lynn • 780 Lynnway, 01905 • 781-592-4300 • From I-90 (toll) Exit 26 follow US-1A N 6.1 miles
☆	2			✓	Methuen • 70 Pleasant Valley St, 01844 • 978-686-2633 • I-93 Exit 48 follow SR-213 E 1.6 miles to Exit 3 then turn left and continue E .2 mile on Pleasant Valley St
●				✓	North Adams • 1415 Curran Memorial Hwy, 01247 • 413-664-4004 • 2 miles south of town center along SR-8
●	1			✓	North Attleboro • 1470 S Washington St, 02760 • 508-699-0277 • I-295 Exit 1A go S 1 mile on US-1
●	3			✓	North Dartmouth • 506 State Rd, 02747 • 508-984-7771 • I-195 Exit 12 go S 1.1 miles on Faunce Corner Rd then W 1.1 miles on US-6
●	5			✓	North Oxford • 742 Main St, 01537 • 508-987-1444 • I-395 Exit 4B go W on Sutton Ave .9 mile then N on Main St 4.1 miles
☆	3				North Reading • 72 Main St, 01864 • 978-664-3262 • I-93 Exit 39 go E on Concord St & Park St for 1.7 miles then N on Main St .5 mile
☆	2			✓	Northampton • 180 N King St, 01060 • 413-587-0001 • I-91 Exit 21 go S on US-5/King St 1.4 miles
●	5			✓	Northborough • 200 Otis St, 01532 • 508-393-4385 • I-495 Exit 23B go W 4.5 miles on SR-9 then N .2 mile on Otis St
☆					Orange • 555 E Main St, 01364 • 978-544-5800 • Jct SR-122/S Main St & SR-2A/E Main St (in town) take E Main St E 1.3 miles
☆					Pittsfield • 555 Hubbard Ave, 01201 • 413-442-1971 • Jct SR-8 & SR-9 (E of town) go E on SR-9 for .4 mile then S on Hubbard Ave .1 mile
●					Plymouth • 300 Colony Place Rd, 02360 • 508-830-9555 • I-495 Exit 4 take SR-105 E 2.9 miles, US-44 E 9.6 miles & SR-80/Commerce Way S .2 mile
☆				✓	Quincy • 301 Falls Blvd, 02169 • 617-745-4390 • Jct SR-53 & SR-3A (in town) go S on SR-53/Quincy Ave .9 mile & W on Falls Blvd .1 mile

☆	♡	⏰	⛽	🚫	Store Details
✪	5	✓		✓	Raynham • 36 Paramount Dr, 02767 • 508-822-4900 • I-495 Exit 6 take US-44 W 3.4 miles, S on Commerce Way .3 mile & W on Paramount Dr .4 mile
✪					Raynham • 160 Broadway, 02767 • 508-692-6046 • I-495 Exit 8 go S 1.8 miles on SR-138/Broadway
☆				✓	Salem • 450 Highland Ave, 01970 • 978-825-1713 • Jct SR-129 & SR-107 (S of town) go N on SR-107/Highland Ave .8 mile
✪	4			✓	Saugus • 770 Broadway, 01906 • 781-816-5370 • About 4 miles south of I-95 Exit 44 along US-1
☆	1			✓	Seekonk • 1180 Fall River Ave, 02771 • 508-336-0290 • I-195 Exit 1 follow SR-114A S .6 mile
✪	3				Springfield • 1105 Boston Rd, 01119 • 413-782-6699 • I-90 (toll) Exit 7 follow SR-21 S 2.2 miles then W on US-20/Boston Rd .6 mile
☆	2				Sturbridge • 100 Charlton Rd, 01566 • 508-347-4993 • I-84 Exit 3A merge onto US-20 E 1.9 miles
✪	1			✓	Swansea • 262 Swansea Mall Dr, 02777 • 774-488-3923 • I-195 Exit 3 go W .3 mile on US-6 then N .5 mile on Maple Ave and E .1 mile on Cousineau St
☆				✓	Teaticket • 137 Teaticket Hwy, 02536 • 508-540-8995 • Jct Sandwich Rd & Teaticket Highway/SR-28 (W of town) go NE on Teaticket Hwy .3 mile
✪	1				Tewksbury • 333 Main St, 01876 • 978-851-6265 • I-495 Exit 38 take SR-38 E .5 mile
✪	2	✓			Walpole • 550 Providence Hwy, 02081 • 508-668-4144 • I-95 Exit 9 follow US-1 N 1.4 miles
✪	6				Ware • 352 Palmer Rd, 01082 • 413-967-0040 • I-90 (toll) Exit 8 follow SR-32 N 6 miles
✪	1		◆	✓	Wareham • 15 Tobey Rd, 02571 • 508-295-8890 • I-195 Exit 21 go W .4 mile on SR-28/Cranberry Hwy and turn left at Tobey Rd
☆	6				West Boylston • 137 W Boylston St, 01583 • 508-835-1101 • I-290 Exit 23 merge onto SR-140 N 4.9 miles then SR-12 S .7 mile
✪	5				Westfield • 141 Springfield Rd, 01085 • 413-572-0400 • I-90 Exit 3 go S 1.8 miles on SR-20/US-202 then E 2.4 miles on US-20
☆				✓	Weymouth • 740 Middle St, 02188 • 781-331-0063 • From Pilgrims Hwy (SR-3) at Main St Exit, go N .2 mile on Main St, E .5 mile on Winter St, S .1 mile on Middle St

☆	♡	⏰	⛽	🚫	Store Details
✪		✓			Whitinsville • 100 Valley Pkwy, 01588 • 508-234-9034 • From SR-146 at Main St Exit, go E .4 mile on Main St
✪	2	✓		✓	Worcester • 25 Tobias Boland Way, 01607 • 774-314-3157 • I-90 Exit 10A take the SR-146 ramp to northbound SR-146 and follow .6 mile then take the Millbury St exit and turn left .2 mile; turn left onto Blackstone River Rd and then first right; store is .4 mile on left.

MICHIGAN

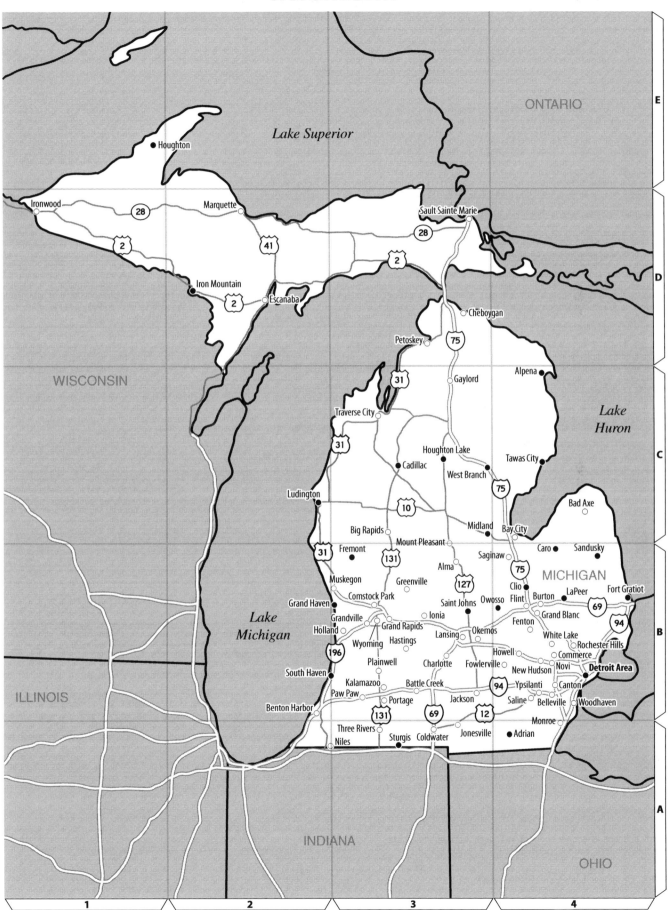

Detroit Metro Area

Chesterfield • Clinton Township • Dearborn • Livonia • Roseville • Shelby Township • Southgate • Sterling Heights • Taylor • Troy • Warren

☆	♡	🕐	⛽	🚫	Store Details
✪		✓	◆		Adrian • 1601 E US Hwy 223, 49221 • 517-265-9771 • Jct SR-34 & US-223 (W of town) go N on US-223 for 1.5 miles
✪		✓			Alma • 7700 N Alger Rd, 48801 • 989-463-6770 • From US-127 at SR-46 (Monroe Rd) Exit, go W .3 mile on Monroe Rd then S .3 mile on Alger Rd
✪		✓	❖		Alpena • 1180 MI Hwy 32 W, 49707 • 989-354-0830 • Jct US-32 & SR-65 (W of town) take SR-65 N 15 miles then SR-32 E 3.3 miles
✪		✓			Bad Axe • 901 N Van Dyke Rd, 48413 • 989-269-9506 • Jct SR-142/Pigeon Rd & SR-53 (N of town) go S on SR-53 for .1 mile
✪	2	✓			Battle Creek • 6020 B Dr N, 49014 • 269-979-1628 • I-94 Exit 97 go E on B Dr N for 1.1 miles
✪	3	✓			Bay City • 3921 Wilder Rd, 48706 • 989-684-0430 • I-75 Exit 164 take Wilder Rd E 2.4 miles
✪	1	✓			Belleville • 10562 Belleville Rd, 48111 • 734-697-2078 • I-94 Exit 190 go N .4 mile on Belleville Rd
✪	1	✓			Benton Harbor • 1400 Mall Dr, 49022 • 269-927-6025 • I-94 Exit 29 go N on Pipestone Rd .2 mile & W on Mall Dr .3 mile
✪		✓			Big Rapids • 21400 Perry Ave, 49307 • 231-796-1443 • From US-131 Exit 139 take SR-20 E .5 mile
✪	1	✓		✓	Burton • 5323 E Court St N, 48509 • 810-744-9690 • I-69 Exit 141 go N .2 mile on Belsay Rd then W .3 mile on Court St
✪		✓	❖		Cadillac • 8917 E 34 Rd, 49601 • 231-775-8778 • US-131 Exit 183 take 34 Rd W for .7 mile
✪	1	✓			Canton • 39500 Ford Rd, 48187 • 734-983-0538 • I-275 Exit 25 go E on Ford Rd .6 mile
✪	3	✓			Canton • 45555 Michigan Ave, 48188 • 734-985-9413 • I-275 Exit 22 go W 2.5 miles on US-12/Michigan Ave
✪		✓	❖		Caro • 1121 E Caro Rd, 48723 • 989-673-7900 • Jct SR-24 & SR-81 (NE of town) go NE on SR-81 for .3 mile
✪	2	✓			Charlotte • 1680 Packard Hwy, 48813 • 517-543-0300 • I-69 Exit 61 go N on Lansing Rd .9 mile then E on Packard Hwy .2 mile

☆	♡	🕐	⛽	🚫	Store Details
✪		✓			Cheboygan • 1150 S Main St, 49721 • 231-627-2769 • I-75 Exit 313 follow SR-27 NE 14.6 miles
✪	1	✓			Chesterfield • 45400 Marketplace Blvd, 48051 • 586-421-0451 • I-94 Exit 240 go W on Rosso Hwy .1 mile & N on Marketplace Blvd .4 mile
✪	5	✓		✓	Clinton Township • 18400 Hall Rd, 48038 • 586-263-7196 • I-94 Exit 240 go W 4.5 miles on SR-59
✪	1	✓	❖		Clio • 11493 N Linden Rd, 48420 • 810-564-3149 • I-75 Exit 131 take SR-57 W .2 mile & S on Linden Rd
✪	1	✓			Coldwater • 800 E Chicago St, 49036 • 517-278-2240 • I-69 Exit 13 take US-12 E .4 mile
✪	6	✓			Commerce • 3301 Pontiac Trail Rd, 48390 • 248-668-0274 • I-96 Exit 164 follow SR-5 N 5.5 miles & NE on Pontiac Trail .3 mile
✪	2	✓			Comstock Park • 3999 Alpine Ave NW, 49321 • 616-784-2047 • I-96 Exit 30 take SR-37 N 1.2 miles then Henze Dr W .2 mile
✪	4				Dearborn • 5851 Mercury Dr, 48126 • 313-441-0194 • I-96 Exit 183 take SR-39 S 2.7 miles to Exit 7 then go E .7 mile on Ford Rd (SR-153)
✪		✓			Escanaba • 601 N Lincoln Rd, 49829 • 906-786-7717 • 1.7 miles northwest of town center, about .5 mile north of US-2/US-41/SR-35 jct
✪				✓	Fenton • 3700 Owen Rd, 48430 • 810-750-1132 • From US-23 Exit 78 take Owen Rd W .2 mile
✪	1	✓		✓	Flint • 4313 Corunna Rd, 48532 • 810-733-5055 • I-75 Exit 118 go W on Corunna Rd .9 mile
✪	4	✓	❖		Fort Gratiot • 4845 24th Ave, 48059 • 810-385-1904 • I-69/94 Exit 274 take I-69/94 BR N then SR-25 N 3.6 miles
✪	1	✓			Fowlerville • 970 Gehringer Dr, 48836 • 517-223-8605 • I-96 Exit 129, north of exit
✪		✓	❖		Fremont • 7083 W 48th St, 49412 • 231-924-5000 • Jct SR-120/Maple Island Rd & SR-82/48th St (W of town) go E on 48th St 3.1 miles
✪	1	✓			Gaylord • 950 Edelweiss Pkwy, 49735 • 989-732-8090 • I-75 Exit 282 merge onto Dickerson Rd S .4 mile then W at Edelweiss Pkwy
✪	2	✓		✓	Grand Blanc • 6170 S Saginaw Rd, 48439 • 810-603-9739 • I-475 Exit 2 go E on Hill Rd 1.7 miles then S on Saginaw Rd .3 mile
✪	10	✓	❖		Grand Haven • 14700 US Hwy 31, 49417 • 616-844-3074 • I-96 Exit 1 follow US-31 S 9.5 miles

☆	🍎	🕐	⛽	🚫	Store Details
☆	1			✓	Grand Rapids • 5859 28th St SE, 49546 • 616-949-7670 • I-96 Exit 43 merge onto 28th St E .7 mile
☆	1				Grandville • 4542 Kenowa Ave SW, 49418 • 616-667-9724 • I-196 Exit 67 go W on 44th St .1 mile then S on Kenowa Ave .2 mile
✪		✓			Greenville • 10772 W Carson City Rd, 48838 • 616-754-3062 • US-131 Exit 101 take SR-57 E 14.5 miles
☆					Hastings • 1618 W MI Hwy 43, 49058 • 269-948-0470 • Jct SR-37 & SR-43 (W of town) go E on SR-37 for .6 mile
✪	7	✓			Holland • 2629 N Park Dr, 49424 • 616-393-2018 • I-196 Exit 55 take I-196 BR W 3.8 miles, 12th Ave N .1 mile, Lakewood Blvd W 1.7 miles & Park Dr N .5 mile
✪		✓	✤		Houghton • 995 Razorback Dr, 49931 • 906-482-0639 • 1.5 miles southwest of town center off SR-26
✪		✓	✤		Houghton Lake • 2129 W Houghton Lake Dr, 48629 • 989-366-9766 • I-75 Exit 227 merge onto SR-55 W 15.3 miles then N on Heightsview Dr .1 mile
✪	5	✓		✓	Howell • 3850 E Grand River Ave, 48843 • 517-548-9500 • I-96 Exit 137 follow CR-D19 N 1.3 miles & Grand River Ave SE 3 miles
✪	5	✓			Ionia • 3062 S State Rd, 48846 • 616-527-1392 • I-96 Exit 67 take SR-66 N 4.7 miles
✪		✓	✤		Iron Mountain • 1920 S Stephenson Ave, 49801 • 906-779-7180 • 1.7 miles southeast of town via US-2/US-141
✪		✓			Ironwood • 10305 Country Club Rd, 49938 • 906-932-0713 • 2 miles east of town off US-2 at Country Club Rd, south of US-2
✪	2	✓		✓	Jackson • 1700 W Michigan Ave, 49202 • 517-817-0326 • I-94 Exit 137 take Airport Rd S .6 mile, Laurence Ave S .7 mile & Michigan Ave E .7 mile
✪		✓			Jonesville • 701 Olds St, 49250 • 517-849-7000 • Jct US-12 & SR-99 (in town) go S on SR-99 for 1.1 miles
✪	4	✓			Kalamazoo • 501 N 9th St, 49009 • 269-544-0718 • I-94 Exit 74 take US-131 N 2.4 miles to Exit 38-Main St W 1 mile & 9th St S .2 mile
✪	6	✓			Kalamazoo • 6065 Gull Rd, 49048 • 269-373-1314 • I-94 Exit 80 take Sprinkle Rd N 4.4 miles then NE on Gull Rd .7 mile
☆					Lansing • 3225 Towne Centre Blvd, 48912 • 517-487-9150 • US-127 Exit 79 go W on Lake Lansing Rd .3 mile & N on Centre Blvd

☆	🍎	🕐	⛽	🚫	Store Details
✪	1	✓			Lansing • 409 N Marketplace Blvd, 48917 • 517-622-1431 • I-69/96 Exit 93 merge E onto Saginaw Hwy .4 mile & S at Marketplace Blvd .2 mile
✪	3	✓	✤		Lapeer • 555 E Genesee St, 48446 • 810-664-3062 • I-69 Exit 155 go N on SR-24 for 2 miles & E on Genesse St .3 mile
✪	2	✓			Livonia • 29555 Plymouth Rd, 48150 • 734-524-0577 • I-96 Exit 176 go S on Middlebelt Rd 1 mile then W at Plymouth Rd .1 mile
✪	4				Livonia • 29574 7 Mile Rd, 48152 • 248-957-0106 • I-19 Exit 176 go N on Middlebelt Rd for 3 miles then W .2 mile on Seven Mile Rd
✪		✓	✤		Ludington • 4854 W US Hwy 10, 49431 • 231-843-1816 • Jct US-31 & US-10 (E of town) go W on US-10 for .8 mile
✪		✓			Marquette • 3225 US Hwy 41 W, 49855 • 906-226-7982 • Jct SR-35 & US-41 (SW of town) go N on US-41 for 4.5 miles
✪		✓	✤		Midland • 910 Joe Mann Blvd, 48642 • 989-835-6069 • I-75 Exit 162 follow US-10 W 16.9 miles, Eastman Ave N .3 mile & Mann Blvd E .5 mile
✪	6	✓			Monroe • 2150 N Telegraph Rd, 48162 • 734-242-2280 • I-275 Exit 2 take US-24 S 5.3 miles
✪		✓			Mount Pleasant • 4730 Encore Blvd, 48858 • 989-772-6300 • 2 miles south of town off US-127 BR at Blue Grass Rd to Encore Blvd
✪	4	✓			Muskegon • 3285 Henry St, 49441 • 231-739-4710 • I-96 Exit 1 continue W on Seaway Dr 3.3 miles, W on Norton .2 mile & N on Henry St .1 mile
✪	3	✓			Muskegon • 1879 E Sherman Blvd, 49444 • 231-739-6202 • I-96 Exit 1 take US-31 N 2.2 miles then Sherman Blvd E .2 mile
✪	1	✓		✓	New Hudson • 30729 Lyon Center Dr E, 48165 • 248-486-0445 • I-96 Exit 155 go S on Milford Rd .2 mile & E on Lynn Center Dr .2 mile
✪		✓	◆	✓	Niles • 2107 S 11th St, 49120 • 269-683-2773 • US-31 Exit 3 take Pulaski Hwy E 3.6 miles & S on 11th St .7 mile
✪	1	✓			Novi • 26090 Ingersol Dr, 48375 • 248-277-4092 • I-96 Exit 162, south of exit
☆	5				Okemos • 5110 Times Square Pl, 48864 • 517-381-5243 • I-69 Exit 94 take Saginaw St S 1.3 miles, Marsh Rd SE 3.1 miles & Times Sq Dr E .3 mile
✪		✓	✤	✓	Owosso • 1621 E MI Hwy 21, 48867 • 989-723-2552 • US-127 Exit 96 follow SR-21 E 19.1 miles

☆	♡	⏱	⛽	🚫	Store Details
✪	1	✓			Paw Paw • 1013 S Kalamazoo St, 49079 • 269-415-6001 • I-94 Exit 60 go S .5 mile on SR-40
✪		✓			Petoskey • 1600 Anderson Rd, 49770 • 231-439-0200 • Jct US-31 & US-131 (W of town) take US-131 S .7 mile & W at Anderson Rd .4 mile
✪		✓			Plainwell • 412 Oaks Crossing, 49080 • 269-685-6191 • Located between Otsego and Plainwell. From US-131 Exit 49, go W .9 mile on SR-89
☆	4				Portage • 8350 Shaver Rd, 49024 • 269-323-2460 • I-94 Exit 76 go S on Westnedge Ave 2.3 miles, continue on Shaver Rd .8 mile
✪	2	✓		✓	Rochester Hills • 2500 S Adams Rd, 48309 • 248-853-0433 • I-75 Exit 77A go E 1.8 miles on SR-59 (Veterans Memorial Fwy) to Adams Rd and go S .2 mile
✪	1	✓		✓	Roseville • 28804 Gratiot Ave, 48066 • 586-777-0221 • I-94 Exit 230 go W .3 mile on Twelve Mile Rd
✪	2	✓			Saginaw • 5650 Bay Rd, 48604 • 989-790-3990 • I-675 Exit 6 go W on Tittabawassee Rd 1.1 miles then N on Bay Rd .7 mile
✪	5	✓			Saginaw • 5825 Brockway Rd, 48638 • 989-497-8102 • I-675 Exit 3 take Davenport Ave W 4.6 miles, S on Wieneke Rd .1 mile & W on Brockway Rd
✪		✓	❖		Saint Johns • 1165 Superior Dr, 48879 • 989-224-8099 • From US-127 Exit 91, follow US-127 BR 5.2 miles then E on Superior Dr .1 mile
✪	4	✓		✓	Saline • 7000 E Michigan Ave, 48176 • 734-944-1053 • I-94 Exit 177 go S 3.5 miles on State St
✪		✓	❖		Sandusky • 655 W Sanilac Rd, 48471 • 810-648-2728 • Jct SR-53 & SR-46 (W of town) go E on SR-46 for 11.6 miles
✪	1	✓			Sault Sainte Marie • 3763 I-75 Business Spur, 49783 • 906-632-0572 • I-75 Exit 392 go E .7 mile on I-75 Business Spur
✪		✓	❖		Shelby Township • 51450 Shelby Pkwy, 48315 • 586-997-6905 • Jct SR-59 & SR-53 (S of town) take SR-53 N 2.7 miles, 23 Mile Rd E .4 mile & Shelby Pkwy N .3 mile
✪	1	✓	❖		South Haven • 201 73rd St, 49090 • 269-639-2260 • I-196 Exit 20 W on Phoenix St & N on 73rd St .1 mile
✪	2	✓			Southgate • 14900 Dix-Toledo Rd, 48195 • 734-286-9594 • I-75 Exit 36 go E 1.4 miles on Eureka Rd then N .2 mile on Dix-Toledo Rd

☆	♡	⏱	⛽	🚫	Store Details
✪	5	✓		✓	Sterling Heights • 33201 Van Dyke Ave, 48312 • 586-939-7208 • I-75 Exit 65 go E 4.5 miles on 14 Mile Rd
☆				✓	Sterling Heights • 44575 Mound Rd, 48314 • 586-323-2394 • I-75 Exit 77 merge onto SR-59 E 9.8 miles, Hall Rd E .2 mile & Mound Rd S .2 mile
✪	3	✓	❖		Sturgis • 1500 S Centerville Rd, 49091 • 269-651-8580 • I-80/90 (toll-IN) Exit 121 take SR-9 N .7 mile & continue on Centerville Rd 1.7 miles
✪		✓	❖		Tawas City • 621 E Lake St, 48763 • 989-984-0854 • Jct SR-55 & US-23 go N on US-23 for .2 mile
✪	1	✓			Taylor • 7555 Telegraph Rd, 48180 • 313-292-3474 • I-94 Exit 202 take US-24 S .9 mile
✪		✓			Three Rivers • 101 S Tolbert Dr, 49093 • 269-273-7820 • 1 mile west of town center off US-131 at Millard Rd
✪		✓			Traverse City • 2640 Crossing Cir, 49684 • 231-933-8800 • 3 miles south of town center, east of US-31/SR-37 at Airport Rd near Grand Traverse Mall
☆	4				Troy • 2001 W Maple Rd, 48084 • 248-435-4035 • I-75 Exit 69 take Big Beaver Rd W 1.2 miles, Livermore Rd S 1 mile & Maple Rd W 1.5 miles
✪	1	✓		✓	Warren • 29176 Van Dyke Ave, 48093 • 586-467-0258 • I-696 Exit 23 go N 1 mile on Van Dyke Ave
✪	1	✓	❖		West Branch • 2750 Cook Rd, 48661 • 989-343-1309 • I-75 Exit 212 go N on Cook Rd .4 mile
✪		✓			White Lake • 9190 Highland Rd, 48386 • 248-698-9601 • I-75 Exit 77B go W 13 miles on SR-59
✪	1	✓			Woodhaven • 23800 Allen Rd, 48183 • 734-675-4360 • I-75 Exit 32 go E .8 mile on West Rd then S .2 mile on Allen Rd
✪		✓			Wyoming • 355 54th St SW, 49548 • 616-552-6224 • US-131 Exit 78, east of exit
✪	2	✓			Ypsilanti • 2515 Ellsworth Rd, 48197 • 734-434-5620 • I-94 Exit 181, NE on Michigan Ave .6 mile, N on Hewitt Rd .2 mile & W on Ellsworth Rd .3 mile; westbound travelers use Exit 181B

MINNESOTA

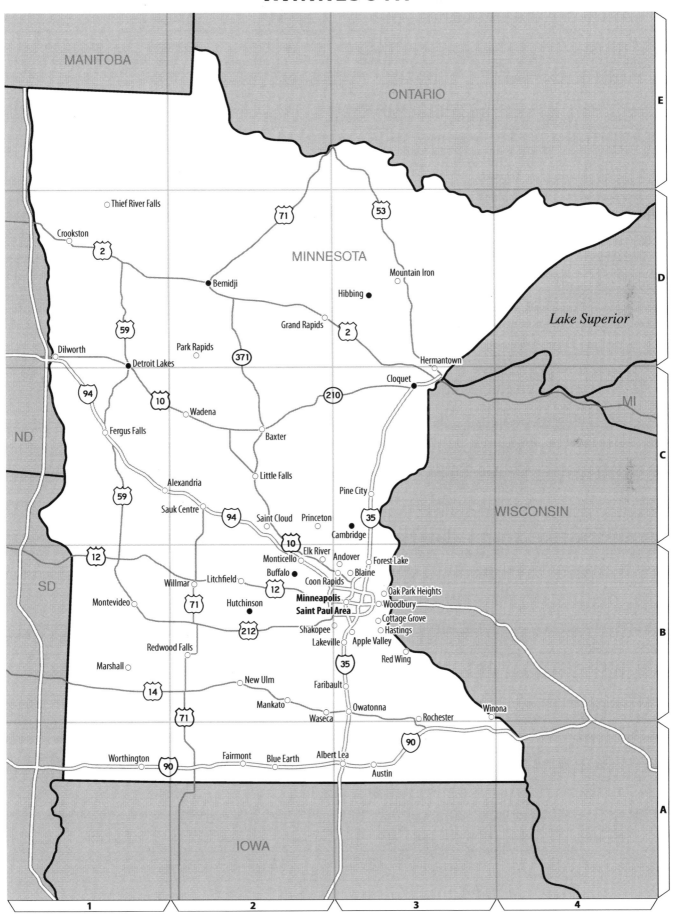

Minneapolis - Saint Paul Metro Area

Bloomington • Brooklyn Center • Brooklyn Park • Burnsville •
Eagan • Eden Prairie • Fridley • Inner Grove Heights • Maple Grove
• Minneapolis • Roseville • Saint Paul • Vadnais Heights

☆	◯	🕐	⛽	🚫	Store Details
✪	1	✓			Albert Lea • 1550 Blake Ave, 56007 • 507-377-2998 • I-35 Exit 11 take CR-46 W .4 mile then S at Olsen Dr .2 mile
✪	1	✓			Alexandria • 4611 MN Hwy 29 S, 56308 • 320-762-8945 • I-94 Exit 103 take SR-29 N .4 mile
✪					Andover • 1851 Bunker Lake Blvd NW, 55304 • 763-354-1559 • From US-10 at Main St, go E .3 mile on Main St then N 1.6 miles on Coon Creek Blvd and turn right .8 mile on Bunker Lake Blvd
✪	3	✓		✓	Apple Valley • 7835 150th St W, 55124 • 952-431-9700 • I-35E Exit 88B go E 2.9 miles on CR-42/Egan Dr then N .1 mile on Pennock Ln
✪	1	✓			Austin • 1000 18th Ave NW, 55912 • 507-434-8159 • I-90 Exit 177 go N .3 mile on US-218 then E .3 mile on 18th Ave
✪		✓			Baxter • 7295 Glory Rd, 56425 • 218-829-2220 • Jct SR-210 & SR-371 (in town) take SR-371 S .5 mile & Glory Rd W .3 mile
✪		✓	❖		Bemidji • 2025 Paul Bunyan Dr NW, 56601 • 218-755-6120 • 2.7 miles northwest of town via SR-197, just east of US-71
✪	5	✓		✓	Blaine • 11505 Ulysses St NE, 55434 • 763-354-1979 • I-35W Exit 33 go N .6 mile on Lexington Ave, W 3.6 mile on 109th Ave, then N .8 mile on Ulysses St
✪	1	✓			Blaine • 4369 Ball Rd NE, 55449 • 763-784-0147 • I-35W Exit 33, south of exit
✪	1	✓		✓	Bloomington • 700 American Blvd E, 55420 • 952-854-5600 • I-494 Exit 3, south of exit
☆	1				Blue Earth • 1210 Giant Dr, 56013 • 507-526-4766 • I-90 Exit 119 take US-169 S .6 mile & W on Fairgrounds Rd
✪	1	✓		✓	Brooklyn Center • 1200 Shingle Creek Crossing, 55430 • 763-354-1941 • I-94 Exit 34 go S 1 mile on Shingle Creek Pkwy
✪	2	✓			Brooklyn Park • 8000 Lakeland Ave N, 55445 • 763-424-4842 • I-94 Exit 31 take CR-81 N .9 mile, 73rd Ave E .1 mile & Broadway S .1 mile
✪	9	✓	❖		Buffalo • 1315 Hwy 25 N, 55313 • 763-682-2958 • I-94 Exit 193 take SR-25 S 8.6 miles

☆	◯	🕐	⛽	🚫	Store Details
✪	1	✓			Burnsville • 12200 River Ridge Blvd, 55337 • 952-356-0018 • I-35W Exit 4A, east of exit
✪		✓	❖		Cambridge • 2101 2nd Ave SE, 55008 • 763-689-0606 • I-35 Exit 147 take SR-95 NW 11.8 miles & S at McKinley .1 mile
✪	2	✓	❖		Cloquet • 1308 Hwy 33 S, 55720 • 218-878-0737 • I-35 Exit 237 merge onto SR-33 N 1.2 miles
☆					Coon Rapids • 13020 Riverdale Dr NW, 55448 • 763-421-2622 • I-35W Exit 30 take US-10 W 10.5 miles, CR-9 N .1 mile & Northdale Blvd W
✪	8	✓			Cottage Grove • 9300 East Point Douglas Rd, 55016 • 651-846-2831 • I-494 Exit 67B go SE 6.7 miles on US-10/US-61 to the Innovation Rd exit and go N to East Point Douglas Rd and go W .4 mile
✪		✓			Crookston • 1930 Sahlstrom Dr, 56716 • 218-281-2970 • 1.7 miles north of town off US-2 at Acres Dr
✪		✓	◆		Detroit Lakes • 1583 Hwy 10 W, 56501 • 218-847-1126 • Jct US-59 & US-10 (NW of town) take US-10 W 1.2 miles, Airport Rd S .1 mile & Frontage Rd E
✪	3	✓			Dilworth • 415 34th St N, 56529 • 218-233-9822 • I-94 Exit 2 go N on 34th St 2.2 miles
☆	1			✓	Eagan • 1360 Town Centre Dr, 55123 • 651-686-7428 • I-35E Exit 97 take Pine Knob Rd S .1 mile, Duckwood Dr E .1 mile & Town Centre Dr N .2 mile
☆	2			✓	Eden Prairie • 12195 Singletree Ln, 55344 • 952-829-9040 • I-494 Exit 11A take US-212 W .9 mile, Prairie Center Dr W .4 mile & Singletree Ln N .2 mile
✪	9	✓		✓	Elk River • 18185 Zane St NW, 55330 • 763-441-3461 • I-94 Exit 207 go N 6.9 miles on SR-101 and .8 mile N on US-169 to Main St then E .1 mile and S .3 mile on Zane St
✪	1	✓			Fairmont • 1250 Goemann Rd, 56031 • 507-235-2500 • I-90 Exit 102, north of exit
✪	1	✓			Faribault • 150 Western Ave NW, 55021 • 507-332-0232 • I-35 Exit 56 take SR-60 E .6 mile & S on Western Ave .2 mile
✪	1	✓			Fergus Falls • 3300 MN Hwy 210 W, 56537 • 218-739-5552 • I-94 Exit 54 take SR-210 W .2 mile
✪	1	✓			Forest Lake • 200 12th St SW, 55025 • 651-464-9740 • I-35 Exit 131 go E .2 mile on Broadway Ave then S .2 mile on 12th St
✪	2			✓	Fridley • 8450 University Ave NE, 55432 • 763-780-9400 • I-694 Exit 37 take University Ave N 1.7 miles

☆	○	⏱	⛽	🚫	Store Details
✪		✓			Grand Rapids • 100 SE 29th St, 55744 • 218-326-9682 • 2.2 miles south of town center via US-169
✪		✓			Hastings • 1752 N Frontage Rd, 55033 • 651-438-2400 • 2 miles west of town off SR-55 at General Sieben Dr
✪	6	✓			Hermantown • 4740 Mall Dr, 55811 • 218-727-1310 • I-35 Exit 255 follow US-53 NW for 5.4 miles
✪		✓	❖	✓	Hibbing • 12080 Hwy 169 W, 55746 • 218-262-2351 • 1 mile west of town along SR-169
✪		✓	❖		Hutchinson • 1300 Hwy 15 S, 55350 • 320-587-1020 • Jct 5th Ave & Main St (in town) go S on Main St for 1.2 miles
☆	3			✓	Inver Grove Heights • 9165 Cahill Ave, 55076 • 651-451-3975 • I-494 Exit 65 take 7th Ave S .6 mile, continue S on Cahill Ave 1.9 miles
✪	1	✓		✓	Lakeville • 20710 Keokuk Ave, 55044 • 612-354-5927 • I-35 Exit 81, west of exit
✪					Litchfield • 2301 E Frontage Rd, 55355 • 320-693-1022 • 1.8 miles east of town center along US-12
✪		✓			Little Falls • 15091 18th St NE, 56345 • 320-632-9268 • 1.8 miles east of town center along SR-27 at 18th St
✪		✓			Mankato • 1881 E Madison Ave, 56001 • 507-625-9318 • Jct US-14 & SR-22 (E of town) take SR-22 S .5 mile
✪	1	✓		✓	Maple Grove • 9451 Dunkirk Ln N, 55311 • 763-420-3500 • I-94 Exit 213 take 95th Ave W .2 mile & Dunkirk Ln S
✪		✓			Marshall • 1221 E Main St, 56258 • 507-532-9383 • Jct US-59 & SR-68 (NW of town) go N on SR-68 for 1 mile
✪		✓			Montevideo • 3001 E Hwy 7, 56265 • 320-269-5390 • 1.5 miles east of town center on SR-7
✪	1	✓			Monticello • 9320 Cedar St, 55362 • 763-295-9800 • I-94 Exit 193 take SR-25 N .3 mile & E at 7th St
✪		✓			Mountain Iron • 8580 Rock Ridge Dr, 55768 • 218-305-3314 • 2.4 miles east of town center off US-169
✪		✓			New Ulm • 1720 Westridge Rd, 56073 • 507-354-0900 • 2.5 miles northwest of town center along US-14
✪	7	✓			Oak Park Heights • 5815 Norell Ave N, 55082 • 651-439-7476 • I-694 Exit 52 take SR-36 E 6.7 miles & S at Norrelle Ave .3 mile
✪	1	✓			Owatonna • 1130 W Frontage Rd, 55060 • 507-455-0049 • I-35 Exit 42 go W on US-14 to Frontage Rd N for .1 mile

☆	○	⏱	⛽	🚫	Store Details
✪		✓			Park Rapids • 1303 Charles St, 56470 • 218-732-0339 • 1.3 miles east of town center off SR-34 at SR-81 (Henrietta Ave)
✪	1	✓			Pine City • 950 11th St SW, 55063 • 320-629-5845 • I-35 Exit 169 take CR-7 W .3 mile & N at 11th St
✪		✓			Princeton • 300 21st Ave N, 55371 • 763-389-7821 • 1 mile west of town center off US-169 at SR-95
✪		✓			Red Wing • 295 Tyler Rd S, 55066 • 651-385-0003 • Jct SR-19 & US-61 (E of town) take US-61 S 2.8 miles & S at Tyler Rd
☆					Redwood Falls • 1410 E Bridge St, 56283 • 507-644-6278 • Jct SR-101 & US-71 (E of town) go E on US-71/Bridge St for .2 mile
✪		✓			Rochester • 3400 55th St NW, 55901 • 507-280-7733 • Jct US-14 & CR-22 (W of town) go N on CR-22 for 3.3 miles
✪	7	✓		✓	Rochester • 25 25th St SE, 55904 • 507-292-0909 • I-90 Exit 218 take US-52 N 5.5 miles then US-63 N .8 mile & 25th St E
✪	1			✓	Roseville • 1960 Twin Lakes Pkwy, 55113 • 612-788-1303 • I-35W Exit 24, east of exit
✪	5	✓			Saint Cloud • 3601 2nd St S, 56301 • 320-345-9810 • I-94 Exit 167B go N 4 miles on SR-15 then E .2 mile on 2nd St
✪	8	✓			Saint Cloud • 21 County Road 120, 56303 • 320-259-1527 • I-94 Exit 167B go N 6.5 miles on SR-15 then NE .6 mile on CR-120
☆	1				Saint Paul • 1450 University Ave W, 55104 • 651-644-0020 • I-94 Exit 239 merge onto St Anthony Ave W .3 mile, Pascal St N .2 mile & University Ave E
✪	2			✓	Saint Paul • 1644 Robert St S, 55118 • 651-453-0343 • I-494 Exit 67 take SR-3 N 1.7 miles
✪	1	✓			Sauk Centre • 205 12th St S, 56378 • 320-352-7954 • I-94 Exit 127 take US-71 N .1 mile & 12th St E .2 mile
✪	7	✓		✓	Shakopee • 8101 Old Carriage Ct, 55379 • 952-445-8013 • I-494 Exit 10 take US-169 S 5.7 miles, CR-18 S .9 mile & Old Carriage Rd W .1 mile
✪		✓			Thief River Falls • 1755 Hwy 59 S, 56701 • 218-683-3643 • Jct CR-7 & US-59 (S of town) take US-59 N 2.6 miles
✪	1				Vadnais Heights • 850 E County Rd E, 55127 • 651-486-7001 • I-35E Exit 115 go W on CR-E .3 mile
✪		✓			Wadena • 100 Juniper Ave, 56482 • 218-631-1068 • Jct US-71 & US-10 (in town) take US-10 W 1 mile, 640th Ave N .6 mile & Juniper Ave E .2 mile

☆	♡	🕐	⛽	🚫	Store Details
✪		✓			Waseca • 2103 State St N, 56093 • 507-835-2250 • I-35 Exit 42 take US-14 W 13.4 miles & SR-13 N 1.3 miles
✪		✓			Willmar • 700 19th Ave SE, 56201 • 320-231-3456 • 2 miles southeast of town center, east of US-71 at 19th Ave
✪	1	✓			Winona • 955 Frontenac Dr, 55987 • 507-452-0102 • I-90 Exit 252 follow SR-43 N 7.2 miles & Frontenac Dr E .2 mile
✪	1			✓	Woodbury • 10240 Hudson Rd, 55129 • 651-735-5181 • I-94 Exit 251 take CR-19 S .3 mile & Hudson Rd E .4 mile
✪	1	✓			Worthington • 1055 Ryans Rd, 56187 • 507-376-6446 • I-90 Exit 43 take US-59 S .3 mile & Ryans Rd E

MISSISSIPPI

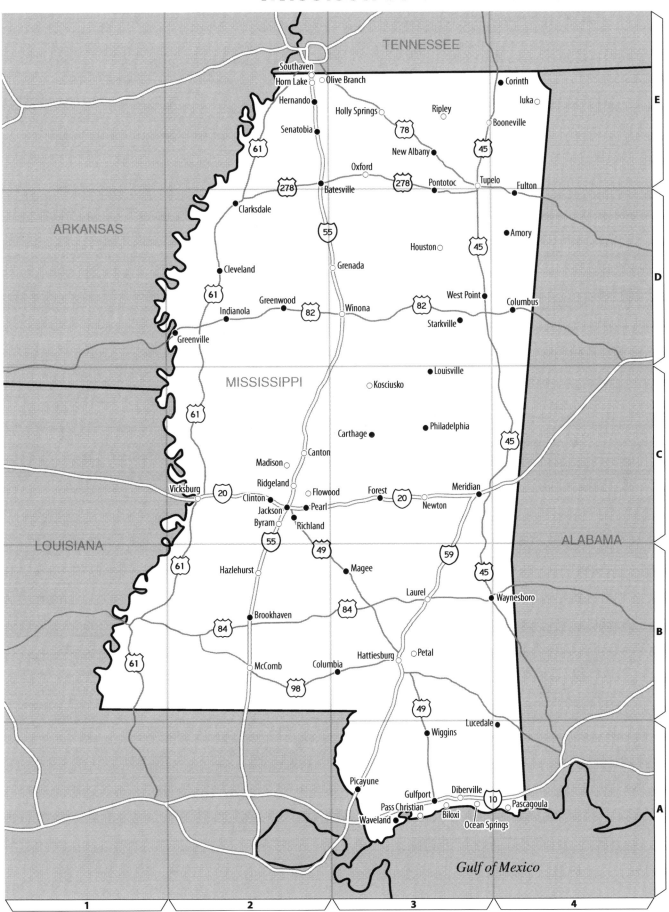

☆	♡	🕐	⛽	🚐	Store Details
●		✓	◆		Amory • 1515 Hwy 278 E, 38821 • 662-256-1590 • Jct SR-25 & US-278 (S of town) go E on US-278 for 2 miles
●	2	✓	❖		Batesville • 205 House Carlson Dr, 38606 • 662-563-3100 • I-55 Exit 243A take US-278 E .7 mile, Medical Center Dr S & House Carlson Dr W .4 mile
●	6	✓			Biloxi • 2681 C T Switzer Sr Dr, 39531 • 228-385-1046 • I-10 Exit 38 go S 2.7 miles on Lorraine Rd; continue S .5 mile on Cowan Rd; go E 1.5 miles on Pass Rd; S .5 mile on De Buys Rd; E .3 mile on C T Switzer Sr Dr
●		✓			Booneville • 300 Walmart Cir, 38829 • 662-728-6211 • From town center go N 1.4 miles on SR-145 then W .2 mile on Walmart Cir
●	1	✓	◆		Brookhaven • 960 Brookway Blvd, 39601 • 601-835-0232 • I-55 Exit 40 take Brookway Blvd E .9 mile
●	1	✓			Byram • 131 Handley Blvd, 39272 • 769-237-4314 • I-55 Exit 85, west of exit
●	1	✓		✓	Canton • 244 Feather Ln, 39046 • I-55 Exit 119 go W .2 mile on Peace St, turn left .1 mile on Commercial Pkwy then left onto Feather Ln for .6 mile
●		✓	◆		Carthage • 905 Hwy 16 W, 39051 • 601-267-8374 • Jct SR-35 & SR-16 (in town) take SR-16 E .3 mile
●		✓	❖		Clarksdale • 1000 S State St, 38614 • 662-627-1133 • Jct US-278 & SR-322 (S of town) follow SR-322 W 4.2 miles
●		✓	❖		Cleveland • 710 N Davis Ave, 38732 • 662-843-6567 • .5 mile north of town along US-61/US-278
●	3	✓	❖	✓	Clinton • 950 Hwy 80 E, 39056 • 601-924-9096 • I-20 Exit 35 take US-80 E 2.2 miles
●		✓	❖		Columbia • 1001 Hwy 98 Byp, 39429 • 601-731-1193 • Jct SR-13 & US-98 (S of town) go E on US-98 for 1.1 miles
●		✓	◆		Columbus • 1913 Hwy 45 N, 39705 • 662-329-4810 • Jct US-82 & US-45 (SW of town) follow US-45 N 5.7 miles
●		✓	◆		Corinth • 2301 S Harper Rd, 38834 • 662-287-3148 • Jct US-72 & CR-404/Harper Rd (SE of town) go S on Harper Rd .2 mile
●	1	✓			Diberville • 3615 Sangani Blvd, 39540 • 228-396-4740 • I-10 Exit 46 take SR-15 N .6 mile then E on Sangani Blvd
●	9	✓			Flowood • 5341 Highway 25, 39232 • 601-992-8898 • I-55 Exit 98B go E 8.5 miles on Lakeland Dr (SR-25)
●	4		❖		Forest • 1309 Hwy 35 S, 39074 • 601-469-2122 • I-20 Exit 88 take SR-35 N 3.6 miles

☆	♡	🕐	⛽	🚐	Store Details
●		✓	❖		Fulton • 100 Interchange Dr, 38843 • 662-862-2143 • From US-78 Exit 104 go S .2 mile on SR-25/Adams St
●		✓	❖		Greenville • 1831 Highway 1 S, 38703 • 662-332-9026 • 4 miles southeast of town center along SR-1
●		✓	❖		Greenwood • 2202 Hwy 82 W, 38930 • 662-453-4656 • Jct US-278 & SR-1 (in town) follow SR-1 S 5 miles & Wilcox Rd E 1.4 miles
●	1	✓			Grenada • 1655 Sunset Dr, 38901 • 662-229-0114 • I-55 Exit 206 take SR-8 E 1 mile
●	2	✓	◆		Gulfport • 9350 Hwy 49, 39503 • 228-864-5197 • I-10 Exit 34 take US-49 S 1.1 miles
●	3	✓			Hattiesburg • 5901 US Hwy 49, 39402 • 601-296-6855 • I-59 Exit 65 go E 1.4 miles on Hardy St then S 1.1 miles on US-49, right on Eddy St, left on Hicks St to store
●	2	✓			Hattiesburg • 6072 US Hwy 98, 39402 • 601-261-9393 • I-59 Exit 65 merge onto US-98 W 1.9 miles
●	1	✓			Hazlehurst • 527 Lake St, 39083 • 601-894-1673 • I-55 Exit 61 take SR-28 E .4 mile then Lake St S .6 mile
●	1	✓	❖		Hernando • 2600 Mcingvale Rd, 38632 • 662-429-3456 • I-55 Exit 280 take SR-340 E .3 mile then Mcingvale Rd S .1 mile
●		✓			Holly Springs • 950 Mackie Dr, 38635 • 662-252-2211 • 1.9 miles south of town center, south of US-78 Exit 30 at SR-4/SR-7
●	4	✓	❖		Horn Lake • 4150 Goodman Rd W, 38637 • 662-253-6184 • I-69 Exit 289 go W 3.5 miles on Goodman Rd
☆					Houston • 660 E Madison St, 38851 • 662-456-5711 • Jct SR-15 & SR-8 go E on SR-8/Madison St .6 mile
●		✓	❖		Indianola • 633 Hwy 82 W, 38751 • 662-887-3320 • Jct US-49W & US-82 (NE of town) take US-82 W .5 mile
☆					Iuka • 1110 Battleground Dr, 38852 • 662-423-3054 • Jct US-72 & SR-25 (S of town) take SR-25 N 1.1 miles
●	1	✓	◆		Jackson • 2711 Greenway Dr, 39204 • 601-922-3406 • I-20 Exit 40B go S on Robinson Rd .5 mile & Greenway Dr W .2 mile
●		✓			Kosciusko • 220 Veterans Memorial Dr, 39090 • 662-289-3422 • Jct SR-12 & SR-35 (in town) follow SR-35 SE for 1.4 miles
●	2	✓			Laurel • 1621 Hwy 15 N, 39440 • 601-649-6191 • I-59 Exit 95 merge onto CR-15 N 1.7 miles

☆	○	🕐	⛽	🚭	Store Details
✪		✓	❖		Louisville • 159 Hwy 15 S, 39339 • 662-773-7823 • 1.8 miles west of town center at SR-14/SR-15 jct
✪		✓	❖		Lucedale • 11228 Old 63 S, 39452 • 601-947-6991 • 1.6 miles south of town center via SR-63
✪		✓			Madison • 127 Grandview Blvd, 39110 • 601-605-9662 • I-20 Exit 48 take SR-468 E 6.9 miles, SR-469 S 2.1 miles, Monterey Rd S 1.9 miles & Grandview Dr W
✪		✓	◆		Magee • 1625 Simpson Hwy 49, 39111 • 601-849-2628 • Jct SR-541 & US-49 (W of town) take US-49 N .4 mile
✪	1	✓			McComb • 1608 Veterans Blvd, 39648 • 601-684-1074 • I-55 Exit 18 go E on Smithdale Rd .5 mile
✪	1	✓	❖		Meridian • 1733 2nd St S, 39301 • 601-485-2250 • I-20 Exit 153 take 22nd Ave NW .7 mile & 2nd St NE .3 mile
✪	3	✓	❖		Meridian • 2400 Hwy 19 N, 39307 • 601-482-0425 • I-20/59 Exit 150 follow SR-19 N 3 miles
✪		✓	◆		Natchez • 314 Sergeant Prentiss Dr, 39120 • 601-442-2895 • Jct US-84/98 & US-61 (W of town) follow US-61 SW 3.9 miles
✪		✓	❖		New Albany • 202 Park Plaza Dr, 38652 • 662-534-9374 • From US-78 Exit 61 take SR-30 W to Park Plaza Dr S .2 mile
✪	2	✓			Newton • 231 Eastside Dr, 39345 • 601-683-3393 • I-20 Exit 109 take SR-15 S 1.5 miles
✪	6	✓			Ocean Springs • 3911 Bienville Blvd, 39564 • 228-875-4036 • I-10 Exit 57 take SR-57 S 2.8 miles then US-90 W 2.5 miles
✪	10	✓		✓	Olive Branch • 7950 Craft Goodman Frontage Rd, 38654 • 662-890-2500 • I-55 Exit 289 take SR-302 E 9 miles then Goodman Rd N .2 mile
✪		✓			Oxford • 2530 Jackson Ave W, 38655 • 662-234-9131 • From US-278/SR-6 (W of town) take Jackson Ave W/SR-6 Bypass .4 mile
✪	9	✓			Pascagoula • 4253 Denny Ave, 39581 • 228-762-9662 • I-10 Exit 75 take Franklin Creek Rd S .5 mile & US-90 W 7.6 miles
✪	8	✓			Pass Christian • 1617 E Beach Blvd, 39571 • 228-452-4948 • I-10 Exit 24 go S 6.2 miles on Menge Ave then E 1.8 miles on Beach Blvd
✪	1	✓	◆	✓	Pearl • 5520 Hwy 80 E, 39208 • 601-939-0281 • I-20 Exit 54 take Greenfield Rd N .3 mile then US-80 W .6 mile
✪	6	✓			Petal • 36 Byrd Blvd, 39465 • 601-584-6025 • I-59 Exit 69 go E 6 miles on SR-42

☆	○	🕐	⛽	🚭	Store Details
✪		✓	◆		Philadelphia • 1002 W Beacon St, 39350 • 601-656-4166 • Jct CR-15 & SR-16 (W of town) take SR-16 E .6 mile
✪	1	✓	◆		Picayune • 235 Frontage Rd, 39466 • 601-799-3455 • I-59 Exit 4 take SR-43 S .3 mile then S on Frontage Rd .6 mile
✪		✓	❖		Pontotoc • 100 McCord Rd, 38863 • 662-489-7451 • From US-78 Exit 64 take SR-15 S 13.2 miles
✪	5	✓	❖		Richland • 200 Marketplace Dr, 39218 • 601-939-0538 • I-20 Exit 47 take US-49 S 4.3 miles
✪	2	✓		✓	Ridgeland • 815 S Wheatley St, 39157 • 601-956-2717 • I-59 Exit 103 go E on County Line Rd .7 mile & N on Wheatley St .6 mile
☆					Ripley • 822 City Ave S, 38663 • 662-837-0014 • Jct SR-4 & SR-15 (in town) take SR-15 S .6 mile
✪	2	✓	◆		Senatobia • 5219 Hwy 51 N, 38668 • 662-562-6202 • I-55 Exit 265 follow SR-4 W 1.5 miles then US-51 N .1 mile
✪	1	✓		✓	Southaven • 6811 Southcrest Pkwy, 38671 • 662-349-1838 • I-55 Exit 289 take SR-302 E .5 mile
✪		✓	❖		Starkville • 1010 Hwy 12 W, 39759 • 662-324-0374 • Jct US-82 & SR-25 (NW of town) take SR-25 S 3.5 miles & SR-12 E .5 mile
✪		✓			Tupelo • 2270 W Main St, 38801 • 662-844-4011 • US-78 Exit 85 take Natchez Trace Pkwy S 3.6 miles then SR-6 E 1.1 miles
✪		✓			Tupelo • 3929 N Gloster St, 38804 • 662-840-8401 • US-78 Exit 86 take US-45 N 1.5 miles, Barnes Crossing W .5 mile & Gloster St S .4 mile
✪	2	✓			Vicksburg • 2150 Iowa Blvd, 39180 • 601-638-9164 • I-20 Exit 1C merge onto Halls Ferry Rd .3 mile, W on Frontage Rd .9 mile & Iowa Ave NW
✪		✓	❖		Waveland • 460 Hwy 90, 39576 • 228-467-4371 • I-10 Exit 2 take SR-607 S 5.8 miles & US-90 E 7.6 miles
✪		✓	❖		Waynesboro • 1350 Azalea Dr, 39367 • 601-735-9716 • Jct US-84 & SR-184 (W of town) go SE on SR-184/Azelea Dr 2.3 miles
✪		✓	❖		West Point • 1313 Hwy 45 S, 39773 • 662-494-1551 • 1.5 miles south of town along US-45/SR-25
✪		✓	❖		Wiggins • 1053 Frontage Dr E, 39577 • 601-928-9119 • 2 miles southwest of town center on US-49, about 1 mile south of SR-26
☆	3				Winona • 620 S Applegate St, 38967 • 662-283-3814 • I-55 Exit 185 take US-82 & US-182 E 1.7 miles & US-51 S 1.2 miles

MISSOURI

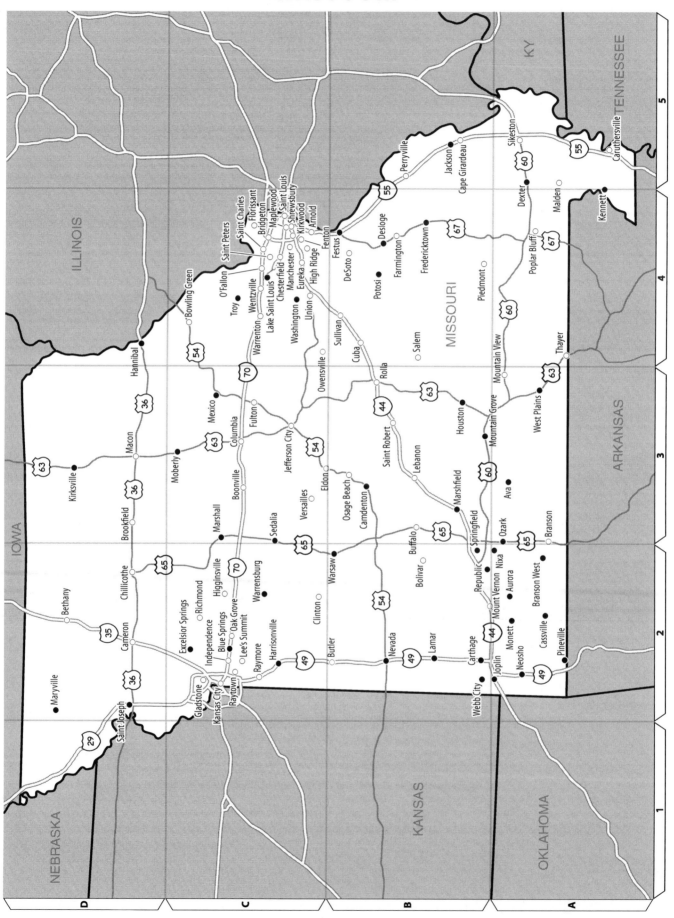

☆	⬭	🕐	⛽	🚫	Store Details
✪	1	✓			Arnold • 2201 Michigan Ave, 63010 • 636-282-0297 • I-55 Exit 191 go E .4 mile on SR-141, S .5 mile on US-61/US-67, W .1 mile on Michigan Ave
✪		✓	❖		Aurora • 3020 S Elliott Ave, 65605 • 417-678-5800 • I-44 Exit 46 follow SR-39 S 12.4 miles
✪		✓	❖		Ava • 1309 NW 12th Ave, 65608 • 417-683-4194 • Jct SR-5 & SR-14 (NW of town) go W on SR-14/12th Ave .2 mile
✪	1	✓			Bethany • 810 S 37th St, 64424 • 660-425-4410 • I-35 Exit 92 go W on US-136 .1 mile then S on 37th St .1 mile
✪	1	✓	❖		Blue Springs • 600 NE Coronado Dr, 64014 • 816-224-4800 • I-70 Exit 21 take Adams Pkwy S .2 mile & Coronado Dr E .1 mile
✪		✓			Bolivar • 2451 S Springfield Ave, 65613 • 417-326-8424 • Jct SR-32 & SR-13/Springfield Ave (in town) go S on SR-13 for 1.7 miles
✪	1	✓			Boonville • 2150 Main St, 65233 • 660-882-7422 • I-70 Exit 103 go N on SR-B 1 mile
✪		✓			Bowling Green • 3 Town Center Dr, 63334 • 573-324-0040 • 1 mile southeast of town center at US-61/US-61-BUS
✪		✓			Branson • 1101 Branson Hills Pkwy, 65616 • 417-334-2137 • West of US-65 at Branson Hills Pkwy exit
☆				✓	Branson • 2050 W Hwy 76, 65616 • 417-334-5005 • Jct US-65 & SR-76 (in town) go W on West 76 Country Blvd 2.2 miles
✪		✓	◆		Branson West • 18401 MO Hwy 13, 65737 • 417-272-8044 • Jct SR-265/413 & SR-13/76 (N of town) go S on SR-13 for .6 mile
✪	1				Bridgeton • 11900 Saint Charles Rock Rd, 63074 • 314-291-2300 • I-70 Exit 234, north of exit
✪		✓		✓	Brookfield • 937 Park Circle Dr, 64628 • 660-258-7416 • 1.3 miles south of town center at US-36/SR-11 jct
☆					Buffalo • 1250 W Dallas St, 65622 • 417-345-6166 • Jct US-65 & SR-32 (W of town) go W on SR-32/Dallas St .1 mile
✪	1	✓			Butler • 400 S Fran Ave, 64730 • 660-679-3151 • I-49 Exit 131, east of exit
✪		✓	❖		Camdenton • 94 Cecil St, 65020 • 573-346-3588 • Jct SR-5/7 & US-54 (in town) take US-54 NE 1.5 miles
✪	1	✓			Cameron • 2000 N Walnut St, 64429 • 816-632-9900 • I-35 Exit 54 follow I-35 BR .8 mile

☆	⬭	🕐	⛽	🚫	Store Details
✪	1	✓			Cape Girardeau • 3439 William St, 63701 • 573-335-4600 • I-55 Exit 96 go W on SR-K .1 mile
✪	1	✓	◆		Carthage • 2705 Grand Ave, 64836 • 417-358-3000 • I-49 Exit 50 go E .7 mile on Fir Rd then N .1 mile on Grand Ave
☆	4				Caruthersville • 1500 State Hwy 84 W, 63830 • 573-333-1262 • I-55 Exit 19 go E 4 miles on SR-84
✪		✓	❖		Cassville • 1401 Old Exeter Rd, 65625 • 417-847-3138 • 1 mile west of town center off SR-37
✪	1	✓		✓	Chesterfield • 100 THF Blvd, 63005 • 636-536-4601 • I-64 Exit 17 take Boones Crossing S .2 mile, Airport Rd E .5 mile & Chesterfield Commons S .1 mile
✪		✓			Chillicothe • 1000 Graves St, 64601 • 660-646-6000 • 1 mile south of town off US-65 near intersection with US-36
✪		✓			Clinton • 1712 E Ohio St, 64735 • 660-885-5536 • Jct SR-7 & SR-13 (E of town) go E on SR-7 for .2 mile
✪	4	✓		✓	Columbia • 1201 Grindstone Pkwy, 65201 • 573-449-0815 • I-70 Exit 128A go S on US-63 for 3 miles then W on SR-AC .8 mile
✪	1	✓			Columbia • 415 Conley Rd, 65201 • 573-499-4935 • I-70 Exit 128A go S on US-63 for .2 mile, W on Interstate Dr .1 mile & S on Conley Rd .5 mile
✪	2	✓		✓	Columbia • 3001 W Broadway, 65203 • 573-445-9506 • I-70 Exit 124 take Stadium Blvd S .9 mile & SR-TT W .5 mile
☆	1				Cuba • 100 Ozark Dr, 65453 • 573-885-2501 • I-44 Exit 208 go S on SR-19 & E on Ozark Dr .1 mile
✪		✓			De Soto • 12862 State Hwy 21, 63020 • 636-586-6878 • Jct SR-CC & SR-21 (S of town) take SR-21 N for 1.6 miles
✪		✓	❖		Desloge • 407 N State St, 63601 • 573-431-5094 • 1.2 miles northeast of town center, just west of US-67 at Cedar Falls Rd Exit
✪		✓	❖		Dexter • 2025 W Business US Hwy 60, 63841 • 573-624-5514 • Jct US-60 & SR-25 (NE of town) take US-60 W 1.7 miles, One Mile Rd S .5 mile & US-60 BR W .3 mile
☆					Eldon • 1802 Business Hwy 54, 65026 • 573-392-3114 • Jct US-54 & US-54 BR (S of town) go N on US-54 BR 2.4 miles
✪	2	✓			Eureka • 131 Eureka Towne Center Dr, 63025 • 636-587-9836 • I-44 Exit 261 go N on Six Flags Rd .2 mile & E on 5th St 1.2 miles

☆	🛡	🕐	⛽	🚫	Store Details
✪	10	✓	❖		Excelsior Springs • 2203 Patsy Ln, 64024 • 816-630-1003 • I-35 Exit 20 merge onto US-69 N 9.4 miles then S at Mc-Cleary Rd .1 mile
✪		✓		✓	Farmington • 701 Walton Dr, 63640 • 573-756-8448 • Jct US-67 & SR-32 (NW of town) take SR-32 SE .5 mile & Walton Dr S .2 mile
✪	4	✓			Fenton • 653 Gravois Bluffs Blvd, 63026 • 636-349-3116 • I-270 Exit 3 follow SR-30 W 2.5 miles, SR-141 S .5 mile & Gravois Blvd E .1 mile
✪	2	✓	◆		Festus • 650 S Truman Blvd, 63028 • 636-937-8441 • I-55 Exit 174A merge onto S Truman Blvd 1.4 miles
✪	5	✓	◆	✓	Florissant • 3390 N Hwy 67, 63033 • 314-824-0023 • I-270 Exit 25 go N 4.2 miles on US-67
✪		✓	❖		Fredericktown • 1025 Walton Dr, 63645 • 573-783-5581 • 1.7 miles west of town center near US-67/SR-72 jct
✪	6	✓			Fulton • 1701 N Bluff St, 65251 • 573-642-6877 • I-70 Exit 148 go S on US-54W 3.7 miles & US-54 BR/Bluff St S 1.5 miles
✪	4	✓			Gladstone • 7207 North M-1 Hwy, 64119 • 816-436-8900 • I-435 Exit 49A go W 1.7 miles on SR-152 then S 1.5 miles on SR-1
✪	1	✓	❖		Hannibal • 3650 Stardust Dr, 63401 • 573-221-5610 • From I-72/US-36 exit at US-61 and go N .5 mile then W at Stardust Dr .5 mile
✪	1	✓	◆		Harrisonville • 1700 N MO Hwy 291, 64701 • 816-884-5635 • I-49 Exit 160, 1/2 mile east of exit
☆	6				Higginsville • 1180 W 19th St, 64037 • 660-584-7717 • I-70 Exit 49 take SR-13 N 5.4 miles then E on 19th St
✪	9	✓			High Ridge • 2700 Ridge Point Dr, 63049 • 636-375-3201 • I-270 Exit 3 go W 8.6 miles on SR-30/Gravois Rd
✪		✓	❖		Houston • 1433 S Sam Houston Blvd, 65483 • 417-967-3302 • Jct SR-17 & US-63 (S of town) go S on US-63 for .3 mile
✪	1	✓			Independence • 4000 S Bolger Rd, 64055 • 816-478-4090 • I-70 Exit 15B take SR-291 N .2 mile, 39th St W .4 mile & Bolger St N .2 mile
✪	2	✓	◆		Jackson • 3051 E Jackson Blvd, 63755 • 573-243-3909 • I-55 Exit 99 follow I-55 BR/Jackson Blvd 1.9 miles
✪		✓			Jefferson City • 401 Supercenter Dr, 65101 • 573-635-3535 • 4 miles east of town center via US-50/US-63
✪		✓			Jefferson City • 724 W Stadium Blvd, 65109 • 573-635-8283 • Jct SR-179 & US-50 BR (W of town) go E on US-50 BR for .9 mile then S at Stadium Blvd

☆	🛡	🕐	⛽	🚫	Store Details
✪		✓	◆		Joplin • 2623 W 7th St, 64801 • 417-206-4644 • I-44 Exit 15 follow I-44 BR/SR-66 W for 10.2 miles
✪	3	✓			Joplin • 1501 S Range Line Rd, 64804 • 417-781-0100 • I-44 Exit 8B go N on Range Line Rd 2.4 miles
✪	1	✓			Kansas City • 11601 E US Hwy 40, 64133 • 816-313-1183 • I-70 Exit 11 take US-40 E .3 mile
✪	4	✓		✓	Kansas City • 1701 W 133rd St, 64145 • 816-942-3847 • I-435 Exit 75B go S on State Line Rd 3.5 miles & E at 133rd St .1 mile
✪	2	✓			Kansas City • 8551 N Boardwalk Ave, 64154 • 816-741-1099 • I-29 Exit 8 go E on Barry Rd 1 mile then N on Boardwalk Ave .2 mile
✪	1	✓			Kansas City • 8301 N Church Rd, 64158 • 816-792-4644 • I-35 Exit 16 go W on Barry Rd .3 mile & S on Church Rd .1 mile
✪		✓	◆		Kennett • 1500 1st St, 63857 • 573-888-2084 • I-55 Exit 17B take US-412 W 16.8 miles, continue on SR-84 .1 mile
✪		✓	◆		Kirksville • 2206 N Baltimore St, 63501 • 660-627-7100 • Jct US-63 & SR-6 (N of town) go S on US-63 for .1 mile
✪	1	✓			Kirkwood • 1202 S Kirkwood Rd, 63122 • 314-835-9406 • I-44 Exit 277 follow US-61 N .3 mile
✪	5	✓	❖		Lake Saint Louis • 6100 Ronald Reagan Dr, 63367 • 636-625-2101 • I-70 Exit 214 take Lake St Louis Blvd SW 3.2 miles then Reagan Dr S .9 mile
✪	1	✓	❖		Lamar • 29 SW 1st Ln, 64759 • 417-682-5516 • I-49 Exit 77, west of exit
✪	1	✓			Lebanon • 1800 S Jefferson Ave, 65536 • 417-588-2268 • I-44 Exit 129 take SR-5 S .5 mile
✪	3	✓			Lees Summit • 1000 NE Sam Walton Ln, 64086 • 816-246-4555 • I-470 Exit 10B merge onto SR-291 for 1.4 miles, Tudor Rd W .1 mile & Sam Walton Way S .3 mile
☆					Macon • 705 E Briggs Dr, 63552 • 660-385-5783 • Jct US-63 & US-36 (in town) go S on US-63 for .2 mile & E on Briggs Dr .2 mile
☆					Malden • 1007 N Douglass St, 63863 • 573-276-5735 • Jct SR-153 & US-62 (E of town) take US-62 W 8.2 miles, SR-25 N 1 mile, Tom St W .7 mile & S on Douglass St
✪	4	✓			Manchester • 201 Highlands Blvd Dr, 63011 • 636-256-0697 • I-270 Exit 9 take SR-100/Manchester Rd W 3.2 miles

☆	◯	🕐	⛽	⊘	Store Details
✪	1	✓			Maplewood • 1900 Maplewood Commons Dr, 63143 • 314-781-2165 • I-64 Exit 33B go S on Big Bend Blvd .4 mile then W on Bruno Ave .6 mile
✪		✓	❖		Marshall • 855 Cherokee Dr, 65340 • 660-886-6852 • I-70 Exit 78B take US-65 N 11.1 miles then W at Cherokee Dr
✪	1	✓	❖		Marshfield • 14740 MO Hwy 38, 65706 • 417-468-3518 • I-44 Exit 100 follow SR-38 W .6 mile
✪		✓	◆		Maryville • 1605 S Main St, 64468 • 660-562-2994 • Jct SR-V & US-71 BR/S Main St (S of town) go S on US-71 BR .3 mile
✪		✓	❖		Mexico • 4820 S Clark St, 65265 • 573-581-4500 • I-70 Exit 148 go N on US-54 for 13.4 miles & US-54 BR N 2.4 miles
✪		✓	◆		Moberly • 1301 E Hwy 24, 65270 • 660-263-3113 • Jct US-63 & US-24 (NE of town) go E on US-24 for .2 mile
✪		✓	❖		Monett • 885 E US Hwy 60, 65708 • 417-235-6292 • I-44 Exit 44 follow SR-H 14.2 miles, Cleveland St W 1 mile, Eisenhower St S .1 mile & Scott St W .2 mile
☆	2	✓			Mount Vernon • 500 W Mount Vernon Blvd, 65712 • 417-461-7005 • I-44 Exit 44 go E 1.4 miles on I-44-BUS/Mount Vernon Blvd; westbound travelers use Exit 46
✪		✓	❖		Mountain Grove • 2100 N Main Ave, 65711 • 417-926-5107 • US-60 at Main St, north of exit
☆					Mountain View • 101 W US Hwy 60, 65548 • 417-934-6000 • Jct SR-17 & US-60 (E of town) go W on US-60 for .8 mile
✪	2	✓	◆		Neosho • 3200 Lusk Dr, 64850 • 417-451-5544 • I-49 Exit 24 go E 1.2 miles on US-60 then S .1 mile on Lusk Dr
✪	1	✓	❖		Nevada • 2250 Lincoln Ave, 64772 • 417-667-3630 • I-49 Exit 101 go W .4 mile on Austin Blvd then S .2 mile on Barrett St
✪		✓	◆		Nixa • 1102 N Massey Blvd, 65714 • 417-724-1097 • Jct SR-14 & US-160 (in town) go N on US-160/Massey Blvd 1.5 miles
✪	1	✓			O'Fallon • 1307 Hwy K, 63366 • 636-980-3700 • I-70 Exit 217 go S on SR-K .6 mile
✪	1	✓			Oak Grove • 201 SE Salem St, 64075 • 816-690-4900 • I-70 Exit 28 go S on SR-H .3 mile, 4th St E .2 mile & Salem St N .2 mile
✪		✓			Osage Beach • 4252 Hwy 54, 65065 • 573-348-6445 • Jct SR-134 & US-54 (N of town) go S on US-54 for .8 mile

☆	◯	🕐	⛽	⊘	Store Details
✪		✓			Owensville • 1888 Hwy 28, 65066 • 573-437-4156 • Jct SR-19 & SR-28 (S of town) go N on SR-28 for .9 mile
✪		✓	❖		Ozark • 2004 W Marler Ln, 65721 • 417-581-2761 • I-44 Exit 82A take US-65 S 17.2 miles, SR-F E .2 mile & Marler Ln S .1 mile
✪	8	✓			Perryville • 1750 S Perryville Blvd, 63775 • 573-547-2577 • I-55 Exit 129 take SR-51 S 7.8 miles
☆					Piedmont • 15 Halls Plaza Dr, 63957 • 573-223-7330 • Jct SR-34 & SR-49 (NE of town) go S on SR-49 for 2 miles & W at Hals Plaza Dr
✪		✓	❖		Pineville • 100 Commercial Ln, 64856 • 417-226-5800 • 9 miles south of town along US-71
✪		✓			Poplar Bluff • 333 S Westwood Blvd, 63901 • 573-686-6420 • Jct US-67 & SR-53 (SW of town) go N on US-67 BR .8 mile
✪		✓	❖		Potosi • 1 Memorial Dr, 63664 • 573-438-5441 • 1.2 miles southeast of town center on SR-21, near the hospital
✪	1	✓			Raymore • 2015 W Foxwood Dr, 64083 • 816-322-5455 • I-49 Exit 174, 1/2 mile east of exit
✪	3	✓			Raytown • 10300 E Hwy 350, 64138 • 816-358-7790 • I-435 Exit 67 go E 1.5 miles on Gregory Blvd then S 1 mile on SR-350/Blue Pkwy
✪		✓	❖		Republic • 1150 US Hwy 60 E, 65738 • 417-732-1473 • Jct SR-M & US-60 (N of town) go SW on US-60 for 1.5 miles
✪		✓			Richmond • 908 Walton Way, 64085 • 816-776-5834 • 1.5 miles southeast of town, south of SR-10/SR-13 jct
✪	2	✓			Rolla • 500 S Bishop Ave, 65401 • 573-341-9145 • I-44 Exit 185 go E on SR-E .3 mile, S on I-44 BR .6 mile & US-63 S .5 mile
✪	1	✓			Saint Charles • 2897 Veterans Memorial Pkwy, 63303 • 636-947-8732 • I-70 Exit 227 go S .1 mile on Zumbehl Rd then go E .3 mile on Veterans Memorial Pkwy
✪	2	✓	❖		Saint Joseph • 3022 S Belt Hwy, 64503 • 816-232-9819 • I-29 Exit 44 follow I-29 BR 1.7 miles
✪	2	✓			Saint Joseph • 4201 N Belt Hwy, 64506 • 816-390-8400 • I-29 Exit 50 follow US-169 S 1.3 miles
✪	1	✓			Saint Louis • 3270 Telegraph Rd, 63125 • 314-845-8544 • I-255 Exit 2 go N on Telegraph Rd .3 mile
✪	1				Saint Louis • 10741 W Florissant Ave, 63136 • 314-521-3422 • I-270 Exit 29 go S on Florissant Ave .4 mile

☆	◯	🕐	⛽	🚭	Store Details
✪	2	✓			Saint Peters • 1661 Jungermann Rd, 63304 • 636-447-4450 • I-70 Exit 225 take Cave Springs Rd S .2 mile, Mexico Rd W .6 mile & Jungermann Rd S 1.1 miles
✪	1	✓			Saint Robert • 185 Saint Robert Blvd, 65584 • 573-336-5103 • I-44 Exit 161B take SR-Y N .1 mile & Saint Robert Blvd W .6 mile
✪		✓		✓	Salem • 1101 W Hwy 32, 65560 • 573-729-6151 • Jct SR-19 & SR-32/72 (S of town) go W on SR-32/72 .6 mile
✪		✓	◆	✓	Sedalia • 3201 W Broadway Blvd, 65301 • 660-826-7800 • I-70 Exit 78A take US-65 S 18.9 miles & US-50 W 1 mile
✪	3				Shrewsbury • 7437 Watson Rd, 63119 • 314-687-1216 • I-44 Exit 280 go S about 1 mile on Elm Ave then E 2 miles on Watson Rd
✪	3	✓			Sikeston • 1303 S Main St, 63801 • 573-472-3020 • I-55 Exit 66B take US-60 W 2.6 miles then N on Kingshighway St
✪	2	✓			Springfield • 1923 E Kearney St, 65803 • 417-865-4545 • I-44 Exit 80A go S .7 mile on Glenstone Ave/I-44-BUS then E .1 mile
✪	1	✓		✓	Springfield • 2825 N Kansas Expy, 65803 • 417-865-8865 • I-44 Exit 77 follow SR-13 S .2 mile
✪		✓			Springfield • 2021 E Independence St, 65804 • 417-886-8209 • I-44 Exit 82A take US-65 S 8.6 miles, follow US-65 BR 1.9 miles & W at Indpendence St .2 mile
✪		✓		✓	Springfield • 3315 S Campbell Ave, 65807 • 417-887-0855 • I-44 Exit 82A take US-65 S 6.4 miles, Battlefld St W 3.9 miles & Campbell Ave S .3 mile
✪	5	✓	❖	✓	Springfield • 3520 W Sunshine St, 65807 • 417-862-7447 • I-44 Exit 72 take Chestnut Expy E 2.1 miles, US-160 S 2 miles & W on Sunshine St
✪	1	✓			Sullivan • 350 Park Ridge Rd, 63080 • 573-468-7030 • I-44 Exit 226 go E on SR-H .2 mile, Service Rd S .1 mile & E toward Park Ridge Rd
☆					Thayer • 333 E Walnut St, 65791 • 417-264-7195 • Jct SR-19 & US-63 (N of town) take US-63 S 1.4 miles & W on Public Rd/Walnut St .3 mile
✪		✓	◆	✓	Troy • 101 Hwy 47 E, 63379 • 636-528-8901 • I-70 Exit 193 follow SR-47 NE 18.9 miles
✪	4	✓			Union • 1445 E Central Ct, 63084 • 636-583-2355 • I-44 Exit 247 take US-50 W 3.2 miles, N on Prairie Dell & E at Central Ct
✪		✓			Versailles • 1003 W Newton St, 65084 • 573-378-4668 • Jct SR-5 & SR-52 (W of town) take SR-52 W for .2 mile

☆	◯	🕐	⛽	🚭	Store Details
✪		✓	◆		Warrensburg • 301 E Cooper St, 64093 • 660-747-1505 • Jct US-50 & SR-13 (N of town) go N on SR-13 for .2 mile
✪	1	✓			Warrenton • 500 Warren County Ctr, 63383 • 636-456-4600 • I-70 Exit 193, north of exit on Service Rd
✪		✓	❖		Warsaw • 103 W Polk St, 65355 • 660-438-7394 • Jct US-65 & SR-7 (N of town) take SR-7 SW 1.3 miles then S on Main St .2 mile
✪		✓	❖		Washington • 1701 Aroy Dr, 63090 • 636-239-1993 • Jct SR-47 & SR-100 (S of town) go E on SR-100 for .3 mile
✪	8	✓	◆		Webb City • 1212 S Madison St, 64870 • 417-673-8288 • I-44 Exit 11 take SR-249 N 3.7 miles, W on Zora St 2.4 miles & N on US-71 BR 1.4 miles
✪	1	✓			Wentzville • 1971 Wentzville Pkwy, 63385 • 636-327-5155 • I-70 Exit 208 go N on Pearce Blvd/Wentzville Pkwy .2 mile
✪		✓	◆		West Plains • 1310 Preacher Roe Blvd, 65775 • 417-257-2800 • 2 miles southwest of town center off US-63 at US-160

MONTANA

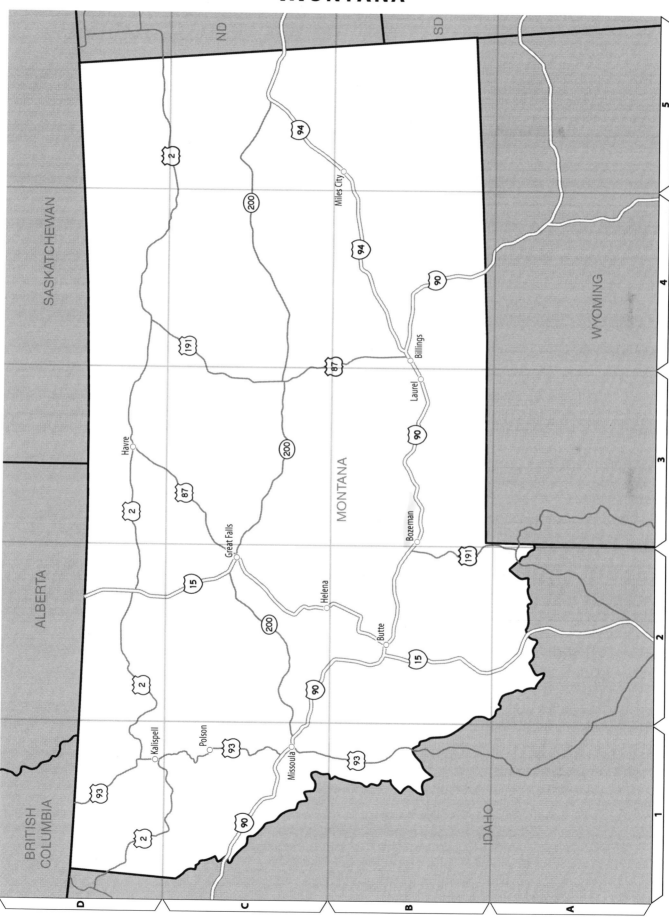

☆	♡	⏲	⛽	🚭	Store Details
✪	2	✓			Billings • 2525 King Ave W, 59102 • 406-652-9692 • I-90 Exit 446 take I-90 BR W .4 mile then King Ave W 1.2 miles
✪	3	✓			Billings • 1649 Main St, 59105 • 406-254-2842 • I-90 Exit 452 follow US-87 N for 2.8 miles
✪	1	✓			Bozeman • 1500 N 7th Ave, 59715 • 406-585-8788 • I-90 Exit 306 go S on 7th Ave .1 mile
✪	2	✓			Butte • 3901 Harrison Ave, 59701 • 406-494-1420 • I-15/90 Exit 127A go S on Harrison Ave 1.3 miles
✪	3	✓			Great Falls • 701 Smelter Ave NE, 59404 • 406-761-5426 • I-15 Exit 280 take Central Ave E 1.2 miles, 3rd St N 1.3 miles & Smelter Ave NE .3 mile
✪		✓			Havre • 3510 US Hwy 2 W, 59501 • 406-262-9162 • Jct US-87 & US-2 (W of town) go E on US-2 for .7 mile
✪	1	✓			Helena • 2750 Prospect Ave, 59601 • 406-443-3220 • I-15 Exit 192 go E on US-12 for .4 mile
✪		✓		✓	Kalispell • 170 Hutton Ranch Rd, 59901 • 406-257-7535 • 2.3 miles north of town along US-93
✪	1	✓			Laurel • 101 Bernhardt Rd, 59044 • 406-628-3000 • I-90 Exit 434 go N .4 mile on 1st Ave then E .5 mile on Railroad St
✪	1	✓			Miles City • 3205 Stower St, 59301 • 406-232-0022 • I-94 Exit 138 take SR-59 N .6 mile
✪	6				Missoula • 4000 US Hwy 93 S, 59804 • 406-251-6060 • I-90 Exit 101 go S 5.8 miles on US-93
✪	4	✓			Missoula • 3555 Mullan Rd, 59808 • 406-829-8489 • I-90 Exit 104 take Orange St S .6 mile, Broadway W 1.3 miles & Mullen Rd W 1.2 miles
✪					Polson • 36318 Memory Ln, 59860 • 406-883-9211 • 2.5 miles east of town along US-93

NEBRASKA

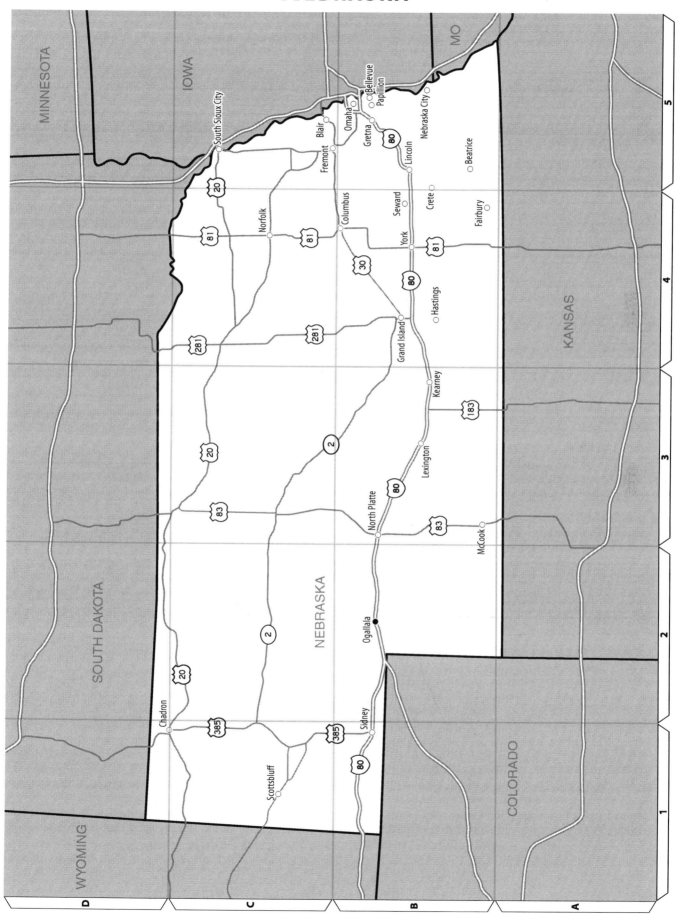

☆	🛡	🕐	⛽	🚭	Store Details
★		✓			Beatrice • 3620 N 6th St, 68310 • 402-228-1244 • Jct SR-34D & US-77 (N of town) go S on US-77 for 5.5 miles
★	6	✓			Bellevue • 10504 S 15th St, 68123 • 402-292-0156 • I-80 Exit 452 take US-75 S 4.9 miles then Cornhusker Rd E .2 mile & 15th St S .3 mile
★		✓			Blair • 1882 Holly St, 68008 • 402-533-8222 • 2 miles south of town center along US-30 at Holly St
★		✓			Chadron • 510 Linden St, 69337 • 308-432-6999 • Jct US-385 & US-20 (W of town) go W on US-20/4th St .3 mile
★		✓			Columbus • 818 E 23rd St, 68601 • 402-564-1668 • Jct SR-15 & US-30 (E of town) go W on US-30 for 14.3 miles
★		✓			Crete • 1800 E 29th St, 68333 • 402-826-1002 • I-80 Exit 388 follow SR-103 S 12.2 miles then go W .6 mile on SR-33/SR-103
★		✓			Fairbury • 2831 Hwy 15, 68352 • 402-729-3394 • 1.5 miles north of town along SR-15
★		✓			Fremont • 3010 E 23rd St, 68025 • 402-727-0414 • Jct US-275 & US-30 BR (E of town) take US-30 BR W 1 mile, Luther Rd S .9 mile, Peterson Ave W .1 mile & 10th St W .3 mile
★	7	✓			Grand Island • 3501 S Locust St, 68801 • 308-381-4970 • I-80 Exit 312 follow US-281 N 4.7 miles then US-34 E 2 miles & Locust St S .1 mile
★	9	✓			Grand Island • 2250 N Diers Ave, 68803 • 308-381-0333 • I-80 Exit 312 follow US-281 N 8.8 miles then Capitol Ave W & Diers Ave S .1 mile
★	1	✓			Gretna • 11350 Wickersham Blvd, 68028 • 402-881-3530 • I-80 Exit 439, west of exit
★		✓			Hastings • 3803 Osborne Dr W, 68901 • 402-462-6000 • I-80 Exit 312 take US-281 S 13.9 miles then 42nd St W & Osborne Dr S .2 mile
★	5	✓			Kearney • 5411 2nd Ave, 68847 • 308-234-8448 • I-80 Exit 272 follow SR-44 N 4.1 miles
★	1	✓			Lexington • 200 Frontier St, 68850 • 308-324-7427 • I-80 Exit 237 go N .4 mile on US-283
★	5	✓			Lincoln • 3400 N 85th St, 68507 • 402-466-0447 • I-80 Exit 409 go SW 2.4 miles on US-6 then S 2.1 miles on 84th St
★	9	✓		✓	Lincoln • 2501 Grainger Pkwy, 68512 • 402-975-6171 • I-80 Exit 397 go S 4.8 miles on US-77; E 2.1 miles on Old Cheney Rd; S 1.9 miles on 27th St
★	2	✓			Lincoln • 4700 N 27th St, 68521 • 402-438-4377 • I-80 Exit 403 take 27th St S 1.8 miles

☆	🛡	🕐	⛽	🚭	Store Details
★		✓			Lincoln • 8700 Andermatt Dr, 68526 • 402-484-6166 • I-80 Exit 397 take US-77 S 2.5 miles, SR-2 SE 8.2 miles & 87th St NE .1 mile
★		✓			McCook • 1902 West B St, 69001 • 308-345-1800 • 1 mile west of town on US-6/US-34
★	6	✓			Nebraska City • 2101 S 11th St, 68410 • 402-874-9080 • I-29 Exit 10 follow SR-2 W 5.1 miles then 11th St N .8 mile
★		✓			Norfolk • 2400 W Pasewalk Ave, 68701 • 402-371-5452 • Jct US-21 & US-275 (S of town) take US-275 W .9 mile then S on Pasewalk Ave .2 mile
★	1	✓			North Platte • 1401 S Dewey St, 69101 • 308-532-5529 • I-80 Exit 177 take US-83 N .5 mile
★	1	✓	◆		Ogallala • 201 Pony Express Ln, 69153 • 308-284-0143 • I-80 Exit 126, south of exit
★	5				Omaha • 5018 Ames Ave, 68104 • 402-970-9301 • I-490 Exit 6 go SE 2 miles on Blair High Rd; contine SE 1 mile on Military Ave; go N .1 mile on 72nd St; E 1.7 miles on Ames Ave
★	6	✓			Omaha • 16960 W Maple Rd, 68116 • 402-289-9238 • I-680 Exit 4 take Maple Rd W 5.6 miles
★	2	✓			Omaha • 1606 S 72nd St, 68124 • 402-393-9560 • I-80 Exit 449 go N 1.4 miles on 72nd St
★	7	✓			Omaha • 18201 Wright St, 68130 • 402-330-4400 • I-80 Exit 445 follow US-275 W 6.8 miles then S on 183rd St & E on Wright St
★	5				Omaha • 5018 Ames Ave, 68104 • 402-970-9301 • I-490 Exit 6 go SE 2 miles on Blair High Rd; contine SE 1 mile on Military Ave; go N .1 mile on 72nd St; E 1.7 miles on Ames Ave
★	1	✓			Omaha • 6304 N 99th St, 68134 • 402-492-9344 • I-680 Exit 6 take SR-133 E .2 mile then 99th St S .3 mile
★	3	✓			Omaha • 12850 L St, 68137 • 402-697-1054 • I-80 Exit 446 take SR-92/L St W 3 miles
★	5	✓			Papillion • 8525 S 71st St Plaza, 68132 • 402-597-8977 • I-80 Exit 449 take 72nd St S 4.2 miles
★		✓			Scottsbluff • 3322 Avenue I, 69361 • 308-632-2666 • 1.9 miles northwest of town center near US-26/SR-71 jct
★	4	✓			Seward • 1326 280th, 68434 • 402-643-6631 • I-80 Exit 379 take SR-15 N 3.9 miles
★	1	✓			Sidney • 3001 Silverberg Dr, 69162 • 308-254-9138 • I-80 Exit 59 follow I-80 BR W .3 mile then E at Old Post Rd

☆	♡	🕐	⛽	🚫	Store Details
✪	2	✓			South Sioux City • 1601 Cornhusker Dr, 68776 • 402-494-8858 • I-129 Exit 1B merge onto US-77 N 1.4 miles & W on 25th St
✪	1	✓			York • 101 E David Dr, 68467 • 402-362-3366 • I-80 Exit 353 take US-81 N .5 mile

Nevada

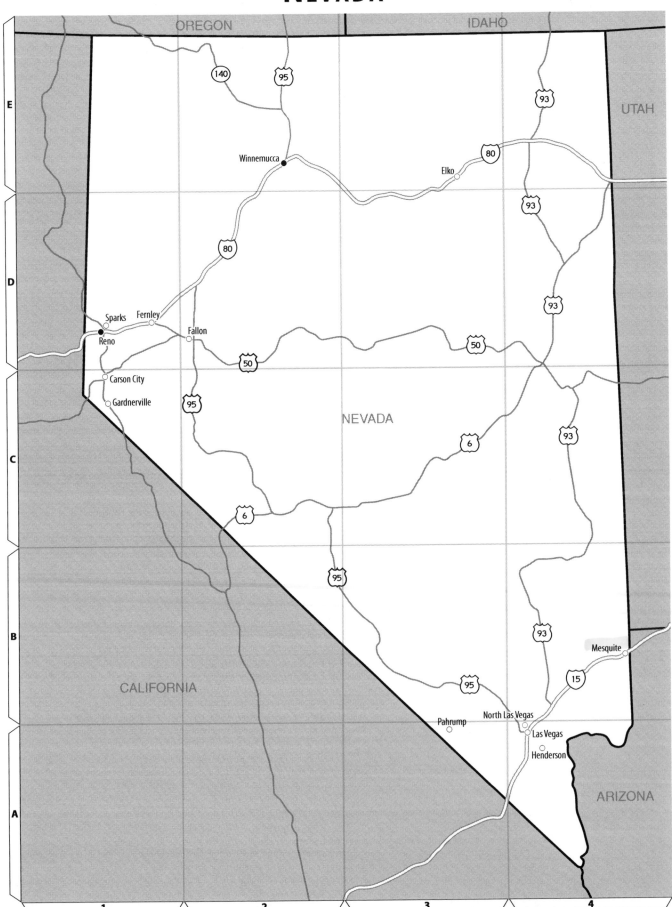

☆	🍎	🕐	⛽	🚫⛽	Store Details
✪		✓			Carson City • 3770 US Hwy 395 S, 89705 • 775-267-2158 • Jct US-50 & US-395 (in town) go S on US-395 for 5.3 miles
✪		✓		✓	Carson City • 3200 Market St, 89706 • 775-883-6415 • US-395 Exit 41 go W .1 mile on College Pkwy
✪	1	✓			Elko • 2944 Mountain City Hwy, 89801 • 775-778-6778 • I-80 Exit 301 take SR-225 N .4 mile
✪		✓			Fallon • 2333 Reno Hwy, 89406 • 775-428-1700 • Jct US-95 & US-50 (in town) go W on US-50 for 1.7 miles
✪	1	✓			Fernley • 1550 Newlands Dr E, 89408 • 775-575-4832 • I-80 Exit 48, south of exit
✪		✓			Gardnerville • 1511 Grant St, 89410 • 775-552-3436 • 2 miles southeast of town along US-395
✪	1	✓		✓	Henderson • 540 Marks St, 89014 • 702-547-0551 • I-515 Exit 64 take Sunset Rd W .3 mile then Marks St S .2 mile
✪	2	✓		✓	Henderson • 300 E Lake Mead Pkwy, 89015 • 702-564-3665 • I-515 Exit 61 take SR-564 E for 2 miles
✪	3	✓		✓	Las Vegas • 4505 W Charleston Blvd, 89102 • 702-258-4540 • I-15 Exit 41 take Charleston Blvd W 2.3 miles
✪	5	✓		✓	Las Vegas • 3615 S Rainbow Blvd, 89103 • 702-367-9999 • I-15 Exit 38A take Flamingo Rd W 3.3 miles & Rainbow Blvd N .8 mile
☆					Las Vegas • 3041 N Rainbow Blvd, 89108 • 702-656-0199 • US-95 Exit 83 take Cheyenne Ave E .2 mile & Rainbow Blvd S .2 mile
☆	3			✓	Las Vegas • 201 N Nellis Blvd, 89110 • 702-452-9998 • I-515 Exit 72 take Charleston Blvd E 1.7 miles & Nellis Blvd N .5 mile
✪	3	✓			Las Vegas • 7200 Arroyo Crossing Pkwy, 89113 • 702-270-6003 • I-15 Exit 34 go W 2.6 miles on SR-215 (Bruce Woodbury Belt) to Exit 15 then S .4 mile
✪	4	✓		✓	Las Vegas • 6005 S Eastern Ave, 89119 • 702-451-8900 • I-515 Exit 68 go W on Tropicana 2 miles & S on Eastern Ave 1.3 miles
✪	4	✓		✓	Las Vegas • 3075 E Tropicana Ave, 89121 • 702-433-4267 • I-15 Exit 37 go E 4 miles on Tropicana Ave
✪	3	✓		✓	Las Vegas • 5198 Boulder Hwy, 89122 • 702-434-5595 • I-515 Exit 70 go S on Boulder Hwy 2.5 miles
✪	1	✓		✓	Las Vegas • 2310 E Serene Ave, 89123 • 702-270-7831 • I-215 Exit 7 take Eastern Ave SE .2 mile & Serene Ave S
✪	1	✓			Las Vegas • 6464 N Decatur Blvd, 89131 • 702-515-7050 • I-215 Exit 13 take Decatur Blvd N .4 mile
✪		✓		✓	Las Vegas • 5200 S Fort Apache Rd, 89148 • 702-367-4001 • US-95 Exit 90 take Ann Rd W 2.5 miles then S on Ft Apache Rd .5 mile
✪	5	✓		✓	Las Vegas • 8060 W Tropical Pkwy, 89149 • 702-839-3620 • I-15 Exit 37 go W on Tropicana 4.8 miles
✪	1	✓			Mesquite • 1120 W Pioneer Blvd, 89027 • 702-346-0208 • I-15 Exit 120, west of exit
✪	4	✓			North Las Vegas • 1807 W Craig Rd, 89032 • 702-633-6521 • I-15 Exit 48 take Craig Rd W 3.7 miles
✪	3	✓			North Las Vegas • 3950 W Lake Mead Blvd, 89032 • 702-631-0421 • I-15 Exit 45 follow Lake Mead Blvd W 3 miles
✪		✓			Pahrump • 300 S Hwy 160, 89048 • 775-537-1400 • Jct SR-372 & SR-160 (in town) go N on SR-160 for .4 mile
✪	1	✓			Reno • 2425 E 2nd St, 89502 • 775-359-8200 • I-580 Exit 67, east of exit
✪	7	✓		✓	Reno • 250 Vista Knoll Pkwy, 89506 • 775-332-0308 • I-80 Exit 15 go N 6.4 miles on US-395
✪		✓			Reno • 4855 Kietzke Lane, 89509 • 775-829-8088 • US-395 Exit 64 go W .2 mile on Moana Ln, S 1 mile on Kietzke Ln, W .1 mile on Redfield Pkwy
✪	9	✓	❖	✓	Reno • 155 Damonte Ranch Pkwy, 89521 • 775-853-6400 • I-80 Exit 15 take US-395 S 8.8 miles to Exit 59-Damonte Pkwy W .2 mile
✪	1	✓			Reno • 5260 W 7th St, 89523 • 775-624-2000 • I-80 Exit 10 go N .9 mile on McCarran Blvd then .1 mile on 7th St
✪	3	✓		✓	Sparks • 5065 Pyramid Way, 89436 • 775-425-9300 • I-80 Exit 18 go N on Pyramid Way 2.9 miles
✪	1	✓	◆		Winnemucca • 3010 Potato Rd, 89445 • 775-625-3777 • I-80 Exit 176 take I-80 BR/W Winnemucca Blvd .4 mile & follow Potato Rd E .5 mile

New Hampshire

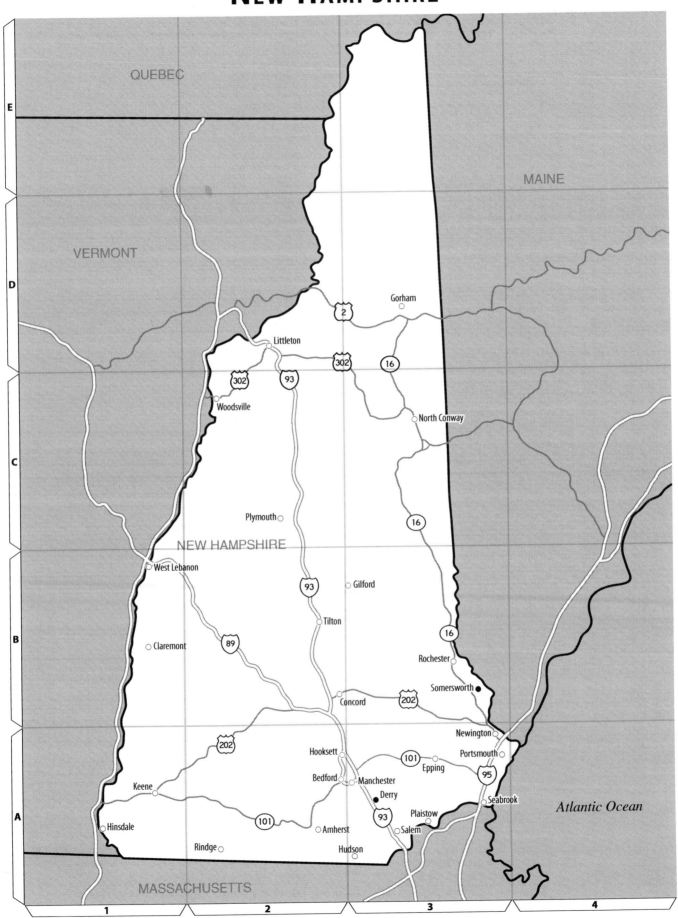

QUEBEC

MAINE

VERMONT

E

D

Gorham

Littleton

302   16

302   93

Woodsville

North Conway

C

NEW HAMPSHIRE

Plymouth

16

West Lebanon

93   Gilford

Tilton

B   89

Claremont

16

Rochester

Somersworth

Concord   202

Newington

202

Hooksett   101   Portsmouth

Epping

Bedford   Manchester   95

Keene   Derry

A   Plaistow

Hinsdale   101   93   Atlantic Ocean

Amherst   Salem   Seabrook

Rindge   Hudson

MASSACHUSETTS

1   2   3   4

☆	🍎	🕐	⛽	🚫	Store Details
❂	5	✓		✓	Amherst • 85 NH Hwy 101A, 03031 • 603-672-3421 • I-293 Exit 8 go W on Southwood Dr .1 mile then follow SR-101A W 4.5 miles
☆	1				Bedford • 17 Colby Ct, 03110 • 603-626-6733 • I-293 Exit 4 follow US-3 S .6 mile then W on Colby Ct
❂	6	✓			Claremont • 14 Bowen St, 03743 • 603-542-2703 • I-91 Exit 8 (in VT) go E on SR-12 3.7 miles, North St S 1.2 miles & SR-11 E .4 mile
❂	2	✓		✓	Concord • 344 Loudon Rd, 03301 • 603-226-9312 • I-393 Exit 2 take Eastside Dr E .4 mile & Louden Rd N 1.5 miles
❂	3		◆		Derry • 11 Ashleigh Dr, 03038 • 603-434-3589 • I-93 Exit 5 follow SR-28 S 2.6 miles
❂		✓			Epping • 35 Fresh River Rd, 03042 • 603-679-5919 • SR-101 Exit 7 take SR-125 N .4 mile then E at Fresh River Rd .2 mile
❂				✓	Gilford • 1458 Lake Shore Rd, 03249 • 603-528-8011 • I-93 Exit 20 follow US-3 NE 12.8 miles
❂		✓			Gorham • 561 Main St, 03581 • 603-752-4621 • 3.3 miles north of town center via US-2/SR-16
❂				✓	Hinsdale • 724 Brattleboro Rd, 03451 • 603-336-5538 • 3.5 miles northwest of town center via SR-119
❂	1			✓	Hooksett • 3 Commerce Dr, 03106 • 603-644-8144 • I-93 Exit 10 go W .5 mile on SR-3A
☆				✓	Hudson • 254 Lowell Rd, 03051 • 603-598-4226 • From Everett Tpk Exit 2 go E 1 mile to SR-3A then S .2 mile on Lowell Rd (SR-3A)
☆				✓	Keene • 350 Winchester St, 03431 • 603-357-7200 • Jct US-12 & SR-101 (S of town) follow SR-12/101 W .8 mile & N on Winchester St
☆	1				Littleton • 615 Meadow St, 03561 • 603-444-6300 • I-93 Exit 42 merge onto US-302 W .2 mile
☆	1				Manchester • 300 Keller St, 03103 • 603-621-9666 • I-293 Exit 1 take SR-28 S .2 mile & W on Auto Center Rd .1 mile
☆	2				Newington • 2200 Woodbury Ave, 03801 • 603-430-9985 • I-95 Exit 7 take Market St W .7 mile, continue W on Woodbury Ave 1.3 miles
❂				✓	North Conway • 46 N South Rd, 03860 • 603-356-0130 • About 3 miles south of town center along US-302
☆	3				Plaistow • 58 Plaistow Rd, 03865 • 603-382-2839 • I-495 Exit 51B (in MA) go N on SR-125 for 2.1 miles

☆	🍎	🕐	⛽	🚫	Store Details
❂	3	✓			Plymouth • 683 Tenney Mountain Hwy, 03264 • 603-536-5352 • I-93 Exit 26 merge onto SR-3A W 3 miles
❂	4				Portsmouth • 2460 Lafayette Rd, 03801 • 603-433-6008 • I-95 Exit 5 take SR-16 S .6 mile then follow US-1 BYP S for 3.1 miles
☆					Rindge • 750 US Hwy 202, 03461 • 603-899-6882 • Jct SR-119 & US-202 (in West Rindge) go S on US-202 for .6 mile
❂					Rochester • 116 Farmington Rd, 03867 • 603-332-4300 • From US-202 (toll) Exit 15 (N of town) go N on SR-11 for 1.4 miles
❂	2	✓		✓	Salem • 326 N Broadway, 03079 • 603-894-5642 • I-93 Exit 3 follow SR-111 E for 1.4 miles then S on Broadway .4 mile
❂	1				Seabrook • 700 Lafayette Rd, 03874 • 603-474-2037 • I-95 Exit 1 go E .5 mile on SR-107
❂		✓	◆		Somersworth • 59 Waltons Way, 03878 • 603-692-6346 • Spaulding Tpk (toll) Exit 9 go E on Indian Brook Dr .6 mile then continue on SR-9 for .7 mile
❂	1			✓	Tilton • 33 Sherwood Dr, 03276 • 603-286-7673 • I-93 Exit 20, west of exit
☆	1				West Lebanon • 285 Plainfield Rd, 03784 • 603-298-5014 • I-89 Exit 20 take SR-12A S .5 mile
❂	5	✓			Woodsville • 4901 Dartmouth College Hwy, 03785 • 603-747-8250 • I-91 Exit 17 (in Vermont) follow US-302 E 4.3 miles then SR-10 S .1 mile

New Jersey

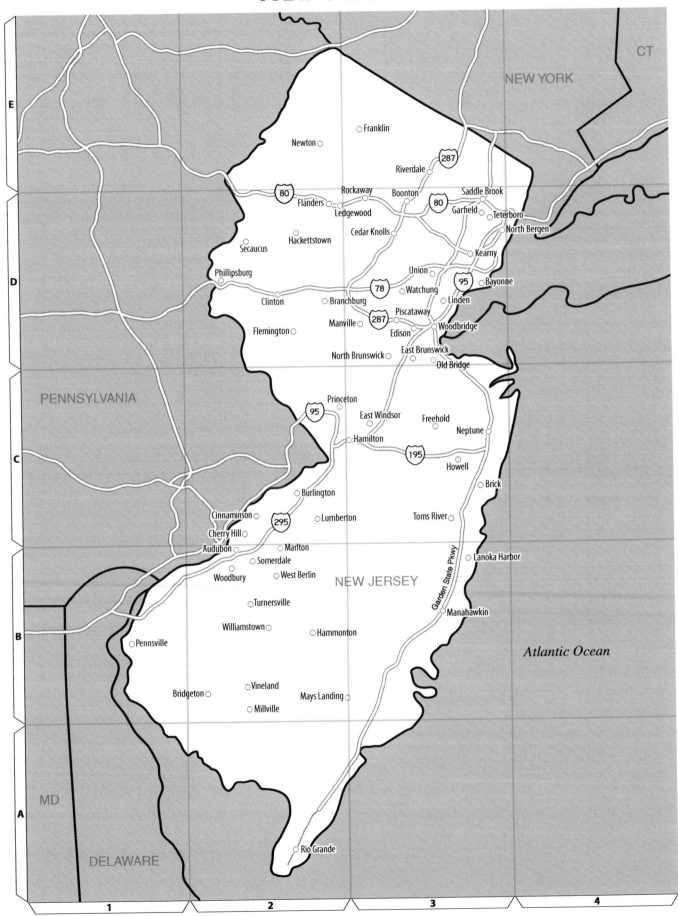

CT

NEW YORK

E

Franklin

Newton

Riverdale

287

80

Rockaway

Boonton

Saddle Brook

Flanders

80

Ledgewood

Garfield

Teterboro

North Bergen

Cedar Knolls

Kearny

D

Hackettstown

Secaucus

Union

95

Bayonne

Phillipsburg

78

Watchung

Linden

Clinton

Branchburg

Piscataway

Manville

287

Woodbridge

Flemington

Edison

East Brunswick

North Brunswick

Old Bridge

PENNSYLVANIA

Princeton

95

East Windsor

Freehold

Hamilton

Neptune

C

195

Howell

Burlington

Brick

Cinnaminson

Lumberton

Toms River

295

Cherry Hill

Lanoka Harbor

Audubon

Marlton

Somerdale

West Berlin

NEW JERSEY

Woodbury

Garden State Pkwy

Turnersville

Manahawkin

B

Williamstown

Hammonton

Atlantic Ocean

Pennsville

MD

Bridgeton

Vineland

Mays Landing

Millville

A

DELAWARE

Rio Grande

1   2   3   4

☆	◯	🕐	⛽	🚫	Store Details
☆	2				Audubon • 130 Black Horse Pike, 08106 • 856-310-1470 • I-295 Exit 28 go N 1.3 miles on Black Horse Pike (or 2 miles north of NJ Tpk Exit 3)
●	2	✓			Bayonne • 500 Bayonne Crossing Way, 07002 • 201-620-6137 • I-78 Exit 14A go S 1.2 miles on Avenue E; E .1 mile on 32nd St; S .2 mile on SR-440; E .4 mile on New Hook Rd
☆	1				Boonton • 300 Wootton St, 07005 • 973-299-3943 • I-287 Exit 45 merge onto Park Ave W .1 mile then Wootton St W .4 mile
☆	5				Branchburg • 3576 US Hwy 22, 08889 • 908-534-7377 • I-78 Exit 24 take CR-523/Oldwick Rd S 2.1 miles & US-22 E 2.2 mile
☆					Brick • 1872 Rt 88, 08724 • 732-840-7772 • Garden State Pkwy Exit 88 take SR-70 E 2.5 miles & SR-88 NE .4 mile
☆					Bridgeton • 1130 Hwy 77, 08302 • 856-453-0418 • From SR-55 Exit 32B follow SR-56 W 7.8 miles then SR-77 S 1 mile
●	1	✓			Burlington • 2106 Mount Holly Rd, 08016 • 609-386-8400 • I-295 Exit 47B go NW .4 mile on Mount Holly Rd
☆	2			✓	Cedar Knolls • 235 Ridgedale Ave, 07927 • 973-889-8646 • I-287 Exit 36B merge onto Lafayette Rd W .4 mile & Ridgedale Ave N 1.3 miles
☆					Cherry Hill • 500 Rt 38, 08002 • 856-665-5430 • New Jersey Tpk (toll) Exit 4 merge onto SR-73 N 1.9 miles then SR-38 W 4.2 miles
☆	6				Cinnaminson • 2501 Rt 130 S, 08077 • 856-303-2119 • I-295 Exit 43 take Creek Rd W 3.6 miles, Bridgeboro St N .4 mile & US-130 S 1.4 miles
☆	1			✓	Clinton • 1 Walmart Plaza, 08809 • 908-730-8665 • I-78 Exit 15 take CR-513 S .1 mile then E on Frontage Dr and immediate right
●	2	✓		✓	East Brunswick • 290 State Rt 18, 08816 • 732-387-1059 • About 1.5 miles southeast of I-95 Exit 9 via SR-18 and Old Bridge Turnpike
☆					East Windsor • 839 US Hwy 130, 08520 • 609-443-6159 • New Jersey Tpk (toll) Exit 8 take SR-33 W .9 mile, Main St S .1 mile, Stockton St W .8 mile & US-130 S .9 mile
☆	1			✓	Edison • 2220 State Hwy 27, 08818 • 732-650-1297 • I-287 Exit 2b (northbound travelers only), west of exit. Southbound travelers use I-287 Exit 3 and go W .3 mile on Durham Rd; turn left at Talmadge Rd 1.3 miles; turn left at Route 27 .5 mile.

☆	◯	🕐	⛽	🚫	Store Details
☆	1				Flanders • 40 International Dr S, 07836 • 973-347-7400 • I-80 Exit 27 take US-206 S .3 mile then Int'l Dr W .5 mile
●	9			✓	Flemington • 150 State Hwy 31, 08822 • 908-788-6769 • I-78 Exit 17 follow SR-31 S 8.3 miles
☆					Franklin • 230 State Hwy 23, 07416 • 973-209-4242 • Jct CR-631/Franklin Ave & SR-23 (E of town) go N on SR-23 for .7 mile
●	9	✓			Freehold • 326 W Main St, 07728 • 732-780-3048 • I-195 Exit 16B follow Monmouth Rd/CR-537 NE 8.7 miles
●	3	✓			Garfield • 174 Passaic St, 07026 • 973-330-3550 • I-80 Exit 63 go N 300 feet on Riverview Ave, W .2 mile on Essex St, S 1.7 miles on Main St, then continue S .7 mile on Passaic Ave
●	8	✓			Hackettstown • 1885 State Route 57, 07840 • 908-979-9342 • I-80 Exit 19 follow CR-517 S 6 miles then SR-57 S 1.8 miles
☆	2				Hamilton • 700 Marketplace Blvd, 08691 • 609-585-1463 • I-195 Exit 5A take US-130 S 1.2 miles, Crosswicks Rd E .2 mile & Marketplace Blvd N .6 mile
☆					Hammonton • 55 S White Horse Pike, 08037 • 609-567-2700 • Atlantic City Expy Exit 28 take SR-54 N 3.2 miles & US-30 E .1 mile
☆	3				Howell • 4900 US Hwy 9, 07731 • 732-886-9100 • I-195 Exit 28A merge onto US-9 S 2.4 miles
●	1	✓			Kearny • 150 Harrison Ave, 07032 • 201-955-0280 • I-280 Exit 17B, west of exit
●		✓			Lanoka Harbor • 580 US Hwy 9, 08743 • 609-242-4231 • Garden State Parkway Exit 74 go E .8 mile on Lacey Rd, N .6 mile on Manchester Ave, E 1 mile on Haines Rd
☆	2				Ledgewood • 461 State Rt 10 Ledgewood Mall #29, 07852 • 973-252-7666 • I-80 Exit 28 take CR-631 S .2 mile then US-46 E .9 mile & SR-10 E .2 mile
☆					Linden • 1601 W Edgar Rd, 07036 • 908-474-9055 • Garden State Pkwy Exit 135 follow CR-613 E 2.7 miles, Grand Ave E .1 mile & US-1 N .6 mile
☆					Lumberton • 1740 Rt 38, 08048 • 609-702-9200 • New Jersey Tpk (toll) Exit 5 follow CR-541 S 3.8 miles then SR-38 E 2.1 miles
☆					Manahawkin • 525 Rt 72 W, 08050 • 609-978-8300 • Garden State Pkwy Exit 63 follow SR-72 E 1.9 miles
●	3			✓	Manville • 100 N Main St, 08835 • 908-575-8997 • I-287 Exit 13 go W 1 mile on SR-28 then S 1.7 miles on Finderne Ave/Main St; northbound travelers use Exit 13B

☆	⬡	🕐	⛽	🚫	Store Details
☆					Marlton • 150 E Rt 70, 08053 • 856-983-2100 • New Jersey Tpk (toll) Exit 4 take SR-70 E 1 mile
☆					Mays Landing • 4620 Black Horse Pike, 08330 • 609-625-8200 • Atlantic City Expy Exit 17 take SR-50 S 2.8 miles then US-322 E 3.4 miles
☆					Millville • 2291 N 2nd St, 08332 • 856-825-4200 • From SR-55 Exit 27 take SR-47 S .4 mile
✪		✓			Neptune • 3575 State Hwy 66, 07753 • 732-922-8084 • Garden State Pkwy (toll) Exit 100A take SR-66 E .6 mile
☆					Newton • 26 Hampton House Rd, 07860 • 973-300-1859 • I-80 Exit 34B take SR-15 N 15.2 miles then SW on SR-94 for 3.6 miles
✪	3	✓		✓	North Bergen • 2100 88th St, 07047 • 201-758-2810 • I-95 at US-46, follow US-46 E for .5 mile then go S on US-1 for 2.5 miles
☆					North Brunswick • 979 Route 1 S, 08902 • 732-545-4499 • New Jersey Tpk (toll) Exit 9 take US-1 S 2.8 miles
☆				✓	Old Bridge • 1126 US Hwy 9, 08857 • 732-525-8030 • Garden State Pkwy (toll) Exit 123 take US-9 S 4.8 miles
✪	9	✓			Old Bridge • 2825 Route 18, 08857 • 732-955-0139 • I-95 Exit 9 go SE for 8.7 miles on SR-18 to Spring Valley Rd
☆	5				Pennsville • 709 S Broadway, 08070 • 856-935-8200 • I-295 Exit 1C go S on N Hood Rd 4.4 miles then S on Broadway .1 mile
✪	1	✓		✓	Phillipsburg • 1300 US Hwy 22, 08865 • 908-454-3622 • I-78 Exit 3, north of exit
☆	1				Piscataway • 1303 Centennial Ave, 08854 • 732-562-1771 • I-287 Exit 5 go S on Stelton Rd .2 mile & W on Centennial Ave .5 mile
☆	3				Princeton • 101 Nassau Park Blvd, 08540 • 609-987-0202 • I-95 Exit 67 take US-1 N 2.1 miles, Quakerbridge Rd W .4 mile & Nassau Park Blvd N .5 mile
☆					Rio Grande • 3159 Route 9 S, 08242 • 609-465-2204 • From Garden State Pkwy Exit 4 go W on Delsea Dr .6 mile then N on US-9 .5 mile
☆	1				Riverdale • 48 State Hwy 23, 07457 • 973-835-5812 • I-287 Exit 52A take SR-23 S .5 mile
☆	2				Rockaway • 220 Enterprise Dr, 07866 • 973-361-6089 • I-80 Exit 35 take Mt Hope Ave S .5 mile, Mt Pleasant Ave W .9 mile & Enterprise Ave N .4 mile

☆	⬡	🕐	⛽	🚫	Store Details
☆	2			✓	Saddle Brook • 189 US Hwy 46, 07663 • 201-226-0575 • I-80 Exit 62B take Railroad Ave E .2 mile, Rochelle Ave & Main St S .7 mile, Outwater Ln W .5 mile & US-46 W .4 mile
✪	2	✓		✓	Secaucus • 400 Park Pl, 07094 • 201-325-9280 • Northbound I-95 travelers use Exit 16E and follow signs for SR-3/Secaucus to Harmon Meadow Blvd, 1.2 miles. Southbound travelers use Exit 17 and follow signs for SR-3/Secaucus to Harmon Meadow Blvd, 1.7 miles.
✪	2	✓			Somerdale • 1 Coopertown Blvd, 08083 • 856-545-9052 • I-295 Exit 29 follow US-30 E 1.8 miles
✪	3	✓			Teterboro • 1 Teterboro Landing Dr, 07608 • 201-375-4002 • I-95 at US-46, go W 2.4 miles on US-46 and turn left onto Industrial Ave
☆				✓	Toms River • 950 Rt 37 W, 08755 • 732-349-6000 • Garden State Pkwy (toll) Exit 82A follow SR-97 W 4.6 miles
✪	9	✓			Turnersville • 3501 Rt 42, 08012 • 856-629-3888 • Jct I-295 & I-76 take I-76 S 1.3 miles, continue S on SR-42 for 7 miles
☆					Union • 900 Springfield Rd, 07083 • 908-624-0644 • Garden State Pkwy (toll) Exit 140A follow US-22 W 2.6 miles
✪		✓			Vineland • 1070 W Landis Ave, 08360 • 856-205-9940 • 1 mile west of town center
☆	3			✓	Watchung • 1501 US Hwy 22, 07069 • 908-756-1925 • I-78 Exit 41 take Plainfield Ave E .9 mile, Bonnie Burn Rd E 1 mile then US-22 S .8 mile
☆					West Berlin • 265 N Rt 73, 08091 • 856-753-8787 • New Jersey Tpk (toll) Exit 4 take SR-73 S for 9.8 miles
✪		✓			Williamstown • 1840 S Black Horse Pike, 08094 • 856-629-2054 • 2.5 miles southeast of town center along US-322
☆					Woodbridge • 306 US Hwy 9 N, 07095 • 732-826-4652 • Jct SR-440 & US-9 (S of town) take US-9 N 1.5 miles
✪	3				Woodbury • 2000 Clements Bridge Rd, 08096 • 856-384-3211 • I-295 Exit 28 go S 1.7 miles on SR-168 then W 1.1 mile on Clements Bridge Rd
✪		✓			Woodbury • 820 Cooper St, 08096 • 856-686-0133 • 1.5 miles southeast of town center

NEW MEXICO

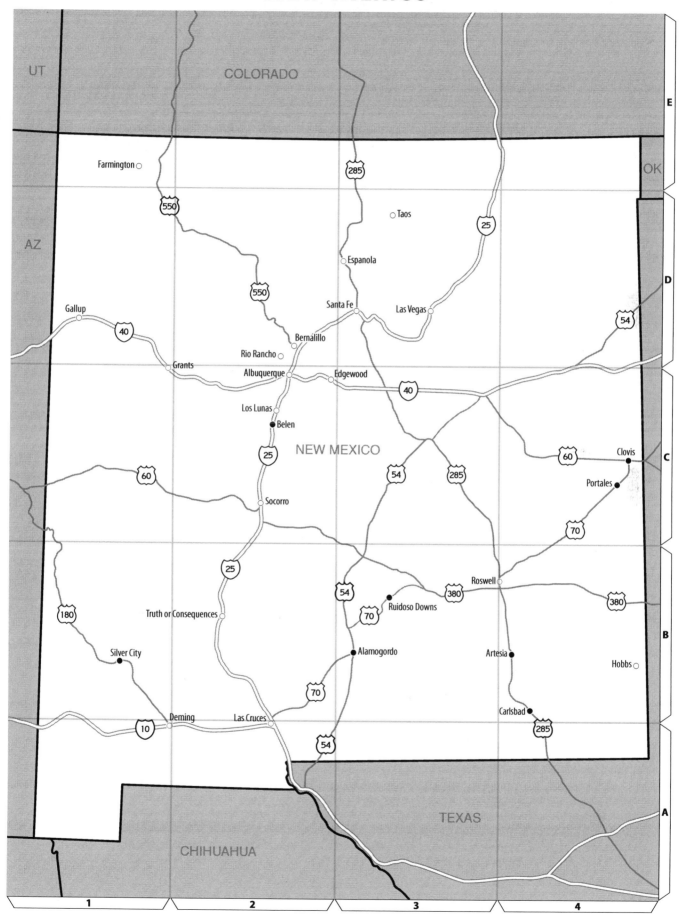

☆	🛡	🕐	⛽	🚫	Store Details
✪		✓	◆		Alamogordo • 233 S New York Ave, 88310 • 575-434-5870 • Jct US-54 & US-70 (S of town) go N on US-54/70/82 for 1.4 miles then E on New York Ave .2 mile
✪	2	✓			Albuquerque • 301 San Mateo Blvd SE, 87108 • 505-268-6611 • I-40 Exit 161A go S on San Mateo Blvd 1.8 miles
✪	1	✓			Albuquerque • 2701 Carlisle Blvd NE, 87110 • 505-884-6650 • I-40 Exit 160 go N on Carlisle Blvd .6 mile
✪	3	✓			Albuquerque • 8000 Academy Rd NE, 87111 • 505-856-5274 • I-25 Exit 230 go SE on San Mateo Blvd .3 mile then E on Academy Rd 1.9 miles
✪	2	✓		✓	Albuquerque • 2266 Wyoming Blvd NE, 87112 • 505-323-4131 • I-40 Exit 164 go N 1.2 miles on Wyoming Blvd
✪	8	✓			Albuquerque • 10224 Coors Byp NW, 87114 • 505-897-1228 • I-40 Exit 155 follow Coors Blvd NW 7.9 miles
✪	1	✓			Albuquerque • 2550 Coors Blvd NW, 87120 • 505-352-1870 • I-40 Exit 155, north of exit
✪	5	✓			Albuquerque • 3500 Coors Blvd SW, 87121 • 505-877-2254 • I-25 Exit 220 go W on Rio Bravo 4 miles
✪	1	✓			Albuquerque • 400 Eubank Blvd NE, 87123 • 505-293-8878 • I-40 Exit 165 go S on Eubank Blvd .5 mile
✪		✓	❖		Artesia • 604 N 26th St, 88210 • 575-746-2184 • Jct US-285 & US-82 (in town) take US-82 W 1.9 miles & 26th St N .3 mile
✪	2	✓	◆		Belen • 1 I-25 Bypass, 87002 • 505-864-9114 • I-25 Exit 195 take I-25-BR E 1.4 miles
✪	3	✓			Bernalillo • 460 NM Hwy 528, 87004 • 505-771-4867 • I-25 Exit 242 follow US-550 W 2.4 miles then SR-528 S .6 mile
✪		✓	◆		Carlsbad • 2401 S Canal St, 88220 • 575-885-0727 • Jct US-285 & US-180 (S of town) go N on US-285/Pecos Hwy 3.5 miles
✪		✓	◆		Clovis • 3728 N Prince St, 88101 • 575-769-2261 • Jct US-60/70/84 & SR-209/Prince St (in town) go N on Prince St 2.6 miles
✪	1	✓			Deming • 1021 E Pine St, 88030 • 575-546-6045 • I-10 Exit 82A go S .1 mile on Pearl St then E .4 mile on Pine St
✪	1	✓			Edgewood • 66 State Road 344, 87015 • 505-286-3043 • I-40 Exit 187 take SR-344 N .5 mile
✪		✓			Espanola • 1610 N Riverside Dr, 87532 • 505-747-0414 • Jct US-285/84 & SR-68 (in town) take SR-68/N Riverside Dr for 1.8 miles

☆	🛡	🕐	⛽	🚫	Store Details
✪		✓			Farmington • 1400 W Main St, 87401 • 505-327-1243 • Jct SR-170 & US-64 (W of town) follow US-64 E 2 miles
✪		✓			Farmington • 4600 E Main St, 87402 • 505-326-1100 • Jct US-64 & SR-516 (E of town) follow SR-516 N 3 miles
✪	1	✓			Gallup • 1650 W Maloney Ave, 87301 • 505-722-2296 • I-40 Exit 20 take US-491 N .1 mile then W on Maloney Ave
✪	2	✓			Grants • 1000 Robert Rd, 87020 • 505-285-3350 • I-40 Exit 85 take I-40 BR W .8 mile & W on Robertas Rd .6 mile
✪		✓			Hobbs • 3800 N Lovington Hwy, 88240 • 575-492-0120 • Jct US-180/62 & W County Rd (W of town) follow County Rd N 3.5 miles then SR-18 NW 3.2 miles
✪	1	✓			Las Cruces • 571 Walton Blvd, 88001 • 575-525-1222 • I-25 Exit 3 go W on Lohman Ave .2 mile & N on Walton Blvd
✪	1	✓			Las Cruces • 1550 S Valley Dr, 88005 • 575-523-4924 • I-10 Exit 140 take SR-28 N .4 mile then I-10 BR E .1 mile
✪	2	✓			Las Cruces • 3331 Rinconada Blvd, 88011 • 575-680-3772 • I-25 Exit 6 go E 1.4 miles then S .1 mile on Rinconada Blvd
✪	4	✓			Las Vegas • 2609 7th St, 87701 • 505-425-5242 • I-25 Exit 347 merge onto I-25 BR S 1.3 miles, SR-329/Mills Ave W .7 mile & SR-519/7th St N 1.1 miles
✪	1	✓		✓	Los Lunas • 2250 Main St NW, 87031 • 505-565-4611 • I-25 Exit 203 take SR-6 W .1 mile
✪		✓	◆		Portales • 1604 E Spruce St, 88130 • 575-359-3420 • Jct SR-467 & US-70 (NE of town) continue S on Kilgore Ave .1 mile & W on Spruce St
✪	10	✓			Rio Rancho • 901 Unser Blvd SE, 87124 • 505-962-9227 • I-25 Exit 233 follow SR-528 W 5 miles, Coors Blvd N 2.2 miles, Southern Blvd W 2.3 miles, and Unser Blvd N .2 mile
✪		✓			Roswell • 4500 N Main St, 88201 • 575-623-2062 • 4 miles north of town center via US-285
✪		✓	◆		Ruidoso Downs • 26180 US Hwy 70 E, 88346 • 575-378-8050 • 1.5 miles west of town center on US-70
☆	4			✓	Santa Fe • 3251 Cerrillos Rd, 87507 • 505-474-4727 • I-25 Exit 278B go N 4 miles on SR-14/Cerrillos Rd
✪	1	✓			Santa Fe • 5701 Herrera Dr, 87507 • 505-424-9304 • I-25 Exit 278B go N .4 mile on SR-14/Cerrillos Rd
✪		✓	❖		Silver City • 2501 Hwy 180 E, 88061 • 575-538-2222 • 2.4 miles northeast of town center via SR-90 and US-180

☆	♡	⏰	⛽	🚫	Store Details
✪	3	✓			Socorro • 700 6th St N, 87801 • 575-838-1415 • I-25 Exit 147 take I-25 BR N 2 miles then E at Neal Ave
☆					Taos • 926 Paseo Del Pueblo Sur, 87571 • 575-758-1136 • 2 miles south of town along SR-68
✪	1	✓			Truth or Consequences • 2001 H.R. Ashbaugh Dr, 87901 • 575-894-0343 • I-25 Exit 79, east of exit

NEW YORK

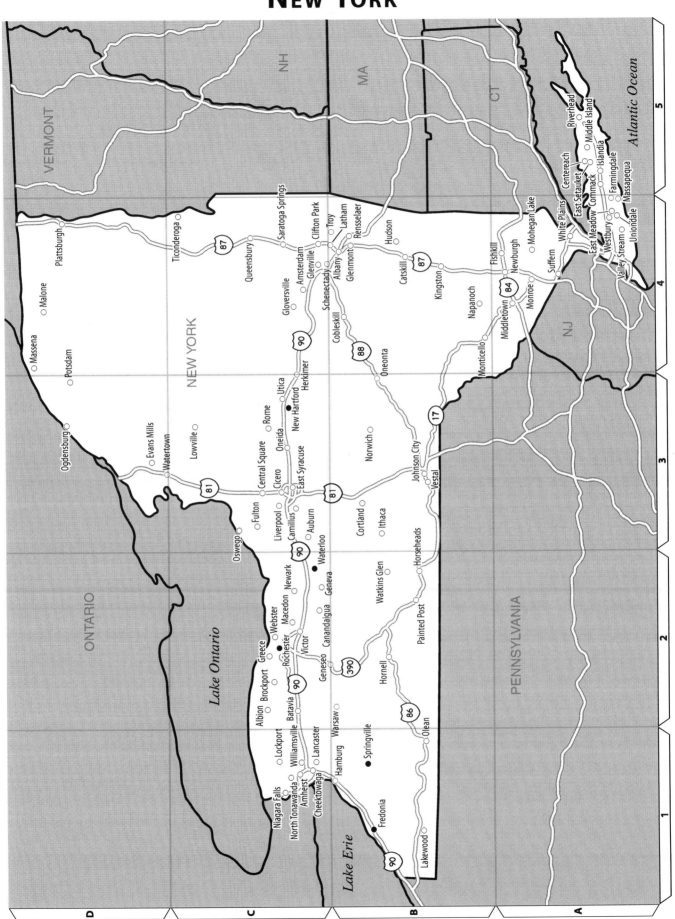

☆	◌	🕐	⛽	🚛	Store Details
✪	2	✓		✓	Albany • 141 Washington Ave Ext, 12205 • 518-869-4694 • Eastbound travelers turn right at I-90 Exit 2 and follow Washington Ave 1.6 miles; Westbound travelers turn left on Fuller Rd from I-90 Exit 2 then right at Washington Ave 1.3 miles
✪		✓			Albion • 13858 State Route 31, 14411 • 585-589-0608 • I-90 Exit 48 take SR-98 N 15.6 miles & SR-31 W 1.7 miles
✪	1	✓			Amherst • 3290 Sheridan Dr, 14226 • 716-691-0195 • I-290 Exit 5A go S .4 mile on SR-263 then W .6 mile on Sheridan Dr/SR-324
✪	3	✓		✓	Amsterdam • 101 Sanford Farms Shpg Ctr, 12010 • 518-843-6890 • I-90/NY State Thruway (toll) Exit 27 take SR-30 N 2.7 miles
✪		✓		✓	Auburn • 297 Grant Ave, 13021 • 315-255-0532 • I-81 Exit 15 take US-20 W 21.3 miles, SR-86 N 1.8 miles, Gates Rd W .9 mile & SR-5 S .4 mile
✪	1	✓			Batavia • 4133 Veterans Memorial Dr, 14020 • 585-345-1050 • I-90 (toll) Exit 48 take Park Rd W .3 mile, continue on Veterans Memorial Dr .3 mile
✪		✓			Brockport • 6265 Brockport Spencerport Rd, 14420 • 585-637-6331 • 1.8 miles southeast of town along SR-31
✪	5	✓		✓	Camillus • 5399 W Genesee St, 13031 • 315-487-0121 • I-690 Exit 6 take SR-695 S 1.9 miles, SR-5 W 1.5 miles, Hinsdale Rd S 1 mile & CR-98 W .5 mile
✪	7				Canandaigua • 4238 Recreation Dr, 14424 • 585-394-5300 • I-90 (toll) Exit 43 take SR-21 S 5.2 miles, CR-22 S .5 mile, CR-4 E .1 mile, CR-10 S 1.7 miles & Recreation Dr E .6 mile
✪	3	✓			Catskill • 30 Catskill Commons, 12414 • 518-943-9423 • I-87 (toll) Exit 21 follow Main St S 1.7 miles then Maple Ave S for .8 miles; continue on Bridge St for .3 miles
☆	4			✓	Centereach • 161 Centereach Mall, 11720 • 631-467-4825 • I-495 Exit 62 take CR-97 N 2.9 miles & SR-25 E .4 mile
✪	1	✓			Central Square • 3018 East Ave, 13036 • 315-668-0400 • I-81 Exit 32 take SR-49 W .2 mile
☆	2				Cheektowaga • 2500 Walden Ave, 14225 • 716-896-3669 • I-90 Exit 52E go E 1.2 miles on Walden Ave
✪	1	✓		✓	Cicero • 8064 Brewerton Rd, 13039 • 315-698-0130 • I-481 Exit 10 take Circle Dr W .1 mile then US-11 N .8 mile
✪	3	✓			Clifton Park • 1549 Route 9, 12065 • 518-373-8457 • I-87 Exit 9E take SR-146 E .6 mile then US-9 S 1.5 miles

☆	◌	🕐	⛽	🚛	Store Details
✪	3	✓			Cobleskill • 139 Merchant Pl, 12043 • 518-234-1090 • I-88 Exit 22 take SR-145 W 2 miles & N on Merchant Pl
☆	1				Commack • 85 Crooked Hill Rd, 11725 • 631-851-0468 • I-495 Exit 52 take Commack Rd/CR-4 N .3 mile, Henry St E .2 mile & Crooked Hill Rd N .2 mile
✪	6	✓		✓	Cortland • 819 Bennie Rd, 13045 • 607-756-1776 • I-81 Exit 12 follow ramp .7 mile to SR-281 then go S 4.5 on SR-281
☆					East Meadow • 2465 Hempstead Tpke, 11554 • 516-579-3307 • From Southern Pkwy Exit 27N merge onto Wantaugh Pkwy N 2.3 miles then SR-24 W .4 mile
☆	6				East Setauket • 3990 Nesconset Hwy, 11733 • 631-474-3287 • I-495 Exit 62 take CR-97 N 4.3 miles, E at Hawkins Rd to Wireless Rd N 1.2 miles then E at Nesconsett Hwy
✪	1	✓		✓	East Syracuse • 6438 Basile Rowe, 13057 • 315-434-9873 • I-690 Exit 17 go N .6 mile on Bridge St/Manlius Center Rd
✪	5	✓		✓	Evans Mills • 25737 US Route 11, 13637 • 315-629-2124 • I-81 Exit 48 take SR-342 E 3.9 miles then US-11 N .4 mile
☆				✓	Farmingdale • 965 Broadhollow Rd, 11735 • 631-752-8768 • From Southern Pkwy Exit 32N go N on Broad Hollow Rd (SR-110) for 1.5 miles
✪	1	✓			Fishkill • 26 W Merritt Blvd, 12524 • 845-896-8192 • I-84 Exit 13 take US-9 N .6 mile then W on Merritt Blvd .3 mile
✪	1	✓	❖		Fredonia • 10401 Bennett Rd, 14063 • 716-679-3150 • I-90 (toll) Exit 59 go S on Bennett Rd .4 mile
✪		✓			Fulton • 1818 State Route 3, 13069 • 315-598-1773 • 2 miles west of town along SR-3 at Hannibal St
✪	4	✓			Geneseo • 4235 Veteran Dr, 14454 • 585-243-4090 • I-390 Exit 8 take US-20A S 3.2 miles, Volunteer Rd W .1 mile & Veteran Dr S .1 mile
✪	9	✓		✓	Geneva • 990 Route 5 & 20, 14456 • 315-781-3253 • I-90 (toll) Exit 42 take SR-14 S 5.8 miles, turn left at Castle St, then right at SR-5/US-20 for 2.5 miles
✪	2	✓			Glenmont • 311 Rt 9 W, 12077 • 518-432-6120 • I-87 (toll) Exit 23 take US-9W S 1.9 miles
✪	3	✓			Glenville • 200 Dutch Meadows Ln, 12302 • 518-344-7035 • I-890 Exit 4C follow SR-5 NW 1 mile, SR-50 N 1 mile & Dutch Meadow Ln E .6 mile
✪					Gloversville • 329 S Kingsboro Ave Ext, 12078 • 518-725-2403 • 1.5 miles south of town center off SR-30A at Kingsboro Ave

☆	🛡	🕐	⛽	🚫	Store Details
✪	7	✓		✓	Greece • 3800 Dewey Ave, 14616 • 585-957-7382 • I-490 Exit 9A go N 4.4 miles on SR-390; E .6 mile on Vintage Ln; E .6 mile on Dorsey Rd; N .6 mile on Dewey Ave
☆	5				Greece • 100 Elm Ridge Center Dr, 14626 • 585-227-0720 • I-490 Exit 8 merge onto SR-531 W .7 mile, SR-386 N 3.9 miles & E at Elm Ridge Center Dr
✪	2	✓		✓	Hamburg • 5360 Southwestern Blvd, 14075 • 716-646-0682 • I-90/NY State Thruway Exit 57 go NW .4 mile on SR-75 then SW .9 mile on US-20/Southwestern Blvd
✪	1	✓			Herkimer • 103 N Caroline St, 13350 • 315-717-0023 • I-90 Exit 30 follow SR-28 N .7 mile
☆	2				Hornell • 1000 NY Hwy 36, 14843 • 607-324-7019 • I-86 Exit 34 merge onto SR-36 S 1.9 miles
✪	2	✓			Horseheads • 1400 County Route 64, 14845 • 607-739-1714 • I-86 Exit 51A go S .2 mile on Chambers Rd then E 1 mile on CR-64/Big Flats Rd
✪		✓			Hudson • 460 Fairview Ave, 12534 • 518-822-0160 • 3.6 miles north of town center via US-9
☆	1				Islandia • 1850 Veterans Memorial Hwy, 11749 • 631-851-0468 • I-495 Exit 57 take SR-454 E .6 mile
✪		✓			Ithaca • 135 Fairgrounds Memorial Pkwy, 14850 • 607-277-4510 • 1.4 miles south of town via SR-34/SR-96
✪	1				Johnson City • 2 Gannett Dr, 13790 • 607-240-5040 • I-86 Exit 71, south of exit
✪		✓			Kingston • 601 Frank Sottile Blvd, 12401 • 845-336-4159 • Jct US-209 & US-9W (N of town) take US-9W S .1 mile then E on Frank Sottile Blvd .9 mile
✪	5	✓			Lakewood • 350 E Fairmount Ave, 14750 • 716-763-0945 • I-86 Exit 12 take SR-60 S 1.7 miles then SR-394 W 3.2 miles
✪	4	✓			Lancaster • 4975 Transit Rd, 14086 • 716-206-3050 • I-90 Exit 52A (NY Thruway) go E .7 mile on William St, S .2 mile on Union Rd, W 2.9 miles on Losson Rd
✪	1				Latham • 800 Loudon Rd, 12110 • 518-783-4086 • I-87 Exit 6 go E .5 mile on SR-2 then S on Loudon Rd
✪		✓			Liverpool • 8770 Dell Center Dr, 13090 • 315-622-5401 • SR-481 Exit 12 go W .6 mile on SR-31 then N .2 mile on Dell Center Dr
✪					Lockport • 5735 S Transit Rd, 14094 • 716-438-2404 • About 2 miles south of town center along SR-78

☆	🛡	🕐	⛽	🚫	Store Details
✪		✓			Lowville • 7155 State Route 12, 13367 • 315-376-7030 • 1.2 miles southeast of town center along SR-12
✪	7	✓			Macedon • 425 NY Hwy 31, 14502 • 315-986-1584 • I-490 Exit 26 go E 6.7 miles on SR-31 (Pittsford-Palmyra Rd)
✪		✓			Malone • 3222 NY Hwy 11, 12953 • 518-483-5968 • Jct CR-28/Town Line Rd & US-11 (N of town) take US-11 N 1.5 miles
☆					Massapequa • 200 Sunrise Mall, 11758 • 516-799-2697 • From Southern Pkwy Exit 32S take SR-110 S 1.3 miles, SR-27 E .7 mile & Hemlock St E .1 mile
✪		✓			Massena • 43 Stephenville St, 13662 • 315-769-1072 • 1.3 miles southeast of town center along SR-37/Seaway Trail
☆	7				Middle Island • 750 Middle Country Rd, 11953 • 631-924-0081 • I-495 Exit 64 take SR-112 N 3.3 miles & SR-25 E 3 miles
✪	2	✓		✓	Middletown • 470 Rt 211 E, 10940 • 845-342-0222 • I-84 Exit 4W take SR-17 NW 1 mile then SR-211 W .5 mile
☆					Mohegan Lake • 3133 E Main St, 10547 • 914-526-1100 • Jct SR-35/Bear Mountain State Pkwy & US-6 (S of town) take US-6 N 1.2 miles
✪	2	✓			Monroe • 288 Larkin Dr, 10950 • 845-783-3505 • I-87 (toll) Exit 16 go W .2 mile on SR-17 then S .3 mile on SR-32 then W .6 mile on Larkin Dr
✪		✓			Monticello • 41 Anawana Lake Rd, 12701 • 845-796-7202 • From SR-17 Exit 105B (N of town) take SR-42 N .1 mile & CR-103 W .2 mile
✪		✓			Napanoch • 7500 Route 209, 12458 • 845-647-2671 • Located along US-209 about 2 miles north of Ellenville
✪	5	✓	◆		New Hartford • 4765 Commercial Dr, 13413 • 315-736-4932 • From I-790 at SR-5A (Oriskany St) in Utica, go W 2.2 miles on Oriskany St then S 2.1 miles on Commercial Dr
✪		✓			Newark • 6788 NY Hwy 31 E, 14513 • 315-331-5081 • I-90/NY State Thruway (toll) Exit 42 take SR-14 N 7.6 miles then SR-31 W 3.9 miles
✪	2	✓			Newburgh • 1201 Route 300, 12550 • 845-567-6007 • I-84 Exit 7B go S 1.3 miles on SR-300
✪	2	✓			Niagara Falls • 1540 Military Rd, 14304 • 716-298-4484 • I-190 Exit 22 go E 1.2 miles on US-62/Niagara Falls Blvd then N .4 mile on SR-265/Military Rd
✪		✓			North Tonawanda • 866 Niagara Falls Blvd, 14120 • 716-243-4138 • 1.6 miles northeast of town center along SR-425

☆	◯	🕐	⛽	🚫	Store Details
✪		✓			Norwich • 5396 NY Hwy 12, 13815 • 607-334-5553 • Jct SR-32A/Hale St & SR-12 (S of town) take SR-12 S 1.8 miles
☆					Ogdensburg • 3000 Ford St Ext, 13669 • 315-394-8990 • Jct SR-68 & SR-37 (E of town) go N on SR-37 for 1.4 miles then W on Ford St
✪	2	✓			Olean • 1869 Plaza Dr, 14760 • 716-373-2781 • I-86 Exit 25 go S .4 mile on Buffalo St, W .9 mile on Constitution Ave, S .2 mile on Independence Dr, and W .2 mile on Cinema Dr
✪	6	✓			Oneida • 2024 Genesee St, 13421 • 315-361-1037 • I-90 (toll) Exit 34 take SR-13 S 1.3 miles & SR-5 E 4.4 miles
✪	1	✓		✓	Oneonta • 5054 State Highway 23, 13820 • 607-431-9557 • I-88 Exit 15 merge onto SR-28/23 E .4 mile
☆				✓	Oswego • 341 State Route 104, 13126 • 315-342-6210 • 1.7 miles east of town center on SR-104
✪	1	✓		✓	Painted Post • 3217 Silverback Ln, 14870 • 607-937-9627 • I-86 Exit 44 take Silverback Ln S .5 mile
✪	1	✓		✓	Plattsburgh • 25 Consumer Sq, 12901 • 518-561-0195 • I-87 Exit 37 take SR-3 E .4 mile then S on Consumer Sq
✪		✓			Potsdam • 7494 US Hwy 11, 13676 • 315-268-6900 • 2 miles west of town center via US-11
✪	1	✓		✓	Queensbury • 891 NY Hwy 9, 12804 • 518-793-0309 • I-87 Exit 19 take SR-254 E .6 mile & US-9 N .4 mile
✪	4	✓			Queensbury • 24 Quaker Ridge Blvd, 12804 • 518-746-4155 • I-87 Exit 19 follow SR-254 E 3.9 miles
✪	1	✓			Rensselaer • 279 Troy Rd, 12061 • 518-283-3055 • I-90 Exit 9 take US-4 S .5 mile
✪	3				Riverhead • 1890 Old Country Rd, 11901 • 631-369-1041 • 3 miles west of town center near junction of I-495 and SR-25
✪	7	✓	◆		Rochester • 1490 Hudson Ave, 14621 • 585-266-2000 • I-490 Exit 21 take SR-590 N 3.9 miles, follow SR-104 W 2.8 miles & N on Hudson Ave
✪	1	✓			Rochester • 1200 Marketplace Dr, 14623 • 585-292-6000 • I-390 Exit 13 go W on Highland Dr .1 mile & N on Marketplace Dr .3 mile
✪	2	✓		✓	Rochester • 2150 Chili Ave, 14624 • 585-429-9640 • I-390 Exit 18B follow SR-204 W 1.8 miles
✪		✓			Rome • 5815 Rome Taberg Rd, 13440 • 315-338-7900 • Jct SR-49 & SR-69 (NW of town) follow SR-69 NW for .5 mile
✪	1	✓			Saratoga Springs • 16 Old Gick Rd, 12866 • 518-581-8035 • I-87 Exit 15 take SR-50 E .3 mile then N on Old Gick Rd .2 mile
☆	3				Schenectady • 1320 Altamont Ave, 12303 • 518-355-2596 • I-890 Exit 6 take Brandywine N 1 mile, SR-146 E .4 mile & Altamont Ave S .9 mile
✪		✓	◆		Springville • 317 S Cascade Dr, 14141 • 716-592-1460 • Jct SR-39 & US-219 (W of town) go S on US-219 for .7 mile
☆	1				Suffern • 250 Route 59, 10901 • 845-368-4705 • I-87 Exit 14B take Airmont Rd S .3 mile & SR-59 E .3 mile
✪		✓			Ticonderoga • 1134 Wicker St, 12883 • 518-585-3060 • I-87 Exit 28 take SR-74 E 17.3 miles then Wicker St S .1 mile
☆	4				Troy • 760 Hoosick Rd, 12180 • 518-279-0685 • I-787 Exit 9E merge onto SR-7 E 3.3 miles
☆					Uniondale • 1123 Jerusalem Ave, 11553 • 516-505-1508 • From Southern Pkwy Exit 24N take Merrick Ave N .1 mile then Jerusalem Ave E .8 mile
✪	1	✓			Utica • 710 Horatio St, 13502 • 315-738-1155 • From I-90 at SR-8/SR-12 go N .7 mile on SR-8/SR-12 to Horatio St
☆					Valley Stream • 77 Green Acres Rd, 11581 • 516-887-0127 • From Belt Pkwy Exit 23B take SR-27 E 1.9 miles & S on Green Acres Rd .1 mile
✪		✓			Vestal • 2405 Vestal Pkwy E, 13850 • 607-798-1011 • From SR-17 Exit 70S merge onto SR-201S 2 miles then SR-434 W 2.3 miles
✪	1			✓	Victor • 441 Commerce Dr, 14564 • 585-398-6038 • I-90 Exit 45 go N .6 mile on I-490 to Exit 29, turn right .1 mile on SR-96
☆					Warsaw • 2348 State Rt 19 N, 14569 • 585-786-0700 • Jct US-20A & SR-19 (in town) go N on SR-19 1.8 miles
✪	4	✓	◆		Waterloo • 1860 North Rd, 13165 • 315-539-2560 • I-90/NY State Thruway Exit 41 go S 4 miles on SR-414
✪	1	✓			Watertown • 20823 NY Hwy 3, 13601 • 315-786-0145 • I-81 Exit 45 take SR-3 W .4 mile
✪		✓		✓	Watkins Glen • 515 E 4th St, 14891 • 607-535-3108 • I-86 Exit 46 follow SR-414 N 20.5 miles
☆	6				Webster • 1902 Empire Blvd, 14580 • 585-787-1370 • I-490 Exit 21 merge onto SR-590 N 2.4 miles then Empire Blvd/SR-404 NE 2.9 miles

☆	◯	🕐	⛽	🚫	Store Details
☆					Westbury • 1220 Old Country Rd, 11590 • 516-794-7280 • From Northern Pkwy Exit 31A take Meadowbrook Pkwy S 1.4 miles, then Exit M1 for Old Country Rd E .7 mile
☆	2			✓	White Plains • 275 Main St, 10601 • 914-285-1070 • I-287 Exit 8, Westchester Ave W 1.2 miles, SR-22 S .1 mile, Martine Ave E .2 mile, SR-125 N & Main St E .2 mile
✪	3	✓		✓	Williamsville • 5033 Transit Rd, 14221 • 716-565-0250 • I-90 (toll) Exit 49 take SR-78/Transit Rd N 2.6 miles

NORTH CAROLINA

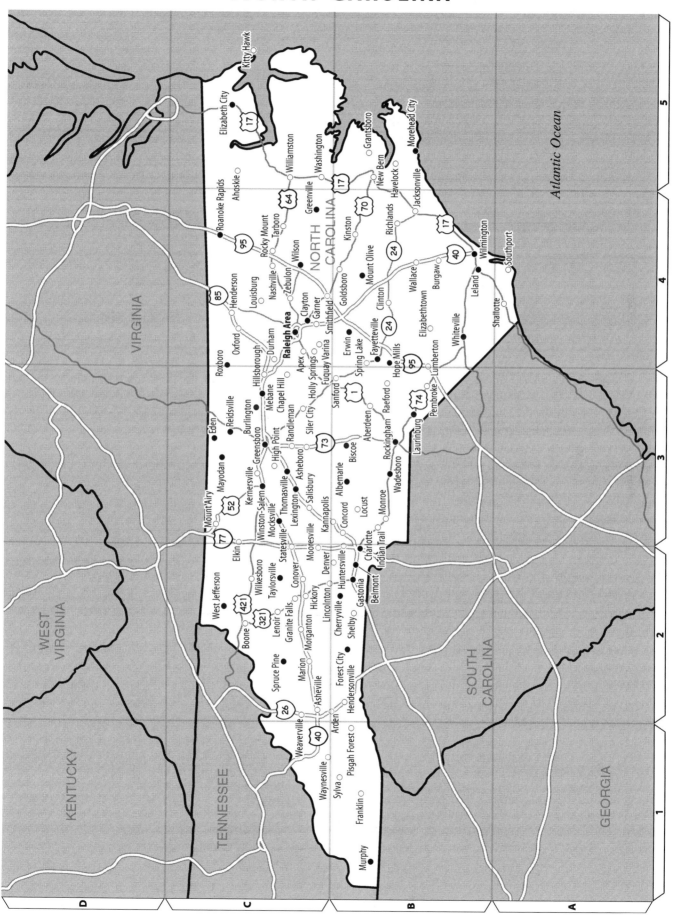

Raleigh Metro Area
Cary · Knightdale · Morrisville · Raleigh · Wake Forest

☆	⬭	🕐	⛽	🚫	Store Details
✪		✓			Aberdeen · 250 Turner St, 28315 · 910-695-1255 · Jct US-1 & US-15/501 (in Midtown) take US-15/501 NE .7 mile then W on Commerce Ave
✪				✓	Ahoskie · 2150 US 13 S, 27910 · 252-332-7773 · 2 miles east of town center along US-13
✪		✓	❖		Albemarle · 781 Leonard Ave, 28001 · 704-983-6830 · Jct US-52 & SR-27 (S of town) go E on SR-27/Spaulding St .9 mile then N on Leonard Ave
✪		✓			Apex · 3151 Apex Peakway, 27502 · 919-362-3737 · From US-1 Exit 95 go N .3 mile on SR-55; turn left at Apex Peakway .3 mile
✪	2	✓		✓	Arden · 60 Airport Rd, 28704 · 828-274-9283 · I-26 Exit 40 go N 1.5 miles on Airport Rd
✪	3	✓			Asheboro · 1226 E Dixie Dr, 27203 · 336-626-0004 · Jct I-73/74 & US-64 take US-64 E 2.5 miles
✪	4	✓		✓	Asheville · 1636 Hendersonville Rd, 28803 · 828-333-9505 · I-40 Exit 50/50A go S 3.3 miles on US-25
✪	2	✓		✓	Asheville · 125 Bleachery Blvd, 28805 · 828-298-8092 · I-240 Exit 8 take US-74A W .4 mile then Bleachery Blvd N .8 mile
✪	1	✓	❖		Belmont · 701 Hawley Ave, 28012 · 704-825-8885 · I-85 Exit 26 take Main St S .3 mile, Wilkerson Blvd E .5 mile & Hawley Ave S .2 mile
✪	2	✓	◆		Biscoe · 201 Montgomery Crossing, 27209 · 910-428-1851 · I-73/I-74 Exit 33 take SR-27/24 W 1.8 miles
✪		✓			Boone · 200 Watauga Village Dr, 28607 · 828-262-0254 · 1.8 miles southeast of town along US-221/US-321
☆	2		◆		Burgaw · 908 NC Hwy 53 E, 28425 · 910-789-6005 · I-40 Exit 398 go S 1.4 miles on SR-53
✪	1	✓			Burlington · 3141 Garden Rd, 27215 · 336-584-6400 · I-40/I-85 Exit 141 take Huffman Mill Rd N .2 mile & Garden Rd W .2 mile
✪	3	✓	❖		Burlington · 530 S Graham Hopedale Rd, 27217 · 336-226-1819 · I-40/I-85 Exit 148 take SR-54 NW 1.1 miles, Main St N .8 mile, W on Providence/N on Washington .2 mile, Graham Hopedale Rd N .7 mile
☆	6				Cary · 2010 Kildaire Farm Rd, 27518 · 919-852-0651 · I-40 Exit 293 follow US-1 S 4.2 miles then Tryon Rd/US-64 E 1 mile & Kildaire Rd S .1 mile
✪	9	✓			Chapel Hill · 12500 US 15/501 N, 27517 · 919-357-9039 · I-40 Exit 270 go S 8.7 miles on US-15
✪	4				Charlotte · 3850 E Independence Blvd, 28205 · 704-535-3708 · I-277 Exit 2B follow US-74 E 3.2 miles
✪	2	✓			Charlotte · 3240 Wilkinson Blvd, 28208 · 704-392-2311 · I-277 Exit 1 take Wilkinson Blvd/US-74 W 1.6 miles
✪	9	✓		✓	Charlotte · 9820 Callabridge Ct, 28216 · 704-392-3338 · I-77 Exit 11B take SR-16 N 8.1 miles, Mt Holly Rd E .2 mile & Callabridge Ct N .2 mile
☆	3				Charlotte · 3209 Pineville Matthews Rd, 28226 · 704-541-7292 · I-485 Exit 57 take SR-16 N 2.8 miles then Pineville Rd W .2 mile
☆	3				Charlotte · 9101 Albemarle Rd, 28227 · 704-531-6588 · I-485 Exit 41 take SR-24/27 W 2.7 miles
✪	2	✓			Charlotte · 7735 N Tryon St, 28262 · 704-547-0525 · I-85 Exit 45A go E .6 mile on Harris Blvd then S .9 mile on Tryon St
✪	3	✓	❖		Charlotte · 1830 Galleria Blvd, 28270 · 704-844-1066 · I-485 Exit 52 take John St N 1.9 miles, continue on Monroe Rd .8 mile & E on Galleria .3 mile
✪	1	✓		✓	Charlotte · 8180 S Tryon St, 28273 · 704-588-2656 · I-485 Exit 1 take Tryon St/SR-49 N .2 mile
✪		✓	❖		Cherryville · 2505 Lincolnton Hwy, 28021 · 704-435-4449 · 2.6 miles east of town center along SR-150
✪	6	✓	❖		Clayton · 805 Town Centre Blvd, 27520 · 919-550-5600 · I-40 Exit 306 merge onto US-70 E 5.6 miles
✪		✓			Clinton · 1415 Sunset Ave, 28328 · 910-592-1818 · I-40 Exit 364 follow SR-24/US-701 BR W 13.2 miles
✪	6	✓			Concord · 150 Concord Commons Pl SW, 28027 · 704-788-3135 · I-85 Exit 58 follow US-29 S 5.4 miles
✪	1	✓		✓	Concord · 5825 Thunder Rd, 28027 · 704-979-2540 · I-85 Exit 49 go W .7 mile on Concord Mills Blvd then N .1 mile on Thunder Rd
✪	1	✓			Conover · 201 Zelkova Ct NW, 28613 · 828-464-4441 · I-40 Exit 132 take Thornberg Dr NW .3 mile & SR-16 S .2 mile
✪	9	✓			Denver · 7131 Hwy 73, 28037 · 704-827-8911 · I-77 Exit 25 take SR-73 W 8.7 miles
✪	1				Durham · 1525 Glenn School Rd, 27704 · 919-688-3595 · I-85 Exit 180 go E .3 mile on Glenn School Rd

☆	🍎	🕐	⛽	🚭	Store Details
✪	1				Durham • 5450 New Hope Commons Dr, 27707 • 919-489-4412 • I-40 Exit 270 take US-501 NE .3 mile, Mt Moriah Rd W .1 mile & New Hope Dr S .1 mile
✪		✓	❖		Eden • 304 E Arbor Ln, 27288 • 336-623-8981 • Jct SR-700/770 & SR-14 (in town) take SR-14 S 1.2 miles then Arbor Ln E
✪		✓	❖		Elizabeth City • 101 Tanglewood Pkwy N, 27909 • 252-338-3367 • 4.6 miles west of town center along SR-344
☆					Elizabethtown • 1347 W Broad St, 28337 • 910-862-8424 • Jct US-701 & SR-41 (N of town) go W on SR-41 for .8 mile
✪	1	✓			Elkin • 548 CC Camp Rd, 28621 • 336-526-2636 • I-77 Exit 85 go W .7 mile on SR-268-BYP
✪	4	✓	❖		Erwin • 590 E Jackson Blvd, 28339 • 910-892-0445 • I-95 Exit 73 follow US-421 N 3.2 miles
✪	9	✓			Fayetteville • 1550 Skibo Rd, 28303 • 910-868-6434 • Jct I-295 & US-401 (N of town) take US-401 S 3.5 miles & US-401 BYP S 5.1 miles
✪		✓	❖	✓	Fayetteville • 7701 S Raeford Rd, 28304 • 910-864-6575 • I-95 Exit 46 take SR-87 5.5 miles to Exit 104 then US-401 BR W 9.5 miles
✪				✓	Fayetteville • 2820 Gillespie St, 28306 • 910-364-0315 • About 4 miles south of town center via I-95-BUS/Gillespie St
✪	3	✓	❖		Fayetteville • 4601 Ramsey St, 28311 • 910-488-1800 • Jct I-295 & US-401 (N of town) take US-401 S 2.2 miles
✪	3	✓	❖		Forest City • 197 Plaza Dr, 28043 • 828-287-7458 • From I-74 Exit 181 (S of town) take US-74 ALT N 2.4 miles & Plaza Dr W .1 mile
✪		✓			Franklin • 273 Commons Dr, 28734 • 828-524-9111 • 2.5 miles southeast of town center along US-441-Bypass/Sylva Rd at Dowdle Mountain Rd
✪		✓			Fuquay Varina • 1051 E Broad St, 27526 • 919-567-2350 • I-40 Exit 312 follow SR-42 W 12.9 miles, Judd Pkwy N .1 mile & Broad St W .2 mile
✪	1	✓			Garner • 5141 NC Hwy 42, 27529 • 919-772-7373 • I-40 Exit 312 go N .4 mile on SR-42
✪	2	✓	❖		Gastonia • 223 N Myrtle School Rd, 28052 • 704-864-6776 • I-85 Exit 14 take SR-274 S .7 mile, Crescent Ln W & Myrtle School Rd S .5 mile
✪	1	✓		✓	Gastonia • 3000 E Franklin Blvd, 28056 • 704-867-2440 • I-85 Exit 20 take SR-279 S .5 mile & Franklin Blvd E .4 mile
✪		✓			Goldsboro • 2908 US Hwy 70 W, 27530 • 919-736-7332 • 5 miles west of town on US-70 at SR-581

☆	🍎	🕐	⛽	🚭	Store Details
✪		✓			Goldsboro • 1002 N Spence Ave, 27534 • 919-778-3324 • Jct SR-111 & US-70/13 (SE of town) take US-70/13 N 3.1 miles then Spence Ave E .2 mile
✪	6	✓			Granite Falls • 4780 Hickory Blvd, 28630 • 828-396-3170 • I-40 Exit 123B take US-321 N 5.9 miles
☆		✓	◆		Grantsboro • 11233 B NC-55 Hwy, 28529 • 252-201-9005 • East of town center on SR-55
✪	6	✓	❖	✓	Greensboro • 2107 Pyramid Village Blvd, 27405 • 336-375-5445 • I-840 Exit 21 take US-70 W 3.8 miles, US-29 N 1.5 miles, then E .2 mile on Cone Blvd
✪	1	✓		✓	Greensboro • 121 W Elmsley St, 27406 • 336-370-0775 • I-85 Exit 124 take Eugene St N .2 mile & Elmsley Dr W .2 mile
✪	1	✓			Greensboro • 4424 W Wendover Ave, 27407 • 336-292-5070 • I-40 Exit 214 go S on Wendover Ave .6 mile
✪	8				Greensboro • 3738 Battleground Ave, 27410 • 336-282-6754 • I-40 Exit 212B follow I-73 N 3.2 miles; Joseph M Bryan Blvd E 1.9 miles; New Garden Rd N 1.8 miles; and Battleground Ave W .4 mile.
✪		✓	❖		Greenville • 210 Greenville Blvd SW, 27834 • 252-355-2441 • Jct SR-11 & US-264 ALT (S of town) go NE on US-264 ALT .7 mile
✪		✓			Greenville • 4600 E 10th St, 27858 • 252-917-6286 • 4.5 miles east of town center on SR-33
✪		✓			Havelock • 566 US Hwy 70 W, 28532 • 252-444-2055 • 3 miles north of town along US-70 at Catawba Rd
✪	1	✓			Henderson • 200 N Cooper Dr, 27536 • 252-438-9004 • I-85 Exit 213 take US-158 BYP .7 mile to Dabney Dr E & Cooper Dr S .1 mile
✪	1	✓			Hendersonville • 250 Highlands Square Dr, 28792 • 828-696-8285 • I-26 Exit 49A take US-64 N .5 mile then W at Highlands Sq Dr .2 mile
✪	1	✓			Hickory • 2525 US Hwy 70 SE, 28602 • 828-326-7060 • I-40 Exit 126 take McDonald Pkwy SE .3 mile & US-70 E .4 mile
✪	3	✓			High Point • 2628 S Main St, 27263 • 336-869-9633 • I-85 Exit 111 take US-311 NW 2.5 miles
✪	8	✓			High Point • 2710 N Main St, 27265 • 336-869-7638 • I-85 Exit 111 take US-311 NW 7.8 miles
✪	1	✓			Hillsborough • 501 Hampton Pointe, 27278 • 919-732-9172 • I-85 Exit 165 take SR-86 S .2 mile then W at Hampton Point Dr .1 mile

☆	◯	🕐	⛽	🚫	Store Details
✪		✓			Holly Springs • 7016 GB Alford Hwy, 27540 • 919-557-9181 • From US-1 Exit 95 (N of town) take SR-55 S 6 miles
✪	4	✓	❖		Hope Mills • 3030 N Main St, 28348 • 910-429-7401 • I-95 Exit 41 go NW on SR-59 for 4 miles
✪	1	✓		✓	Huntersville • 11145 Bryton Town Center Dr, 28078 • 704-977-2040 • I-77 Exit 19A go N .5 mile on SR-115/Old Statesville Rd then E .3 mile on Eastfield Rd
✪	4	✓			Indian Trail • 2101 Younts Rd, 28079 • 704-882-5566 • I-485 Exit 51 follow US-74 SE 3.4 miles, Indian Trail Rd E .2 mile & Younts Rd N .1 mile
✪		✓			Jacksonville • 561 Yopp Road, 28540 • 910-346-1889 • Jct US-258 & SR-24 (W of town) take US-258 E .5 mile then Yopp Rd S .4 mile
✪		✓			Jacksonville • 2025 N Marine Blvd, 28546 • 910-455-2358 • Jct SR-24 & US-17 (S of town) take Marine Blvd/US-17 N 4.7 miles
✪	1	✓		✓	Kannapolis • 2420 Supercenter Dr NE, 28083 • 704-792-9800 • I-85 Exit 60, west of exit
✪	6	✓			Kernersville • 1130 S Main St, 27284 • 336-992-2343 • I-40 Exit 206 merge onto I-40 BR W 4.5 miles to Exit 14 - Main St S .6 mile
✪		✓			Kinston • 4101 W Vernon Ave, 28504 • 252-527-3100 • Jct US-70 & US-258 (W of town) take US-70 E .3 mile
☆				✓	Kitty Hawk • 5400 N Croatan Hwy, 27949 • 252-261-6011 • Jct US-64 & US-158 (S of Nags Head) take US-158 N for 15.3 miles
☆	2				Knightdale • 7106 Knightdale Blvd, 27545 • 919-217-0490 • I-540 Exit 24B take US-64 BR E 1.6 miles
✪	1	✓	❖		Laurinburg • 901 US Hwy 401 S, 28352 • 910-277-7770 • I-74 Exit 183, north of exit
✪		✓	❖		Leland • 1112 New Pointe Blvd, 28451 • 910-383-1769 • Jct US-74/76 & US-17 (S of town) follow US-17 S 1.2 miles
✪		✓			Lenoir • 935 Blowing Rock Blvd, 28645 • 828-754-0763 • 2 miles north of town via US-321
✪	1	✓	❖		Lexington • 160 Lowes Blvd, 27292 • 336-243-3051 • I-85 Exit 91 take SR-8 N .5 mile & E on Lowes Blvd
✪		✓			Lincolnton • 306 N Generals Blvd, 28092 • 704-732-3090 • 1.3 miles northeast of town center off US-321 at Main St
✪		✓		✓	Locust • 1876 Main St W, 28097 • 704-781-0426 • 2 miles west of town center via SR-24/SR-27

☆	◯	🕐	⛽	🚫	Store Details
✪					Louisburg • 705 Retail Way, 27549 • 919-496-2221 • 2 miles south of town center via US-401/SR-56
✪	1	✓			Lumberton • 5070 Fayetteville Rd, 28358 • 910-738-2595 • I-95 Exit 22 take Fayettville Rd E .2 mile
✪	1				Marion • 2875 Sugar Hill Rd, 28752 • 828-659-3200 • I-40 Exit 81, north of exit
✪		✓	❖		Mayodan • 6711 NC Hwy 135, 27027 • 336-548-6540 • Jct US-220 & SR-135 (E of town) take SR-135 W 1.3 miles
✪	1	✓	❖		Mebane • 1318 Mebane Oaks Rd, 27302 • 919-304-0171 • I-40/I-85 Exit 154 go S on Mebane Oaks Rd .3 mile
✪	1	✓	❖		Mocksville • 261 Cooper Creek Dr, 27028 • 336-751-1266 • I-40 Exit 170 take US-601 N .3 mile then Cooper Creek Dr E .4 mile
✪		✓			Monroe • 2406 W Roosevelt Blvd, 28110 • 704-289-5478 • I-485 Exit 51 follow US-74 E 10.5 miles
✪	1	✓			Mooresville • 169 Norman Station Blvd, 28117 • 704-664-5238 • I-77 Exit 36 take SR-150 E .3 mile then Norman Station Blvd S .1 mile
✪		✓	❖		Morehead City • 300 NC Hwy 24, 28557 • 252-247-0511 • Jct US-70 & SR-24 (W of town) take SR-24 W .6 mile
☆	1				Morganton • 1227 Burkemont Ave, 28655 • 828-433-7696 • I-40 Exit 103 take US-64 S .2 mile
✪	2	✓		✓	Morrisville • 1001 Shiloh Glenn Dr, 27560 • 919-474-2285 • I-40 Exit 281 go S 1.9 miles on Miami Blvd/SR-1959
✪	2	✓			Mount Airy • 2241 Rockford St, 27030 • 336-719-2300 • I-74 Exit 11 take US-601 N 1.6 miles
✪	10	✓	❖		Mount Olive • 308 NC Hwy 55 W, 28365 • 919-658-1701 • I-40 Exit 355 take I-40 Connector N 5 miles, US-117 N 4.4 miles, SR-55 W .5 mile
✪		✓	❖		Murphy • 2330 US 19, 28906 • 828-837-9184 • Jct US-64/74 & US-129/19 (S of town) take US-19 S 1.9 miles
✪	4	✓			Nashville • 1205 Eastern Ave, 27856 • 252-459-0020 • I-95 Exit 138 follow US-64 W 3.2 miles, S .3 mile on US-64 BR, then E .1 mile on Eastern Ave/Sunset Ave
✪		✓			New Bern • 3105 Martin Luther King Jr Blvd, 28562 • 252-637-6699 • Jct US-70 & US-17 (W of town) take MLK Jr Blvd/US-17 S .3 mile
✪	1				Oxford • 1015 Lewis St, 27565 • 919-693-2900 • I-85 Exit 202 go N .7 mile on US-15
✪	8	✓			Pembroke • 930 Hwy 711 E, 28372 • 910-522-1321 • I-95 Exit 17 follow SR-711 W 7.9 miles

☆	◯	🕐	⛽	🚫	Store Details
☆					Pisgah Forest • 177 Forest Gate Ctr, 28768 • 828-885-7900 • I-26 Exit 40 go S 16 miles on SR-280
✪		✓			Raeford • 4545 Fayetteville Rd, 28376 • 910-683-6056 • 4 miles northeast of town via US-401
✪	3			✓	Raleigh • 4500 Fayetteville Rd, 27603 • 919-772-8751 • I-40 Exit 298A go S 2.3 miles on US-70/US-401
✪	1	✓		✓	Raleigh • 1725 New Hope Church Rd, 27609 • 919-790-6910 • I-440 Exit 10 take Wake Forest Rd N .9 mile & New Hope Rd E .1 mile
✪	2	✓	❖		Raleigh • 4431 New Bern Ave, 27610 • 919-212-6442 • I-440 Exit 13B merge onto New Bern Ave E 1.6 miles
☆	3				Raleigh • 6600 Glenwood Ave, 27612 • 919-783-5552 • I-440 Exit 7 take US-70 W 2.9 miles
✪	1	✓		✓	Raleigh • 8000 Town Dr, 27616 • 919-424-6235 • I-540 Exit 17, south of exit
✪	1	✓		✓	Raleigh • 10050 Glenwood Ave, 27617 • 919-596-5790 • I-540 Exit 4B take US-70 W .7 mile
✪	1	✓			Randleman • 1021 High Point St, 27317 • 336-495-6278 • I-73/I-74 Exit 66 take Academy St E .4 mile & S at High Pt St
✪		✓	❖		Reidsville • 1624 NC Hwy 14, 27320 • 336-349-6569 • Jct US-29 & US-158 (NE of town) take US-158 W/SR-14 N 5.8 miles
✪		✓	❖	✓	Richlands • 349 Kinston Hwy, 28574 • 910-324-6508 • 1.5 miles west of town center along SR-24/US-258
✪	1	✓	❖		Roanoke Rapids • 251 Premier Blvd, 27870 • 252-535-3151 • I-95 Exit 173 take US-158 W .1 mile & Premier Blvd S .4 mile
✪		✓	❖		Rockingham • 720 E US Hwy 74, 28379 • 910-582-3996 • Jct US-220 & US-74 BR (in town) take US-74 BR N 1 mile
✪	6	✓		✓	Rocky Mount • 1511 Benvenue Rd, 27804 • 252-985-2254 • I-95 Exit 138 merge onto US-64 E 4.3 miles then SR-43/48 N 1.4 miles
✪		✓	❖		Roxboro • 1049 Durham Rd, 27573 • 336-597-2909 • Jct US-158 & US-501 (S of town) take US-501 S .1 mile
✪	1	✓			Salisbury • 323 S Arlington St, 28144 • 704-639-9718 • I-85 Exit 76 take Innes St W .1 mile & Arlington St S .3 mille
✪		✓			Sanford • 3310 NC 87 S, 27330 • 919-776-9388 • 2.4 miles southeast of town along SR-87
✪		✓			Shallotte • 4540 Main St, 28470 • 910-754-2880 • Jct SR-130 & US-17 (in town) take US-17 BR NE 1.3 miles

☆	◯	🕐	⛽	🚫	Store Details
✪		✓			Shelby • 705 E Dixon Blvd, 28152 • 704-484-0021 • I-85 Exit 10B merge onto US-74 W 11.7 miles, continue on US-74 BYP 3 miles
✪		✓			Siler City • 14215 US Hwy 64 W, 27344 • 919-663-6000 • From US-421 Exit 171 (E of town) go E on US-64 for .3 mile
✪	2	✓			Smithfield • 1299 N Brightleaf Blvd, 27577 • 919-989-6455 • I-95 Exit 97 go W on US-70 for .6 mile then US-301 S .7 mile
✪		✓			Southport • 1675 N Howe St, 28461 • 910-454-9909 • Jct SR-133/Dosher Cutoff & SR-211 (N of town) take SR-211/ Howe St S .4 mile
✪		✓			Spring Lake • 670 Lillington Hwy, 28390 • 910-436-1199 • .5 mile northeast of town on SR-210
✪		✓	◆		Spruce Pine • 2514 Halltown Rd, 28777 • 828-766-9991 • I-40 Exit 86 follow SR-226 N for 19.4 miles then E at Halltown Rd .2 mile
✪	1	✓			Statesville • 1116 Crossroads Dr, 28625 • 704-871-9833 • I-40 Exit 151 take US-21 N .3 mile
✪		✓			Sylva • 210 Walmart Plz, 28779 • 828-586-0211 • From US-23/74 Exit 85 (N of town) take US-23 BR 1.8 miles, SR-107 S 1.1 miles & Connor Rd W
✪		✓			Tarboro • 110 River Oaks Dr, 27886 • 252-824-8170 • From US-64 Exit 485 (S of town) go S on US-258 for .3 mile
✪		✓	❖		Taylorsville • 901 NC Hwy 16 S, 28681 • 828-632-4176 • Jct SR-90 & SR-16 (NW of town) go N on SR-16 for 1.3 miles
✪	1	✓	❖		Thomasville • 1585 Liberty Dr, 27360 • 336-474-2239 • I-85 Exit 103 take SR-109 E .3 mile then N at Liberty Dr .2 mile
✪			❖		Wadesboro • 2004 US Hwy 74 W, 28170 • 704-694-6530 • 1.7 miles west of town on US-74
✪	7	✓	❖		Wake Forest • 2114 S Main St, 27587 • 919-562-2921 • I-540 Exit 16 take US-1 N 6 miles & NE on Main St .4 mile
✪	2	✓			Wallace • 5625 S Hwy 41, 28466 • 910-285-2078 • I-40 Exit 385 go SW 1.6 miles on SR-41
✪		✓			Washington • 570 Pamlico Plz, 27889 • 252-975-2083 • Jct US-17 & SR-32/3rd St (in town) go S on SR-32 for 2.9 miles then E at Pamlico Dr .2 mile
✪	9	✓			Waynesville • 135 Town Center Loop, 28786 • 828-456-4828 • I-40 Exit 27 go S 8.1 miles on US-74 then E on SR-23
✪	1	✓			Weaverville • 25 Northridge Commons Pkwy, 28787 • 828-645-5028 • I-26 Exit 19, north of exit

☆	♡	🕐	⛽	🚫	Store Details
✪		✓	❖		West Jefferson • 1489 Mount Jefferson Rd, 28694 • 336-246-3920 • From US-221/SR-163 jct (south of town) go N .6 mile on US-221 and turn right at SR-1250, continue N .2 mile Mount Jefferson Rd
✪		✓	❖		Whiteville • 200 Columbus Corners Dr, 28472 • 910-640-1393 • Jct US-701 BR & SR-130 (in S Whiteville) continue S on US-701 BR .2 mile
✪		✓		✓	Wilkesboro • 1801 US Hwy 421, 28697 • 336-667-7691 • 2 miles west of town via US-421
✪		✓			Williamston • 1529 Washington St, 27892 • 252-792-9033 • 1.5 miles south of town center via US-17 BR
✪	3	✓	❖		Wilmington • 5226 Sigmon Rd, 28403 • 910-392-4034 • I-40 Exit 420 continue on US-117 S 2.2 miles, Imperial Dr W .1 mile, Van Campen Blvd N .3 mile & Sigmon Rd W
✪	6	✓		✓	Wilmington • 8035 Market St, 28411 • 910-821-6009 • I-40 Exit 416B go E about 5 miles on US-17 then S about 1 mile on Market St
✪	10	✓	❖		Wilmington • 5135 Carolina Beach Rd, 28412 • 910-452-0944 • I-40 Exit 420 continue S on US-117 for 9.3 miles then US-421 N .6 mile
✪	4	✓	❖	✓	Wilson • 2500 Forest Hills Rd W, 27893 • 252-243-9300 • I-95 Exit 121 take US-264 ALT E 3.7 miles then S on SR-1183 for .3 mile
✪	2	✓			Winston Salem • 4550 Kester Mill Rd, 27103 • 336-760-9868 • I-40 Exit 188 take US-421 N 1 mile to Exit 239-Jonestown Rd S .3 mile
✪	10	✓			Winston Salem • 320 E Hanes Mill Rd, 27105 • 336-377-9194 • I-40 Exit 193B take US-52 N 9.2 miles then Exit 115A-University Pkwy .5 mile N to Hanes Mill Rd E
✪	3	✓	❖		Winston Salem • 3475 Parkway Village Ct, 27127 • 336-771-1011 • I-40 Exit 192 go S 2.3 miles on SR-150 then W .1 mile on Stafford Village Blvd
✪		✓			Zebulon • 841 East Gannon Ave, 27597 • 919-269-2221 • 1 mile east of town center via SR-97/Gannon Ave near jct with US-64

NORTH DAKOTA

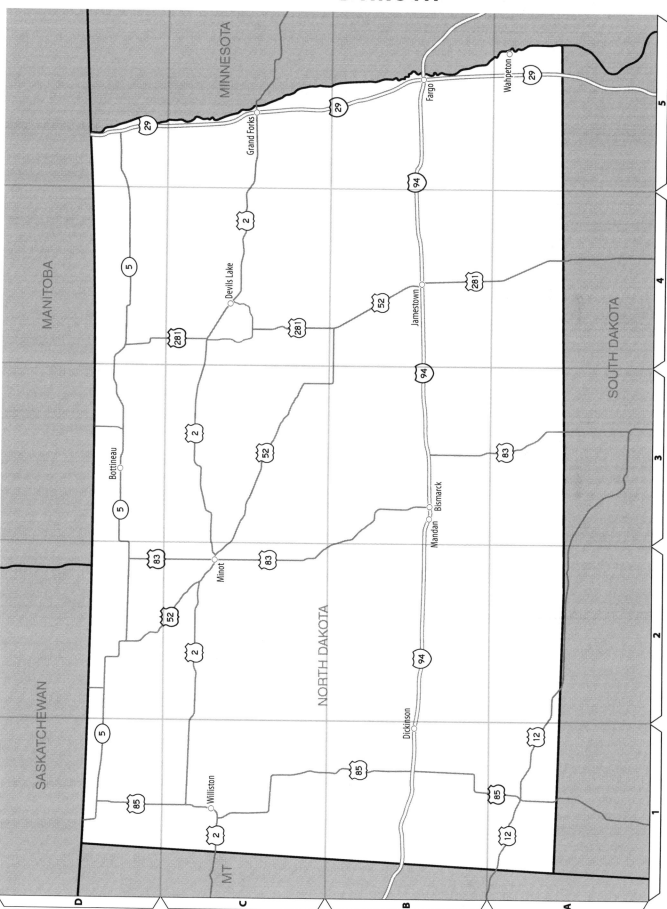

☆	♡	⏰	⛽	🚫	Store Details
✪	2	✓			Bismarck • 1400 Skyline Blvd, 58503 • 701-323-0530 • I-94 Exit 159 go N 1.7 miles on US-83
✪	3	✓			Bismarck • 2717 Rock Island Pl, 58503 • 701-223-3066 • I-94 Exit 161 go S 2.9 miles on Bismarck Expy
✪		✓			Bottineau • 912 11th St E, 58318 • 701-228-5276 • .5 mile east of town along SR-5
☆					Devils Lake • 210 Hwy 2 W, 58301 • 701-662-5203 • Jct SR-20 & US-2 (SE of town) go W on US-2 for .2 mile
✪	1	✓		✓	Dickinson • 2456 3rd Ave W, 58601 • 701-225-8504 • I-94 Exit 61 take SR-22 N .8 mile
✪	2	✓			Fargo • 4731 13th Ave S, 58103 • 701-281-3971 • I-94 Exit 348 go N on 45th St 1.1 miles then W on 13th Ave .2 mile
✪	1	✓			Fargo • 3757 55th Ave S, 58104 • 701-526-1167 • I-29 Exit 60, west of exit
✪	1	✓			Grand Forks • 2551 32nd Ave S, 58201 • 701-746-7225 • I-29 Exit 138 take 32nd Ave E 1 mile
✪	1	✓			Grand Forks • 5755 Gateway Dr, 58203 • 701-620-6003 • I-29 Exit 141 go W .9 mile on US-2
✪	1	✓			Jamestown • 921 25th St SW, 58401 • 701-252-6778 • I-94 Exit 258 take US-281 S .2 mile then 25th St W .2 mile
✪	1			✓	Mandan • 1000 Old Red Trl NW, 58554 • 701-354-6961 • I-94 Exit 152, north of exit
✪		✓			Minot • 3900 S Broadway, 58701 • 701-838-2176 • Jct US-2 & US-83 (S of town) take US-83 S 1 mile
✪		✓			Wahpeton • 1625 Commerce Dr, 58075 • 701-642-9086 • I-29 Exit 23A follow SR-13 E 10 miles, SR-210 N 1.3 miles, W at 16th Ave .2 mile
✪		✓			Williston • 4001 2nd Ave W, 58801 • 701-572-8550 • Jct 2nd Ave/US-2 & 28th St (N of town) go N on 2nd Ave for .8 mile

OHIO

MICHIGAN

ONTARIO

Lake Erie

PA

IN

Bryan

Wauseon ⑧⑨ Holland Toldeo ○ Oregon
Perrysburg
Napoleon
Ⓤ24 Bowling Green Fremont Sandusky Lorain Avon Cleveland
Defiance Norwalk Oberlin Elyria Parma
Ottawa Findlay Tiffin
Ⓤ30 Van Wert Upper Sandusky Bucyrus Ontario
Lima Ⓤ30 Mansfield
Wapakoneta Kenton Marion
Celina
Ⓤ75 Sidney Bellefontaine Ⓤ33 Delaware
Piqua Marysville
Greenville Troy Urbana Dublin Lewis Center Newark
Newburgh Springfield Ⓤ70 Westerville Heath
Clayton Huber Heights London Columbus Whitehall
Ⓤ70 Dayton Beavercreek Grove City Reynoldsburg Ⓤ70 Zanesville
Eaton Morain Xenia Canal Winchester Lancaster
Oxford Franklin Ⓤ71 Circleville Logan
Middletown Lebanon Washington Court House Ⓤ33 Athens Marietta
Hamilton West Chester Wilmington
Mason Chillicothe
Cincinnati Milford Hillsboro
Amelia Waverly
Ⓤ32 Jackson Ⓤ32
Gallipolis
West Union New Boston

Ashtabula
Madison Ⓤ90
Eastlake Mentor
North Olmsted South Euclid Chardon
Mayfield Heights Middlefield
Macedonia Aurora
Strongsville Streetsboro Cortland Ⓤ80
Medina Stow Youngstown
Wadsworth Fairlawn Kent Ⓤ76 Austintown
Akron Poland
Wooster North Canton Alliance
Ashland Ⓤ71 Salem
Massillon Canton
Millersburg East Liverpool
Mount Vernon New Philadelphia Ⓤ77
Coshocton Steubenville
Cambridge Ⓤ70 Saint Clairsville
Ⓤ77

OHIO

WEST VIRGINIA

South Point

KENTUCKY

1   2   3   4

☆	🛡	🕐	⛽	🚫	Store Details
✪	1	✓			Akron • 2887 S Arlington Rd, 44312 • 330-645-9556 • I-77 Exit 120, east of exit
✪		✓			Alliance • 2700 W State St, 44601 • 330-821-0026 • Jct US-62F & US-62 (W of town) go E on US-62/State St for .5 mile
✪	7	✓	❖		Amelia • 1815 E Ohio Pike, 45102 • 513-797-5700 • I-275 Exit 65 go SE on SR-125 for 6.8 miles
✪	3	✓			Ashland • 1996 E Main St, 44805 • 419-281-9537 • I-71 Exit 186 take US-250 W 2.5 miles
✪	5	✓			Ashtabula • 3551 N Ridge Rd E, 44004 • 440-998-4000 • I-90 Exit 228 merge onto SR-46 N 3.9 miles then US-20 E .7 mile
✪		✓			Athens • 929 E State St, 45701 • 740-594-3398 • From US-50 Exit 16A (E of town) go N on US-33 for .2 mile then E on State St .7 mile
✪		✓		✓	Aurora • 7235 Market Place Dr, 44023 • 330-562-0000 • 3 miles northwest of town along SR-43
✪	3	✓			Austintown • 6001 Mahoning Ave, 44515 • 330-270-0001 • I-80 Exit 224 merge onto SR-11 S 1.8 miles then Mahoning Ave W 1 mile
✪	1	✓		✓	Avon • 35901 Chester Rd, 44011 • 440-937-4750 • I-90 Exit 153 take US-83 N .2 mile then Chester Rd E .2 mile
✪	1	✓			Beavercreek • 3360 Pentagon Blvd, 45431 • 937-426-8227 • I-675 Exit 17 go S on Fairfield Rd .3 mile then W on Pentagon Blvd .2 mile
✪		✓	❖		Bellefontaine • 2281 US Highway 68 S, 43311 • 937-592-4700 • 2.3 miles south of town center on US-68
✪	2	✓	❖		Bowling Green • 131 W Gypsy Lane Rd, 43402 • 419-352-3776 • I-75 Exit 179 merge onto US-6 W 1.4 miles then US-25 N .5 mile
✪		✓			Bryan • 1215 S Main St, 43506 • 419-636-1535 • I-80/90 (toll) Exit 13 take SR-15 S 10.4 miles
✪		✓			Bucyrus • 1875 E Mansfield St, 44820 • 419-562-8101 • Jct US-30 & CR-330/US-30 BR (E of town) go W on US-30 BR .7 mile
✪	1	✓	❖		Cambridge • 61205 Southgate Rd, 43725 • 740-439-5743 • I-70 Exit 178 take SR-209 S .5 mile
✪	5	✓			Canal Winchester • 6674 Winchester Blvd, 43110 • 614-833-3930 • I-270 Exit 46 go E 4.6 miles on US33; S .2 mile on SR-74; E .2 mile on Winchester Blvd
✪	5	✓	❖		Canton • 3200 Atlantic Blvd NE, 44705 • 330-489-9035 • I-77 Exit 107B merge onto US-62 E 4.1 miles

☆	🛡	🕐	⛽	🚫	Store Details
✪	2	✓	❖		Canton • 4004 Tuscarawas St W, 44708 • 330-479-9620 • I-77 Exit 105 take SR-172 W 1.3 miles
✪		✓	❖		Celina • 1950 Havemann Rd, 45822 • 419-586-3777 • I-75 Exit 11 take US-33 & SR-29 W for 19.6 miles
✪	7	✓			Chardon • 223 Meadowlands Dr, 44024 • 440-286-2250 • I-90 Exit 200 take SR-44 S 6 miles then W on Meadowlands Dr .3 mile
✪		✓	❖		Chillicothe • 85 River Trace Ln, 45601 • 740-774-4800 • 1 mile north of town center near junction of US-35 and SR-159/Bridge St
✪	2	✓			Cincinnati • 4000 Red Bank Rd, 45227 • 513-351-9818 • I-71 Exit 9 go S 1.8 miles on Red Bank Rd
✪	5				Cincinnati • 2322 Ferguson Rd, 45238 • 513-922-8881 • I-74 Exit 14 go S on Bend Rd for 2 miles; E on Harrison Ave for .2 miles; S on Boudinot Ave for 1.7 miles; E on Glenhills Way for .3 mile
✪	3	✓			Cincinnati • 8451 Colerain Ave, 45239 • 513-245-9458 • I-275 Exit 33 go SE on US-27 (Colerain Ave) 2.4 miles
✪	2	✓			Cincinnati • 1143 Smiley Ave, 45240 • 513-825-4423 • I-275 Exit 39 follow Winton Rd S 1.2 miles then NE at Smiley Ave .2 mile
✪	1	✓		✓	Cincinnati • 2801 Cunningham Rd, 45241 • 513-769-1124 • I-75 Exit 14 go E .8 mile on Glendale Milford Rd
✪	2	✓		✓	Cincinnati • 4370 Eastgate Square Dr, 45245 • 513-753-3200 • I-275 Exit 63B merge onto SR-32 E 1.3 miles then S at Eastgate Sq Dr .1 mile
✪	1	✓			Cincinnati • 10240 Colerain Ave, 45251 • 513-385-0083 • I-275 Exit 33, north of exit
✪		✓			Circleville • 1470 S Court St, 43113 • 740-477-3678 • Jct US-22/Main St & CR-188/Court St (in town) take Court St S 1.2 miles
✪	1	✓	❖		Clayton • 7725 Hoke Rd, 45315 • 937-836-9405 • I-70 Exit 26 go N on Hoke Rd .1 mile
✪	1	✓		✓	Cleveland • 3400 Steelyard Dr, 44109 • 216-661-2406 • I-71 Exit 247A (northbound exit only) follow Steelyard Dr E .2 mile and then S .4 mile
✪	1	✓			Cleveland • 10000 Brookpark Rd, 44130 • 216-741-7340 • I-480 Exit 13 go S .5 mile on Tiedeman Rd then E .2 mile on Brookpark Rd
☆	2				Columbus • 3579 S High St, 43207 • 614-409-0683 • I-270 Exit 52A merge onto US-23 N 1.2 miles

☆	◯	🕐	⛽	🚭	Store Details
✪	1	✓			Columbus • 3900 Morse Rd, 43219 • 614-476-2070 • I-270 Exit 32 go W on Morse Rd .7 mile
✪	4	✓			Columbus • 2700 Bethel Rd, 43220 • 614-326-0083 • I-270 Exit 20 take Sawmill Rd S 2.8 miles, Resler Rd E .3 mile, Picforde Dr S .2 mile & Bethel Rd W .2 mile
✪	1	✓			Columbus • 1221 Georgesville Rd, 43228 • 614-275-9811 • I-270 Exit 5 take Georgesville Rd N .6 mile
✪	1	✓			Columbus • 5200 West Pointe Plaza, 43228 • 614-876-7850 • I-70 Exit 91 (Exit 91B for westbound travelers) go N .3 mile on Hilliard Rome Rd then E .2 mile on Renner Rd
✪		✓			Cortland • 2016 Millenium Blvd, 44410 • 330-372-1772 • 3.7 miles northeast of Warren via Elm Rd and SR-5
✪		✓	❖		Coshocton • 23605 Airport Rd, 43812 • 740-622-1278 • I-77 Exit 65 take US-36 W 16.6 miles
✪	1	✓			Dayton • 3465 York Commons Blvd, 45414 • 937-454-6240 • I-75 Exit 59 take Benchwood Rd W .2 mile, Commerce Center N .2 mile & York Commons W .1 mile
✪	2	✓			Dayton • 8800 Kingsridge Dr, 45458 • 937-435-2222 • I-75 Exit 44 go E .4 mile on Miamisburg Centerville Rd, .5 mile S on Springboro Pike, then E .4 mile on Kingsridge Dr
✪	1	✓			Dayton • 6244 Wilmington Pike, 45459 • 937-848-3188 • I-675 Exit 7 take Wilmington Pike S .4 mile
✪		✓			Defiance • 1804 N Clinton St, 43512 • 419-784-2390 • 1 mile north of town along SR-66 (Clinton St)
☆	10				Delaware • 1760 Columbus Pike, 43015 • 740-363-9931 • I-71 Exit 131 take US-36 W 7.5 miles then US-23 S 2.4 miles
✪	1	✓			Dublin • 5900 Britton Pkwy, 43016 • 614-717-9660 • I-270 Exit 15 take Tuttle Crossing Blvd W .3 mile & Britton Pkwy S .2 mile
✪	1	✓		✓	Dublin • 7730 Sawmill Rd, 43016 • 614-943-6503 • I-270 Exit 20 go N 1 mile on Sawmill Rd
✪		✓			East Liverpool • 16280 Dresden Ave, 43920 • 330-386-4002 • Jct US-30 & SR-170 (N of town) go E on SR-170 & S on Dresden Ave .1 mile
✪	5	✓		✓	Eastlake • 33752 Vine St, 44095 • 440-269-8827 • I-90 Exit 185 take SR-2 E 3.1 miles, SR-91 N .5 mile & Vine St W .5 mile
✪	6	✓			Eaton • 100A E Washington Jackson Rd, 45320 • 937-456-1777 • I-70 Exit 10 take US-127 S 4.9 miles & Washington Jackson Rd W .6 mile

☆	◯	🕐	⛽	🚭	Store Details
✪	7	✓			Elyria • 1000 Chestnut Commons Dr, 44035 • 440-365-0135 • I-80 Exit 145 follow SR-57 S 5.8 mile, E .1 mile on Chestnut Ridge Rd, N .3 mile on Chestnut Commons Dr
☆	1				Fairlawn • 3750 W Market St, 44333 • 330-668-1129 • I-77 Exit 137A follow SR-18 E .7 mile
✪	1	✓	❖		Findlay • 1161 Trenton Ave, 45840 • 419-425-2186 • I-75 Exit 159 take US-224 W .3 mile
✪	5	✓			Findlay • 2500 Tiffin Ave, 45840 • 419-425-1300 • I-75 Exit 157 follow SR-12 West & North 1.2 miles, Center St E .3 mile, continue on Tiffin Ave 2.7 miles
✪	1	✓	❖		Franklin • 1275 E 2nd St, 45005 • 937-704-0568 • I-75 Exit 38 take 2nd St W .4 mile
✪	2	✓	❖	✓	Fremont • 2052 N State Rt 53, 43420 • 419-334-3190 • I-80/90 (toll) Exit 91 merge onto SR-53 S 1.7 miles
✪		✓			Gallipolis • 2145 Eastern Ave, 45631 • 740-441-0406 • 2 miles northeast of town center along SR-7
✪		✓			Greenville • 1501 Wagner Ave, 45331 • 937-547-9644 • 2 miles north of town center along US-127-BUS
✪	1	✓		✓	Grove City • 1693 Stringtown Rd, 43123 • 614-539-8560 • I-71 Exit 100 take Stringtown Rd E .2 mile
✪	9	✓	❖		Hamilton • 3201 Princeton Rd, 45011 • 513-869-8400 • I-75 Exit 24 take SR-129 W 7.8 miles & SR-4 BYP N .3 mile
✪		✓			Hamilton • 1505 Main St, 45013 • 513-737-0564 • I-75 Exit 24 take SR-129 W 12.2 miles, continue W on Main St 1.8 miles
✪	7	✓			Heath • 911 Hebron Rd, 43056 • 740-522-5841 • I-70 Exit 129B take SR-79 N 6.6 miles
✪		✓	❖		Hillsboro • 540 Harry Sauner Rd, 45133 • 937-840-0208 • Jct US-50 & US-62 (in town) take US-62 N 1.9 miles & Sauner Rd W .5 mile
✪	1	✓			Holland • 1355 S McCord Rd, 43528 • 419-867-0155 • I-475 Exit 8B follow SR-2 W .5 mile & McCord Rd N .4 mile
✪	1	✓			Huber Heights • 7680 Brandt Pike, 45424 • 937-237-1988 • I-70 Exit 38 take SR-201 S .2 mile
✪		✓	❖		Jackson • 100 Walmart Dr, 45640 • 740-288-2700 • 1.9 miles southeast of town center via SR-93
✪	1	✓			Kent • 250 Tallmadge Rd, 44240 • 330-673-3142 • I-76 Exit 31 take Tallmadge Rd W .4 mile
✪		✓	❖		Kenton • 1241 E Columbus St, 43326 • 419-675-1156 • Jct US-68 & SR-67 (in town) take SR-67 E .7 mile

☆	◯	🕐	⛽	🚫	Store Details
✪		✓			Lancaster • 2687 N Memorial Dr, 43130 • 740-687-0323 • 2.6 miles northwest of town center via US-33 BR/Memorial Dr
✪	5	✓			Lebanon • 1530 Walmart Dr, 45036 • 513-932-4236 • I-71 Exit 32 follow SR-123 W 2.4 miles then US-42 BYP N 1.9 miles & US-42 N .2 mile
✪	5	✓			Lewis Center • 8659 Columbus Pike, 43035 • 740-657-1341 • I-270 Exit 23 take US-23 N 4.4 miles
✪	1	✓	❖		Lima • 2400 Harding Hwy, 45804 • 419-222-4466 • I-75 Exit 175 follow SR-309 E .6 mile
✪	5	✓			Lima • 2450 Allentown Rd, 45805 • 419-224-3168 • I-75 Exit 125 (Exit 125B for southbound travelers) follow SR-117/SR-309 W 1.3 miles; continue W on Market St for .4 miles; go N on Central Ave .2 mile; then W on North St/SR-81 for 2.7 miles
✪		✓	❖		Logan • 12910 OH Hwy 664 S, 43138 • 740-380-1472 • Jct US-33 & SR-664 (W of town) take SR-664 N .3 mile
✪	5	✓			London • 375 Lafayette St, 43140 • 740-852-1507 • I-70 Exit 79 take US-42 S 4.5 miles
✪	4	✓			Lorain • 4380 Leavitt Rd, 44053 • 440-324-4104 • I-80/I-90 Exit 140 go N 3.7 miles on SR-58
✪	1	✓			Macedonia • 8160 Macedonia Commons Blvd, 44056 • 330-468-0200 • Southbound I-271 travelers use Exit 19 and go W to Macedonia Commons Blvd then S .3 mile; Northbound travelers use Exit 18 and go W .3 mile on SR-8 then N .4 mile on Macedonia Commons Blvd
✪	5	✓	❖		Madison • 6067 N Ridge Rd, 44057 • 440-417-0010 • I-90 Exit 212 follow SR-528 N 3 miles & US-20 W 1.2 miles
✪	1	✓	❖		Mansfield • 2485 Possum Run Rd, 44903 • 419-756-2850 • I-71 Exit 169 take SR-13 E .2 mile & Possum Run Rd S .3 mile
✪	1	✓			Marietta • 804 Pike St, 45750 • 740-376-9030 • I-77 Exit 1 take SR-7 E .5 mile
✪		✓			Marion • 1546 Marion Mount Gilead Rd, 43302 • 740-389-3404 • Jct US-23 & SR-95 (E of town) take SR-95 W .6 mile
✪		✓	❖		Marysville • 555 Colemans Crossing Blvd, 43040 • 937-644-2800 • 1.6 miles east of town center off 5th St at Colemans Crossing Blvd
✪	2	✓		✓	Mason • 5303 Bowen Dr, 45040 • 513-583-9330 • I-71 Exit 19 go N on Mason-Montgomery Rd 1.2 miles then W at Bowen Dr .2 mile
✪	8	✓			Massillon • 1 Massillon Marketplace Dr SW, 44646 • 330-834-0500 • I-77 Exit 104 take US-30 W 7.2 miles, SR-21 N .6 mile & Erie St S .2 mile
☆	1				Mayfield Heights • 6594 Mayfield Rd, 44124 • 440-446-0668 • I-271 Exit 34 merge onto US-322 E .2 mile
✪		✓		✓	Medina • 4141 Pearl Rd, 44256 • 330-723-1122 • 1.6 miles north of town center along US-42
☆	4		◆		Mentor • 9303 Mentor Ave, 44060 • 440-974-3300 • I-90 Exit 195 take SR-615 N 1.5 miles then US-20 E 1.9 miles
✪		✓			Middlefield • 15050 S Springdale Ave, 44062 • 440-632-0383 • Jct CR-608/State Ave & SR-87/High St (in town) take High St W .6 mile then Springdale Ave S .3 mile
✪	1	✓			Middletown • 2900 Towne Blvd, 45044 • 513-423-6785 • I-75 Exit 32 take SR-122 W .1 mile then Towne Blvd S .7 mile
✪	1	✓			Milford • 201 Chamber Dr, 45150 • 513-248-0067 • I-275 Exit 59 take Milford Pkwy W .7 mile then left at Chamber Dr
✪		✓			Millersburg • 1640 S Washington St, 44654 • 330-674-2888 • Jct US-62 & SR-83 (S of town) take SR-83 N 1.6 miles
✪	3	✓	❖		Moraine • 1701 W Dorothy Ln, 45439 • 937-643-2124 • I-75 Exit 47 go E on Dixie Ave .6 mile; N on Springboro Pike 1.6 miles; E on Dorothy Ln .7 mile
✪		✓			Mount Vernon • 1575 Coshocton Ave, 43050 • 740-392-3800 • Jct CR-308 & US-36 (E of town) take US-36 W 1.8 miles
✪		✓	❖	✓	Napoleon • 1815 Scott St, 43545 • 419-599-1973 • I-80/90 (toll) Exit 34 follow SR-108 S 13.8 miles
✪		✓			New Boston • 4490 Gallia St, 45662 • 740-456-8257 • .5 mile east of town on US-52
✪	1	✓			New Philadelphia • 231 Bluebell Dr NW, 44663 • 330-339-3991 • I-77 Exit 81 take SR-250 BR E .2 mile & Bluebell Dr N .2 mile
✪		✓	❖		Newark • 1315 N 21st St, 43055 • 740-364-9090 • I-70 Exit 132 follow SR-13 N 8.2 miles, Granville St NW 1.2 miles & 21st St N 1.3 miles
☆	1	✓			North Canton • 4572 Mega St NW, 44720 • 330-305-9527 • I-77 Exit 111 take Portage St W .2 mile, Strip Ave S .6 mile & Mega St W .1 mile

☆	⬡	🕐	⛽	🚫	Store Details
✪	1	✓		✓	North Olmsted · 24801 Brookpark Rd, 44070 · 440-979-9234 · I-480 Exit 6 (Exit 6B for westbound travelers) take SR-252 N .3 mile then Brookpark Rd E .2 mile
✪	6	✓			Norwalk · 340 Westwind Dr, 44857 · 419-663-2212 · I-80/90 (toll) take US-250 S 5.9 miles
✪	10	✓	❖		Oberlin · 46440 US Hwy 20, 44074 · 440-774-6720 · I-80/90 (toll) take Baumhart Rd S 7.3 miles then US-20 E 2.6 miles
✪	10	✓			Ontario · 359 N Lexington Springmill Rd, 44906 · 419-529-2950 · I-71 Exit 176 go W on US-30 for 7.9 miles; continue W on SR-309 for 1.6 miles; go S on Lexington-Springmill Rd for .4 miles
✪	2	✓			Oregon · 3721 Navarre Ave, 43616 · 419-698-2034 · I-280 Exit 7 take SR-2 E 1.7 miles
✪		✓			Ottawa · 1720 N Perry St, 45875 · 419-523-6995 · Jct SR-15 & SR-65 (N of town) go N on SR-65 for .9 mile
✪		✓			Oxford · 5720 College Corner Pike, 45056 · 513-524-4122 · Jct CR-732/N Main St & W Church St (in town) take Church St W .4 mile then US-27 NW for 1.8 miles
☆	7			✓	Parma · 8303 W Ridgewood Dr, 44129 · 440-884-5641 · I-77 Exit 153 take Pleasant Valley Rd W 4.4 miles, Ridge Rd N 1.4 miles & Ridgewood Dr W .4 mile
✪	1	✓			Perrysburg · 10400 Fremont Pike, 43551 · 419-874-0291 · I-75 Exit 193 take US-20 E .5 mile
✪	1	✓	❖		Piqua · 1300 E Ash St, 45356 · 937-615-9924 · I-75 Exit 82 take US-36 E .7 mile
✪	1	✓			Poland · 1300 Doral Dr, 44514 · 330-758-0011 · I-680 Exit 11 (Exit 11B for southbound travelers) go W .2 mile on Boardman Poland Rd then N .3 mile on Tiffany Blvd
✪		✓		✓	Port Clinton · 2826 E Harbor Rd, 43452 · 419-732-3369 · Jct US-2 & SR-163 (E of town) take SR-163 E 1.4 miles
✪	7	✓			Ravenna · 2600 OH Hwy 59, 44266 · 330-677-0338 · I-76 Exit 38 go N .7 mile on SR-44 (Ravenna Louisville Rd), continue N 2.6 miles on Prospect St, then go W 3.1 miles on SR-59
✪	1	✓			Reynoldsburg · 2793 Taylor Rd Ext, 43068 · 614-367-1015 · I-70 Exit 112 take SR-256 N .2 mile & Taylor Rd E .1 mile
✪	1	✓			Saint Clairsville · 50739 Valley Plaza Dr, 43950 · 740-695-8410 · I-70 Exit 218 take Mall Rd N .4 mile & Valley Centre Blvd W .3 mile
✪		✓	❖	✓	Salem · 2875 E State St, 44460 · 330-337-8313 · 2 miles east of town center along SR-14
✪	7	✓	❖		Sandusky · 5500 Milan Rd, 44870 · 419-627-8778 · I-80/90 (toll) take US-250 N 6.8 miles
✪	1	✓	❖		Sidney · 2400 Michigan St, 45365 · 937-498-2371 · I-75 Exit 92 take SR-47 W .5 mile
✪	6			✓	South Euclid · 1868 Warrensville Center Rd, 44121 · 216-382-1657 · I-271 Exit 34 go W 4.7 miles on Mayfield Rd then S .8 mile on Warrensville Center Rd
✪	3	✓			South Point · 354 Private Drive 288, 45680 · 740-894-3235 · I-64 Exit 6 (in WV) follow US-52 NW 3.5 miles
✪	4	✓	❖		Springfield · 200 S Tuttle Rd, 45503 · 937-325-2111 · I-70 Exit 62 go W 3.2 miles on US-40/National Rd
✪	4	✓			Springfield · 2100 N Bechtle Ave, 45504 · 937-399-0370 · I-70 Exit 52 take US-68 N 2.1 miles, US-40 E 1 mile & Bechtle Ave N .4 mile
✪		✓			Steubenville · 100 Mall Dr, 43952 · 740-266-7136 · Jct SR-43 & US-22 (W of town) take US-22 E 2.4 miles, Lovers Ln S 1.5 miles & Mall Dr E .5 mile
✪	7	✓			Stow · 3520 Hudson Dr, 44224 · 330-923-8232 · I-80 Exit 180 go S 6 miles on SR-8 to Graham Rd Exit and go W .1 mile then N .1 mile on Hudson Dr
✪	1	✓		✓	Streetsboro · 905 Singletary Dr, 44241 · 330-626-9990 · I-80 (toll) Exit 187, south of exit
✪	1	✓		✓	Strongsville · 8585 Pearl Rd, 44136 · 440-826-0004 · I-71 Exit 234 take US-42 SW .8 mile
✪		✓	❖	✓	Tiffin · 2801 W OH Hwy 18, 44883 · 419-448-4402 · Jct US-224 & SR-18 (W of town) take SR-18 N .2 mile
✪	5	✓			Toledo · 2925 Glendale Ave, 43614 · 419-380-0994 · I-75 Exit 201A take SR-25 S 3.5 miles then Glendale Ave W .9 mile
✪	1	✓			Toledo · 5821 W Central Ave, 43615 · 419-536-9105 · I-475 Exit 13 take US-20 E .8 mile
✪	1	✓			Troy · 1801 W Main St, 45373 · 937-339-7211 · I-75 Exit 74 take SR-41 W .4 mile
✪		✓			Upper Sandusky · 1855 E Wyandot Ave, 43351 · 419-294-3404 · Jct US-23/30 & CR-182 (W of town) take US-23/30 N .2 mile then Wyandot Ave E .1 mile
✪		✓			Urbana · 1840 E US Hwy 36, 43078 · 937-653-5313 · Jct SR-29 & US-36 (E of town) go E on US-36 for .6 mile

☆	♡	🕐	⛽	🚫	Store Details
✪		✓	❖		Van Wert • 301 Town Center Blvd, 45891 • 419-238-5662 • Jct US-127 & SR-116 (S of town) go W on Fox Rd .9 mile
✪	1	✓		✓	Wadsworth • 222 Smokerise Dr, 44281 • 330-336-5170 • I-76 Exit 9 take SR-94 N .4 mile & Smokerise Dr W .2 mile
✪	1	✓	❖		Wapakoneta • 1257 Bellefontaine St, 45895 • 419-738-0474 • I-75 Exit 111 go W on Bellefontaine Rd .4 mile
✪		✓	❖		Washington Court House • 1397 Leesburg Ave, 43160 • 740-333-3171 • I-71 Exit 65 take US-35 E 10.1 miles & US-62 N .5 mile
✪	2	✓	❖		Wauseon • 485 Airport Hwy, 43567 • 419-337-8900 • I-80 (toll) Exit 34 take SR-108 S 1.3 miles then US-20 ALT E .4 mile
✪		✓			Waverly • 990 W Emmitt Ave, 45690 • 740-947-1700 • Jct SR-220 & US-23 (in town) go S on US-23 .7 mile
✪	1	✓		✓	West Chester • 8288 Cincinnati Dayton Rd, 45069 • 513-777-2397 • I-75 Exit 21 go N on Cincinnati Dayton Rd .2 mile
✪		✓			West Union • 11217 OH Hwy 41, 45693 • 937-544-7198 • Jct SR-125 & SR-41 (W of town) take SR-41 S 1.6 miles
✪	1	✓		✓	Westerville • 50 E Schrock Rd, 43081 • 614-948-4402 • I-270 Exit 29 go N .7 mile on State St to Schrock Rd and turn right
✪	4	✓	❖		Whitehall • 3657 E Main St, 43213 • 614-239-7509 • I-270 Exit 41 follow US-40 W 3.4 miles
✪	8	✓	❖		Wilmington • 2825 Progress Way, 45177 • 937-382-4919 • I-71 Exit 50 follow US-68 SE 5.2 miles; US-22 E 2.6 miles; and Progress Way S .2 mile
✪		✓			Wooster • 3883 Burbank Rd, 44691 • 330-345-8955 • I-71 Exit 204 follow SR-83 E 10.9 miles
✪	9		❖		Xenia • 70 Hospitality Dr, 45385 • 937-376-9878 • I-675 Exit 13A take US-35 E 6.9 miles, US-35 BR E 1.1 miles & S on Progress Dr/ W on Harner
✪	1	✓			Youngstown • 200 Goldie Rd, 44505 • 330-759-2066 • I-80 eastbound travelers use Exit 229, turn right at exit and follow Liberty St to Belmont Ave then go S .4 mile; westbound travelers use Exit 229 and go S .8 mile on Belmont Ave
✪	3	✓			Zanesville • 2850 Maple Ave, 43701 • 740-455-9001 • I-70 Exit 153B merge onto Maple Ave N 2.1 miles
✪	5	✓	❖		Zanesville • 2850 Maysville Pike, 43701 • 740-452-3282 • I-70 Exit 155 take SR-146/60 S .6 mile, follow US-22 S 4.2 miles

OKLAHOMA

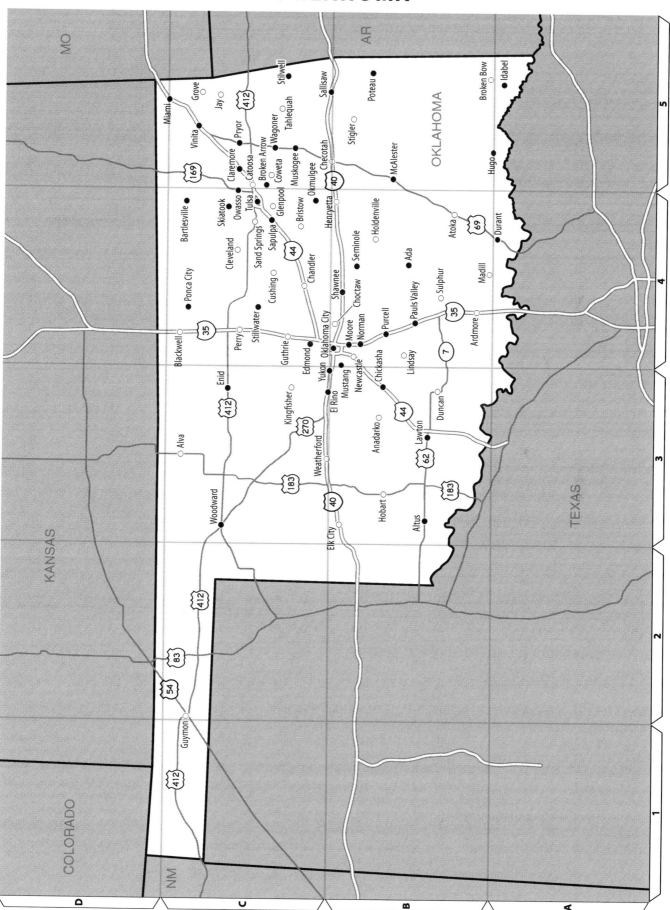

☆	◯	◷	⛽	🚫	Store Details
⚫		✓	◆		Ada • 1419 N Country Club Rd, 74820 • 580-332-2232 • Jct SR-1 & US-377 (N of town) go E on US-377 for .5 mile, continue E on Abbott Blvd 1 mile & CC Rd S .1 mile
⚫		✓	◆		Altus • 2500 N Main St, 73521 • 580-482-8189 • Jct SR-62 & US-283 (in town) take US-283 N 1.7 miles
⚫		✓			Alva • 914 E Oklahoma Blvd, 73717 • 580-327-4021 • At Jct US-64 & US-281 (E of town)
⚫		✓			Anadarko • 1201 W Petree Rd, 73005 • 405-247-2535 • Jct US-62 & SR-8 (E of town) take SR-8/7th St S 1 mile then Petree Rd W .6 mile
⚫	2	✓			Ardmore • 1715 N Commerce St, 73401 • 580-226-1257 • I-35 Exit 33 take SR-142 E 1.3 miles & US-77 S .7 mile
☆					Atoka • 1901 S Mississippi Ave, 74525 • 580-889-6676 • Jct SR-7 & US-75/69 (S of town) go S on US-75/69 for .5 mile
⚫		✓	❖		Bartlesville • 4000 SE Green Country Rd, 74006 • 918-335-6600 • Jct US-60 & US-75 (E of town) take US-75 S .2 mile & Green Country Rd E .2 mile
☆	3			✓	Blackwell • 1219 W Doolin Ave, 74631 • 580-363-4111 • I-35 Exit 222 take SR-11 E 2.2 miles
⚫	7	✓			Bristow • 105 W Hwy 16, 74010 • 918-367-3335 • I-44 (toll) Exit 196 take SR-48 S 1.3 miles & follow SR-16 5.3 miles
⚫		✓	❖		Broken Arrow • 6310 S Elm Pl, 74011 • 918-455-4354 • From I-44 at Exit 34 follow Creek Tpk for 15 miles to Elm Pl then go S .2 mile
⚫		✓	❖		Broken Arrow • 2301 W Kenosha St, 74012 • 918-259-9126 • Jct US-169 & SR-51 (NE of town) take SR-51 E 2.5 miles & Aspen Ave S 1.2 miles
⚫	8	✓			Broken Arrow • 3900 E Hillside Dr, 74014 • 918-355-1024 • From I-44 at Creek Turnpike, follow turnpike S 7.5 miles to Kenosha St exit and go W .1 mile
☆					Broken Bow • 501 S Park Dr, 74728 • 580-584-3324 • Jct SR-3 & US-259/70 (S of town) go S on US-259/70 for .2 mile
⚫	1	✓		✓	Catoosa • 19801 Robson Rd, 74015 • 918-739-7001 • I-44 Exit 240, north of exit
⚫	2	✓			Chandler • 3100 E 1st St, 74834 • 405-258-0541 • I-44 (toll) Exit 166 follow SR-18 S .7 mile then E on 1st St 1 mile
⚫	2	✓			Checotah • 131 Paul Carr Dr, 74426 • 918-473-2201 • I-40 Exit 264B take US-69 N 1.2 miles & US-266 E to Paul Carr Dr (frontage road)
⚫	1	✓	❖		Chickasha • 2001 S 1st St, 73018 • 405-224-1867 • I-44 (toll) Exit 80 merge onto US-277 N .5 mile then Grand Ave E .1 mile

☆	◯	◷	⛽	🚫	Store Details
⚫		✓			Choctaw • 14185 Mack Harrington Dr, 73020 • 405-390-4262 • West of town center off US-62 at Henney Rd
⚫	3	✓	❖		Claremore • 1500 S Lynn Riggs Blvd, 74017 • 918-341-2765 • I-44 (toll) Exit 255 go W 1.4 miles on Will Rogers Blvd, S 1.2 miles on Lynn Riggs Blvd and left onto frontage road
⚫		✓			Cleveland • 772 N Airport Rd, 74020 • 918-358-3553 • 1 mile south of town center along US-64
⚫		✓			Coweta • 11207 S Hwy 51, 74429 • 918-486-6511 • From Muskogee Tpk Exit 13 go W on SR-51 for 7 miles
⚫		✓			Cushing • 3100 E Main St, 74023 • 918-225-0578 • 2.6 miles east of town along SR-33 (Main St)
⚫		✓			Duncan • 1845 N Hwy 81, 73533 • 580-255-5455 • Jct SR-7 & US-81 (N of town) take US-81 S 4.7 miles
⚫		✓	❖		Durant • 3712 W Main St, 74701 • 580-920-0234 • Jct US-69 & US-70 (W of town) take US-70 W .6 mile
⚫	7	✓	❖	✓	Edmond • 2200 W Danforth Rd, 73003 • 405-216-0520 • I-35 Exit 143 take Covell Rd W 4.4 miles, Kelly Ave S 1 mile & Danforth Rd W .9 mile
⚫	1	✓		✓	Edmond • 1225 W I-35 Frontage Rd, 73034 • 405-348-8005 • I-35 Exit 140, west of exit
⚫	1	✓	❖		El Reno • 2400 S Country Club Rd, 73036 • 405-262-7354 • I-40 Exit 123 go N on Country Club Rd .2 mile
⚫	1				Elk City • 20221 E 1110 County Rd, 73644 • 580-225-3003 • I-40 Exit 40, south of exit
⚫		✓	❖		Enid • 5505 W Owen K Garriott Rd, 73703 • 580-237-7963 • Jct US-81 & US-60 (S of town) take US-60 W 3.3 miles
⚫		✓			Glenpool • 12200 S Waco, 74033 • 918-299-8030 • 2 miles north of town at US-75/SR-117 jct
⚫		✓			Grove • 2115 S Main St, 74344 • 918-786-8561 • I-44 (toll) Exit 302 follow US-59 S 16.1 miles
⚫	3	✓			Guthrie • 1608 S Division St, 73044 • 405-282-7900 • I-35 Exit 153 follow US-77 N 3 miles
⚫		✓			Guymon • 2600 N Hwy 64, 73942 • 580-338-1611 • 1.7 miles north of town center along US-64/US-412
☆	1				Henryetta • 605 E Main St, 74437 • 918-652-9676 • I-40 Exit 240B follow I-40 BR W .3 mile
☆					Hobart • 923 W 11th St, 73651 • 580-726-5693 • Jct US-183 & SR-9 (SE of town) go W on SR-9 for 2.3 miles

☆	♡	⏰	⛽	🚫	Store Details
☆					Holdenville • 500 E Hwy 270, 74848 • 405-379-6688 • Jct US-270 & US-270 BR (W of town) continue W on US-270 BR .8 mile
✪		✓	❖		Hugo • 1911 E Jackson St, 74743 • 580-326-6494 • Jct SR-93 & US-70 (E of town) take US-70 W .4 mile & US-70 BR NW 1 mile
✪		✓	❖		Idabel • 1907 SE Washington St, 74745 • 580-286-6696 • Jct SR-3 & US-259 (E of town) take SR-3 W 1.1 miles
☆					Jay • 1107 S Main St, 74346 • 918-253-4861 • Jct SR-127 & US-59 (SW of town) go N on US-59 for .3 mile
✪		✓			Kingfisher • 200 Starlite Dr, 73750 • 405-375-5743 • 2.3 miles south of town center along US-81
✪	3	✓			Lawton • 1002 NW Sheridan Rd, 73505 • 580-355-9070 • I-44 (toll) Exit 39A merge onto NW Cache Rd W 2 miles & Sheridan Rd S .3 mile
✪	5	✓	❖		Lawton • 6301 NW Quannah Parker Trl, 73505 • 580-510-9130 • I-44 (toll) Exit 39A follow Old US-62 W 4.7 miles
☆					Lindsay • 401 Linwood Plz, 73052 • 405-756-9535 • East end of town near jct of SR-76 and SR-19
✪		✓			Madill • 1100 South 1st St, 73446 • 580-795-7383 • 1.5 miles south of town center via US-70
✪		✓	◆		McAlester • 432 S George Nigh Expy, 74501 • 918-423-8585 • From Indian Nation Tpk Exit 63 take US-69 N 5.6 miles
✪	4	✓	❖		Miami • 2415 N Main St, 74354 • 918-542-6654 • I-44 (toll) Exit 313 take SR-10 W 1.4 miles & US-69 N 2.3 miles
✪	1	✓	◆	✓	Moore • 501 SW 19th St, 73160 • 405-790-0021 • I-35 Exit 116 take 19th St W .1 mile
✪		✓	❖		Muskogee • 1000 W Shawnee St, 74401 • 918-687-0058 • Jct SR-165 & US-62 (NW of town) take US-62 W 4 miles
✪	9	✓	❖		Mustang • 951 E OK Hwy 152, 73064 • 405-376-4549 • I-44 Exit 116B take SR-152 W 8.8 miles
✪	1	✓			Newcastle • 3300 Tri City Dr, 73065 • 405-387-3400 • I-44 Exit 108 take SR-37 W .1 mile then N on Tri City Dr .1 mile
✪	2	✓	◆	✓	Norman • 333 N Interstate Dr, 73069 • 405-329-4000 • I-35 Exit 109 merge E onto Main St .9 mile & N on Interstate Dr .3 mile
✪	6	✓	❖	✓	Norman • 3651 Classen Blvd, 73071 • 405-515-7024 • I-35 Exit 108A go E on SR-9 for about 4.5 miles then S .6 mile on US-77

☆	♡	⏰	⛽	🚫	Store Details
✪	5	✓	◆		Norman • 601 12th Ave NE, 73071 • 405-579-5203 • I-35 Exit 109 take Main St W 4.2 miles
✪	1	✓			Oklahoma City • 5401 Tinker Diagonal St, 73115 • 405-670-1007 • I-40 Exit 156A merge onto Tinker Diagonal W .3 mile
✪	1	✓			Oklahoma City • 1801 Belle Isle Blvd, 73118 • 405-841-6502 • I-44 Exit 125C take Belle Isle Blvd E .3 mile
✪	1	✓			Oklahoma City • 6100 W Reno Ave, 73127 • 405-491-0320 • I-40 Exit 144 take MacArthur Blvd N .3 mile & Reno Ave W .3 mile
✪	7	✓			Oklahoma City • 7800 NW Expressway, 73132 • 405-773-2625 • I-44 Exit 125C follow SR-3 NW for 6.9 miles
✪	9	✓			Oklahoma City • 2000 W Memorial Rd, 73134 • 405-752-1900 • I-44 Exit 123B take SR-74 N 6.8 miles, Kilpatrick Tpk (toll) W 1.3 miles & Penn Ave/Memorial Rd W .2 mile
✪	5	✓	❖	✓	Oklahoma City • 9011 NE 23rd St, 73141 • 405-769-2164 • I-35 Exit 130 take US-62 E 4.8 miles
✪	1	✓	❖		Oklahoma City • 100 E I-240 Service Rd, 73149 • 405-631-0746 • I-240 Exit 5 go NW to Service Rd .2 mile
✪		✓	◆		Okmulgee • 1800 S Wood Dr, 74447 • 918-756-6790 • I-40 Exit 240B follow US-75 N 12.6 miles
✪	10	✓	❖		Owasso • 12101 E 96th St N, 74055 • 918-272-6609 • I-244 Exit 13C take US-169 N 9.4 miles & 96th St W .4 mile
✪	2	✓	❖		Pauls Valley • 2008 W Grant Ave, 73075 • 405-238-7353 • I-35 Exit 72 take SR-19 E 1.1 miles
☆	2				Perry • 1506 Fir St, 73077 • 580-336-4491 • I-35 Exit 186 take Fir St/US-64 E 1.5 miles
✪		✓	◆		Ponca City • 1101 E Prospect Ave, 74601 • 580-762-0395 • Jct US-60 & US-60 BR (W of town) take US-60 BR E 3.1 miles, Union St N 2.4 miles & Prospect St E .7 mile
✪		✓	◆		Poteau • 3108 N Broadway St, 74953 • 918-647-5040 • Jct SR-112 & US-59 (N of town) take US-59 S .1 mile
✪		✓	❖		Pryor • 4901 S Mill St, 74361 • 918-825-6000 • I-44 (toll) Exit 255 take US-20 E 15.4 miles & US-69 S 3.2 miles
✪	1	✓	❖		Purcell • 2015 S Green Ave, 73080 • 405-527-5621 • I-35 Exit 91 take SR-74 N .7 mile
✪	1	✓	❖		Sallisaw • 1101 W Ruth Ave, 74955 • 918-775-4492 • I-40 Exit 308 take US-59 N .2 mile

☆	🛡	🕐	⛽	🚫	Store Details
✪	10	✓			Sand Springs • 220 S Hwy 97, 74063 • 918-245-0213 • I-44 (toll) Exit 215 follow SR-97 N 9.1 miles
✪	3	✓	◆		Sapulpa • 1002 W Taft St, 74066 • 918-224-8080 • I-44 (toll) Exit 215 take SR-97 S 1.8 miles then SR-117 E .7 mile
✪		✓	❖		Seminole • 1500 E Wrangler Blvd, 74868 • 405-382-5290 • I-40 Exit 200 take US-377 S 9.4 miles then SR-9 E .9 mile
✪	1	✓	❖		Shawnee • 196 Shawnee Mall Dr, 74804 • 405-275-1030 • I-40 Exit 186 go W to Shawnee Mall Dr .6 mile
✪		✓	❖		Skiatook • 700 W Rogers Blvd, 74070 • 918-396-1244 • Jct US-75 & SR-20 (E of town) follow SR-20 W 5.1 miles
✪		✓			Stigler • 1312 E Main St, 74462 • 918-967-4637 • 1 mile east of town along SR-9 (Main St)
✪		✓			Stillwater • 4545 W 6th Ave, 74074 • 405-707-0744 • Jct SR-51 & US-177 (E of town) take SR-51 W 3.8 miles
✪		✓	◆		Stillwater • 111 N Perkins Rd, 74075 • 405-372-2897 • Jct SR-51 & US-177 (E of town) take US-177 N .5 mile
✪		✓	❖		Stilwell • RR 6 Box 1895, 74960 • 918-696-3141 • 1.5 miles south of town via US-59
✪	10	✓			Sulphur • 2705 W Broadway Ave, 73086 • 580-622-6146 • I-35 Exit 55 go E 10 miles on SR-7
✪		✓			Tahlequah • 2020 S Muskogee Ave, 74464 • 918-456-8804 • Jct SR-51 & US-62 (S of town) go S on US-62 for .1 mile
✪	1	✓	❖		Tulsa • 207 S Memorial Dr, 74112 • 918-834-8700 • I-244 Exit 12A take Memorial Dr S .4 mile
✪	8	✓	❖		Tulsa • 10938 S Memorial Dr, 74133 • 918-394-4000 • I-44 Exit 231 follow US-64 SE 7.8 miles
✪	4	✓			Tulsa • 6625 S Memorial Dr, 74133 • 918-294-3800 • I-44 Exit 231 take SR-51 S .9 mile then Memorial Dr S 2.9 miles
✪	6	✓	◆		Tulsa • 2019 E 81st St, 74137 • 918-488-8791 • I-44 Exit 229 take Yale Ave S 2.3 miles, 71st St W 2 miles, Lewis Ave S 1 mile & 81st St W .2 mile
✪	1	✓	❖		Vinita • 268 S 7th St, 74301 • 918-256-7505 • I-44 (toll) Exit 289 take US-60/69 W .3 mile then S4410 Rd/7th St S .2 mile
✪		✓	◆		Wagoner • 410 S Dewey Ave, 74467 • 918-485-9515 • Jct SR-51 & US-69 (W of town) take US-69 S .1 mile
✪	1	✓			Weatherford • 1349 E Eagle Ave, 73096 • 580-772-1408 • I-40 Exit 82 go S .3 mile on Washington Ave then E .1 mile on Eagle Rd

☆	🛡	🕐	⛽	🚫	Store Details
✪		✓	◆		Woodward • 3215 Williams Ave, 73801 • 580-254-3331 • Jct US-412 & US-270 (in town) go S on US-270 for 1.4 miles
✪	1	✓	◆		Yukon • 1200 Garth Brooks Blvd, 73099 • 405-350-1900 • I-40 Exit 136 take SR-92 N .4 mile

OREGON

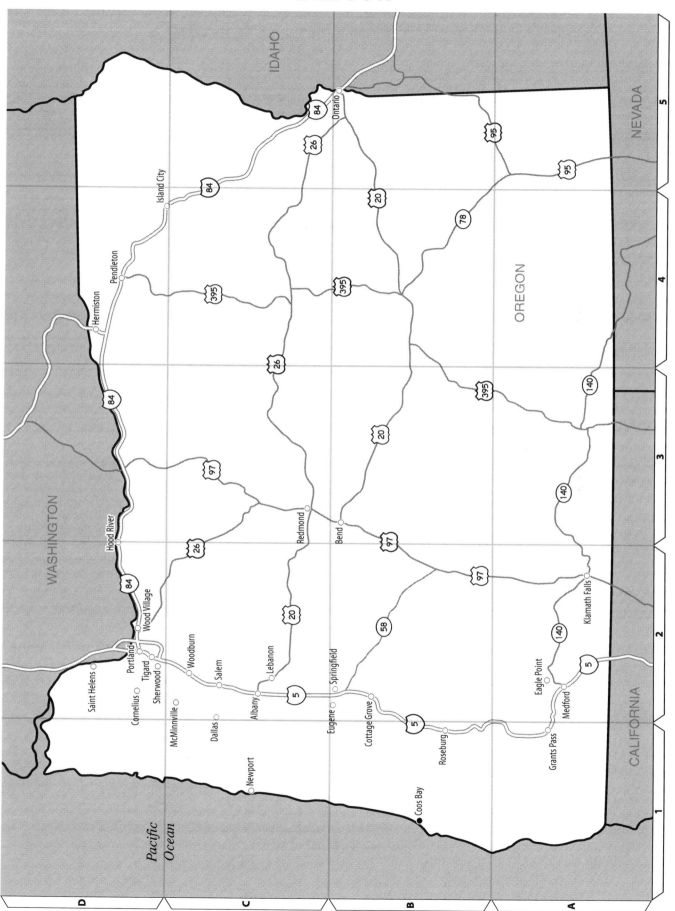

☆	◎	🕐	⛽	🚫⛽	Store Details
✪	1	✓		✓	Albany • 1330 Goldfish Farm Rd SE, 97322 • 541-971-4052 • I-5 Exit 233, go .7 miles E on US-20 and turn right on Goldfish Farm Rd
✪		✓			Bend • 20120 Pinebrook Blvd, 97702 • 541-389-8184 • 2.5 miles south of town center off Bend Pkwy at Pinebrook Blvd
✪		✓	◆		Coos Bay • 2051 Newmark Ave, 97420 • 541-888-5488 • From US-101 at Newmark St, go W 1.6 miles on Newmark St (which becomes Newmark Ave)
✪		✓			Cornelius • 220 N Adair St, 97113 • 503-207-0626 • From town center go E 2.2 miles on SR-8 then N .1 mile on 4th Ave
✪	1	✓		✓	Cottage Grove • 901 Row River Rd, 97424 • 541-942-4600 • I-5 Exit 174, east of exit
☆					Dallas • 321 NE Kings Valley Hwy, 97338 • 503-623-0490 • 1 mile northeast of town center on Kings Valley Hwy
✪	10	✓			Eagle Point • 11500 Hannon Rd, 97524 • 541-826-2210 • I-5 Exit 30 go N 9.6 miles on Crater Lake Hwy (SR-62)
✪		✓		✓	Eugene • 4550 W 11th Ave, 97402 • 541-344-2030 • 4 miles west of town along SR-126, east of the Beltline Hwy
☆	3			✓	Eugene • 1040 Green Acres Rd, 97408 • 541-343-6977 • I-5 Exit 195B go W 2.4 miles on Beltline Hwy, N .1 mile on Delta Hwy, and E .3 mile on Green Acres Rd
✪	1	✓		✓	Grants Pass • 135 NE Terry Ln, 97526 • 541-471-2822 • I-5 Exit 55 go W .5 mile on Grants Pass Pkwy
✪	8	✓			Hermiston • 1350 N 1st St, 97838 • 541-567-4854 • I-84 Exit 188 take US-395 N for 7.6 miles (located on US-395 north of town)
☆	1			✓	Hood River • 2700 Wasco St, 97031 • 541-387-2300 • I-84 Exit 62, go S .5 mile to Wasco St and turn left
✪	1				Island City • 11619 Island Ave, 97850 • 541-963-6783 • I-84 Exit 261, go NE .7 mile on Island Ave
✪		✓		✓	Klamath Falls • 3600 Washburn Way, 97603 • 541-885-6890 • From Jct US-97/SR-140, E on SR-140 2.5 miles, N on Washburn Way 1.4 miles
✪	10	✓			Lebanon • 3290 S Santiam Hwy, 97355 • 541-258-7400 • I-5 Exit 228 go E 7.7 miles on SR-34 then S 2.3 miles on US-20
☆					McMinnville • 2375 NE Hwy 99W, 97128 • 503-434-9233 • 2 miles northeast of town center along SR-99W

☆	◎	🕐	⛽	🚫⛽	Store Details
✪	1	✓		✓	Medford • 1360 Center Dr, 97501 • 541-772-2060 • I-5 Exit 27 go W .3 mile on Garfield St then N .1 mile on Center Dr
☆	2			✓	Medford • 3615 Crater Lake Hwy, 97504 • 541-770-2010 • I-5 Exit 30, follow SR-62 (Crater Lake Hwy) NE about 2 miles
✪		✓		✓	Newport • 160 NW 25th St, 97365 • 541-265-6560 • 1.3 miles north of town center along US-101
✪	1	✓			Ontario • 1775 E Idaho Ave, 97914 • 541-889-7400 • I-84 Exit 376B go N .4 mile
✪	1	✓			Pendleton • 2203 SW Court Ave, 97801 • 541-966-9970 • I-84 Exit 209 go N to SW 20th St and turn left .3 mile
✪	1			✓	Portland • 1123 Hayden Meadows Dr, 97217 • 503-205-8844 • I-5 Exit 306 go E on Victory Blvd; S .2 mile on Whitaker Rd; E .3 mile on Hayden Meadows Dr
✪	1			✓	Portland • 4200 SE 82nd Ave, 97266 • 503-788-0200 • I-205 Exit 19 go W .6 mile on Powell Blvd then S .4 mile on 82nd Ave
☆	1			✓	Portland • 10000 SE 82nd Ave, 97286 • 503-788-4748 • I-205 Exit 16 go W .3 mile on Johnson Creek Blvd then S .4 mile on 82nd Ave
✪		✓		✓	Redmond • 300 NW Oaktree Ln, 97756 • 541-923-5972 • 1.5 miles north of town center, east of US-97 at Maple Ave
✪	1	✓		✓	Roseburg • 2125 NW Stewart Pkwy, 97470 • 541-957-8550 • I-5 Exit 125 go W .7 mile on Garden Valley Blvd then N .2 mile on Stewart Pkwy
☆				✓	Saint Helens • 2295 Gable Rd, 97051 • 503-366-5866 • 2 miles southwest of town center at US-30/Gable Rd jct
✪	1	✓			Salem • 1940 Turner Rd SE, 97302 • 503-391-0394 • I-5 Exit 253 go W .8 mile on SR-22 then S .6 mile on Turner Rd
✪	2	✓			Salem • 3025 Lancaster Dr NE, 97305 • 503-378-7424 • I-5 Exit 256 go E .3 mile on Market St then N 1 mile on Lancaster Dr
☆	2			✓	Salem • 5250 Commercial St SE, 97306 • 503-378-1336 • I-5 Exit 252 go W 1.6 miles on Kuebler Blvd then S .2 mile on Commercial St
✪	5			✓	Sherwood • 21320 SW Langer Farms Pkwy, 97140 • 503-825-4050 • I-5 Exit 289 go W 4.3 miles on Nyberg St/Tualatin-Sherwood Rd
✪	4	✓			Springfield • 2659 Olympic St, 97477 • 541-744-3004 • I-5 Exit 194A go E 2.4 miles on OR-126 (McKenzie Hwy), S .2 mile on Mohawk Blvd, E .6 mile on Olympic St

☆	♡	🕐	⛽	🚫	Store Details
✪	1				Tigard • 7600 SW Dartmouth St, 97223 • 503-268-5270 • Southbound I-5 Exit 293 go W .3 mile on Dartmouth St; northbound I-5 Exit 293 go W .2 mile on Haines St, S .2 mile on 68th Ave, and W .3 mile on Dartmouth St
✪	1	✓			Wood Village • 23500 NE Sandy Blvd, 97060 • 503-665-9200 • I-84 Exit 16 go N .2 mile on 238th Dr then W .2 mile on Sandy Blvd
✪	1	✓			Woodburn • 3002 Stacey Allison Way, 97071 • 503-981-9622 • I-5 Exit 271 go E .1 mile on Newberg Hwy, S .1 mile on Lawson Ave, W .2 mile on Stacey Allison Way

PENNSYLVANIA

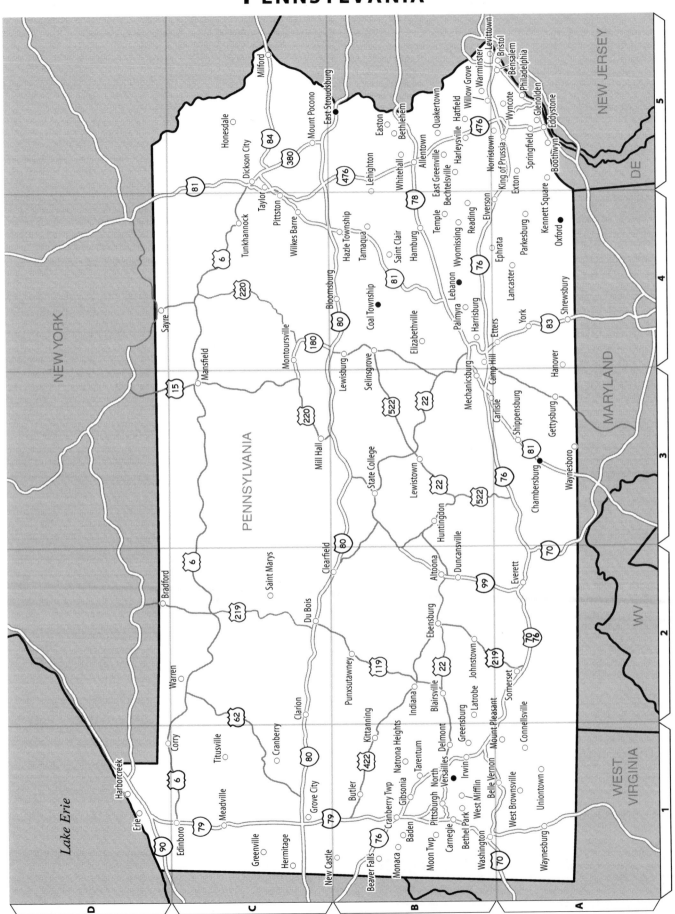

☆	♡	⏰	⛽	🚫⛽	Store Details
✪	4	✓			Allentown • 1091 Millcreek Rd, 18106 • 610-530-1400 • I-78 Exit 49A take SR-100 S 1.9 miles, continue S on Trexlertown Rd .2 mile then E on Cetronia Rd 1.1 miles
✪	1	✓			Altoona • 2600 Plank Rd Commons, 16601 • 814-949-8980 • I-99 Exit 31 take Plank Rd S .6 mile
✪		✓			Baden • 1500 Economy Way, 15005 • 724-390-9016 • 2 miles north of town via SR-65 and Economy Way
✪	7	✓			Beaver Falls • 100 Chippewa Town Ctr, 15010 • 724-843-1100 • I-76 Exit 10 take SR-60 (toll) S 5.6 miles to Exit 29-SR-51 N 1.4 miles
✪		✓			Bechtelsville • 567 Rt 100 N, 19505 • 610-367-1005 • Jct US-422 & SR-100 (S of town) follow SR-100 N 10.6 miles
✪	1	✓		✓	Belle Vernon • 100 Sara Way, 15012 • 724-929-2424 • I-70 Exit 43A (Exit 43 for eastbound travelers) take SR-201 S .2 mile & W at Sara Way .2 mile
☆	3				Bensalem • 3461 Horizon Blvd, 19020 • 215-942-4005 • I-276 (toll) Exit 351 take US-1 S .8 mile, SR-132 N .2 mile, Old Lincoln Hwy E .8 mile & Rockhill Dr S .3 mile
☆	8				Bethel Park • 5055 Library Rd, 15102 • 412-831-0459 • I-79 Exit 54 go E .2 mile on SR-50, N .4 mile on Washington Pike, E 1.6 miles on Bower Hill Rd, turn right and continue E 2.4 miles on Painters Run Rd/Gilkeson Rd, continue E 2.2 miles on Connor Rd/Yellow Belt, then S .5 mile on Library Rd/PA-88
☆	8			✓	Bethlehem • 3926 Linden St, 18020 • 610-867-1300 • I-78 Exit 71 take SR-33 N 3.9 miles, US-22 W 3.1 miles & SR-191 S .3 mile
✪		✓			Blairsville • 300 Resort Plaza Dr, 15717 • 724-459-3349 • Jct US-119 & US-22 (E of town) go W on US-22 for .6 mile then S at Resort Plaza Dr
✪	1	✓			Bloomsburg • 100 Lunger Dr, 17815 • 570-389-5750 • I-80 Exit 232 go E on Lunger Dr .3 mile
☆	3				Boothwyn • 605 Conchester Hwy, 19061 • 610-494-2535 • I-95 Exit 3A take US-322 W 2.3 miles
✪		✓			Bradford • 50 Foster Brook Blvd, 16701 • 814-368-4600 • Jct SR-219 & SR-346 (N of town) take Jackson Ave SW 1.5 miles, School St W .4 mile & Interstate Pkwy NW .2 mile
☆	3				Bristol • 100 Commerce Cir, 19007 • 215-788-5600 • I-95 Exit 40 follow SR-413 S 2.4 miles then E at Commerce Cir .2 mile

☆	♡	⏰	⛽	🚫⛽	Store Details
✪		✓			Butler • 400 Butler Commons, 16001 • 724-282-4060 • 2.8 miles northwest of town center along SR-356
✪	4	✓			Camp Hill • 3400 Hartzdale Dr, 17011 • 717-409-3102 • I-76 Exit 236 go N 2.9 miles on US-15 to Lower Allen Dr and turn right to Hartzdale Dr and turn left (north) for .6 miles
✪	1	✓		✓	Carlisle • 60 Noble Blvd, 17013 • 717-258-1250 • I-81 Exit 47B take SR-34 N .2 mile then W on Noble Blvd
☆	1				Carnegie • 2200 Washington Pike, 15106 • 412-429-1285 • I-79 Exit 55 follow US-50 N 1 mile
✪	2	✓	◆		Chambersburg • 1730 Lincoln Way E, 17201 • 717-264-2300 • I-81 Exit 16 take US-30 E 1.6 miles
✪	1	✓			Clarion • 63 Perkins Rd, 16214 • 814-226-0809 • I-80 Exit 62 go N on SR-68 for .5 mile
✪	1	✓			Clearfield • 100 Supercenter Dr, 16830 • 814-765-8089 • I-80 Exit 120 go S on SR-879
✪		✓	◆		Coal Township • 3300 State Route 61, 17866 • 570-648-6700 • 1.8 miles east of town on SR-61
✪		✓			Connellsville • 1450 Morrell Ave, 15425 • 724-626-4470 • Jct SR-201/Vanderbilt Rd & US-119/Morrell Rd (S of town) follow US-119 S 1 mile
✪		✓			Corry • 961 E Columbus Ave, 16407 • 814-663-8070 • 2.3 miles northeast of town center on US-6
✪		✓			Cranberry • 10 Kimberly Ln, 16319 • 814-678-0037 • Jct SR-257 & US-322 (N of town) take US-322 W .4 mile then Ross Dr S
✪	2	✓			Cranberry Twp • 20245 Rt 19, 16066 • 724-772-4550 • I-79 Exit 78 take SR-228 W .4 mile, Dutilh Rd N .6 mile & US-19 S .3 mile
✪		✓			Delmont • 6700 Hollywood Blvd, 15626 • 724-468-6274 • I-76 (toll) Exit 57 follow US-22 E 10.1 miles then Hollywood Blvd S .6 mile
✪	2	✓			Dickson City • 900 Commerce Blvd, 18519 • 570-383-2354 • I-81 Exit 191A take US-6 BR E .8 mile, Viewmont Dr S .2 mile & Commerce Blvd E .4 mile
✪	2	✓			Du Bois • 20 Industrial Dr, 15801 • 814-375-5000 • I-80 Exit 101 go S 1.7 miles on SR-255 then turn right on Industrial Dr .3 mile.
✪	1	✓			Duncansville • 200 Commerce Dr, 16635 • 814-693-0531 • I-99 at Exit 23, east of exit

☆	◯	🕐	⛽	🚫	Store Details
✪	6	✓			East Greenville • 620 Gravel Pike, 18041 • 215-679-2782 • I-476 Exit 44 take SR-663 W 4.5 miles, Quakertown Ave W .4 mile, Main St N .1 mile & Gravel Pike N .1 mile
✪	1	✓	◆		East Stroudsburg • 355 Lincoln Ave, 18301 • 570-424-8415 • I-80 Exit 308 merge onto Prospect St W .1 mile & N on Forge Rd/Lincoln Ave .9 mile
✪	10	✓			Easton • 3722 Easton Nazareth Hwy, 18045 • 610-250-8603 • I-78 Exit 3 follow US-22 W 7.9 miles & SR-248 NW 2.2 miles
✪		✓			Ebensburg • 300 Walmart Dr, 15931 • 814-471-0200 • I-99 Exit 28 go N on US-32 .8 mile then US-22 W 19.3 miles
☆	2				Eddystone • 1570 Chester Pike, 19022 • 610-447-1860 • I-95 Exit 8 take Stewart Ave W .2 mile & US-13 S .9 mile
✪	1	✓			Edinboro • 108 Washington Towne Blvd N, 16412 • 814-734-0900 • I-79 Exit 166, east of exit
✪		✓			Elizabethville • 200 Kocher Ln, 17023 • 717-362-3696 • 1.4 miles northeast of town center via US-209
✪	2	✓			Elverson • 100 Crossings Blvd, 19520 • 610-913-2000 • I-76 (toll) Exit 298 follow SR-10 E .3 mile, Quarry Rd S .4 mile, Morgan Way W .2 mile & Main St E .7 mile
✪		✓		✓	Ephrata • 890 E Main St, 17522 • 717-721-6680 • Jct US-222 & US-322 (SE of town) go NW on US-322 for .6 mile
✪	5	✓			Erie • 2711 Elm St, 16504 • 814-459-3625 • I-79 Exit 182 take US-20/26th St E 4.7 miles then S on Elm St
✪	5	✓			Erie • 5350 W Ridge Rd, 16506 • 814-835-0556 • I-79 Exit 182 go W 4.1 miles on US-20
✪	1	✓			Erie • 1825 Downs Dr, 16509 • 814-864-7330 • I-90 Exit 24 go N .2 mile on US-19 then E .1 mile on Downs Dr
✪	1	✓			Etters • 50 Newberry Pkwy, 17319 • 717-932-4384 • I-83 Exit 33, east of exit
☆	5				Everett • 72 Bedford Sq, 15537 • 814-623-3332 • Jct I-99/US-220 & US-30 (W of town) take US-30 E 4.5 miles & S at Bedford Sq
☆					Exton • 270 Indian Run St, 19341 • 484-875-9053 • Jct US-202 & US-30 (E of town) take US-30 W .4 mile, Lincoln Hwy W 2 miles, Commerce Dr S .3 mile & Indian Run W .1 mile
☆				✓	Gettysburg • 1270 York Rd, 17325 • 717-334-2000 • Jct US-15 & US-30 (E of town) go W on US-30 .5 mile
☆	1				Gibsonia • 300 Walmart Dr, 15044 • 724-449-2700 • I-76 (toll) Exit 39 take SR-8 N .6 mile then W at Theater Dr

☆	◯	🕐	⛽	🚫	Store Details
☆	6				Glenolden • 50 N Macdade Blvd, 19036 • 610-583-2682 • I-476 (toll) Exit 3 follow E Baltimore Pike E 1.9 miles, Woodland/Kedron Ave SE 1.8 miles & Macdade Blvd E 1.4 miles
✪	6	✓		✓	Greensburg • 2200 Greengate Centre Cir, 15601 • 724-830-2440 • I-76 Exit 67 take US-30 E 5.5 miles then Greengate Centre Dr N .2 mile
✪		✓			Greenville • 45 Williamson Rd, 16125 • 724-589-0211 • I-79 Exit 130 follow SR-358 W 11.8 miles then Williamson Rd N .1 mile
☆	4				Grove City • 1566 W Main St Ext, 16127 • 724-458-5877 • I-79 Exit 113 take SR-208 NE 2 miles, Irishtown Rd N 1.3 miles & Main St S .6 mile
✪	1	✓			Hamburg • 1800 Tilden Ridge, 19526 • 484-668-4001 • I-78 Exit 29 go N 1 mile on SR-61
✪		✓			Hanover • 1881 Baltimore Pike, 17331 • 717-630-8211 • Jct Grandview Rd & SR-94 (S of town) go S on SR-94 for .9 mile
✪		✓			Hanover • 495 Eisenhower Dr, 17331 • 717-632-8444 • Jct US-15 & US-30 (NW of town) take US-30 E 9 miles, SR-94 S 3.7 miles & Eisenhower Dr E 1 mile
✪	5	✓			Harborcreek • 5741 Buffalo Rd, 16421 • 814-899-6255 • I-90 Exit 32 take SR-430 N .3 mile, Hannon Rd N 2.9 miles & US-20 W .9 mile
☆	4				Harleysville • 651 Main St, 19438 • 215-513-0205 • I-476 (toll) Exit 31 take SR-63 NW 3.9 miles
✪	3	✓			Harrisburg • 6535 Grayson Rd, 17111 • 717-561-8402 • I-83 Exit 47 take US-322 E 2.7 miles, Mushroom Hill Rd N .2 mile & Grayson Rd E .1 mile
✪		✓			Hatfield • 1515 Bethlehem Pike, 19440 • 215-997-2929 • I-276 (toll) Exit 339 take SR-309 N 12 miles
✪	2	✓			Hazle Township • 87 Airport Rd, 18202 • 570-454-8322 • I-81 Exit 145 go E .5 mile on SR-93 then N .7 mile on Airport Rd
✪	6	✓			Hermitage • 1275 N Hermitage Rd, 16148 • 724-346-5940 • I-80 Exit 4B take SR-60 N .8 mile & SR-18 N 4.6 miles
✪		✓			Honesdale • 777 Old Willow Ave, 18431 • 570-251-9543 • I-84 Exit 30 take SR-402 N 4.5 miles, follow US-6 N 11.6 miles & E at Brook Rd .3 mile
✪		✓			Huntingdon • 6716 Towne Center Blvd, 16652 • 814-644-6910 • 1.8 miles west of town center via SR-26

☆	◯	🕐	⛽	🚐	Store Details
✪		✓		✓	Indiana • 3100 Oakland Ave, 15701 • 724-349-3565 • Jct US-422 & SR-286 (S of town) take SR-286/Oakland Ave N .2 mile
✪	1	✓			Irwin • 915 Mills Dr, 15642 • 724-382-3160 • I-76 Exit 67 go W on US-30 .1 mile, left onto Ronda Ct .1 mile, right onto Mills Dr .1 mile
✪		✓			Johnstown • 150 Town Centre Dr, 15904 • 814-266-6996 • Jct US-219 & SR-756 (SE of town) go E on SR-756 for .2 mile & S at Town Center Dr
✪					Kennett Square • 516 School House Rd, 19348 • 610-444-2268 • 2 miles east of town center off US-1
✪	1	✓			King of Prussia • 275 N Gulph Rd, 19406 • 610-768-0530 • I-76 Exit 327, south of exit
✪		✓			Kittanning • 1 Hilltop Plaza, 16201 • 724-543-2023 • 2 miles west of town center via US-422-BUS
☆				✓	Lancaster • 2030 Fruitville Pike, 17601 • 717-581-0200 • From US-30 (NW of town) take Fruitviille Pike N .6 mile
✪		✓			Lancaster • 2034 Lincoln Hwy E, 17602 • 717-390-1738 • Jct US-222 & US-30 (NE of town) take US-30 E for 4.1 miles & Lincoln Hwy E .2 mile
✪		✓			Latrobe • 100 Colony Ln, 15650 • 724-537-0928 • Jct SR-982 & US-30 (S of town) take US-30 W .9 mile & S at Colony Lane
✪	10	✓	◆		Lebanon • 1355 E Lehman St, 17046 • 717-228-1221 • I-76 (toll) Exit 266 follow SR-72 N 7.4 miles, US-422 E 1.8 miles, Cumberland St .3 mile, 11th Ave N .2 mile & Lehman St E .3 mile
✪	5	✓			Lehighton • 1731 Blakeslee Blvd Dr E, 18235 • 570-386-3356 • I-476 Exit 74 go W 2 miles on US-209 then continue W 2.4 miles on SR-443/Blakeslee Blvd Dr
✪	3	✓			Levittown • 180 Levittown Pkwy, 19007 • 215-949-6600 • I-276 Exit 359 go N 2.2 miles on US-13/Bristol Pike then W .2 mile on Levittown Pkwy
✪	6	✓			Lewisburg • 120 AJK Blvd, 17837 • 570-522-8200 • I-80 Exit 210A follow US-15 S 5.2 miles
✪		✓			Lewistown • 10180 US Hwy 522 S, 17044 • 717-242-6201 • Jct US-22 & US-522 (in town) go SW on US-522/US-22 BR 2.8 miles
✪		✓			Mansfield • 1169 S Main St, 16933 • 570-662-1115 • Jct SR-660 & US-15 (S of town) take SR-660/US-15 BR N 1.1 miles
✪	3	✓			Meadville • 16086 Conneaut Lake Rd, 16335 • 814-724-6267 • I-79 Exit 147B take US-6 W 2.3 miles

☆	◯	🕐	⛽	🚐	Store Details
✪	2	✓			Mechanicsburg • 6520 Carlisle Pike, 17050 • 717-691-3150 • I-81 Exit 57 follow SR-114 E 1.7 miles & US-11 E .2 mile
✪	1	✓		✓	Milford • 220 Rt 6 & 209, 18337 • 570-491-4940 • I-84 Exit 46 merge onto US-6 E .5 mile
✪	6	✓			Mill Hall • 167 Hogan Blvd, 17751 • 570-893-4627 • I-80 Exit 178 take US-220 N 4.8 miles then Mill Hall Rd/SR-150 N .7 mile
✪	2	✓			Monaca • 3942 Brodhead Rd, 15061 • 724-773-2929 • I-376 Exit 39 go E on SR-18 for 1.5 miles
☆	1				Montoursville • 1015 N Loyalsock Ave, 17754 • 570-368-5450 • I-180 Exit 21 take Loyalsock Ave S .3 mile
✪	9	✓			Moon Township • 7500 University Blvd, 15108 • 412-893-0143 • I-79 Exit 60 follow SR-60 W 1.3 miles then right 7 miles on Beaver Grade Rd
✪	9	✓			Mount Pleasant • 2100 Summit Ridge Plz, 15666 • 724-542-7300 • I-70/76 (toll) Exit 75 follow US-119 S 7.5 miles & SR-819 NE .6 mile
✪	2	✓			Mount Pocono • 3271 Route 940, 18344 • 570-895-4700 • I-380 Exit 3 take SR-940 E 1.9 miles
✪		✓			Natrona Heights • 4015 Freeport Rd, 15065 • 724-226-6949 • From SR-28 Exit 15 go E .8 mile on Burtner Rd then N 1.2 miles on Freeport Rd
✪		✓			New Castle • 2501 W State St, 16101 • 724-657-9390 • I-80 Exit 4A take SR-60 S 13.5 miles & US-224 E .3 mile
☆	4				Norristown • 53 W Germantown Pike, 19401 • 610-275-0222 • I-276 (toll) Exit 333 take Plymouth Rd E .2 mile & Germantown Pike NW 2.9 miles
✪	5	✓			Norristown • 650 S Trooper Rd, 19403 • 610-631-6750 • I-76 Exit 328A take US-422 W 3 miles then follow SR-363 N 1.5 miles
✪	10	✓	◆		North Versailles • 100 Walmart Dr, 15137 • 412-816-0301 • I-76 (toll) Exit 67 take US-30 W 9 miles & Greensburg Ave N .6 mile
✪		✓	◆		Oxford • 800 Commons Dr, 19363 • 484-702-7206 • .7 mile north of town center along SR-10
✪	9	✓			Palmyra • 100 N Londonderry Sq, 17078 • 717-838-0800 • I-81 Exit 85 follow SR-934 S 5 miles, Clearspring Rd S 2 miles, and US-422 W 1.2 miles
✪		✓			Parkesburg • 100 Commons Dr, 19365 • 610-857-0500 • Jct US-30 & SR-10 (N of town) go S on SR-10/Octorara Trl .1 mile

☆	♥	🕐	⛽	🚫	Store Details
☆	4				Philadelphia • 9745 Roosevelt Blvd, 19114 • 215-698-0350 • I-95 Exit 32 take Academy Rd N 2.2 miles, Grant Ave W 1.4 miles & Roosevelt Blvd N .4 mile
✪	1	✓		✓	Philadelphia • 4301 Byberry Rd, 19154 • 215-281-3159 • I-95 Exit 35 go NW .5 mile on SR-63 to the Franklin Mills Blvd/Millbrook Rd exit and turn right
☆	6				Philadelphia • 4600 Roosevelt Blvd, 19124 • 215-288-0700 • I-76 Exit 340B merge onto US-1 N 6 miles
✪	1				Philadelphia • 2200 Wheatsheaf Ln, 19137 • 215-613-2236 • I-95 Exit 26 follow Aramingo Ave southwest for .5 mile
✪	1	✓		✓	Philadelphia • 1675 S Columbus Blvd, 19148 • 215-468-4220 • I-95 Exit 20 take Columbus Blvd S 1 mile
☆	8			✓	Pittsburgh • 877 Freeport Rd, 15238 • 412-782-4444 • From I-579 take SR-28 N 7.3 miles to Exit 8, then Freeport Rd E .5 mile
✪	5	✓			Pittsburgh • 250 Summit Park Dr, 15275 • 412-788-9055 • I-79 Exit 59B take US-22 W 4 miles, US-60 N .3 mile to Exit 1, follow Summit Park Dr W .6 mile
✪	1	✓			Pittston • 390 Highway 315, 18640 • 570-883-9400 • Southbound I-81 travelers use Exit 175B and go W 400 feet on SR-315; Northbound travelers use Exit 175 and follow SR-315 for .9 mile
✪		✓			Punxsutawney • 21920 Rt 119, 15767 • 814-938-3500 • Jct SR-36 & US-119 (in town) take US-119 S 1.2 miles
☆	4				Quakertown • 195 N West End Blvd, 18951 • 215-529-7689 • I-476 (toll) Exit 44 follow SR-663 E 3.5 miles then N on West End Blvd .2 mile
✪	4	✓			Reading • 5900 Perkiomen Ave, 19606 • 610-582-0505 • I-176/Morgantown Expy Exit 11A merge onto US-422 E 3.5 miles
✪	5	✓			Saint Clair • 500 Terry Rich Blvd, 17970 • 570-429-1959 • I-81 Exit 124A follow SR-61 S 4.4 miles
✪		✓			Saint Marys • 1102 Million Dollar Hwy, 15857 • 814-781-1344 • Jct SR-120 & SR-255 (in town) go S on SR-255 for 2.6 miles
✪		✓			Sayre • 1887 Elmira St, 18840 • 570-888-9791 • 1.6 miles west of town center off US-220 along Elmira St
✪		✓			Selinsgrove • 980 N Susquehanna Trail, 17870 • 570-374-1230 • 2 miles north of town along US-11/US-15
✪	1	✓			Shippensburg • 100 S Conestoga Dr, 17257 • 717-532-4240 • I-81 Exit 29 take SR-174 W .9 mile then N at Conestoga Dr .1 mile

☆	♥	🕐	⛽	🚫	Store Details
✪	1	✓			Shrewsbury • 698 Shrewsbury Commons Ave, 17361 • 717-235-6363 • I-83 Exit 4 merge onto SR-851 W .2 mile & S on Mt Airy Rd .3 mile
✪	3	✓			Somerset • 2028 N Center Ave, 15501 • 814-443-6962 • I-70/76 (toll) Exit 110 go N on Center Ave 2.5 miles
✪	1	✓		✓	Springfield • 400 S State Rd, 19064 • 610-605-3154 • I-476 Exit 5 go E .5 mile on US-1
✪		✓		✓	State College • 373 Benner Pike, 16801 • 814-235-9306 • I-80 Exit 161 follow US-220 S 7.2 miles to Exit 78A, SR-150 S for 3.3 miles
✪		✓			State College • 1665 N Atherton St, 16803 • 814-237-8401 • I-80 Exit 161 follow US-220 S 14.9 miles, Waddle Rd S .8 mile & Vaero Rd W .2 mile
✪		✓			Tamaqua • 35 Plaza Dr, 18252 • 570-668-2054 • 2.9 miles north of town via SR-309
✪		✓			Tarentum • 2010 Village Center Dr, 15084 • 724-274-0260 • From SR-28/Allegheny Valley Expy Exit 12A go W .5 mile on Pittsburgh Mills Blvd then S at Village Center Dr .3 mile
✪	4	✓			Taylor • 1325 Main, 18517 • 570-309-3510 • I-81 Exit 182 go W 1.7 miles on Davis St then N 1.4 miles on Main St
✪		✓			Temple • 5370 Allentown Pike, 19560 • 610-939-0601 • I-78 Exit 29A take SR-61 S 12.3 miles, Tuckerton Rd E .5 mile & 5th St N .6 mile
✪		✓			Titusville • 11415 Hydetown Rd, 16354 • 814-827-0850 • Jct SR-27 & SR-8 (in town) go NW on SR-8 for 1.4 miles
✪		✓			Tunkhannock • 808 Hunter Hwy, 18657 • 570-836-8064 • 1 mile south of town center along SR-29/Hunter Hwy
✪		✓			Uniontown • 355 Walmart Dr, 15401 • 724-438-3344 • 2 miles northwest of town center along US-40, west side of highway
✪	8	✓			Warminster • 100 E Street Rd, 18974 • 215-442-5670 • I-276 (toll) Exit 351 take US-1 S .6 mile & SR-132 W 7.3 miles
✪		✓			Warren • 2901 Market St, 16365 • 814-723-2640 • 2.7 miles north of town via US-62
✪	1	✓			Washington • 30 Trinity Point Dr, 15301 • 724-229-4020 • I-70 Exit 19B take US-19 N .4 mile then Trinity Pt Dr E .3 mile
✪		✓			Waynesboro • 12751 Washington Township Blvd, 17268 • 717-762-2282 • 3.3 miles east of town center via SR-16
✪	1	✓			Waynesburg • 405 Murtha Dr, 15370 • 724-627-3496 • I-79 Exit 14 go E .5 mile on SR-21 then south to store.

☆	◯	🕐	⛽	🚭	Store Details
✪	8	✓			West Brownsville • 134 Daniel Kendall Dr, 15417 • 724-364-4076 • I-70 Exit 37A go S 5.8 miles on SR-43 then E 1 mile on US-40/SR-88
✪		✓			West Mifflin • 2351 Century Dr, 15122 • 412-655-3404 • Jct SR-51 & SR-885/ Yellow Belt (W of town) take SR-885 E .2 mile & S on Mt View/Century Dr .5 mile
☆				✓	Whitehall • 2601 Macarthur Rd, 18052 • 610-266-9645 • I-78 Exit 71 take SR-33 N 4.2 miles, US-22 W 11.4 miles & Macarthur Rd N 1.4 miles
✪	2	✓		✓	Wilkes Barre • 2150 Wilkes Barre Township Market Pl, 18702 • 570-821-6180 • I-81 Exit 165 merge onto SR-309 N 1.3 miles
✪	2	✓			Willow Grove • 2101 Blair Mill Rd, 19090 • 215-830-8370 • I-276/PA Tpk Exit 343 go N .5 mile on SR-611 then W 1 mile on Blair Mill Rd
☆	5				Wyncote • 1000 Easton Rd, 19095 • 215-887-6737 • I-276 (toll) Exit 339 follow SR-309 S 4.5 miles, exit at Easton Rd and go SW .3 mile
☆					Wyomissing • 1135 Berkshire Blvd, 19610 • 610-376-5848 • Jct US-422 & US-222, take US-222 S .7 mile, Papermill Rd W .3 mile, Woodland Rd S .2 mile, Ridgewood Rd W .2 mile
✪	2	✓		✓	York • 2801 E Market St, 17402 • 717-755-1600 • I-83 Exit 18 take SR-124 E .2 mile, Haines Rd N 1 mile, Mills St N .1 mile & SR-462 W .3 mile
✪	3	✓		✓	York • 1800 Loucks Rd, 17408 • 717-764-1485 • I-83 Exit 21B take US-30 W 2.3 miles, Kenneth Rd N .2 mile & Loucks Rd W .1 mile

RHODE ISLAND

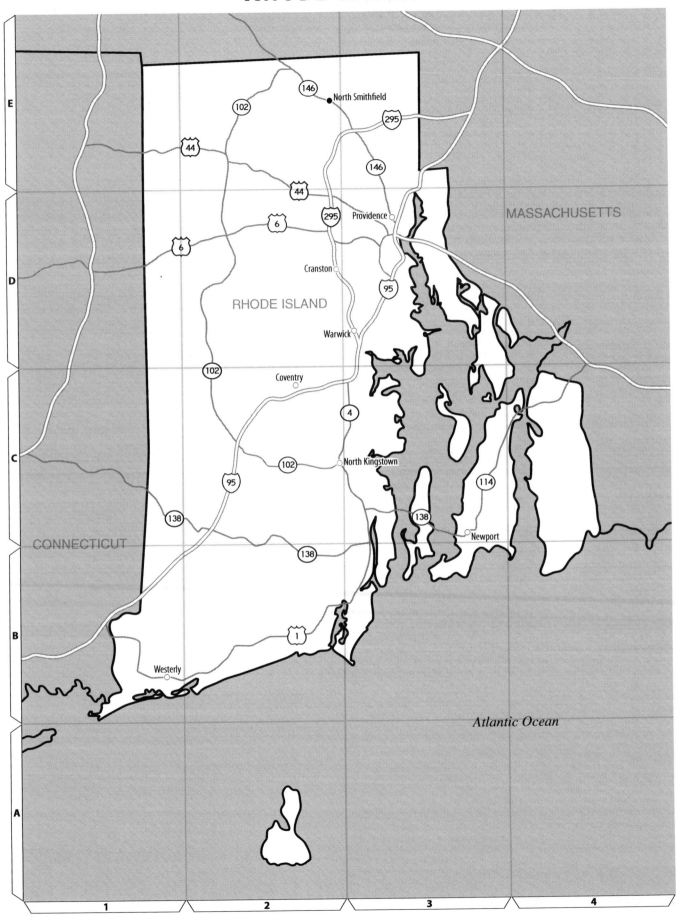

☆	♡	🕐	⛽	�̸	Store Details
✪	1				Coventry • 650 Centre Of New England Blvd, 02816 • 401-823-7780 • I-95 Exit 6A go N on Hopkins Hill Rd .8 mile & E on Centre Of New England Blvd .2 mile
✪	1			✓	Cranston • 1776 Plainfield Pike, 02921 • 401-946-2030 • I-295 Exit 4 take SR-14 E .3 mile
☆				✓	Newport • 199 Connell Hwy, 02840 • 401-848-5167 • 2 miles north of town center; from the Claiborne Pell Bridge, follow SR-138 1 mile to Admiral Kalbfus Rd then go W .2 mile and N .2 mile on Connell Hwy
✪	10				North Kingstown • 1031 Ten Rod Rd, 02852 • 401-294-0025 • I-95 Exit 5A go E on SR-102 for 9.5 miles
✪	3		◆		North Smithfield • 7 Dowling Village Blvd, 02896 • 401-766-1961 • I-295 Exit 9B follow SR-146 (Eddie Dowling Hwy) NW for 2.3 miles then continue on SR-146A for .5 mile
☆	1			✓	Providence • 51 Silver Spring St, 02904 • 401-272-5047 • I-95 Exit 24 take Branch Ave W .4 mile & Silver Sprg St S .2 mile
☆	1			✓	Warwick • 650 Bald Hill Rd, 02886 • 401-821-1766 • I-295 Exit 2 merge onto Bald Hill Rd S .6 mile
☆	3			✓	Warwick • 840 Post Rd, 02888 • 401-781-2233 • I-95 Exit 14 take SR-37 E .9 mile & US-1 N 1.2 miles
✪		✓		✓	Westerly • 258 Post Rd, 02891 • 401-322-0790 • Jct SR-78/Westerly BYP & US-1, follow US-1 NE 2.9 miles

SOUTH CAROLINA

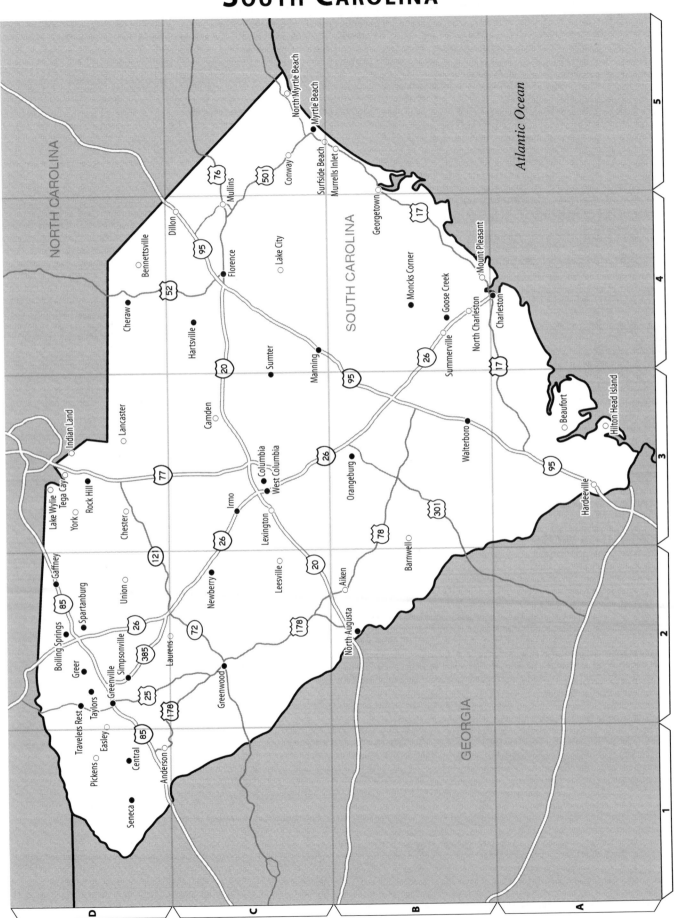

☆	♡	🕐	⛽	🚭	Store Details
✪	10	✓			Aiken • 3581 Richland Ave W, 29801 • 803-648-5551 • I-20 Exit 18 take SR-19 S 4.4 miles, SR-118 SW 4.6 miles & US-1 E .6 mile
✪		✓			Aiken • 2035 Whiskey Rd, 29803 • 803-648-9197 • I-20 Exit 22 take US-1 S 8.1 miles then SR-19 S 3 miles
✪	3	✓			Anderson • 3812 Liberty Hwy, 29621 • 864-225-1800 • I-85 Exit 21 take US-178 E 2.2 miles
✪	8	✓			Anderson • 651 Hwy 28 Byp, 29624 • 864-261-7420 • I-85 Exit 19A go E on SR-28 for 1.9 miles & continue on SR-28 BYP 5.7 miles
✪		✓			Barnwell • 11391 Dunbarton Blvd, 29812 • 803-259-2000 • Jct US-278 & SR-64 (W of town) go W on SR-64/Dunbarton Blvd 1.3 miles
✪		✓			Beaufort • 350 Robert Smalls Pkwy, 29906 • 843-522-8221 • Jct US-21 & US-17 (N of town) take US-21 S 11.8 miles, SR-280 S 1.2 miles & SR-170 SW .2 mile
✪		✓			Bennettsville • 1250 Bennettsville Sq, 29512 • 843-479-0002 • 2 miles north of town center along SR-9
✪	3	✓	❖		Boiling Springs • 4000 Hwy 9, 29316 • 864-814-2889 • I-85 Exit 75 follow SR-9 N 2.9 miles
✪	5	✓			Camden • 2240 W Dekalb St, 29020 • 803-425-5746 • I-20 Exit 98 merge onto US-521 N 2.6 miles then US-601 W 2.4 miles
✪		✓	❖		Central • 1286 Eighteen Mile Rd, 29630 • 864-639-2525 • I-85 Exit 19B follow US-76 W 6.4 miles, SR-28 BR W 1.3 miles, SR-88 NW 3.9 miles & SR-18 N 1.3 miles
✪	7				Charleston • 1231 Folly Rd, 29412 • 843-762-9034 • I-26 Exit 221A take US-17 S 1.8 miles & Folly Rd S 4.4 miles
✪		✓	❖		Charleston • 3951 W Ashley Cir, 29414 • 843-763-5554 • I-26 Exit 221A follow US-17 S 1.8 miles, Folly Rd/Center St S 9.3 miles & Ashley Ave W .9 mile
✪		✓	❖		Cheraw • 1040 Chesterfield Hwy, 29520 • 843-537-6381 • 3 miles west of town along SR-9
✪	10				Chester • 1691 J A Cochran Byp, 29706 • 803-581-6278 • I-77 Exit 65 go W 9.7 miles on SR-9 then S on J A Cochran Bypass
✪	1	✓			Columbia • 321 Killian Rd, 29016 • 803-754-8884 • I-77 Exit 22, west of exit
✪	1	✓			Columbia • 5420 Forest Dr, 29206 • 803-782-0323 • I-77 Exit 12 take Forest Dr W .4 mile
✪	1	✓	❖		Columbia • 7520 Garners Ferry Rd, 29209 • 803-783-1277 • I-77 Exit 9B take US-378/US-76 E .2 mile

☆	♡	🕐	⛽	🚭	Store Details
✪	1	✓	❖		Columbia • 1326 Bush River Rd, 29210 • 803-750-3097 • I-26 Exit 108A, west of exit
✪	1	✓			Columbia • 360 Harbison Blvd, 29212 • 803-781-0762 • I-26 Exit 103 take Harbison Blvd S .2 mile
✪	4	✓	❖		Columbia • 10060 Two Notch Rd, 29223 • 803-736-8123 • I-77 Exit 17 take US-1 NE 3.8 miles
✪		✓			Conway • 2709 Church St, 29526 • 843-365-0303 • Jct US-378 & US-501 (in town) go N on US-501 for 2.7 miles
✪		✓			Conway • 151 Myrtle Ridge Dr, 29526 • 843-234-2040 • 6 miles southeast of town center via US-501
✪	1	✓			Dillon • 805 Enterprise Rd, 29536 • 843-841-9800 • I-95 Exit 193 go S .4 mile on SR-9/SR-57 then W .3 mile on Enterprise Rd
✪		✓			Easley • 115 Rolling Hills Cir, 29640 • 864-859-8595 • 3 miles east of town center along US-123
✪	2	✓			Florence • 230 Beltline Dr, 29501 • 843-664-2020 • I-95 Exit 160A take David McLeod Blvd E for 1.2 miles then N on Beltline Dr for .4 mile
✪	6	✓	❖		Florence • 2014 S Irby St, 29505 • 843-292-0862 • I-95 Exit 164 follow US-52 E 6 miles
✪	1	✓	❖		Gaffney • 165 Walton Dr, 29341 • 864-487-3769 • I-85 Exit 92 follow SR-11 S .6 mile
✪		✓			Georgetown • 1310 N Fraser St, 29440 • 843-527-9970 • Jct SR-51 & US-701 (N of town) go S on US-701 for 1.8 miles
✪	7	✓	◆	✓	Goose Creek • 605 Saint James Ave, 29445 • 843-553-5421 • I-26 Exit 199B take US-17Alt N 3.9 miles & US-176 E 3.1 miles
✪	1	✓			Greenville • 1451 Woodruff Rd, 29607 • 864-297-3031 • I-385 Exit 35 take SR-146 E .5 mile
✪	5	✓	❖	✓	Greenville • 6134 White Horse Rd, 29611 • 864-295-3181 • I-185 Exit 15 take US-25 W 4.2 miles
✪	2	✓			Greenville • 11410 Anderson Rd, 29611 • 864-605-6039 • I-85 Exit 40 go W 1.3 miles on SR-153
✪	1				Greenville • 3925 Pelham Rd, 29615 • 864-288-8081 • I-85 Exit 54, west of exit
✪					Greenwood • 300 Bypass 25 NE, 29646 • 864-321-6028 • 1.7 miles east of town center along US-178 at Cambridge Ave
✪		✓	◆		Greenwood • 508 NW Bypass 72, 29649 • 864-229-2232 • 3 miles northwest of town center along SR-72

☆	⛨	🕐	⛽	🚫	Store Details
✪	8	✓	❖		Greer • 14055 E Wade Hampton Blvd, 29651 • 864-877-1928 • I-85 Exit 66 merge onto SR-29 S 7.3 miles
✪	1	✓			Hardeeville • 4400 US Hwy 278, 29927 • 843-208-3000 • I-95 Exit 8 take US-278 E .2 mile
✪		✓	❖		Hartsville • 1150 S 4th St, 29550 • 843-383-4891 • I-20 Exit 131 take SR-403 N 7.8 miles, US-15 N 4.3 miles & SR-151 BR NW .2 mile
✪				✓	Hilton Head Island • 25 Pembroke Dr, 29926 • 843-681-3011 • I-95 Exit 8 go E 20.8 miles on US-278 then continue E 1.3 miles on William Hilton Pkwy
✪	8				Indian Land • 10048 Charlotte Highway, 29707 • 803-802-6666 • I-77 Exit 85 go E 7 miles on SR-160 then N .8 mile on US-521
✪	4		❖		Irmo • 1180 Dutch Fork Rd, 29063 • 803-781-7775 • I-26 Exit 101A go W 3.2 miles on US-76/US-176
✪		✓		✓	Lake City • 900 Highway 52, 29560 • 843-394-7405 • 1.8 miles north of town center via US-52 at US-378
✪					Lake Wylie • 175 Highway 274, 29710 • 803-619-7021 • 2.5 miles west of town via SR-49 and SR-274
✪		✓			Lancaster • 805 Hwy 9 Bypass W, 29720 • 803-286-5445 • 1.7 miles northwest of town center via US-521 and SR-9 Bypass
✪	6	✓			Laurens • 922 E Main St, 29360 • 864-682-8100 • I-385 Exit 9 take SR-221 S 3.6 miles then US-76 BYP E 1.8 miles & US-76 for .1 mile
✪	9	✓			Leesville • 115 E Church St, 29070 • 803-532-5332 • I-20 Exit 39 take US-178 N 5.1 miles, SR-245 N 3.1 miles & Church St W .8 mile
✪	5	✓		✓	Lexington • 5556 Sunset Blvd, 29072 • 803-808-3740 • I-20 Exit 61 merge onto US-378 W 4.9 miles
✪	4	✓			Lexington • 1780 S Lake Dr, 29073 • 803-957-2557 • I-20 Exit 55 go S on SR-6 for 3.4 miles
✪	2		❖		Manning • 2010 Paxville Hwy, 29102 • 803-435-4323 • I-95 Exit 119 take SR-261 E 1.2 miles
✪		✓	❖	✓	Moncks Corner • 511 N Hwy 52, 29461 • 843-899-5701 • Jct SR-402 & US-52 (N of town) go S on US-52 1.1 miles
✪	1	✓			Mount Pleasant • 1481 N Hwy 17, 29464 • 843-881-6100 • I-526 Exit 30, east of exit
✪	5	✓			Mount Pleasant • 3000 Proprietors Pl, 29466 • 843-884-2844 • I-526 Exit 30 follow US-17 N 5 miles

☆	⛨	🕐	⛽	🚫	Store Details
✪		✓			Mullins • 305 Commerce Dr, 29571 • 843-423-9444 • 5 miles west of town via US-76
✪		✓			Murrells Inlet • 545 Garden City Connector, 29576 • 843-357-6560 • 3 miles north of town near intersection of US-17-BUS and Garden City Connector
✪		✓	◆		Myrtle Beach • 10820 Kings Rd, 29572 • 843-449-0502 • Jct SR-22 & US-17 go E on Kings Rd .2 mile
✪		✓			Myrtle Beach • 541 Seaboard St, 29577 • 843-445-7781 • Jct US-501 & US-17 go E on US-501 for .8 mile then S on Grissom Pkwy .5 mile & E on Pine Island Rd .3 mile
✪	3	✓	◆		Newberry • 2812 Main St, 29108 • 803-276-4411 • I-26 Exit 76 take SR-219 S 3 miles
✪	1	✓			North Augusta • 1041 Edgefield Rd, 29860 • 803-613-3082 • I-20 Exit 5 go N .4 mile on Edgefield Rd then right on Market Place Dr
✪	5	✓	❖		North Augusta • 1201 Knox Ave, 29841 • 803-279-0545 • I-20 Exit 5 follow US-25 S 4.6 miles
✪	1	✓		✓	North Charleston • 7400 Rivers Ave, 29406 • 843-572-9660 • I-26 Exit 209B go E .6 mile on Ashley Rd
✪	2	✓			North Charleston • 4920 Centre Pointe Dr, 29418 • 843-740-1112 • I-26 Exit 213 (eastbound travelers use I-26 Exit 213A) go S .4 mile on Montague Ave, W .4 mile on International Blvd, N .7 mile on Coliseum Dr
✪		✓			North Myrtle Beach • 550 Hwy 17 N, 29582 • 843-281-8352 • Jct SR-22 & US-17 (S of town) take US-17 N 6.4 miles
✪	8	✓	❖		Orangeburg • 2795 North Rd, 29118 • 803-533-0645 • I-26 Exit 149 take SR-33 S 3.5 miles & US-178 W 3.9 miles
✪		✓			Pickens • 2637 Gentry Memorial Hwy, 29671 • 864-644-9020 • 1.5 miles southeast of town center SR-8
✪	1	✓	❖		Rock Hill • 2377 Dave Lyle Blvd, 29730 • 803-366-9431 • I-77 Exit 79 take SR-122 E .5 mile
✪	6	✓			Rock Hill • 4875 Old York Rd, 29732 • 803-323-2080 • I-77 Exit 82C go W 5.8 miles on SR-161
✪		✓	❖		Seneca • 1636 Sandifer Blvd, 29678 • 864-885-0408 • Jct SR-59 & Wells Hwy (S of town) go NW on Wells Hwy 3 miles then S on Sandifer Blvd .2 mile
✪	1	✓	◆		Simpsonville • 3950 Grandview Dr, 29680 • 864-963-0049 • I-385 Exit 26 merge onto Harrison Bridge Rd W .5 mile & N at Grandview Dr .3 mile

☆	◯	🕐	⛽	🚫	Store Details
✪	1	✓			Spartanburg • 141 Dorman Centre Dr, 29301 • 864-574-6452 • I-26 Exit 21B take US-29 N .6 mile & Dorman Centre Dr E .2 mile
✪	4	✓	❖		Spartanburg • 2151 E Main St, 29307 • 864-529-0156 • I-585 Exit 25B continue on Pine St 1.2 miles then Main St NE 2.4 miles
✪	8	✓			Summerville • 9880 Dorchester Rd, 29418 • 843-871-3303 • I-26 Exit 209B go W 3.8 miles on Ashley Phosphate Rd then N 3.7 miles on Dorchester Rd
✪	1	✓			Summerville • 1317 N Main St, 29483 • 843-821-1991 • I-26 Exit 199A take US-17 ALT S .1 mile
✪		✓	❖		Sumter • 1283 Broad St, 29150 • 803-905-5500 • I-95 Exit 135 merge onto US-378 W 18.5 miles
✪		✓			Surfside Beach • 2751 Beaver Run Blvd, 29575 • 843-650-4800 • US-17 at SR-544, east of exit
✪	5	✓	❖		Taylors • 3027 Wade Hampton Blvd, 29687 • 864-292-8155 • I-385 Exit 40A take SR-291 N 1.6 miles then Wade Hampton Blvd NW 2.5 miles
✪	2	✓		✓	Tega Cay • 1151 Stonecrest Blvd, 29708 • 803-578-4140 • I-77 Exit 85 go W 2 miles on SR-160
✪		✓	❖		Travelers Rest • 9 Benton Rd, 29690 • 864-834-7179 • I-185 Exit 15 take US-25 N 17 miles
✪					Union • 513 N Duncan Bypass, 29379 • 864-429-0598 • 1.7 miles northwest of town center via SR-215 at US-176
✪	1	✓	❖		Walterboro • 2110 Bells Hwy, 29488 • 843-539-1550 • I-95 Exit 57 take SR-64 W .4 mile
✪	1	✓	◆		West Columbia • 2401 Augusta Rd, 29169 • 803-796-9144 • I-26 Exit 111B merge onto US-1 N .4 mile
✪		✓			York • 970 E Liberty St, 29745 • 803-684-5486 • I-77 Exit 82 follow SR-161 W 12.8 miles & continue on SR-161 BR .8 mile

SOUTH DAKOTA

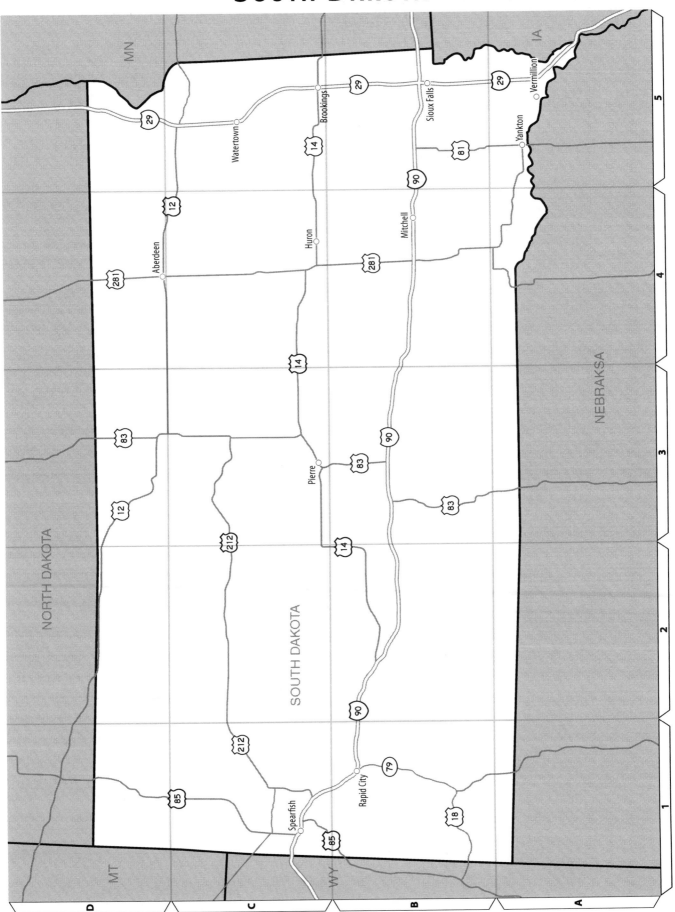

☆	◯	🕐	⛽	🚭	Store Details
✪		✓			Aberdeen • 3820 7th Ave SE, 57401 • 605-229-2345 • 2.5 miles east of town center along US-12
✪	1	✓			Brookings • 2233 6th St, 57006 • 605-692-6332 • I-29 Exit 132 take US-14 W .3 mile
✪		✓			Huron • 2791 Dakota Ave S, 57350 • 605-353-0891 • Jct US-14 & SR-37 (N of town) take SR-37 S for 2.5 miles
✪	1	✓			Mitchell • 1101 E Spruce St, 57301 • 605-995-6840 • I-90 Exit 332 take SR-37 S .4 mile & W on Spruce St .6 mile
✪		✓			Pierre • 1730 N Garfield Rd, 57501 • 605-224-8830 • Jct SR-34/Wells Ave & US-18 (SE of town) go N on US-18 BYP 2.4 miles
✪	1	✓		✓	Rapid City • 1200 N Lacrosse St, 57701 • 605-342-9444 • I-90 Exit 59 take La Crosse St S .5 mile
✪		✓		✓	Rapid City • 100 Stumer Rd, 57701 • 605-877-3291 • 4 miles south of town center via 5th St
✪	1	✓			Sioux Falls • 3209 S Louise Ave, 57106 • 605-362-1002 • I-29 Exit 77 go E on 41st St .4 mile then N .2 mile on Louise Ave
✪	1	✓			Sioux Falls • 5200 W 60th St N, 57107 • 605-906-6078 • I-29 Exit 83 go W .8 mile on 60th St
✪	2	✓			Sioux Falls • 5521 E Arrowhead Pkwy, 57110 • 605-367-3140 • I-229 Exit 6 follow SR-42 E 1.7 miles
✪	1	✓		✓	Spearfish • 2825 1st Ave, 57783 • 605-642-2460 • I-90 Exit 14 go N .2 mile on 27th St then 1st Ave E .2 mile
✪	9	✓			Vermillion • 1207 Princeton Ave, 57069 • 605-624-0215 • I-29 Exit 42 take SR-50 W 7.7 miles & Princeton Ave N 1.2 miles
✪	1	✓			Watertown • 1201 29th St SE, 57201 • 605-882-0801 • I-29 Exit 177 take US-212 W .6 mile then 29th St S .2 mile
✪		✓		✓	Yankton • 3001 Broadway Ave, 57078 • 605-665-1425 • Jct SR-50 & US-81 (N of town) take US-81 S for .3 mile

TENNESSEE

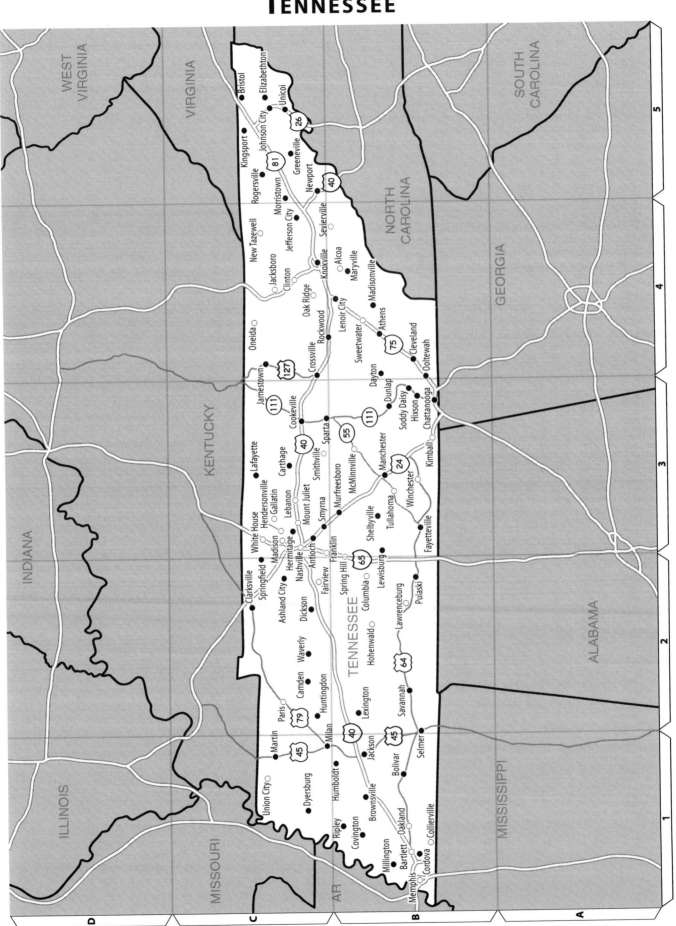

☆	◯	🕐	⛽	🚫	Store Details
✪	5	✓		✓	Alcoa • 1030 Hunters Crossing, 37701 • 865-984-1099 • I-140 Exit 11A take US-129 S 4.8 miles then Louisville Rd W & Hunters Crossing S .1 mile
✪	3	✓	❖		Antioch • 3035 Hamilton Church Rd, 37013 • 615-360-2228 • I-24 Exit 59 take SR-254 NE 1.2 miles, Zelida Ave E .3 mile & Hamilton Church N .6 mile
✪		✓	❖		Ashland City • 1626 Hwy 12 S, 37015 • 615-792-7782 • Jct SR-249/49 & SR-12 (in town) take SR-12 SE 2.6 miles
✪	2	✓	❖		Athens • 1815 Decatur Pike, 37303 • 423-745-0395 • I-75 Exit 49 take SR-30 E 1.3 miles
✪	1	✓		✓	Bartlett • 8400 US Hwy 64, 38133 • 901-382-6101 • I-40 Exit 18 follow US-64 W .8 mile
✪		✓	❖		Bolivar • 1604 W Market St, 38008 • 731-658-7794 • Jct SR-100 & US-64 (NW of town) go SE on US-64 for 8.3 miles
✪	2	✓	❖		Bristol • 220 Century Blvd, 37620 • 423-968-2777 • I-81 Exit 69 take SR-394 SE 3.9 miles, Exide Dr E 1.5 miles & US-11E N 1.9 miles
✪		✓	❖		Brownsville • 1100 S Dupree Ave, 38012 • 731-772-9551 • US-40 Exit 60 follow SR-19 NW 3.6 miles
✪		✓	❖		Camden • 2200 Hwy 641 N, 38320 • 731-584-4445 • 3.2 miles north of town center along US-641 at McKelvy Rd
✪	5	✓	◆		Carthage • 1 Myers St, 37030 • 615-735-2049 • I-40 Exit 258 go N 4.7 miles on SR-53/Gordonsville Hwy
✪	5	✓			Chattanooga • 501 Signal Mountain Rd, 37405 • 423-756-7202 • I-24 Exit 178 follow US-27 N 4 miles then Signal Mountain Rd W .9 mile
✪	2	✓	❖		Chattanooga • 490 Greenway View Dr, 37411 • 423-892-8911 • I-24 Exit 184 take Moore Rd N .4 mile, Brainerd Rd E 1.1 miles & Greenway View S .3 mile
✪	1	✓			Chattanooga • 3550 Cummings Hwy, 37419 • 423-821-1556 • I-24 Exit 174 go E on Cummings Hwy/US-41 .5 mile
✪	1	✓		✓	Chattanooga • 2020 Gunbarrel Rd, 37421 • 423-899-7021 • I-75 Exit 5 go E .4 mile on Shallowford Rd then S .6 mile on Gunbarrel Rd
✪	1	✓	◆		Clarksville • 3050 Wilma Rudolph Blvd, 37040 • 931-553-8127 • I-24 Exit 4 take US-79 S .7 mile
✪	9	✓	◆		Clarksville • 1680 Fort Campbell Blvd, 37042 • 931-645-8439 • I-24 Exit 86 (in KY) follow Fort Campbell Blvd S 8.7 miles
✪	4	✓	❖		Clarksville • 2315 Madison St, 37043 • 931-552-1010 • I-24 Exit 11 merge onto SR-76 W/76 CONN W 3.5 miles

☆	◯	🕐	⛽	🚫	Store Details
✪	2	✓	◆		Cleveland • 4495 Keith St NW, 37312 • 423-472-1436 • I-75 Exit 27 take Huff Pkwy SE 1.4 miles
✪	5	✓	❖		Cleveland • 2300 Treasury Dr SE, 37323 • 423-472-9660 • I-75 Exit 20 follow SR-311 E 5 miles
✪	1	✓			Clinton • 150 Tanner Ln, 37716 • 865-457-4121 • I-75 Exit 122, west of exit
✪		✓			Collierville • 560 W Poplar Ave, 38017 • 901-854-5100 • I-240 Exit 16 merge onto Morris Pkwy E 12.5 miles then Byhalia Rd N .9 mile & Poplar Ave E .5 mile
✪		✓			Columbia • 2200 Brookmeade Dr, 38401 • 931-381-6892 • I-65 Exit 37 take SR-50 NW 11.6 miles & W at Brookmeade .1 mile
✪	4	✓	❖		Cookeville • 589 W Main St, 38501 • 931-537-3880 • I-40 Exit 288 take SR-111 N 3.3 miles, then E on Main St .3 mile
✪	1	✓	❖		Cookeville • 768 S Jefferson Ave, 38501 • 931-520-0232 • I-40 Exit 287 take SR-136 N .6 mile
✪	4	✓	❖	✓	Cordova • 577 Germantown Pkwy, 38018 • 901-758-1591 • I-40 Exit 16A take SR-177 S 3.8 miles
✪		✓	❖		Covington • 201 Lanny Bridges Ave, 38019 • 901-476-4492 • I-40 Exit 35 follow SR-59 NW 17.2 miles, Main St/Sherrod Ave N 1.7 miles & E at College St .4 mile
✪	2	✓	❖		Crossville • 168 Obed Plaza, 38555 • 931-484-9745 • I-40 Exit 317 take US-127 S 1.4 miles
✪		✓	❖		Dayton • 3034 Rhea County Hwy, 37321 • 423-775-4448 • Jct SR-60 & US-27 (S of town) take US-27 S 2.2 miles
✪	5	✓	❖		Dickson • 175 Beasley Dr, 37055 • 615-446-4588 • I-40 Exit 172 take SR-46 N 3.7 miles & Beasley Dr W .5 mile
✪		✓	❖		Dunlap • 16773 Rankin Ave, 37327 • 423-949-7778 • Jct SR-111 & US-127 (in town) take US-127 S 2.1 miles
✪	1	✓	◆		Dyersburg • 2650 Lake Rd, 38024 • 731-285-3700 • I-155 Exit 13 take SR-78 S .4 mile
✪	7	✓	❖		Elizabethton • 1001 Over Mountain Dr, 37643 • 423-543-8133 • I-26 Exit 24 follow US-321 N 6.4 miles then W .2 mile on Over Mountain Dr
✪	7	✓			Fairview • 7100 Hopgood Rd, 37062 • 615-387-7020 • I-40 Exit 182 go S 4.5 miles on SR-96 then W 2 miles on Hopgood Rd
✪		✓	◆		Fayetteville • 1224 Huntsville Hwy, 37334 • 931-433-3010 • Jct SR-15 BYP & US-431 (SW of town) take US-431 S .4 mile

☆	🛡	🕐	⛽	🚫	Store Details
✪	1	✓			Franklin • 3600 Mallory Ln, 37067 • 615-771-0929 • I-65 Exit 67 go W on McEwen Dr .3 mile & N on Mallory Ln .3 mile
✪		✓			Gallatin • 1112 Nashville Pike, 37066 • 615-452-8452 • Jct SR-109 & US-31E (W of town) go SW on US-31E .5 mile
✪		✓	❖		Greeneville • 3755 E Andrew Johnson Hwy, 37745 • 423-639-8181 • I-81 Exit 30 take SR-70 S 10.1 miles then US-11 E 5.6 miles
✪	7	✓		✓	Hendersonville • 204 N Anderson Ln, 37075 • 615-264-0770 • I-65 Exit 95-97 take SR-386 E 5.8 miles & Callender Ln/Indian Lake Blvd S 1 mile
✪	4	✓	❖		Hermitage • 4424 Lebanon Pike, 37076 • 615-883-0201 • I-40 Exit 221 take SR-45 N 2.2 miles then Lebanon Pike E 1.5 miles
✪		✓	❖		Hixson • 5764 Hwy 153, 37343 • 423-870-1680 • I-75 Exit 4 take SR-153 N 10.5 miles
✪		✓			Hohenwald • 612 E Main St, 38462 • 931-796-3282 • Jct SR-20 & US-412 (in town) take US-412 E 1.5 miles
✪		✓	❖		Humboldt • 2716 N Central Ave, 38343 • 731-784-0025 • I-40 Exit 80B take US-45 BYP N 4.6 miles then go N 9.6 miles on US-45/US-45-W
✪		✓	❖		Huntingdon • 180 Veterans Dr N, 38344 • 731-986-4439 • 1.4 miles west of town center off US-70 at Veterans Dr
✪	4	✓		✓	Jacksboro • 2824 Appalachian Hwy, 37757 • 423-566-5318 • I-75 Exit 134 go N 3.6 miles on US-25-W
✪	1	✓	❖		Jackson • 2171 S Highland Ave, 38301 • 731-422-1614 • I-40 Exit 82A merge onto US-45 S .8 mile
✪	2	✓		✓	Jackson • 2196 Emporium Dr, 38305 • 731-664-1157 • I-40 Exit 82B go N .1 mile on US-45 then W 1.6 miles on Vann Dr
✪		✓	❖		Jamestown • 539 E Central Ave, 38556 • 931-879-4767 • .4 mile east of town center on Central Ave near US-127 jct
✪	8	✓	❖		Jefferson City • 630 E Broadway Blvd, 37760 • 865-475-0730 • I-40 Exit 417 take SR-92 N 6.3 miles & US-11 E 1.5 miles
✪	4	✓	❖		Johnson City • 2915 W Market St, 37604 • 423-434-2250 • I-26 Exit 23 take SR-91 & US-11 W 3.3 miles
✪	1	✓	◆		Johnson City • 3111 Browns Mill Rd, 37604 • 423-282-5376 • I-26 Exit 19 go NE on SR-381 for .2 mile then W on Browns Mill Rd .2 mile
✪	1	✓			Kimball • 525 Kimball Crossing Dr, 37347 • 423-837-6732 • I-24 Exit 152 take US-72 E .5 mile then S on Kimball Crossing .2 mile

☆	🛡	🕐	⛽	🚫	Store Details
✪	2	✓	❖		Kingsport • 2500 W Stone Dr, 37660 • 423-246-4676 • I-26 Exit 1 take Stone Dr W 1.4 miles
✪	4	✓			Kingsport • 3200 Fort Henry Dr, 37664 • 423-392-0600 • I-81 Exit 59 take SR-36 N 3.1 miles
☆	1	✓		✓	Knoxville • 2501 University Commons Way, 37919 • 865-824-4453 • I-40 Exit 386B go S .5 mile on US-129; E .1 mile on US-11 and S .2 mile on University Commons Way
✪	3	✓			Knoxville • 6777 Clinton Hwy, 37912 • 865-938-6760 • I-75 Exit 110 take Callahan Dr SW 1.8 miles & Clinton Hwy W .8 mile
✪	7	✓	❖		Knoxville • 7420 Chapman Hwy, 37920 • 865-577-2596 • I-40 Exit 388 take US-441 S 7 miles
✪	1	✓			Knoxville • 8445 Walbrook Dr, 37923 • 865-690-8986 • I-40 Exit 379 merge onto Walbrook Dr N .1 mile
✪	1	✓			Knoxville • 3051 Kinzel Way, 37924 • 865-544-7710 • I-640 Exit 8 take Millertown Pike NE .1 mile & Kenzel Way S .2 mile
✪	1	✓		✓	Knoxville • 10900 Parkside Dr, 37934 • 865-777-5171 • I-40/I-75 Exit 374 take SR-131 S .5 mile & Parkside Dr W .5 mile
✪	5	✓			Knoxville • 7550 Norris Fwy, 37938 • 865-922-6031 • I-75 Exit 112 go NE 4.6 miles on SR-131 then N on Norris Fwy .4 mile
✪		✓	❖		Lafayette • 419 Hwy 52 Byp W, 37083 • 615-666-2135 • Jct SR-10 & SR-52 (W of town) go W on SR-52 BYP for .2 mile
✪		✓			Lawrenceburg • 2130 N Locust Ave, 38464 • 931-762-1094 • Jct US-64 & US-43 (in town) take US-43 N 2.4 miles
✪	1	✓			Lebanon • 615 S Cumberland St, 37087 • 615-444-0471 • I-40 Exit 238 take US-231 N .9 mile
✪	2	✓	❖		Lenoir City • 911 Hwy 321 N, 37771 • 865-986-9002 • I-75 Exit 81 take US-321 S 1.1 miles
✪	7	✓	❖		Lewisburg • 1334 N Ellington Pkwy, 37091 • 931-359-9568 • I-65 Exit 32 take SR-373 E 3.7 miles, SR-417 NE 1.9 miles & US-431 SE .5 mile
✪		✓	❖		Lexington • 547 W Church St, 38351 • 731-968-5212 • I-40 Exit 108 take SR-22 S 9.8 miles then US-412 W 1 mile
✪	2	✓			Madison • 2232 Gallatin Pike N, 37115 • 615-859-7212 • I-65 Exit 96 go E .8 mile on Rivergate Pkwy then N 1 mile on Gallatin Pike Rd

☆	◯	⏰	⛽	🚫	Store Details
✪		✓	❖		Madisonville • 4525 Hwy 411, 37354 • 423-442-5237 • Jct SR-68 & US-411 (in town) go N on US-411 for 1 mile
✪	1	✓	❖		Manchester • 2518 Hillsboro Blvd, 37355 • 931-728-6000 • I-24 Exit 114 take US-41 E .2 mile
✪		✓	❖		Martin • 134 Courtright Rd, 38237 • 731-587-3843 • 2 miles west of town center via University St (SR-431) at Courtright Rd
✪		✓	❖		Maryville • 2410 US Hwy 411 S, 37801 • 865-982-3660 • 3.3 miles southwest of town center via US-129/US-411
✪		✓			McMinnville • 915 N Chancery St, 37110 • 931-473-0826 • 1.6 miles northwest of town center via Chancery St
✪	3	✓			Memphis • 5255 Elvis Presley Blvd, 38116 • 901-346-4994 • I-55 Exit 2B take SR-175 W 1.1 miles then S on Presley Blvd 1.1 miles
✪	6	✓			Memphis • 7525 Winchester Rd, 38125 • 901-757-1442 • I-240 Exit 16 take SR-385 E 5 miles then Winchester Rd W .1 mile
✪	4	✓			Memphis • 3950 Austin Peay Hwy, 38128 • 901-377-1211 • I-40 Exit 8 follow SR-14 N 3.8 miles
✪		✓	❖		Milan • 15427 S First St, 38358 • 731-686-9557 • Jct SR-187 & US-45E (S of town) go S on US-45E .4 mile
✪		✓	◆		Millington • 8445 US Hwy 51 N, 38053 • 901-872-6100 • I-40 Exit 2A take SR-300 W .7 mile & US-51 N 13.4 miles
✪		✓			Morristown • 4331 W Andrew Johnson Hwy, 37814 • 423-254-6671 • 4 miles southwest of town center along US-11E
✪	6	✓	❖		Morristown • 475 S Davy Crockett Pkwy, 37813 • 423-587-0495 • I-81 Exit 8 take US-25E N 5.7 miles
✪	1	✓			Mount Juliet • 300 Pleasant Grove Rd, 37122 • 615-758-1121 • I-40 Exit 226 go N .5 mile on Mount Juliet Rd then W .3 mile on Pleasant Grove Rd
✪	3	✓			Murfreesboro • 140 Joe B Jackson Pkwy, 37127 • 615-867-7512 • I-24 Exit 81 go S 2.4 miles on US-231/Church St; eastbound travelers use Exit 81A
✪	1	✓	◆		Murfreesboro • 2000 Old Fort Pkwy, 37129 • 615-893-0175 • I-24 Exit 78B take SR-96 E .8 mile
✪	5	✓	❖		Murfreesboro • 2900 S Rutherford Blvd, 37130 • 615-896-4650 • I-24 Exit 81B take US-231 N .8 mile then NE on Rutherford Blvd 3.6 miles
✪	5	✓			Murfreesboro • 2012 Memorial Blvd, 37129 • 615-995-7092 • I-24 Exit 78B go E 4.2 miles on SR-96 and Memorial Blvd

☆	◯	⏰	⛽	🚫	Store Details
✪	1	✓			Nashville • 2421 Powell Ave, 37204 • 615-383-3844 • I-65 Exit 79, go E on Amory Dr .2 miles then N on Powell Ave for .8 miles
✪	1				Nashville • 3458 Dickerson Pike, 37207 • 615-873-2222 • I-65 Exit 90A follow US-41/Dickerson Pike N .25 mile
✪	1	✓			Nashville • 7044 Charlotte Pike, 37209 • 615-352-1240 • I-40 Exit 201 take US-70 SW .3 mile
✪	2	✓			Nashville • 4040 Nolensville Pike, 37211 • 615-831-0133 • I-24 Exit 56 take SR-255 W 1.6 miles & N on Nolensville Rd .2 mile
✪	4	✓			Nashville • 5824 Nolensville Pike, 37211 • 615-331-4666 • I-24 Exit 59 take SR-254 W 2.6 miles, continue W on Old Hickory Blvd .6 mile, then S on Nolensville Rd .2 mile
☆					New Tazewell • 432 S Broad St, 37825 • 423-626-6550 • Jct US-25E & SR-33 (N of town) go S on SR-33 for 2.7 miles
✪	1	✓	◆		Newport • 1075 Cosby Hwy, 37821 • 423-623-0429 • I-40 Exit 435 take US-321 S .5 mile
✪		✓			Oak Ridge • 373 S Illinois Ave, 37830 • 865-481-2503 • I-40 Exit 376 take SR-162 N 6.3 miles then SR-62 W 5.3 miles
✪		✓			Oakland • 105 Chickasaw Ridge Dr, 38060 • 901-465-0225 • I-40 Exit 25 take SR-205 S 4 miles then US-64 E 7.3 miles
✪		✓			Oneida • 19740 Alberta St, 37841 • 423-569-6228 • I-75 Exit 141 follow SR-63 W for 16.2 miles then US-27 N 8 miles
✪	1	✓	❖		Ooltewah • 5588 Little Debbie Pkwy, 37363 • 423-238-1036 • I-75 Exit 11 take US-11 N .1 mile & E on Little Debbie .1 mile
✪		✓			Paris • 1210 Mineral Wells Ave, 38242 • 731-644-0290 • Jct US-79 & US-641 (in town) go S on US-641 for .7 mile
✪		✓	◆		Pulaski • 1655 W College St, 38478 • 931-363-7618 • I-65 Exit 14 follow US-64 W 13.5 miles
✪		✓	◆		Ripley • 628 Hwy 51 N, 38063 • 731-635-8904 • Jct SR-19 BYP & US-51 (SW of town) take US-51 N .8 mile
✪	6	✓	❖		Rockwood • 1102 N Gateway Ave, 37854 • 865-354-0863 • I-40 Exit 347 follow US-27 S 5.2 miles
✪		✓	❖		Rogersville • 4331 Hwy 66 S, 37857 • 423-272-7707 • I-81 Exit 23 take US-11E NW 3.8 miles then SR-66 NE 11.5 miles
✪		✓	❖		Savannah • 175 JI Bell Ln, 38372 • 731-925-3020 • Jct SR-128 & US-64 (E of town) take US-64 W 3.5 miles & Bell Ln S .2 mile

☆	♡	🕐	⛽	🚭	Store Details
✪		✓	◆	✓	Selmer • 1017 Mulberry Ave, 38375 • 731-645-7938 • Jct US-64 & US-45 (S of town) go S on US-45 1.4 miles
✪		✓		✓	Sevierville • 1414 Parkway, 37862 • 865-429-0029 • I-40 Exit 407 follow SR-66 S 8.5 miles then US-441 S 2.1 miles
✪		✓	❖		Shelbyville • 1880 N Main St, 37160 • 931-685-0499 • I-24 Exit 81A take US-231 S 21.3 miles
✪		✓			Smithville • 515 W Broad St, 37166 • 615-215-7550 • I-40 Exit 273 take SR-56 S 13 miles then US-70 W .9 mile
✪	4	✓	◆		Smyrna • 570 Enon Springs Rd E, 37167 • 615-355-1029 • I-24 Exit 70 take SR-102 NE 3.9 miles & Enon Springs Rd W .1 mile
✪		✓	❖		Soddy Daisy • 9334 Dayton Pike, 37379 • 423-332-2412 • I-24 Exit 178 take US-27 N 17 miles, Harrison Ln W .3 mile & Dayton Pike S .2 mile
✪		✓	❖		Sparta • 202 Sam Walton Dr, 38583 • 931-738-3225 • I-49 Exit 287 follow SR-136 S 15.7 miles
✪	6	✓			Spring Hill • 4959 Main St, 37174 • 615-435-2443 • I-65 Exit 59B go 2 miles on SR-840 then S 4 miles on US-31
✪		✓	❖		Springfield • 3360 Tom Austin Hwy, 37172 • 615-384-9561 • I-24 Exit 35 take US-431 N 11.7 miles
✪	3	✓			Sweetwater • 935 US Hwy 11 S, 37874 • 423-337-7636 • I-75 Exit 60 go E 2.6 miles on SR-68 then S .4 mile on SR-2/US-11
✪		✓			Tullahoma • 2111 N Jackson St, 37388 • 931-455-1382 • I-24 Exit 111 take SR-55 W 13.1 miles then US-41 ALT N 2.1 miles
✪	1	✓	❖		Unicoi • 110 Rocky Bottom Dr, 37692 • 423-743-8780 • I-26 Exit 34, south of exit
✪		✓		✓	Union City • 1601 W Reelfoot Ave, 38261 • 731-884-0114 • Jct SR-431 & US-51 (S of town) take US-51 S .7 mile
✪		✓	❖		Waverly • 275 Walton Dr, 37185 • 931-296-9235 • 2.2 miles west of town via US-70 at Browntown Rd
✪	1	✓			White House • 222 Wilkinson Ln, 37188 • 615-672-6773 • I-65 Exit 108 go E .4 mile on SR-76 then N on Wilkinson Ln .3 mile
✪		✓			Winchester • 2675 Decherd Blvd, 37398 • 931-967-0207 • I-24 Exit 127 follow SR-50 W 14 miles then US-41 ALT 1 mile

Texas

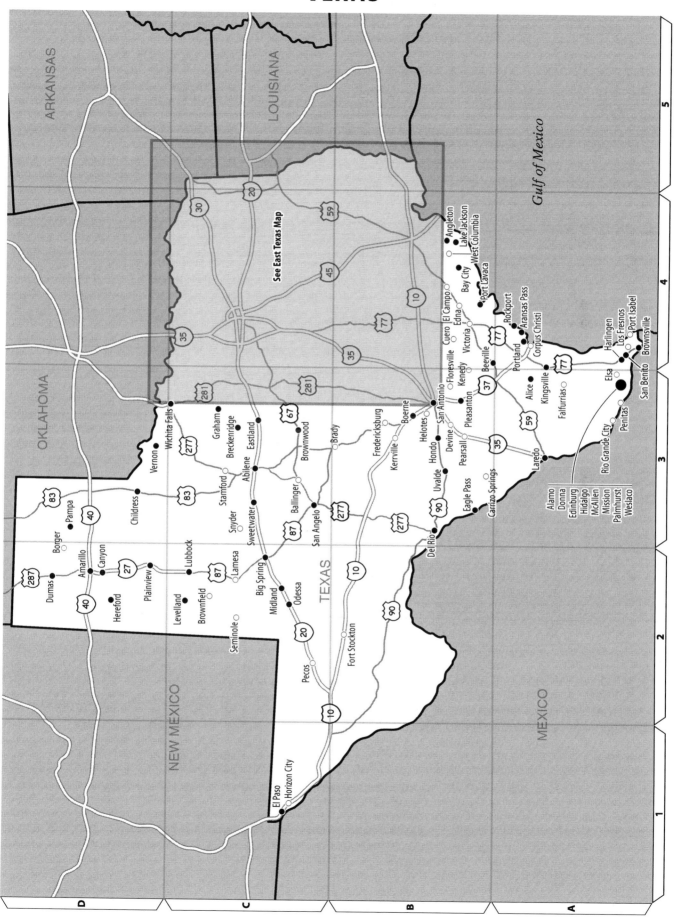

EAST TEXAS

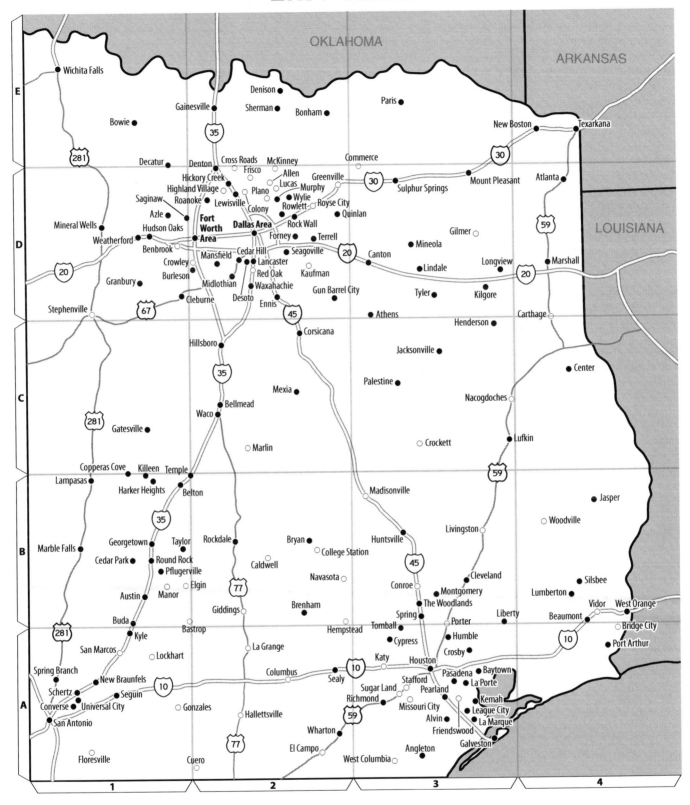

Dallas Metro Area

Balch Springs • Carrollton • Dallas • Garland • Grand Prairie • Grapevine • Irving • Mesquite • Sachse

Fort Worth Metro Area

Arlington • Bedford • Fort Worth • Hurst • Lake Worth • North Richland Hills • Westworth Village

☆	♡	🕐	⛽	🚫	Store Details
✪	1	✓	❖		Abilene • 1650 TX Hwy 351, 79601 • 325-677-5584 • I-20 Exit 288 on SR-351 N of I-20
✪	6	✓			Abilene • 4350 Southwest Dr, 79606 • 325-695-3092 • I-20 Exit 283A follow US-83 S 4.3 miles then Southwest Dr W 1 mile
✪		✓	❖		Alamo • 1421 Frontage Rd, 78516 • 956-782-0034 • Jct US-281 & US-83 (W of town) go E on US-83 for 3.5 miles, exit toward Alamo Rd to S Frontage Rd .1 mile
✪		✓	❖		Alice • 2701 E Main St, 78332 • 361-668-0441 • Jct SR-459 & SR-44 (E of town) merge onto SR-359 W/SR-44 W 1.8 miles
✪		✓		✓	Allen • 730 W Exchange Pkwy, 75013 • 972-649-0356 • US-75 Exit 36, west of exit
✪	10	✓	❖		Alvin • 400 Hwy 35 Byp N, 77511 • 281-585-2825 • I-45 Exit 19 take FM-517 W 9 miles, CR-142 S .6 mile & SR-6 N .4 mile
✪	1	✓	◆	✓	Amarillo • 3700 E I-40, 79103 • 806-342-3030 • I-40 Exit 72B take Interstate Dr E .2 mile
✪	2	✓	❖		Amarillo • 5730 W Amarillo Blvd, 79106 • 806-354-9454 • I-40 Exit 66 go N on Bell St 1.5 miles
✪	1	✓	❖		Amarillo • 4215 Canyon Dr, 79110 • 806-352-6360 • I-27 Exit 121A merge onto Canyon Dr N .3 mile
✪	1	✓	❖		Amarillo • 4610 S Coulter St, 79119 • 806-354-9300 • I-27 Exit 115 take Sundown Ln W .2 mile & Coulter Rd S .6 mile
✪		✓	◆	✓	Angleton • 1801 N Velasco St, 77515 • 979-849-4604 • Jct FM-523 & SR-288 BR (N of town) go S on SR-288 BR 1.4 miles
✪		✓	❖		Aransas Pass • 2501 W Wheeler Ave, 78336 • 361-758-2920 • Jct FM-136 & SR-35 (W of town) take SR-35 E 5 miles then SR-35 BR SE .9 mile
✪	2	✓			Arlington • 915 E Randol Mill Rd, 76011 • 817-274-1040 • I-30 Exit 29 take Ballpark Way S .9 mile & Randol Mill Rd W .9 mile

☆	♡	🕐	⛽	🚫	Store Details
✪	2	✓		✓	Arlington • 4800 S Hwy 287, 76017 • 817-563-1005 • I-20 Exit 445 follow Frontage Rd W .4 mile then S on Little Rd .7 mile
✪	2	✓		✓	Arlington • 4801 S Cooper St, 76017 • 817-465-1000 • I-20 Exit 449 follow FM-157 S 1.2 miles
✪		✓	◆		Athens • 1405 E Tyler St, 75751 • 903-677-5400 • Jct FM-317 Loop & SR-31 (NE of town) go SW on SR-31/Tyler St 1.5 miles
✪		✓	◆		Atlanta • 201 US Hwy 59 Loop, 75551 • 903-796-7916 • Jct FM-2328 & US-59 (SW of town) follow US-59 N 3.5 miles
✪	2	✓	❖	✓	Austin • 710 E Ben White Blvd, 78704 • 512-443-6601 • I-35 Exit 231 (southbound travelers) follow I-35 service road S 1.1 miles then go W .3 mile on Ben White Blvd. Northbound travelers use I-35 Exit 230, go N on service road 1.1 miles then W .3 mile on Ben White Blvd.
✪	8	✓			Austin • 13201 Ranch Road 620 N, 78717 • 512-331-9924 • I-35 Exit 250 follow SR-45 (toll) and FM-620 W for 7.1 miles then go S .1 mile on Lake Creek Pkwy
✪	5	✓			Austin • 5017 W Hwy 290, 78735 • 512-892-6086 • I-35 Exit 230 follow US-290 W 5 miles
✪	1	✓	❖		Austin • 9300 S I-35, 78748 • 512-292-6973 • On west side of I-35 at Slaughter Ln (northbound travelers use Exit 227, southbound use Exit 226B)
✪	1	✓	❖	✓	Austin • 1030 Norwood Park Blvd, 78753 • 512-339-6060 • I-35 Exit 241 go E on Norwood Park Blvd .4 mile
✪	1	✓	❖		Austin • 12900 N I-35 Service Rd, 78753 • 512-837-9886 • I-35 Exit 245 (southbound travelers) follow I-35 service road S .4 mile. Northbound travelers use I-35 Exit 246, W on Howard Ln then S .7 mile on I-35 service road
✪	3	✓		✓	Austin • 2525 W Anderson Ln, 78757 • 512-354-3702 • Southbound I-35 travelers use Exit 240A and follow Anderson Ln W for 2.5 miles; Northbound travelers use Exit 240B and follow US-183 W 1 mile to Anderson Square, turn left then right onto Anderson Ln for 1.2 miles
✪		✓	❖		Azle • 721 Boyd Rd, 76020 • 817-270-5716 • I-820 Exit 10A follow SR-199 W 11.1 miles then FM-730 N .3 mile
✪	1	✓	❖		Balch Springs • 12300 Lake June Rd, 75180 • 972-286-8600 • I-635 Exit 2 go W on Lake June Rd .3 mile
☆					Ballinger • 2005 Hutchins Ave, 76821 • 325-365-5731 • Jct US-83 & US-67 (in town) go S on US-67 for 1.1 miles

☆	⛉	🕐	⛽	🚫⛽	Store Details
✪		✓			Bastrop • 488 Hwy 71 W, 78602 • 512-321-2288 • Jct FM-969 & SR-71 (W of town) go E on SR-71 for 1.7 miles
✪		✓	✤		Bay City • 4600 7th St, 77414 • 979-245-0196 • Jct FM-457 & SR-35 (E of town) go N on SR-35 for .4 mile
✪	2	✓	✤		Baytown • 4900 Garth Rd, 77521 • 281-421-4859 • I-10 Exit 792 take Garth Rd S 2 miles
✪	1	✓			Baytown • 8700 N Hwy 146, 77523 • 281-918-3023 • I-10 Exit 797 go S .3 mile on SR-146; westbound travelers use Exit 798
✪	3	✓	◆		Beaumont • 4145 Dowlen Rd, 77706 • 409-899-9203 • I-10 Exit 853A take US-287 N 2.2 miles then Dowlen Rd W .8 mile
✪	8	✓		✓	Bedford • 4101 Hwy 121, 76021 • 817-571-7928 • I-820 Exit 22B follow SR-121 NE 7.8 miles & W at Cheek-Sparger Rd
✪		✓	✤		Beeville • 502 E FM 351, 78102 • 361-358-4764 • I-37 Exit 56 follow US-59 N 16.7 miles then FM-351 NW 2.6 miles
✪	1	✓	◆		Bellmead • 1521 I-35 N, 76705 • 254-867-8084 • I-35 Exit 338B go N .5 mile
✪	3	✓	✤		Belton • 2604 N Main St, 76513 • 254-939-0962 • I-35 Exit 294A take Central Ave W .6 mile & SR-317 N 1.8 miles
✪	1	✓			Benbrook • 8840 Benbrook Blvd, 76126 • 682-233-6820 • I-20 Exit 429A go S .6 mile on US-377/Benbrook Hwy
✪	4	✓	◆		Big Spring • 201 W Marcy Dr, 79720 • 432-267-3363 • I-20 Exit 179 take I-20 BR W 1.6 miles & US-87 S 1.6 miles
✪	1	✓	✤		Boerne • 1381 S Main St, 78006 • 830-249-6195 • I-10 Exit 540 take SR-46 E .6 mile then US-87 BR S .1 mile
✪		✓	✤		Bonham • 2021 N TX Hwy 121, 75418 • 903-583-9591 • Jct US-82 & SR-121 (NW of town) take SR-121 N .9 mile
✪		✓			Borger • 1501 Roosevelt St, 79007 • 806-274-7257 • 1.3 miles southwest of town center along SR-136/Wilson St
✪		✓	✤		Bowie • 1341 Highway 287 N, 76230 • 940-872-1166 • 1.8 miles southeast of town center at US-81/US-287 junction
✪		✓			Brady • 2207 S Bridge St, 76825 • 325-597-3406 • 1.8 miles south of town center via US-87
✪		✓	✤		Breckenridge • 3800 W Walker St, 76424 • 254-559-6579 • 2.7 miles west of town center via US-180/Walker St
✪		✓	◆	✓	Brenham • 203 US Loop 290 W, 77833 • 979-836-1118 • 2 miles south of town center off US-290 at SR-36
☆	8				Bridge City • 795 Texas Ave, 77611 • 409-735-2417 • I-10 Exit 873 follow SR-73 S 7.1 miles

☆	⛉	🕐	⛽	🚫⛽	Store Details
☆					Brownfield • 1405 Tahoka Rd, 79316 • 806-637-8778 • Jct US-385 & US-380 (in town) take US-380 E 1 mile
✪		✓			Brownsville • 2205 E Ruben Torres Sr Blvd, 78526 • 956-509-2077 • From US-83/I-69E at Ruben Torres Sr Blvd, go E 1.3 miles
✪		✓		✓	Brownsville • 3500 W Alton Gloor Blvd, 78520 • 956-350-0022 • Jct US-83/77 & FM-3248/Alton Gloor Blvd (N of town) go W on Gloor Blvd .2 mile
✪		✓	✤		Brownsville • 2721 Boca Chica Blvd, 78521 • 956-544-0394 • Jct US-83/77 & SR-48/Boca Chica Blvd (in town) go E on Boca Chica .7 mile
✪		✓	◆		Brownwood • 401 W Commerce St, 76801 • 325-643-9727 • Jct US-183 & US-84 (NE of town) follow US-84 SW 1.2 miles
✪		✓	◆		Bryan • 2200 Briarcrest Dr, 77802 • 979-776-6441 • Located 3 miles east of town center, southwest of SR-6 on Briarcrest Dr
✪		✓			Bryan • 643 N Harvey Mitchell Pkwy, 77807 • 979-599-5877 • Located 3.2 miles south of town center along FM-2818/Harvey Mitchell Pkwy
✪	1	✓	✤	✓	Buda • 690 Old San Antonio Rd, 78610 • 512-295-1670 • I-35 Exit 220 go W .5 mile on Cabelas Dr then turn right .5 mile at Old San Antonio Rd
✪	3	✓	◆		Burleson • 951 SW Wilshire Blvd, 76028 • 817-572-9574 • I-35W Exit 36 take SR-50 Spur W .8 mile & SR-174 S 1.3 miles
☆			◆		Caldwell • 475 TX Hwy 36 N, 77836 • 979-567-9807 • Jct SR-21 & SR-36 (N of town) go NW on SR-36 for .1 mile
✪	3	✓	◆		Canton • 603 E Hwy 243, 75103 • 903-567-5744 • I-20 Exit 528 take FM-17 S 1.6 miles, SR-64 SE .4 mile & SR-243 W .5 mile
✪	4	✓	✤		Canyon • 1701 N 23rd St, 79015 • 806-655-1175 • I-27 Exit 110 follow US-87 S 4 miles
☆					Carrizo Springs • 2214 N 1st St, 78834 • 830-876-2462 • 2 miles northeast of town center along US-83
✪	3	✓			Carrollton • 1213 E Trinity Mills Rd, 75006 • 972-466-2228 • I-35E Exit 445 take Bush Tpk (toll) E 1.4 miles then Josey Ln N .4 mile & Trinity Mills W .8 mile
✪		✓			Carthage • 4609 NW Loop 436, 75633 • 903-693-8881 • 2.6 miles west of town center via US-79-BR and LaSalle Pkwy/SR-149/Loop 436
✪	7	✓	✤		Cedar Hill • 621 Uptown Blvd, 75104 • 469-272-7344 • I-20 Exit 464 follow US-67 S 5.9 miles. FM-1382 W .4 mile & Uptown Blvd S .3 mile

☆	♡	🕐	⛽	🚫	Store Details
✪	9	✓	❖		Cedar Park • 201 Walton Way, 78613 • 512-528-8746 • I-35 Exit 257 take FM-1431 W 8.7 miles & Walton Way N .2 mile
✪	6	✓			Cedar Park • 2801 E Whitestone Blvd, 78613 • 512-690-9340 • I-35 Exit 256 go W 5.9 miles on SM-1431
✪		✓	❖		Center • 810 Hurst St, 75935 • 936-598-6131 • Jct SR-87 & US-96 (NW of town) go S on US-96/Hurst St .2 mile
✪		✓	❖		Childress • 2801 Avenue F NW, 79201 • 940-937-6166 • Jct US-62 & US-287/Ave F (NW of town) go NW on Ave F .8 mile
✪		✓	❖		Cleburne • 1616 W Henderson St, 76033 • 817-645-1575 • I-35W Exit 26 follow US-67 W 6.3 miles & US-67-BR W 6.2 miles
✪		✓	❖		Cleveland • 831 Hwy 59 S, 77327 • 281-592-2654 • Jct SR-105 & US-59 (SW of town) take US-59 S 1.6 miles
✪		✓			College Station • 1815 Brothers Blvd, 77845 • 979-693-3095 • 2.8 miles southeast of town center along Texas Ave
✪	2	✓			Colony • 4691 TX Hwy 121, 75056 • 972-625-6000 • I-35E Exit 448A take SR-121 W 1.1 miles
☆	1				Columbus • 2103 Milam St, 78934 • 979-732-8341 • I-10 Exit 696 take SR-71 BR N .1 mile to Milam St N
✪	9	✓			Commerce • 2701 TX Hwy 50, 75428 • 903-886-3108 • I-30 Exit 101 go N 9 miles on SR-50
✪	1	✓			Conroe • 1407 N Loop 336 W, 77304 • 936-788-5400 • I-45 Exit 88 take SR-336 Loop W .2 mile
✪	4	✓	❖		Converse • 8315 FM 78, 78109 • 210-666-6066 • I-35 Exit 172 take SR-1604 S 2.8 miles then FM-78 SW 1.2 miles
✪		✓	◆		Copperas Cove • 2720 E Hwy 190, 76522 • 254-542-7600 • Jct FM-116 & US-190 (in town) go E on US-190 for 1 mile
✪	2	✓			Corpus Christi • 3829 US Hwy 77, 78410 • 361-387-0599 • I-37 Exit 14 follow US-77 S 1.4 miles
✪	10	✓			Corpus Christi • 4109 S Staples St, 78411 • 361-994-9010 • I-37 Exit 4A follow SR-358 SE for 8.5 miles; N .8 mile on Everhart Rd; W .3 mile on Staples St
✪		✓			Corpus Christi • 6101 Saratoga Rd, 78412 • 361-445-3240 • I-37 Exit 4A go SE 9.5 miles on SR-358; S 1.7 miles on Staples St; E .7 mile on Saratoga Blvd
✪	6	✓			Corpus Christi • 1821 S Padre Island Dr, 78416 • 361-854-0943 • I-37 Exit 4A follow SR-358 SE for 4.4 miles; take the Greenwood Rd Exit and follow S Padre Island Dr .4 miles

☆	♡	🕐	⛽	🚫	Store Details
✪		✓			Corpus Christi • 1250 Flour Bluff Dr, 78418 • 361-937-2643 • I-37 Exit 4A follow SR-358 SE for 14.3 miles then Flour Bluff Dr S .2 mile
✪	5	✓	❖		Corsicana • 3801 W TX Hwy 31, 75110 • 903-872-6691 • I-45 Exit 231 merge onto Frontage Rd S .3 mile then SR-31 W 4.4 miles
✪		✓			Crockett • 1225 E Loop 304, 75835 • 936-544-5121 • Jct US-287 & SR-304 Loop (SE of town) go N on SR-304 for .8 mile
✪	8	✓	❖		Crosby • 14215 FM 2100 Rd, 77532 • 281-328-4836 • I-10 Exit 787 take I-10 Frontage W .4 mile then FM-2100 N 7 miles
✪		✓			Cross Roads • 11700 US Highway 380, 76227 • 940-488-7008 • I-35 Exit 469 go E 11.3 miles on US-380
✪	1	✓			Crowley • 1221 FM 1187, 76036 • 682-233-7834 • I-35W Exit 39 go W 1 mile on Crowley Plover Rd
☆					Cuero • 1202 E Broadway St, 77954 • 361-275-5796 • Jct US-183 & US-87 (in town) take US-87 E 1.1 miles
✪		✓	❖		Cypress • 26270 Northwest Fwy, 77429 • 281-256-8038 • I-10 Exit 747A take Fry Rd N 14.1 miles & US-290 E .2 mile
✪	1	✓	❖		Dallas • 1521 N Cockrell Hill Rd, 75211 • 214-330-7249 • I-30 Exit 39 go S on Cockrell Hill Rd .3 mile
✪	4				Dallas • 9410 Webb Chapel Rd, 75220 • 972-629-0007 • I-35E Exit 438 go E 2.4 miles on Walnut Hill Ln then S 1.2 miles on Marsh Ln
✪	1	✓			Dallas • 7401 Samuell Blvd, 75228 • 214-319-2616 • I-30 Exit 52B take Thornton Fwy E .1 mile, St Francis Ave S .1 mile & Samuell Blvd E .2 mile
✪	4			✓	Dallas • 6185 Retail Rd, 75231 • 972-656-2196 • I-635 Exit 16 go S 3.6 miles on Skillman Rd
✪	1				Dallas • 200 Short St, 75232 • 972-232-6400 • I-35E Exit 421B, west of exit
✪	1	✓	❖		Dallas • 3155 W Wheatland Rd, 75237 • 972-709-1400 • I-20 Exit 465 take Wheatland Rd W .4 mile
✪	2	✓			Dallas • 13739 N Central Expy, 75243 • 972-656-2501 • North of I-635 Exits 19A/B off US-75 at Spring Valley Rd
✪	1	✓	◆		Dallas • 9301 Forest Ln, 75243 • 972-437-9146 • I-635 Exit 17, west of exit
✪	1	✓	◆	✓	Dallas • 4122 Lyndon B. Johnson Frwy, 75244 • 972-980-2195 • I-635 Exit 23 go S .2 mile on Midway Rd and turn right at Harvest Hill Rd

☆	○	🕐	⛽	🚫	Store Details
✪	2	✓		✓	Dallas • 15220 Montford Rd, 75248 • 972-233-0438 • I-635 Exit 22C take Dallas North Tollway (toll) N 1.4 miles, Belt Line Rd E .2 mile & Montford Dr N .1 mile
✪	3	✓			Dallas • 7075 W Wheatland Rd, 75249 • 469-608-6240 • I-20 Exit 461 go S for .6 mile on Cedar Ridge Dr, W 1 mile on Camp Wisdom Rd, then S .9 mile on Clark Rd
✪	4	✓	❖		Dallas • 18121 Marsh Ln, 75287 • 972-307-6978 • I-35E Exit 445B take Bush Tpk (toll) E 3.5 miles, Frankford Rd E .2 mile & Marsh Ln S .1 mile
✪		✓	◆		Decatur • 800 S Hwy 287, 76234 • 940-627-5546 • Jct US-380 & US-81 (W of town) go S on US-81 for .6 mile
✪		✓	❖		Del Rio • 2410 Dodson Ave, 78840 • 830-774-6034 • Jct US-90 & US-277 (E of town) go N on Bedell Ave 1.1 miles then N on Dodson 1.1 miles
✪		✓	◆		Denison • 401 N US Hwy 75, 75020 • 903-465-9744 • Jct SR-503 & US-75 (S of town) take US-75 N 2.2 miles
✪	1	✓			Denton • 2750 W University, 76201 • 940-735-3119 • I-35 Exit 469 go E .3 mile on US-380
✪	1	✓	◆		Denton • 1515 S Loop 288, 76205 • 940-484-1717 • I-35E Exit 462 take SR-288 Loop E 1 mile
✪	4	✓	❖		Desoto • 951 W Belt Line Rd, 75115 • 972-223-1711 • I-35 Exit 414 take FM-1382 W 3.2 miles
✪	1				Devine • 175 Interstate 35 N, 78016 • 830-663-5944 • I-35 Exit 122, west of exit
✪		✓			Donna • 900 N Salinas Blvd, 78537 • 956-461-2906 • About 2 miles northeast of town center on Salinas Blvd just north of I-2/US-83
✪		✓	❖		Dumas • 2003 S Dumas Ave, 79029 • 806-935-9075 • Jct FM-722 & US-287/87 (S of town) go S on US-287/87 for .6 mile
✪		✓	❖		Eagle Pass • 496 S Bibb Ave, 78852 • 830-773-9403 • Jct US-277 & FM-375 (in town) take FM-375/Bibb Ave S .4 mile
✪	1	✓	❖		Eastland • 1410 E Main St, 76448 • 254-629-3371 • I-20 Exit 343 take FM-570 W .3 mile
✪		✓	❖		Edinburg • 1724 W University Dr, 78539 • 956-381-6674 • Jct US-281 & SR-107/University Dr (in town) go W on University Dr 2 miles
✪		✓			Edinburg • 2812 S Expressway 281, 78542 • 956-252-2047 • 2.8 miles southeast of town center off US-281 at Canton Rd, east side of highway
✪		✓	❖		Edinburg • 4101 S McColl Rd, 78539 • 956-618-2018 • Jct US-83 & SR-2061/McColl Rd (in McAllen) take McColl Rd N 7 miles

☆	○	🕐	⛽	🚫	Store Details
☆					Edna • 1002 N Wells St, 77957 • 361-782-5223 • At Jct US-59 & SR-111 (N of town)
✪		✓			El Campo • 3413 W Loop St, 77437 • 979-543-7286 • Jct US-59 & SR-525 Loop (SW of town) take SR-525 E 1.5 miles then N at FM-2765 for 2.5 miles
✪	3	✓		✓	El Paso • 5631 Dyer St, 79904 • 915-245-3510 • I-10 Exit 22B go N 2.4 miles to Exit 24; W .4 mile on Fred Wilson Ave; N .2 mile on Dyer St
✪	3	✓	❖		El Paso • 9441 Alameda Ave, 79907 • 915-860-7171 • I-10 Exit 34 take SR-375 Loop S 2.2 miles then Alameda Ave W .2 mile
✪	1	✓			El Paso • 7555 N Mesa St, 79912 • 915-833-1335 • I-10 Exit 11 take Mesa St E .2 mile
✪	9	✓	◆		El Paso • 4530 Woodrow Bean Dr, 79924 • 915-757-0151 • I-10 Exit 22B go N on US-54/Patriot Fwy for 8 miles to Exit 9 then go E on SR-375 Loop .2 mile
✪	1	✓			El Paso • 7101 Gateway Blvd W, 79925 • 915-779-6664 • I-10 Exit 26 merge onto Gateway Blvd W .8 mile
✪	1	✓	❖		El Paso • 10727 Gateway Blvd W, 79935 • 915-594-0243 • I-10 Exit 28B merge onto Gateway Blvd W .1 mile
✪	4	✓	◆		El Paso • 1850 N Zaragoza Rd, 79936 • 915-855-6405 • I-10 Exit 34 merge onto Gateway Blvd W 2.1 miles then Zaragosa Rd S 1.3 miles
✪	8	✓			El Paso • 12236 Montana Ave, 79938 • 915-255-4031 • I-10 Exit 34 go N 7.5 miles on SR-375 then E .5 mile on US-62/US-180
✪		✓		✓	Elgin • 1320 W Hwy 290, 78621 • 512-285-3397 • West end of town at US-290 and SR-95 junction
✪		✓	◆		Elsa • 411 S Broadway St, 78543 • 956-262-9407 • Located on FM-88 about .5 mile south of town center
✪	1	✓	❖		Ennis • 700 E Ennis Ave, 75119 • 972-875-9671 • I-45 Exit 251B go W on Ennis Ave .4 mile
☆					Falfurrias • 2535 US Hwy 281 S, 78355 • 361-325-3601 • 1 mile south of town along US-281
✪		✓			Floresville • 305 10th St, 78114 • 830-393-4417 • 3 miles northwest of town center on US-181
✪	5	✓	❖		Forney • 802 E US Hwy 80, 75126 • 972-564-1867 • I-20 Exit 490 take FM-741 N 2.8 miles, FM-548 N 1.2 miles & US-80 W .9 mile
✪	1	✓			Fort Stockton • 2610 W Dickinson Blvd, 79735 • 432-336-3389 • I-10 Exit 257 follow US-285 E .3 miles then go S .3 mile on 14th St

☆	♡	◷	⛽	🚫	Store Details
●	8	✓		✓	Fort Worth • 2401 Avondale Haslet Rd, 76052 • 817-302-1724 • I-35W Exit 60 follow US-287 NW for 8 miles to Avondale Haslet Rd and turn right
●	5	✓			Fort Worth • 2245 Jacksboro Hwy, 76114 • 817-569-6238 • I-35W Exit 54 go W 3.8 miles on SR-183 to SR-199 and turn left .3 miles
●	3	✓			Fort Worth • 2900 Renaissance Sq, 76105 • 817-900-1909 • I-35W Exit 48A go E 2.3 miles on Berry St
●	1	✓	❖		Fort Worth • 9500 Clifford St, 76108 • 817-367-0042 • I-820 Exit 5A go W on Clifford St .4 mile
●	2	✓	❖		Fort Worth • 3851 Airport Fwy, 76111 • 817-759-2047 • I-30 Exit 16C go N on Beach St 1.8 miles then W at Airport Fwy .2 mile
●	1	✓			Fort Worth • 8401 Anderson Blvd, 76120 • 817-276-9021 • I-30 Exit 24, north of exit
●	2	✓			Fort Worth • 6300 Oakmont Blvd, 76132 • 817-263-4065 • I-20 Exit 433 take Hulen St S 1.4 miles then W at Oakmont Blvd
●	3	✓	❖	✓	Fort Worth • 7451 McCart Ave, 76133 • 817-361-6032 • I-35W Exit 43 go W on Sycamore School Rd 2.8 miles then N at McCart Ave
●	3	✓	❖	✓	Fort Worth • 8520 N Beach St, 76137 • 817-514-9793 • I-35W Exit 61 (northbound travelers) go E 1.6 miles on Tarrant Pkwy then N .2 mile on Beach St. Southbound travelers use I-35W Exit 63 go W 1.6 miles on Heritage Trace Pkwy then S 1.3 miles on Beach St
●		✓		✓	Fredericksburg • 1435 E Main St, 78624 • 830-997-2633 • Jct US-87 & US-290 (in town) go S on US-290 for 1.3 miles
●	1	✓			Friendswood • 150 W El Dorado Blvd, 77546 • 281-480-6134 • I-45 Exit 27 take El Dorado Blvd W .2 mile
●		✓		✓	Frisco • 12220 FM 423, 75034 • 469-362-8542 • From Dallas North Tollway at Eldorado Pkwy go W 2.8 miles on Eldorado Pkwy then N .1 mile on FM-423
●		✓		✓	Frisco • 8555 Preston Rd, 75034 • 469-237-3768 • 1.2 miles east of town center near intersection of Main St and Preston Rd
●	2	✓	❖		Gainesville • 1800 Lawrence St, 76240 • 940-668-6898 • I-35 Exit 498A take US-82 E 1.1 miles
●	2	✓	❖		Galveston • 6702 Seawall Blvd, 77551 • 409-744-8677 • I-45 Exit 1A take 61st St S 1.6 miles then Seawall Blvd S .4 mile

☆	♡	◷	⛽	🚫	Store Details
●		✓			Garland • 5302 N Garland Ave, 75040 • 972-496-2711 • I-635 Exit 19A take US-75 N 7 miles, Bush Tpk (toll) E 4.3 miles & Garland Ave S .4 mile
●	1	✓		✓	Garland • 1801 Marketplace Dr, 75041 • 972-279-8700 • I-635 Exit 11B go E .4 mile on Eastgate Dr then S .1 mile on Plaza Dr
●	1	✓			Garland • 555 W I-30, 75043 • 972-303-5865 • I-30 at Exit 59, north of exit
●		✓	❖		Gatesville • 2805 S TX Hwy 36, 76528 • 254-865-8991 • Jct US-84 & SR-36 (S of town) take SR-36 S 1.8 miles
●	1	✓	❖		Georgetown • 620 S I-35, 78626 • 512-863-4855 • I-35 Exit 261, west side of highway
☆					Giddings • 2374 E Austin St, 78942 • 979-542-1375 • Jct US-77 & US-290 (in town) take US-290 E 1.4 miles
●		✓			Gilmer • 1923 N Wood St, 75644 • 903-797-6501 • Jct SR-155 & US-271 (in town) take US-271 N 1.7 miles
●		✓			Gonzales • 1114 E Sarah Dewitt Dr, 78629 • 830-672-7573 • I-10 Exit 632 go SE on US-183 for 12.7 miles then E on Sarah Dewitt Dr for .8 mile
●		✓	❖		Graham • 2121 Hwy 16 S, 76450 • 940-549-7714 • Jct SR-380 & SR-16 (N of town) go S on SR-16 for 2.2 miles
●		✓	◆		Granbury • 735 E Hwy 377, 76048 • 817-573-3791 • Jct US-377 & SR-144 (in town) go E on US-377 for .8 mile
●	1	✓		✓	Grand Prairie • 2225 W I-20, 75052 • 972-660-4200 • I-20 Exit 454, south of exit on I-20 service road
●	6	✓			Grapevine • 1601 W TX Hwy 114, 76051 • 817-421-4770 • I-635 Exit 36A take SR-121 S 1.4 miles, SR-114 W 4 miles, exit at Southlake Blvd W .1 mile & E at SR-114 for .2 mile
●	1	✓			Greenville • 7401 I-30, 75402 • 903-455-1792 • I-35 Exit 93A, south of exit
●		✓	◆		Gun Barrel City • 1200 W Main St, 75156 • 903-887-4180 • Jct US-175 & FM-85 (E of town) take FM-85 W 5.4 miles
☆					Hallettsville • 1506 N Texana St, 77964 • 361-798-4377 • Jct US-90A & US-77 (in town) take US-77 N 1 mile
●		✓	❖		Harker Heights • 2020 Heights Dr, 76548 • 254-699-1021 • From Central Texas Expy/US-190 at FM-2410 go S .2 mile, turn right at Triangle Rd 318 feet then Commercial Dr W .2 mile
●		✓	❖		Harlingen • 1801 W Lincoln St, 78552 • 956-428-0734 • Jct US-83 & US-77 (W of town) go S on US-77/83 for .4 mile & Lincoln St W .1 mile

☆	🛡	🕐	⛽	🚫	Store Details
✪	6	✓			Helotes • 12550 Leslie Rd, 78023 • 210-507-4979 • I-10 Exit 556A go W 4.2 miles on SR-1604 then N .9 mile on Bandera Rd
☆					Hempstead • 625 Hwy 290 E, 77445 • 979-826-3344 • Jct US-290 & SR-6 (N of town) take US-290 S .5 mile
✪		✓	❖		Henderson • 2121 US Hwy 79 S, 75654 • 903-657-5707 • Jct US-259 & US-79 (S of town) take US-79 SW 1 mile
✪		✓	❖		Hereford • 300 W 15th St, 79045 • 806-364-5712 • Jct US-60 & US-385 (in town) take US-385 N 1.8 miles then W on 15th St .2 mile
✪	1	✓	❖	✓	Hickory Creek • 1035 Hickory Creek Blvd, 75065 • 940-321-5363 • I-35E Exit 457B take Swisher Rd W .3 mile & Hickory Creek Blvd S .1 mile
✪		✓			Hidalgo • 3000 N Jackson Rd, 78557 • 956-904-4826 • From US-281 at Dicker Dr in Pharr, Texas, go W 1.3 miles to store on left
✪	4	✓		✓	Highland Village • 3060 Justin Rd, 75077 • 972-317-4951 • I-35E Exit 454A take Justin Rd/FM-407 W 3.2 miles
✪	1	✓	❖		Hillsboro • 401 Coke Ave, 76645 • 254-582-2523 • I-35 Exit 368A take SR-171/22 W .3 mile & S at Coke Ave
✪		✓	❖		Hondo • 109 22nd St, 78861 • 830-426-4356 • Jct US-90 & SR-173 (E of town) take US-90 W .9 mile then S on Ave D .3 mile
✪	4	✓			Horizon City • 13900 Horizon Blvd, 79928 • 915-206-6199 • I-10 Exit 37 go E 3.3 miles on Horizon Blvd
✪	1	✓		✓	Houston • 111 Yale St, 77007 • 713-860-0700 • I-10 Exit 766, south of exit
✪	1	✓			Houston • 13750 E Freeway, 77015 • 713-453-5018 • I-10 Exit 780 (westbound travelers), south of exit; eastbound travelers use I-10 Exit 780 and follow the frontage road E for 1 mile
✪	3	✓	❖		Houston • 5655 E Sam Houston Pkwy N, 77015 • 713-450-2222 • I-10 Exit 781B take Houston Pkwy N 2.4 miles then Beltway N .3 mile
✪	1	✓			Houston • 4412 North Freeway, 77022 • 713-300-0511 • I-45 Exit 52B, east of exit
✪	1				Houston • 2391 S Wayside Dr, 77023 • 713-300-3653 • I-45 Exit 41B, east of exit at Wayside Dr. Southbound travelers can use Exit 42
✪	1	✓			Houston • 10411 North Fwy 45, 77037 • 281-999-9920 • I-45 Exit 59 (southbound travelers) follow frontage road S .6 mile; northbound travelers use Exit 60A
✪	5	✓			Houston • 13484 Northwest Fwy, 77040 • 713-690-0666 • I-610 Exit 13B take US-290 NW 4.5 miles, exit at Tidwell & continue on NW Fwy .5 mile
☆	1				Houston • 10750 Westview Dr, 77043 • 713-984-2773 • I-10 Exit 756A take Houston Pkwy N .4 mile then Westview Dr W .1 mile
✪	1	✓			Houston • 1118 Silber Rd, 77055 • 713-797-2245 • I-10 Exit 762 go N .3 mile on Silber Rd
✪	5	✓			Houston • 2727 Dunvale Rd, 77063 • 713-977-2099 • I-10 Exit 760 take Bingle Rd/Voss Rd S 3.2 miles, Westheimer Rd W .8 mile, Dunvale Rd S .1 mile
✪		✓	❖		Houston • 12353 FM 1960 Rd W, 77065 • 832-912-7320 • I-10 Exit 756B take Houston Tollway N 6.4 miles, US-29 NW 4.9 miles & FM-1960 E .9 mile
✪	4	✓	❖		Houston • 3450 FM 1960 Rd W, 77068 • 281-440-4482 • I-45 Exit 66 take FM-1960 W 3.8 miles then Walters Rd N .2 mile
✪	1	✓	❖		Houston • 9598 Rowlett Rd, 77075 • 832-386-0103 • I-45 Exit 34 take Gulf Fwy S .4 mile then Rowlett Rd S .1 mile
✪	3	✓			Houston • 2700 S Kirkwood Rd, 77077 • 281-558-5670 • I-10 Exit 754 take Kirkwood Rd S 2.7 miles
✪	1			✓	Houston • 5405 S Rice Ave, 77081 • 713-860-9242 • I-610 Exit 7 go W .4 mile on Fournace Pl then N .5 mile on Rice Ave
✪	5	✓	❖		Houston • 3506 Hwy 6 S, 77082 • 281-561-0866 • I-10 Exit 753A take SR-6 S 4.3 miles
✪	6	✓		✓	Houston • 13003 Tomball Pkwy, 77086 • 281-668-2952 • I-45 Exit 60B/C, follow Sam Houston Tollway W 3.4 miles to Antoine Dr, go S 1.9 miles then W .6 mile on Tomball Pkwy
✪	7	✓	❖		Houston • 15955 FM 529 Rd, 77095 • 281-855-1604 • I-10 Exit 753A take SR-6 N 6.5 miles then FM-529 W .3 mile
☆	1			✓	Houston • 9555 S Post Oak Rd, 77096 • 713-551-9148 • I-610 Exit 4A take Post Oak Rd S .4 mile
✪	8	✓	❖		Houston • 9460 W Sam Houston Pkwy S, 77099 • 281-568-3710 • I-10 Exit 756B take Houston Pkwy (toll) S 7.3 miles & Beltway S .6 mile
✪	2	✓	❖		Hudson Oaks • 2801 E I-20, 76087 • 817-599-7490 • I-20 Exit 413 (eastbound travelers) go N .1 mile on Lakeshore Dr then W .8 mile on I-20 Service Rd; westbound travelers use Exit 414 and continue W .8 mile on US-180/Fort Worth Hwy, S .1 mile on Lakeshore Dr then W .8 mile on I-20 Service Rd

☆	◯	⏲	⛽	🚭	Store Details
✪	9	✓			Humble • 9451 FM 1960 Bypass, 77338 • 281-540-8838 • I-45 Exit 66 take FM-1960 E for 9 miles
✪		✓	❖		Humble • 6626 FM 1960 Rd E, 77346 • 281-852-4648 • I-45 Exit 66 take FM-1960 E 10.7 miles
✪	10	✓	◆		Humble • 9235 N Sam Houston Pkwy E, 77396 • 281-441-2209 • I-45 Exit 60B (northbound use Exit 60D) go E 10 miles on Sam Houston Pkwy
✪	2	✓	◆		Huntsville • 141 I-45 S, 77340 • 936-293-1066 • I-45 Exit 118 go S on I-45 Service Rd/US-190 for 1.7 miles
✪	3	✓	❖		Hurst • 1732 Precinct Line Rd, 76054 • 817-503-7152 • I-820 Exit 22B take SR-121/183 E 1.8 miles then Precinct Line Rd N .5 mile
✪	7	✓		✓	Irving • 4100 W Airport Fwy, 75062 • 972-313-0707 • I-635 Exit 29A follow Bush Tpk & SR-161 S 6 miles then Airport Fwy E .8 mile
✪	1	✓		✓	Irving • 1635 Market Place Blvd, 75063 • 214-574-4517 • I-635 Exit 31, north side of highway at MacArthur Blvd
✪		✓	❖		Jacksonville • 1311 S Jackson St, 75766 • 903-589-3434 • Jct US-79 & US-69 (in town) take US-69 S .9 mile
✪		✓	❖		Jasper • 800 W Gibson St, 75951 • 409-384-1707 • Jct US-96 & US-190 (in town) go W on US-190 for 1.2 miles
✪	1	✓		✓	Katy • 1313 N Fry Rd, 77449 • 281-579-3373 • I-10 Exit 747A take Fry Rd N .2 mile
✪	6	✓		✓	Katy • 6060 N Fry Rd, 77449 • 281-550-4446 • I-10 Exit 747A go N 5.2 miles on Fry Rd
✪	1	✓	❖		Katy • 25108 Market Place Dr, 77494 • 281-644-6404 • I-10 Exit 741 take US-90 W .1 mile, cross over to I-10 Service Rd E .3 mile then Katy Fort Bend Rd S .2 mile
✪		✓			Kaufman • 300 Kings Fort Pkwy, 75142 • 469-595-7068 • 1.5 miles south of town center via Washington St to Kings Fort Pkwy
✪	7	✓	❖		Kemah • 255 FM 518 Rd, 77565 • 281-538-9778 • I-45 Exit 22 take Calder Dr N 1.1 miles then follow FM-518 E 5.8 miles
✪		✓		✓	Kenedy • 200 Business Park Blvd, 78119 • 830-583-9825 • 1 mile northwest of town along US-181
✪	3	✓			Kerrville • 1216 Junction Hwy, 78028 • 830-895-7900 • I-10 Exit 505 take FM-783 S 2.8 miles then W on SR-27 .2 mile
✪	4	✓	❖		Kilgore • 1201 Stone St, 75662 • 903-983-1494 • I-20 Exit 587 take SR-42 S 2.9 miles & E on Stone St .2 mile

☆	◯	⏲	⛽	🚭	Store Details
✪		✓			Killeen • 1400 Lowes Blvd, 76542 • 254-526-4102 • I-35 Exit 293A take US-190 W 17 miles, exit S at Trimmel Rd to US-190 E .3 mile & S at Walmart Blvd .1 mile
✪		✓	❖		Killeen • 3404 W Stan Schlueter Loop, 76549 • 254-669-6168 • 5.7 miles southwest of town center via SR-195 and Stan Schlueter Loop
✪		✓	◆		Kingsville • 1133 E General Cavazos Blvd, 78363 • 361-595-4146 • Jct SR-425 & US-77 (S of town) take US-77 S .6 mile then W on Cavazos Blvd .5 mile
✪	1	✓	❖		Kyle • 5754 Kyle Pkwy, 78640 • 512-268-1451 • I-35 Exit 215 go E .2 mile on Kyle Pkwy
✪		✓			La Grange • 1915 W State Hwy 71, 78945 • 979-968-8426 • Located about 1.8 miles west of town center via Travis St (SR-71-BR)
✪	1	✓	❖	✓	La Marque • 6410 I-45, 77568 • 409-986-6000 • I-45 Exit 15, west of exit
✪		✓	❖		La Porte • 9025 Spencer Hwy, 77571 • 281-479-9636 • I-10 Exit 781B follow Houston Pkwy S 7.2 miles then E on Spencer Hwy 3.5 miles
✪		✓	◆	✓	Lake Jackson • 121 Hwy 332 W, 77566 • 979-297-9757 • Jct FM-2004 & SR-288 (NW of town) take FM-2004 S .8 mile, Lake Rd S .3 mile & SR-332 E .2 mile
✪	2	✓			Lake Worth • 6360 Lake Worth Blvd, 76135 • 817-237-0400 • I-820 Exit 10A take SR-199 W 1.6 miles
☆					Lamesa • 2406 Lubbock Hwy, 79331 • 806-872-9576 • Jct US-180 & US-87 (in town) take US-87 N 1 mile
✪		✓	❖		Lampasas • 1710 Central Texas Expy, 76550 • 512-556-8217 • Jct US-183 & US-190 (S of town) go E on US-190 for 1.2 miles
✪	1	✓	◆		Lancaster • 150 N Interstate 35 E, 75146 • 972-223-9791 • I-35E Exit 414, east side of highway at Belt Line Rd
☆	1				Laredo • 5610 San Bernardo Ave, 78041 • 956-718-2441 • I-35 Exit 3B merge onto San Bernardo Ave S .4 mile
✪	4	✓	❖	✓	Laredo • 2320 Bob Bullock Loop, 78043 • 956-791-3303 • I-35 Exit 2 take US-59 E 3.5 miles & Bullock Loop S .5 mile
✪	2	✓		✓	Laredo • 2615 NE Bob Bullock Loop, 78045 • 956-231-5575 • I-35 Exit 8B go E 2 miles on SR-20 (southbound travelers use Exit 9)
✪		✓	❖		Laredo • 4401 Highway 83 South, 78046 • 956-727-0492 • 5.7 miles southeast of town center via US-83
✪	1	✓	❖		League City • 1701 W FM 646 Rd, 77573 • 281-337-9700 • I-45 Exit 20 take FM-646 SW 1 mile

☆	◯	⏱	⛽	🚫	Store Details
✪		✓	❖		Levelland • 407 E State Highway 114, 79336 • 806-894-2993 • Northeast of town center; .3 mile east of US-385/SR-114 junction
✪	2	✓	❖		Lewisville • 190 E Round Grove Rd, 75067 • 972-315-3398 • I-35E Exit 448B take FM-3040 W 1.4 miles
✪	1	✓			Lewisville • 801 W Main St, 75067 • 972-436-3099 • I-35E Exit 452 take FM-1171 W .2 mile
✪		✓	❖		Liberty • 2121 Hwy 146 Byp, 77575 • 936-336-5601 • From town center go E 1.5 miles on US-90/SR-146 then N 1.3 miles on SR-146
✪	1	✓	❖		Lindale • 105 Centennial Blvd, 75771 • 903-882-0740 • I-20 Exit 556 take US-69 N .5 mile
✪		✓			Livingston • 1620 W Church St, 77351 • 936-327-6370 • Jct US-59 & US-190 (W of town) take US-190 W .2 mile
✪					Lockhart • 1904 S Colorado St, 78644 • 512-398-2333 • 2 miles south of town center on US-183
✪	1	✓	❖		Longview • 4006 Estes Pkwy, 75603 • 903-236-0947 • I-20 Exit 595A take SR-322 S .8 mile
✪	10	✓	❖		Longview • 2440 Gilmer Rd, 75604 • 903-297-1121 • I-20 Exit 589B take SR-31 NE 4.5 miles, SR-281 Loop N 4.7 miles then SR-300 N .7 mile
✪	8	✓			Longview • 515 E Loop 281, 75605 • 903-663-4446 • I-20 Exit 599 take SR-281 Loop NW 7.4 miles
✪		✓		✓	Los Fresnos • 1004 W Ocean Blvd, 78566 • 956-233-1742 • From US-77 at SR-100, go E 5.5 miles on SR-100
✪	1	✓	❖		Lubbock • 1911 Marsha Sharp Fwy, 79415 • 806-747-3454 • I-27 Exit 4 go W 1 mile on 4th St (US-82)
✪	6	✓			Lubbock • 702 W Loop 289, 79416 • 806-793-9686 • I-27 Exit 6B take SR-289 Loop W 4.5 miles, merge onto Service Rd W 1.1 miles
✪	3	✓	◆		Lubbock • 4215 S Loop 289, 79423 • 806-793-2091 • I-27 Exit 1A take SR-289 Loop W 2.6 miles
✪	3	✓	❖		Lubbock • 6315 82nd St, 79424 • 806-698-6394 • I-27 Exit 1 continue on US-87 S .8 mile then 82nd St W 1.7 miles
✪		✓		✓	Lucas • 2662 W Lucas Rd, 75002 • 469-675-8801 • US-75 Exit 33 go E 3.7 miles on Bethany Dr
✪		✓	❖		Lufkin • 2500 Daniel McCall Dr, 75904 • 936-639-9600 • Jct SR-287 Loop & US-59 (S of town) continue S on US-59 for .4 mile then McCall Dr W .2 mile
✪		✓	❖		Lumberton • 100 N LHS Dr, 77657 • 409-755-1963 • I-10 Exit 853A follow US-69 N 12.1 miles

☆	◯	⏱	⛽	🚫	Store Details
☆	1				Madisonville • 1620 E Main St, 77864 • 936-348-3715 • I-45 Exit 142 take US-190 W .9 mile
✪		✓			Manor • 11923 US Hwy 290 E, 78653 • 512-651-9100 • Located 1 mile east of town on US-290
✪	8	✓	◆		Mansfield • 930 N Walnut Creek Dr, 76063 • 817-473-1189 • I-20 Exit 444 take US-287 S 7.9 miles & S at Walnut Creek Dr .1 mile
✪		✓	◆		Marble Falls • 2700 N Hwy 281, 78654 • 830-693-4461 • Jct SR-71 & US-281 (S of town) take US-281 N 6.7 miles
☆					Marlin • 600 N State Hwy 6, 76661 • 254-883-5556 • 1.5 miles east of town center at SR-6/SR-7 jct
✪	5	✓	◆	✓	Marshall • 1701 E End Blvd N, 75670 • 903-938-0072 • I-20 Exit 617 follow US-59 N 4.8 miles
✪		✓			McAllen • 1200 E Jackson Ave, 78503 • 956-686-4311 • Jct US-281 & US-83 (in town) take US-83 W 2 miles then E at Jackson Ave .1 mile
✪		✓	❖		McAllen • 2800 W Nolana Ave, 78504 • 956-687-8285 • Jct US-83 & US-281 (in town) take US-281 N 2 miles & SR-3461/Nolana Blvd W 3.5 miles
✪		✓			McKinney • 2041 N Redbud Blvd, 75069 • 972-542-9585 • From US-75 Exit 41 (N of town) go E at Bray Dr .4 mile & S at Rosebud Blvd .1 mile
✪		✓	❖	✓	McKinney • 5001 McKinney Ranch Pkwy, 75070 • 972-529-5046 • From US-75 Exit 38A (in town) take SR-121 SW 2.4 miles, Lake Forest Dr N 1 mile & McKinney Pkwy W .2 mile
✪		✓	❖		McKinney • 1721 N Custer Rd, 75071 • 972-548-7270 • From US-75 Exit 41 take US-380 W 5.6 miles
✪	2	✓	◆		Mesquite • 200 US Hwy 80 E, 75149 • 972-329-0191 • I-635 Exit 6B merge onto US-80 E 2 miles
✪		✓	◆		Mexia • 1406 E Milam St, 76667 • 254-562-3831 • I-45 Exit 219A take SR-14 S 16.1 miles, CR-243 SE 1.8 miles then US-84 E 1 mile
✪	1	✓	❖		Midland • 200 W I-20, 79701 • 432-684-3910 • I-20 Exit 136, north of exit
✪	7	✓	◆		Midland • 4517 N Midland Dr, 79707 • 432-697-0871 • I-20 Exit 131 take SR-250 Loop NE 6.1 miles, Northcrest Dr N .3 mile, Briarwood E .2 mile & Midland Dr S .1 mile
✪		✓	❖		Midlothian • 400 N Hwy 67, 76065 • 972-775-6755 • I-20 Exit 464B take US-67 S 14.6 miles
✪		✓	◆		Mineola • 135 NE Loop 564, 75773 • 903-569-0180 • Jct US-80 & FM-564 Loop NE 2.5 miles

☆	♡	🕐	⛽	🚫	Store Details
✪		✓	❖		Mineral Wells • 601 FM 1821, 76067 • 940-325-7808 • I-20 Exit 386 take US-281 N 14.3 miles, US-180 E 1.8 miles & FM-1821 N .2 mile
✪		✓	❖		Mission • 2410 E Expressway 83, 78572 • 956-580-3393 • Jct SR-107 & US-83 (in town) take US-83 E 2.6 miles
✪		✓			Missouri City • 5501 Hwy 6, 77459 • 281-403-5000 • Jct US-59 & SR-6 (W of town) go E on SR-6 for 3.4 miles
✪	8	✓		✓	Missouri City • 9929 Hwy 6, 77459 • 281-835-0001 • I-69 at SR-6, follow SR-6 SE for 7.7 miles
✪		✓	❖		Montgomery • 18700 Hwy 105 W, 77356 • 936-582-1551 • I-45 Exit 88 take SR-336 Loop W 1.3 miles & SR-105 W 10.2 miles
✪	4	✓	◆		Mount Pleasant • 2311 S Jefferson Ave, 75455 • 903-572-0018 • I-30 Exit 160 follow US-271 S 3.4 miles
✪		✓	❖	✓	Murphy • 115 W FM Rd 544, 75094 • 972-633-0257 • US-75 at Plano Pkwy, go E 4 miles on Plano Pkwy; continue E 1.5 miles on FM-544
✪		✓			Nacogdoches • 4810 North St, 75965 • 936-560-6969 • Jct US-59 & US-259 (N of town) take US-59 BR S 2.5 miles
☆					Navasota • 1712 E Washington Ave, 77868 • 936-825-7541 • Jct FM-3455 & SR-90 (E of town) go W on SR-90 for 1.5 miles
✪	1	✓	❖		New Boston • 800 James Bowie Dr, 75570 • 903-628-5557 • I-30 Exit 201 take SR-8 S .1 mile & Bowie Dr E .2 mile
✪	1	✓	❖		New Braunfels • 1209 S I-35, 78130 • 830-629-0129 • I-35 at Exit 186 on E Service Rd
✪	1	✓		✓	North Richland Hills • 6401 NE Loop 820, 76180 • 817-577-2100 • I-820 Exit 20B merge onto NE Loop 820 Service Rd .5 mile
✪	7	✓	❖		North Richland Hills • 9101 N Tarrant Pkwy, 76180 • 817-605-1717 • I-820 Exit 22B take SR-121 N 1.8 miles, Precinct Line Rd N 4.5 miles & Tarrant Pkwy W .1 mile
✪	4	✓			Odessa • 4210 John Ben Shepperd Pkwy, 79762 • 432-363-9663 • I-20 Exit 121 take Loop 338 N 2.3 miles then SR-191 W .9 mile
✪	3	✓	◆		Odessa • 2450 NW Loop 338, 79763 • 432-332-6016 • I-20 Exit 113 take SR-338 Loop N 3 miles
✪		✓	◆		Palestine • 2223 S Loop 256, 75801 • 903-729-4441 • Jct US-84 & SR-256 Loop (W of town) go E on SR-256 Loop 2.6 miles
✪		✓	❖	✓	Palmhurst • 215 E Mile 3 Rd, 78573 • 956-519-8453 • Jct US-281 & US-83 go W on US-83 for 5.3 miles, Ware Rd N 3.8 miles & 3 Mile Rd W 1.3 miles
✪		✓	❖		Pampa • 2801 N Charles St, 79065 • 806-665-0727 • 3 miles north of town center off SR-70 at 28th Ave
✪		✓	◆		Paris • 3855 Lamar Ave, 75462 • 903-785-7168 • Jct US-82 & SR-286 Loop (E of town) continue E on US-82/Lamar Ave .2 mile
✪	9	✓	❖	✓	Pasadena • 5200 Fairmont Pkwy, 77505 • 281-998-1077 • I-10 Exit 781A take SR-8/Houston Pkwy S 8.4 miles, then Fairmont Pkwy W .3 mile
✪	9	✓			Pasadena • 1107 Shaver St, 77506 • 713-534-6660 • I-10 Exit 781A take SR-8 S 4 miles, SR-225 W 3.4 miles & Shaver St S 1.2 miles
✪	5	✓	❖	✓	Pearland • 1710 Broadway St, 77581 • 281-482-5016 • I-45 Exit 31 take Dixie Farm Rd W 3.9 miles & Broadway St W .2 mile
✪	7	✓	❖		Pearland • 1919 N Main St, 77581 • 281-485-0877 • I-45 Exit 32 take Houston Tollway W 4.4 miles then SR-35 S 1.9 miles
✪		✓			Pearland • 10505 Broadway St, 77584 • 713-436-2899 • I-45 Exit 32 take Houston Tollway W 9 miles, FM-865 S 2.8 miles & FM-518 W 2.1 miles
☆	4				Pearsall • 819 N Oak St, 78061 • 830-334-9451 • I-35 Exit 104 take I-35 BR S 3.1 miles
☆	1				Pecos • 1903 S Cedar St, 79772 • 432-445-4231 • I-20 Exit 42 take US-285 W .7 mile
✪		✓			Penitas • 1705 W Expressway 83, 78576 • 956-580-6840 • On US-83 about 6.3 miles west of Mission, Texas
✪	6	✓	❖		Pflugerville • 1548 FM 685, 78660 • 512-252-0112 • I-35 Exit 247 follow FM-1825 E 3.7 miles then FM-685 N 1.3 miles
✪	1	✓	❖		Plainview • 1501 N I-27, 79072 • 806-293-4278 • I-27 Exit 49 take the W Service Rd N 1 mile
✪		✓		✓	Plano • 6000 Coit Rd, 75023 • 972-612-9637 • From US-75 Exit 28B take Bush Tpk (toll) W 2.3 miles then Coit Rd N 3.9 miles
✪		✓		✓	Plano • 6001 N Central Expy, 75023 • 972-422-3000 • I-635 Exit 19A take US-75 N 10.4 miles
✪		✓			Plano • 8801 Ohio Dr, 75024 • 972-731-9576 • I-35E Exit 448A take SR-121 NE 12.4 miles then Ohio Dr S .2 mile

☆	⬤	🕐	⛽	🚫	Store Details
✪		✓			Plano • 425 Coit Rd, 75075 • 972-599-1650 • From US-75 Exit 28B take Bush Tpk (toll) W 2.3 miles then Coit Rd N .7 mile
✪	8	✓		✓	Plano • 1700 Dallas Pkwy, 75093 • 972-931-9846 • I-635 Exit 22C take Dallas Tollway N 7.4 miles
✪	8	✓	◆		Pleasanton • 2151 W Oaklawn Rd, 78064 • 830-569-3879 • I-37 Exit 103 take US-281 N 5.1 miles then SR-97 W 2.2 miles
✪		✓	�		Port Arthur • 8585 Memorial Blvd, 77640 • 409-727-4667 • I-10 Exit 849 follow US-287 S 12.7 miles
✪		✓	✤		Port Arthur • 4999 N Twin City Hwy, 77642 • 409-962-7858 • I-10 Exit 849 take US-287 S 5.5 miles then SR-347 E 9.1 miles
✪		✓			Port Isabel • 1401 Hwy 100, 78578 • 956-943-1387 • 1 mile west of town center via SR-100
✪		✓	✤		Port Lavaca • 400 Tiney Browning Blvd, 77979 • 361-552-4116 • From town center go N .9 mile on FM-1090/Virginia St then E .8 mile on SR-35
✪		✓			Porter • 23561 Hwy 59, 77365 • 281-354-3400 • Jct FM-1960 & US-59 (S of town) take US-59 N 6.2 miles
✪		✓	✤		Portland • 2000 Hwy 181, 78374 • 361-643-5342 • Jct FM-2986 & US-181 (in town) go N on US-181 .4 mile
✪		✓	✤		Quinlan • 8801 Hwy 34 S, 75474 • 903-356-1000 • I-30 Exit 85 take FM-36 S 8.7 miles then SR-276 W 2.6 miles
✪	1	✓		✓	Red Oak • 100 Ryan Dr, 75154 • 972-515-2062 • I-35E Exit 410B, east of exit
✪		✓	◆		Richmond • 5330 FM 1640 Rd, 77469 • 281-232-8396 • Jct US-59 & FM-762 (E of town) take FM-762 NW 1.3 miles & FM-1640 W .3 mile
✪	6	✓			Richmond • 5660 Grand Pkwy S, 77469 • 832-595-0322 • I-10 Exit 743 go S 6 miles on Grand Pkwy
✪		✓			Rio Grande City • 4534 E Hwy 83, 78582 • 956-487-0090 • On US-83/2nd St E of town
✪	3	✓	✤		Roanoke • 1228 N Hwy 377, 76262 • 682-831-9338 • I-35W Exit 74 take FM-1171 E 2.6 miles then US-377 S .2 mile
✪		✓	✤		Rockdale • 709 W US Hwy 79, 76567 • 512-446-5851 • Jct US-77 & US-79 (E of town) take US-79 E .5 mile
✪		✓	✤		Rockport • 2401 Hwy 35 N, 78382 • 361-729-9277 • Jct FM-3036 & SR-35 BR (NE of town) take SR-35 BR S 1 mile
✪	1	✓	✤		Rockwall • 782 E I-30, 75087 • 972-771-8309 • I-30 Exit 68 take the Service Rd/US-67 S 1 mile

☆	⬤	🕐	⛽	🚫	Store Details
✪	1	✓			Round Rock • 2701 S I-35, 78664 • 512-310-9024 • I-35 Exit 250 (northbound travelers) follow I-35 Service Rd N 1 mile; southbound travelers use Exit 250B or Exit 251
✪	5	✓	✤		Round Rock • 4700 E Palm Valley Blvd, 78664 • 512-218-1018 • I-35 Exit 253 take Palm Valley Blvd W 4.6 miles, continue on US-79 E .3 mile
✪	6	✓	✤		Rowlett • 2501 Lakeview Pkwy, 75088 • 214-607-9839 • I-30 Exit 60A take Rosehill Rd N .7 mile, Rowlett Rd NE 3.9 miles & SR-66 W .5 mile
✪	1	✓			Royse City • 494 W Interstate 30, 75189 • 972-635-2728 • I-30 Exit 76, north of exit
✪		✓		✓	Sachse • 8015 Woodbridge Pkwy, 75048 • 469-440-0290 • 2 miles northeast of town center along SR-78 at Woodbridge Pkwy
✪	5	✓	✤		Saginaw • 1401 N Saginaw Blvd, 76179 • 817-306-1468 • I-820 Exit 13 take US-287 BR N 4.5 miles
✪		✓	✤		San Angelo • 610 W 29th St, 76903 • 325-655-4949 • 1.6 miles north of town center off US-87 at 29th St
✪		✓	◆		San Angelo • 5501 Sherwood Way, 76904 • 325-949-9201 • Jct SR-306 Loop & US-67 (SW of town) take US-67 S .5 mile
✪	2	✓	✤		San Antonio • 1430 Austin Hwy, 78209 • 210-637-1700 • I-410 Exit 24 take Wurzbach Rd S 1.6 miles & Austin Hwy W .2 mile
✪	1	✓	◆		San Antonio • 8538 I-35 S, 78211 • 210-810-3199 • Southbound I-35 travelers use Exit 149 to Poteet Jourdanton Fwy and go south. Northbound travelers use Exit 148 and follow frontage road to store
✪	3	✓	✤		San Antonio • 1603 Vance Jackson Rd, 78213 • 210-738-8218 • I-10 Exit 565B follow Vance Jackson Rd N 2 miles
✪	4	✓	✤		San Antonio • 1200 SE Military Dr, 78214 • 210-921-0800 • I-35 Exit 135 take SR-13 W 3.7 miles
✪	2	✓	◆		San Antonio • 8500 Jones Maltsberger Rd, 78216 • 210-377-1899 • I-410 Exit 20 take 410 Service Rd E 1.1 miles then Jones Maltsberger Rd S .3 mile
✪	2				San Antonio • 4331 Thousand Oaks Dr, 78217 • I-35 Exit 167 go W 1.8 miles on Thousand Oaks
✪	2			✓	San Antonio • 5626 Walzem Rd, 78218 • 210-507-0650 • I-35 Exit 165 go E 1.4 miles on Walzem Rd
✪	1	✓	✤		San Antonio • 2100 SE Loop 410, 78220 • 210-648-7194 • I-410 Exit 35 take Service Rd N .3 mile

☆	♡	🕐	⛽	🚫	Store Details
✪	1	✓			San Antonio • 3302 SE Military Dr, 78223 • 210-337-1946 • I-37 Exit 135 take SR-13 W .3 mile
✪	3				San Antonio • 918 Bandera Rd, 78228 • 210-536-0576 • I-10 Exit 567 go W 2.4 miles on Woodlawn Ave to Bandera Rd and turn right. Westbound travelers use I-10 Exit 567B
☆	1				San Antonio • 5025 NW Loop 410, 78229 • 210-523-1091 • I-410 Exit 14A take Service Rd W .6 mile
✪	4				San Antonio • 12639 Blanco Rd, 78231 • 210-591-6282 • I-10 Exit 561 go N 3.3 mile on Wurzbach Rd then E .1 mile on Blanco Rd
✪	1	✓	◆		San Antonio • 7239 SW Loop 410, 78242 • 210-247-5905 • I-410 Exit 3, west of exit
✪	2	✓			San Antonio • 4096 N Foster Rd, 78244 • 210-507-4958 • I-10 Exit 583 go N 1.3 miles on Foster Rd
✪	1	✓	❖	✓	San Antonio • 8923 W Military Dr, 78245 • 210-675-5092 • I-410 Exit 9A go W on Military Dr .7 mile
✪	3	✓	◆		San Antonio • 16503 Nacogdoches Rd, 78247 • 210-646-6077 • I-35 Exit 172 take SR-1604 Loop W 2.5 miles then FM-2252 W .3 mile
✪	1	✓		✓	San Antonio • 5555 De Zavala Rd, 78249 • 210-558-2007 • I-10 Exit 558 merge N onto McDermott Fwy .5 mile then E on DeZavala Rd .3 mile
✪	4	✓	❖		San Antonio • 8030 Bandera Rd, 78250 • 210-520-6517 • I-410 Exit 13A take Bandera Rd/SR-16 N 3.1 miles
✪	4	✓			San Antonio • 9427 Culebra Rd, 78251 • 210-526-6000 • I-410 Exit 10 go W 3.5 miles on Culebra Rd
✪	5	✓			San Antonio • 11210 Potranco Rd, 78253 • 210-679-7184 • I-410 Exit 9 take SR-151 W 1.4 miles then Potranco Rd W 3.1 miles
✪	9	✓	◆		San Antonio • 6703 Leslie Rd, 78254 • 210-688-3626 • I-10 Exit 556A follow SR-1604 (Charles Anderson Loop) W 9 miles
✪	10	✓			San Antonio • 1515 N Loop 1604 E, 78258 • 210-491-0291 • I-35 Exit 72 follow SR-1604-LOOP W for 9.7 miles
✪		✓	❖		San Benito • 1126 W Hwy 77, 78586 • 956-399-1373 • From US-77 take SR-486 E 1 mile then US-77 BR S .8 mile
✪	1	✓			San Marcos • 1015 Hwy 80, 78666 • 512-353-0617 • I-35 Exit 205 take SR-80 E .3 mile
✪	1	✓	❖	✓	Schertz • 6102 FM 3009, 78154 • 210-651-8217 • I-35 Exit 175 take FM-3009 W .3 mile
✪	7	✓	❖		Seagoville • 220 N Hwy 175, 75159 • 972-287-3917 • I-20 Exit 479B take US-175 S 6.7 miles
✪	1	✓	❖		Sealy • 310 Overcreek Way, 77474 • 979-627-7758 • I-10 Exit 720, go S .4 mile on SR-36
✪	3	✓	❖		Seguin • 550 S Hwy 123 Byp, 78155 • 830-372-5993 • I-10 Exit 610 take SR-123 S 2.6 miles
☆				✓	Seminole • 2000 Hobbs Hwy, 79360 • 432-758-9215 • 1.3 miles west of town center along US-62/US-180
✪		✓	◆		Sherman • 401 E US Hwy 82, 75090 • 903-813-4825 • From US-75 Exit 63 (N of town) take US-82 W .3 mile
✪		✓	❖		Silsbee • 1100 Hwy 96 N, 77656 • 409-385-0782 • Jct US-96 & US-96 BR (S of town) take US-96 BR N 1.7 miles
☆					Snyder • 4515 College Ave, 79549 • 325-573-1967 • Jct SR-1605/37th St & SR-350 (S of town) take SR-350/College Ave S .6 mile
✪	1	✓			Spring • 155 Louetta Crossing, 77373 • 281-651-9963 • I-45 Exit 68 take Louetta Rd E .4 mile, Whitewood Dr S .3 mile & Louetta Crossing W .1 mile
✪	5	✓	❖		Spring • 21150 Kuykendahl Rd, 77379 • 281-288-6437 • I-45 Exit 70 take FM-2920 W 4.7 miles & Kuykendahl Rd N .3 mile
✪	1	✓		✓	Spring • 1025 Sawdust Rd, 77380 • 281-298-4306 • I-45 Exit 73 take Sawdust Rd W 1 mile
✪			◆		Spring Branch • 305 Singing Oaks, 78070 • 830-438-4380 • In the northwest corner of US-281 and SR-46 junction about 30 miles north of San Antonio
✪	10	✓			Stafford • 11210 W Airport Blvd, 77477 • 281-933-7800 • I-610 Exit 8A take US-59 S 8.7 miles then Wilcrest Dr/FM-1092 S .8 mile & Airport Blvd W .5 mile
✪		✓			Stamford • 2614 N Swenson St, 79553 • 325-773-2775 • About 2 miles north of town center off US-277 at SR-6
✪		✓			Stephenville • 2765 W Washington St, 76401 • 254-965-7766 • Jct SR-108 & S Loop US-87 (S of town) go W on US-87 for 2.6 miles
✪		✓			Sugar Land • 345 Hwy 6, 77478 • 281-340-0900 • I-610 Exit 8A take US-59/SW Fwy S 13.6 miles then SR-6 S 1.5 miles
✪	1	✓	◆		Sulphur Springs • 1750 S Broadway St, 75482 • 903-439-3144 • I-30 Exit 124 take SR-154 S .8 mile
✪	1	✓	❖		Sweetwater • 407 NE Georgia Ave, 79556 • 325-236-9562 • I-20 Exit 246 merge onto Service Rd W 1 mile

☆	◌	🕐	⛽	🚫	Store Details
★		✓	❖		Taylor • 3701 N Main St, 76574 • 512-352-5505 • Jct SR-29 & SR-95 (N of town) take SR-95 S 3.5 miles
★	2	✓			Temple • 3401 S 31st St, 76502 • 254-778-9235 • I-35 Exit 299 take US-190 E 1.6 miles then FM-1741 S .3 mile
★	4	✓	◆		Temple • 6801 W Adams Ave, 76502 • 254-598-7593 • I-35 Exit 301 go W 3.4 miles on Adams Ave
★	2	✓	◆	✓	Terrell • 1900 W Moore Ave, 75160 • 972-563-7638 • I-20 Exit 499A take FM-148 N 1.5 miles then Moore Ave W .2 mile
★	1	✓	◆		Texarkana • 4000 New Boston Rd, 75501 • 903-838-4007 • I-30 Exit 220A take US-59 S .7 mile, Bishop Rd S & New Boston Rd W .1 mile
★	9	✓	❖		The Woodlands • 10001 Woodlands Pkwy, 77382 • 281-419-0162 • I-45 Exit 76B go W about 9 miles on Woodlands Pkwy
★	1	✓	❖		The Woodlands • 3040 College Park Dr, 77384 • 936-321-9922 • I-45 Exit 79 take College Pk Dr W .2 mile
★		✓	❖		Tomball • 22605 State Hwy 249, 77375 • 281-374-9449 • From town center go W 1.1 miles on Main St then S 5.7 miles on SR-249 (Tomball Pkwy)
★		✓	◆		Tomball • 27650 State Hwy 249, 77375 • 281-351-2616 • From town center go W 1.1 miles on Main St then S 1 mile on SR-249 (Tomball Pkwy)
★		✓			Tyler • 6801 S Broadway Ave, 75703 • 903-581-4296 • Jct SR-49 & US-69 (S of town) take US-69 N 2.6 miles
★		✓	❖		Tyler • 3820 TX Hwy 64 W, 75704 • 903-597-2888 • Jct FM-2661 & SR-64 (W of town) go E on SR-64 for 1.1 miles
★		✓	❖		Tyler • 5050 Troup Hwy, 75707 • 903-534-1333 • Jct SR-64 & SW Loop 323 (W of town) go E on Loop 323 for 7.3 miles & S on SR-110 for 1.3 miles
★	1		❖	✓	Universal City • 510 Kitty Hawk Rd, 78148 • 210-536-8548 • I-35 Exit 172 go SE on SR-1604 .7 mile to Kitty Hawk Rd and go E .2 mile
★		✓	❖		Uvalde • 3100 E Main St, 78801 • 830-278-9117 • Jct US-83 & US-90 (in town) take US-90 E 2.2 miles
★		✓	❖		Vernon • 3800 US Hwy 287 W, 76384 • 940-552-8029 • Jct US-283/183 & US-287/70 (N of town) go W on N Frontage Rd 1.2 miles
★		✓			Victoria • 4101 Houston Hwy, 77901 • 361-827-7272 • 2.5 miles east of town center along Houston Highway
★		✓			Victoria • 9002 N Navarro St, 77904 • 361-573-0041 • Jct SR-463 & US-77 (N of town) go N on US-77 1 mile
☆	1				Vidor • 1350 N Main St, 77662 • 409-769-6233 • I-10 Exit 861A take FM-105 N .8 mile
★	3	✓			Waco • 4320 Franklin Ave, 76710 • 254-751-0464 • I-35 Exit 331 take New Rd W 2.1 miles then Franklin Ave N .1 mile
★	4	✓	❖		Waco • 600 Hewitt Dr, 76712 • 254-666-9021 • I-35 Exit 328 take Sun Valley Dr W 1.7 miles & Hewitt Dr NW 2.1 miles
★	5	✓	◆		Waxahachie • 1200 N Hwy 77, 75165 • 972-937-3460 • I-35 Exit 397 merge onto US-77 N for 4.6 miles
★	1	✓	◆		Weatherford • 1836 S Main St, 76086 • 817-594-9193 • I-20 Exit 408 take SR-171 N .5 mile
★		✓	◆		Weslaco • 1310 N Texas Blvd, 78596 • 956-968-6357 • Jct US-83 & SR-88 go S on SR-88/Texas Blvd .1 mile
☆					West Columbia • 301 N Columbia Dr, 77486 • 979-345-3147 • Jct FM-1301 & SR-36 (W of town) go N on SR-36 for .2 mile
★	4	✓	◆		West Orange • 3115 Edgar Brown Dr, 77630 • 409-883-5244 • I-10 Exit 877 follow SR-87 S 3.2 miles
★	3	✓		✓	Westworth Village • 6770 Westworth Blvd, 76114 • 817-570-9538 • I-30 Exit 7B follow SR-183 N 2.2 miles
★		✓	❖		Wharton • 10388 US 59 Road, 77488 • 979-532-3986 • 1.5 miles west of town at US-59/SR-102 jct
★		✓	❖		Wichita Falls • 5131 Greenbriar Rd, 76302 • 940-397-9650 • South of town center about .5 mile west of US-281 via SR-369
★	1	✓	◆		Wichita Falls • 2700 Central Fwy, 76306 • 940-851-0629 • I-44 Exit 3C merge onto Central Fwy S .2 mile
★	6	✓			Wichita Falls • 3130 Lawrence Rd, 76308 • 940-692-0771 • I-44 Exit 3C take US-287 S 1.8 miles & follow US-82 W 2.8 miles then Lawrence Rd N .7 mile
★		✓			Woodville • 115 Cobb Mill Rd, 75979 • 409-283-8248 • Jct US-190 & S Beech St (in town) take S Beech St .6 mile then Cobb Rd E .2 mile
★		✓	❖	✓	Wylie • 2050 N Hwy 78, 75098 • 972-429-3526 • Jct CR-434 & SR-78 (N of town) go W on SR-78 for 1.5 miles

UTAH

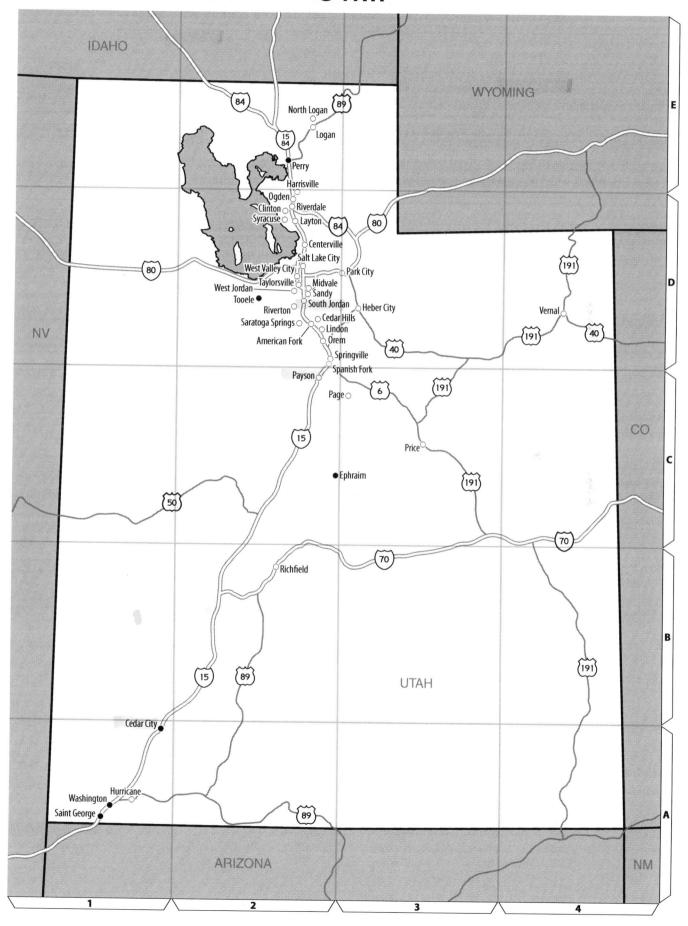

IDAHO

WYOMING

NV

CO

UTAH

NM

ARIZONA

North Logan
Logan
Perry
Harrisville
Ogden
Riverdale
Clinton
Syracuse
Layton
Centerville
Salt Lake City
West Valley City
Park City
Taylorsville
Midvale
West Jordan
Sandy
Tooele
South Jordan
Heber City
Riverton
Cedar Hills
Saratoga Springs
Lindon
Orem
American Fork
Springville
Spanish Fork
Payson
Page
Vernal
Price
Ephraim
Richfield
Cedar City
Hurricane
Washington
Saint George

☆	⬭	🕐	⛽	🚐	Store Details
✪	1	✓			American Fork • 949 W Grassland Dr, 84003 • 801-492-1102 • I-15 Exit 279 take SR-73 E .4 mile, US-89 S .2 mile
✪	1	✓	◆		Cedar City • 1330 S Providence Center Dr, 84720 • 435-586-0172 • I-15 Exit 57 go W on Sage Way .1 mile & S at Providence Center Dr
✪	8	✓			Cedar Hills • 4689 W Cedar Hills Dr, 84062 • 801-756-2372 • I-15 Exit 284 go E 6.2 miles on SR-92 (Highland Hwy) then S 1.1 miles on N 4800 W
✪	1	✓		✓	Centerville • 221 W Parrish Ln, 84014 • 801-294-0587 • I-15 Exit 319 go E on Parrish Ln .4 mile
✪	3	✓			Clinton • 1632 N 2000 W, 84015 • 801-779-3165 • I-15 Exit 335 take SR-126 N .2 mile, W800N W 2 miles & Two Mile Rd N .8 mile
✪		✓	◆		Ephraim • 777 N Main St, 84627 • 435-283-8189 • Jct SR-132 & US-89 (N of town) take US-89 S for 3.8 miles
✪	4	✓			Harrisville • 534 N Harrisville Rd, 84404 • 801-737-0092 • I-15 Exit 344 take W1200S E 1.9 miles, Wall Ave N 1.6 miles, North Rd E .2 mile & Harrisville Rd N .1 mile
✪		✓			Heber City • 1274 S US Hwy 189, 84032 • 435-709-3015 • From town center go S .8 mile on US-40/US-189
✪	.6	✓			Hurricane • 180 N 3400 W, 84737 • 435-635-6945 • I-15 Exit 16 go E 5.2 miles on SR-9/State St
✪	1	✓			Layton • 745 W Hill Field Rd, 84041 • 801-546-1992 • I-15 Exit 331 take SR-232 W .1 mile
✪	3	✓			Lindon • 585 N State St, 84042 • 801-785-7683 • I-15 Exit 273 take W1600N E 1.1 miles & US-89 N 1.8 miles
✪		✓			Logan • 1150 S 100 W, 84321 • 435-753-2111 • 1.7 miles south of town center via US-89/US-91
✪	1	✓			Midvale • 7250 Union Park Ave, 84047 • 801-255-0224 • I-215 Exit 9 follow Union Park Ave S 1 mile
✪		✓			North Logan • 1550 N Main St, 84341 • 435-753-0880 • Jct SR-30 & US-91 (S of town) go N on US-91 for 4.4 miles, E on SR-237 for .7 mile & N on Main St .3 mile
✪	2				Ogden • 1959 Wall Ave, 84401 • 801-917-1026 • I-15/84 Exit 343 go E 1.8 miles on SR-104 then N .1 mile on Wall Ave
✪	1	✓			Orem • 1355 Sandhill Rd, 84058 • 801-221-0600 • I-15 Exit 269 take SR-265 E .3 mile & Sandhilol Rd S .2 mile
✪	1	✓		✓	Park City • 6545 Landmark Dr, 84098 • 435-647-9909 • I-80 Exit 145 take SR-224 S .2 mile & Landmark Dr NW .2 mile

☆	⬭	🕐	⛽	🚐	Store Details
✪	1	✓			Payson • 1052 Turf Farm Rd, 84651 • 801-465-8246 • I-15 Exit 248 take W800S E .2 mile & Turf Farm Rd S .3 mile
✪	2	✓	◆		Perry • 1200 S Commerce Way, 84302 • 435-734-9660 • I-15 Exit 362 merge onto US-91 E 1.3 miles & S at Commerce Way
✪		✓			Price • 255 S Hwy 55, 84501 • 435-637-6712 • Jct SR-10 & US-6/191 (S of town) take US-6/191 E 1.1 miles & US-6 BR N .8 mile
✪	1	✓			Richfield • 10 E 1300 S, 84701 • 435-893-8164 • I-70 Exit 37 go E 1 mile on 1300 S St
✪	1	✓			Riverdale • 4848 S 900 W, 84405 • 801-627-0066 • I-84 Exit 81 go E .5 mile on SR-26 (Riverdale Rd) then S .1 mile on S900W Rd
✪	6	✓			Riverton • 13502 Hamilton View Rd, 84065 • 801-446-2981 • I-15 Exit 289 go W 5.4 miles on SR-154
✪	1	✓	❖	✓	Saint George • 2610 Pioneer Rd, 84790 • 435-674-0459 • I-15 Exit 4 go W .3 mile then S on Pioneer Rd .5 mile
✪	1	✓		✓	Salt Lake City • 2705 E Parleys Way, 84109 • 385-313-3942 • I-80 Exit 129, north of exit
✪	1	✓		✓	Salt Lake City • 350 Hope Ave, 84115 • 801-484-7311 • I-15 Exit 305C go E on W1300S .1 mile & S on S400W .2 mile
✪	3	✓		✓	Salt Lake City • 4627 S 900 E, 84117 • 801-261-3695 • I-15 Exit 301 take SR-266 E 1.9 miles & S900E S .3 mile
✪	2	✓			Sandy • 9151 S Quarry Blvd, 84094 • 801-352-4200 • I-15 Exit 295 take SR-209 E 2 miles
✪	5	✓			Saratoga Springs • 136 W State Hwy 73, 84045 • 801-766-4272 • I-15 Exit 279 go W 4.7 miles on SR-73
✪	2	✓			South Jordan • 11328 S Jordan Gateway, 84095 • 801-553-2266 • I-15 Exit 293 take SR-151 W .2 mile then Jordan Gateway S 1.1 miles
✪	4	✓			South Jordan • 3590 W South Jordan Pkwy, 84095 • 801-601-3098 • I-15 Exit 293 go W 4 miles on South Jordan Pkwy
✪	1	✓			Spanish Fork • 1206 N Canyon Creek Pkwy, 84660 • 801-804-3505 • I-15 Exit 257B go E .1 mile on US-6 then N .2 mile on Canyon Creek Pkwy
✪	1	✓			Springville • 660 S 1750 W, 84663 • 801-489-6293 • I-15 Exit 260 take SR-77 E .4 mile & S1750W S .3 mile
✪	5	✓			Syracuse • 2228 W 1700 S, 84075 • 801-775-9688 • I-15 Exit 332 follow SR-108 W 3.9 miles & continue on W1700S .2 mile

☆	♡	🕐	⛽	🚫	Store Details
✪	2	✓		✓	Taylorsville • 5469 S Redwood Rd, 84123 • 801-264-9666 • I-15 Exit 297 take W7200/W7000 W 1.8 miles
✪		✓	◆		Tooele • 99 W 1280 N, 84074 • 435-833-9017 • I-80 Exit 99 merge onto SR-36 S 10.5 miles then E at W1280N
✪		✓		✓	Vernal • 1851 W Hwy 40, 84078 • 435-789-9784 • Jct US-191 & US-40 (in town) go W on US-191/US-40 for 2.3 miles
✪	1	✓	◆		Washington • 625 W Telegraph St, 84780 • 435-628-2802 • I-15 Exit 10 go E .1 mile on Green Spring Dr then N .2 mile on SR-212 (Telegraph St)
✪	6	✓			West Jordan • 7671 S 3800 W, 84084 • 801-282-4066 • I-15 Exit 295 take SR-209 W 4 miles, SR-154 N 1.5 miles, W7800S W .3 mile & S3800W S .1 mile
✪	6	✓			West Valley City • 5675 W 6200 S, 84118 • 801-965-0125 • I-215 Exit 13 take SR-68 S .6 mile then W6200S W 4.6 miles
✪	5	✓		✓	West Valley City • 3180 S 5600 W, 84120 • 801-966-2986 • I-215 Exit 18B take SR-171 W 3.8 miles & S5600W N .4 mile

VERMONT

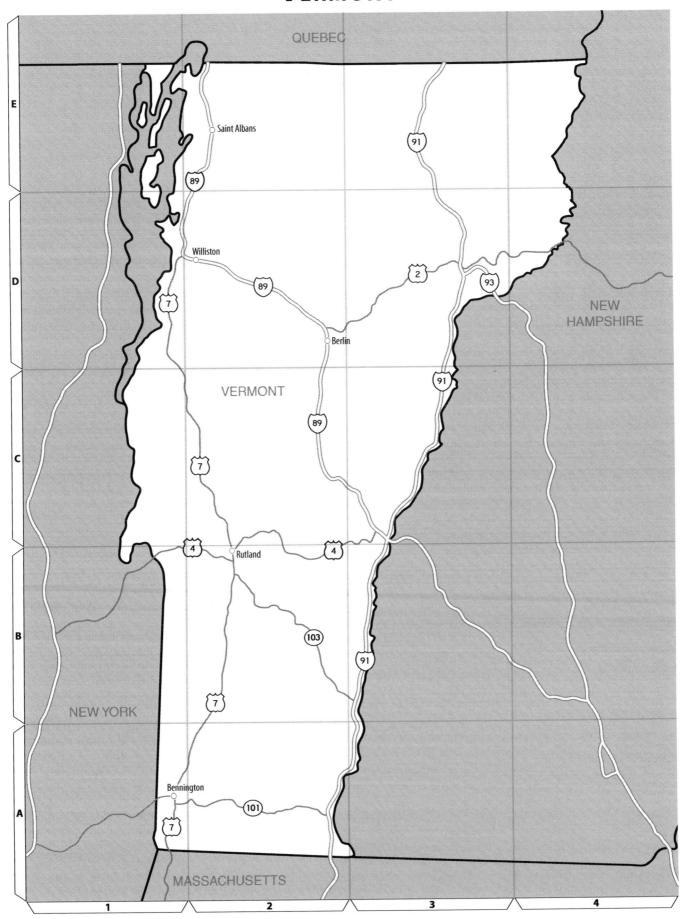

QUEBEC

E

Saint Albans

89

D

Williston

89

7

2

93

NEW
HAMPSHIRE

Berlin

VERMONT

91

89

C

7

91

4

4

Rutland

B

103

91

NEW YORK

7

91

A

Bennington

101

7

MASSACHUSETTS

1 2 3 4

☆	◯	🕐	⛽	🚫	Store Details
☆					Bennington • 210 Northside Dr, 05201 • 802-447-1614 • From US-7 Exit 2 (N of town) go S on SR-7A for 1.6 miles
☆	2				Berlin • 282 Berlin Mall Rd, 05602 • 802-229-7792 • I-89 Exit 7 take SR-62 E .9 mile then N on Berlin Mall Rd .2 mile
☆					Rutland • 1 Rutland Shopping Plz, 05701 • 802-773-0200 • From town center go S .3 mile on Main St (US-4/US-7) then W .3 mile on Washington St
☆	1			✓	Saint Albans • 700 Tuckers Way, 05478 • 802-528-4110 • I-89 Exit 20 go W .2 mile on SR-207 then N .2 mile on US-7
☆	1				Williston • 863 Harvest Ln, 05495 • 802-878-5233 • I-89 Exit 12 take SR-2A N .3 mile, Marshall Ave W .3 mile & Harvest Ln S .3 mile

VIRGINIA

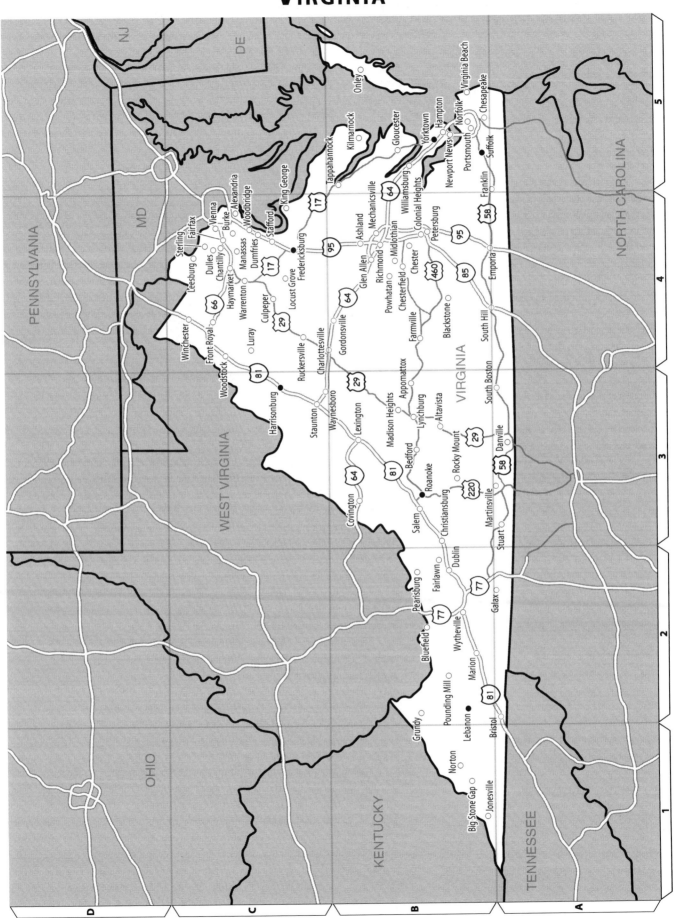

☆	🛡	🕐	⛽	🚫	Store Details
☆	5				Alexandria • 7910 Richmond Hwy, 22306 • 703-799-8815 • I-95 Exit 177 take US-1 S 4.5 miles
✪	2	✓		✓	Alexandria • 6303 Richmond Hwy, 22306 • 703-253-9901 • I-95/495 Exit 177A go S 1.5 miles on US-1
☆	2			✓	Alexandria • 5885 Kingstowne Blvd, 22315 • 703-924-8800 • I-95 Exit 173 follow Van Dorn St S 1.5 miles then SW on Kingstowne Blvd .3 mile
✪		✓			Altavista • 125 Clarion Rd, 24517 • 434-309-2245 • Jct SR-43 & US-29 (W of town) take US-29 N 2 miles & S on Clarion Rd .3 mile
✪					Appomattox • 505 Oakville Rd, 24522 • 434-352-6066 • 1 mile northwest of town along SR-26/Oakville Rd
✪	3	✓			Ashland • 145 Hill Carter Pkwy, 23005 • 804-798-2511 • I-95 Exit 89 take Lewistown Rd E .4 mile, Ashcake Rd NW 2 miles & Hill Carter Pkwy N .6 mile
✪		✓			Bedford • 1126 E Lynchburg Salem Tpke, 24523 • 540-586-6176 • Jct US-221 & US-460 (SE of town) take US-460 E .4 mile
☆					Big Stone Gap • 1941 Neeley Rd, 24219 • 276-523-5026 • From town center, follow US-23-BR/US-23-ALT E 1.2 miles then go S .2 mile on Neely Rd
✪		✓			Blackstone • 1451 S Main St, 23824 • 434-292-5898 • Jct SR-46 & SR-40 (S of town) go W on SR-40 for .2 mile
✪	10	✓			Bluefield • 4001 College Ave, 24605 • 276-322-3144 • I-77 Exit 66 take SR-598 W 6.3 miles, US-460 W 2.2 miles & SR-102 NW 1.4 miles
✪	1	✓			Bristol • 13245 Lee Hwy, 24202 • 276-466-0290 • I-81 Exit 7 go W on Old Airport Rd .1 mile & NW on Lee Hwy .7 mile
☆	8				Burke • 6000 Burke Commons Rd, 22015 • 703-250-9280 • I-95 Exit 169 take SR-644 W 5.5 miles, SR-643 W 1.7 miles & N on Burke Commons Rd .3 mile
✪	3	✓			Chantilly • 4368 Chantilly Shopping Ctr, 20151 • 571-392-3081 • I-66 Exit 53B go N 2.6 miles on SR-28 then E .3 mile on Willard Rd to Chantilly Shopping Center
✪	8	✓		✓	Charlottesville • 975 Hilton Heights Rd, 22901 • 434-973-1412 • I-64 Exit 118B follow US-29 N 7.5 miles
✪	1	✓			Chesapeake • 1521 Sams Cir, 23320 • 757-436-6055 • I-64 Exit 290B take SR-168 BR S .1 mile & E at Walmart Way
✪	2	✓			Chesapeake • 2448 Chesapeake Square Ring Rd, 23321 • 757-488-6098 • I-664 Exit 11B take SR-337 E 1.1 miles, Capri Cir N .2 mile & Ring Rd N .4 mile

☆	🛡	🕐	⛽	🚫	Store Details
✪	4	✓			Chesapeake • 632 Grassfield Pkwy, 23322 • 757-312-8309 • I-464 Exit 15B take US-17 S 3.4 miles & Grassfield Pkwy E .2 mile
✪	8	✓			Chesapeake • 201 Hillcrest Pkwy, 23322 • 757-421-3689 • I-64 Exit 291B follow SR-168 S for 8 miles to Hillcrest Pkwy exit
✪	5	✓			Chester • 12000 Iron Bridge Rd, 23831 • 804-768-0060 • I-95 Exit 61B follow SR-10 W 4.7 miles
✪		✓			Chesterfield • 14501 Hancock Village St, 23832 • 804-256-0844 • I-95 Exit 62 follow SR-288 W 13 miles to US-360/Hull St and continue W 3.2 miles
✪	6	✓			Christiansburg • 2400 N Franklin St, 24073 • 540-381-3705 • I-81 Exit 118 take US-460 W 4.2 miles then US-460 BR W 1.2 miles
✪	1	✓			Colonial Heights • 671 Southpark Blvd, 23834 • 804-526-0844 • I-95 Exit 53 take Southpark Blvd NE .3 mile
✪	1	✓			Covington • 313 Thacker Ave, 24426 • 540-962-6670 • I-64 Exit 14 take SR-154 S .1 mile, continue S on Durant Rd .1 mile
✪		✓			Culpeper • 801 James Madison Hwy, 22701 • 540-825-2723 • Jct US-15/29 & US-15/29 BR (E of town) take US-15/29 BR W 2.1 miles
✪		✓			Danville • 515 Mount Cross Rd, 24540 • 434-799-6902 • Jct US-58 & US-29 (S of town) take US-29 BR N 3.3 miles, Piedmont Dr NW 1.3 miles & Mt Cross Rd W .1 mile
✪	1	✓		✓	Dublin • 5225 Alexander Rd, 24084 • 540-674-5385 • I-81 Exit 98 take SR-100 N .4 mile then W at Alexander Rd .2 mile
✪		✓			Dulles • 24635 Dulles Landing Dr, 20166 • 571-367-3036 • I-66 Exit 57B go NW on US-50 for 10.7 miles and turn right onto Dulles Landing Dr
✪	2				Dumfries • 17041 Jefferson Davis Hwy, 22026 • 703-221-4116 • I-95 Exit 152A go E .6 mile on SR-234 then N .6 mile on US-1
✪	1	✓			Emporia • 303 Market Dr, 23847 • 434-336-9269 • I-95 Exit 11A take US-58 E .5 mile & Market Dr N .2 mile
✪	2	✓			Fairfax • 11181 Lee Hwy, 22030 • 703-995-5061 • I-66 Exit 60 go S .3 mile on Chain Bridge Rd/SR-123 then W 1.4 miles on Lee Hwy/US-29
✪	2				Fairfax • 13059 Fair Lakes Pkwy, 22033 • 703-631-9450 • I-66 Exit 55B follow SR-7100 N .7 mile then W on Fair Lakes Pkwy .9 mile

☆	🛡	🕐	⛽	🚫	Store Details
✪	6	✓			Fairlawn • 7373 Peppers Ferry Blvd, 24141 • 540-731-3378 • I-81 Exit 105 take SR-232 N 3.9 miles, US-11 NW 1.1 miles & SR-114 N .3 mile
✪		✓			Farmville • 1800 Peery Dr, 23901 • 434-392-5334 • 1.8 miles south of town center via US-15-BR
✪		✓			Franklin • 1500 Armory Dr, 23851 • 757-562-6776 • Jct US-58 & SR-671 (W of town) go NE on SR-671/Armory Dr .5 mile
✪	3	✓	◆		Fredericksburg • 1800 Carl D Silver Pkwy, 22401 • 540-786-2090 • I-95 Exit 130B take SR-3 W .9 mile, Bragg Ave/Fan Hill Ave N 1.1 miles & Silver Pkwy SE .2 mile
✪	4	✓			Fredericksburg • 125 Washington Square Plz, 22405 • 540-899-8890 • I-95 Exit 130A go E 4 miles on SR-3
✪	3	✓			Fredericksburg • 11 Village Pkwy, 22406 • 540-752-2125 • I-95 Exit 133B go W 3 miles on US-17
✪	1	✓			Fredericksburg • 10001 Southpoint Pkwy, 22407 • 540-834-4142 • I-95 Exit 126 take US-17 S .3 mile & Southpoint Pkwy W .6 mile
✪	1	✓			Front Royal • 10 Riverton Commons Dr, 22630 • 540-635-4140 • I-66 Exit 6, north of exit off US-340/US-522/Winchester Rd
✪	8	✓			Galax • 1140 E Stuart Dr, 24333 • 276-236-7113 • I-77 Exit 14 follow US-58 W 7.4 miles
✪	1	✓			Glen Allen • 11400 W Broad St, 23060 • 804-360-9777 • I-64 Exit 178A take US-250 W 1 mile
✪		✓			Gloucester • 6819 Walton Ln, 23061 • 804-694-0110 • Jct US-17 & SR-216 take US-17 S 1.8 miles then W at Walton St
✪	1	✓		✓	Gordonsville • 164 Camp Creek Pkwy, 22942 • 540-832-1259 • I-64 Exit 136, north of exit
✪					Grundy • 1179 Riverview St, 24614 • 276-244-3007 • In town center near intersection of US-460 and SR-83
✪	2	✓			Hampton • 1900 Cunningham Dr, 23666 • 757-826-6377 • I-64 Exit 263 merge onto SR-134 SE 1.2 miles & S on Cunningham Dr
✪	1	✓	◆		Harrisonburg • 171 Burgess Rd, 22801 • 540-433-0808 • I-81 Exit 247A merge onto US-33 E .4 mile & S at Burgess Rd .2 mile
✪	3	✓			Harrisonburg • 2160 John Wayland Hwy, 22801 • 540-438-0349 • I-81 Exit 245 take Pt Republic Rd/Maryland Ave W .9 mile & SR-42 SW 1.6 miles

☆	🛡	🕐	⛽	🚫	Store Details
✪	1	✓			Haymarket • 6530 Trading Sq, 20169 • 703-468-2445 • I-66 Exit 40, south of exit
✪		✓			Jonesville • 468 Trade Center Ln, 24263 • 276-346-2860 • From town center, follow Main St E .6 mile then go NE 3.1 miles on US-58-ALT
✪		✓			Kilmarnock • 200 Old Fairgrounds Way, 22482 • 804-435-6148 • 1.2 miles north of town along SR-3
✪		✓			King George • 16375 Merchant Ln, 22485 • 540-413-3037 • I-95 Exit 133 go E 25.4 miles on SR-218 then E .6 mile on SR-206 then E 1.2 miles on US-301
✪		✓	◆		Lebanon • 1050 Regional Park Rd, 24266 • 276-889-1654 • Jct SR-656 & US-19 (N of town) take US-19 S 1.7 miles, US-19 BR S .6 mile & S at Cedar Heights .2 mile
☆					Leesburg • 950 Edwards Ferry Rd NE, 20176 • 703-779-0102 • 1.4 miles east of town center via Edwards Ferry Rd at US-15
✪	1	✓		✓	Lexington • 1233 N Lee Hwy, 24450 • 540-464-3535 • I-64 Exit 55 take US-11 N .5 mile
✪		✓			Locust Grove • 2533 Germanna Hwy, 22508 • 540-317-2185 • I-95 Exit 130B go W 16.6 miles on SR-3
✪	9	✓			Luray • 1036 US Hwy 211 W, 22835 • 540-743-4111 • I-81 Exit 264 follow US-211 E 8.4 miles
✪		✓		✓	Lynchburg • 3227 Old Forest Rd, 24501 • 434-200-9132 • From town center go NW .3 mile on Main St, turn left at 5th St .8 mile and continue .4 mile on Memorial Ave, turn right at Langhorne Rd and follow 1.8 miles, turn left at Cranehill Dr .4 mile, take second left onto Linkhorne Dr .6 mile and continue onto Old Forest Rd .6 mile
✪		✓		✓	Lynchburg • 3900 Wards Rd, 24502 • 434-832-0304 • From town center follow US-29 S for 5.3 miles
✪		✓			Madison Heights • 197 Madison Heights Sq, 24572 • 434-846-9650 • Jct US-29 & Amelon Hwy (NE of town) go W on Amelon Hwy 2 miles then S on US-29 BR .5 mile
✪	2				Manassas • 8386 Sudley Rd, 20109 • 703-330-5253 • I-66 Exit 47 go S 2 miles on Sudley Rd
✪	8				Manassas • 9401 Liberia Ave, 20110 • 703-257-0403 • I-66 Exit 53A follow SR-28 S 6.6 miles then Liberia Ave E 1 mile
☆	2				Marion • 1193 N Main St, 24354 • 276-783-4244 • I-81 Exit 47 follow US-11 S 1.1 miles

☆	⬭	🕐	⛽	🚫	Store Details
✪		✓			Martinsville • 976 Commonwealth Blvd, 24112 • 276-634-5110 • Jct US-58 & US-58 BR (E of town) go W on US-58 BR 4.6 miles then N on Chatham Rd .3 mile
✪	1	✓		✓	Mechanicsville • 7430 Bell Creek Rd, 23111 • 804-730-8877 • I-295 Exit 37A go E .3 mile on US-360, N .1 mile on Sandy Ln, E .1 mile on Bell Creek Rd
✪		✓			Midlothian • 12200 Chattanooga Plz, 23112 • 804-744-8437 • I-95 Exit 62 take SR-288 NW 12.6 miles then Warbro Rd N .1 mile
✪		✓			Midlothian • 900 Walmart Way, 23113 • 804-378-9001 • I-64 Exit 175 take SR-288 S 11.4 miles then US-60 E 3.7 miles & N at Walmart Way
✪	1	✓			Newport News • 12401 Jefferson Ave, 23602 • 757-874-4434 • I-64 Exit 255 take SR-143 W .9 mile
✪	4			✓	Newport News • 6111 Jefferson Ave, 23605 • 757-637-4205 • I-64 Exit 263A go 3.4 miles SW on US-258 then right on Jefferson Ave
✪	2	✓			Norfolk • 1170 N Military Hwy, 23502 • 757-461-6330 • I-64 Exit 281 follow Military Hwy S 1.3 miles (or from I-264 Exit 13B go N 1.3 miles on Military Hwy)
✪	1	✓			Norfolk • 7530 Tidewater Dr, 23505 • 757-480-0587 • I-64 Exit 277B merge onto Tidewater Dr NE .7 mile
✪		✓			Norton • 780 Commonwealth Dr, 24273 • 276-679-7327 • 2 miles northeast of town via US-23 at SR-657
✪					Onley • 26036 Lankford Hwy, 23418 • 757-302-4089 • .5 mile southwest of town center on US-13/Lankford Hwy
✪		✓			Pearisburg • 160 Kinter Way, 24134 • 540-921-1204 • Jct US-460 & US-460 BR (E of town) go W on US-460 BR 1 mile & N on Kinter Way
✪	2	✓			Petersburg • 3500 S Crater Rd, 23805 • 804-957-6444 • I-95 Exit 48B take Wagner Rd W .4 mile & Crater Rd/US-301 S .7 mile
✪	1	✓			Portsmouth • 1098 Fredrick Blvd, 23707 • 757-399-1795 • I-264 Exit 5 take US-17 N 1 mile
✪		✓			Pounding Mill • 13320 G C Peery Hwy, 24637 • 276-596-9706 • Jct SR-16 ALT & US-460/US-19 (NE of town) take US-460/US-19 SW 7.7 miles
✪		✓			Powhatan • 1950 Anderson Hwy, 23139 • 804-464-9887 • 9 miles east of town center along US-60
✪		✓			Richmond • 2501 Sheila Ln, 23225 • 804-320-6991 • I-95 Exit 67 take SR-150 NW 10.8 miles then Forest Hill Ave W .2 mile & Sheila Ln S .2 mile

☆	⬭	🕐	⛽	🚫	Store Details
✪	1	✓			Richmond • 7901 Brook Rd, 23227 • 804-553-8432 • I-95 Exit 83B go W .4 mile on SR-73/Parham Rd then S .2 mile on US-1/Brook Rd
✪	2	✓			Richmond • 1504 N Parham Rd, 23229 • 804-270-6034 • I-64 Exit 181 take Parham Rd S 1.6 miles
✪	1				Richmond • 6920 Forest Ave, 23230 • 804-288-1279 • I-64 Exit 183 (westbound travelers use Exit 183A) go S .3 mile on Glenside Dr then E .2 mile on Forest Ave
✪	6	✓			Roanoke • 4524 Challenger Ave, 24012 • 540-977-3745 • I-81 Exit 150A take US-220 S 5.1 miles & US-221 S .7 mile
✪	1	✓	◆		Roanoke • 4807 Valley View Blvd NW, 24012 • 540-265-5600 • I-581 Exit 3E take SR-101 E .4 mile then Valley View Blvd S .6 mile
✪		✓		✓	Roanoke • 5350 Clearbrook Village Ln, 24014 • 540-772-3892 • I-81 Exit 143 follow I-581/US-220 S 12.6 miles
✪		✓			Rocky Mount • 550 Old Franklin Tpk, 24151 • 540-484-1002 • Jct SR-122 & SR-40 (NE of town) go E on SR-40 for 4.8 miles
✪		✓			Ruckersville • 135 Stoneridge Dr, 22968 • 434-990-6013 • I-64 Exit 118B go N 14 miles on US-29 then W .2 mile on US-33
✪	1	✓			Salem • 1851 W Main St, 24153 • 540-375-2919 • I-81 Exit 137 take SR-112 S .4 mile & US-11/US-460 E .4 mile
✪		✓			South Boston • 3471 Old Halifax Rd, 24592 • 434-575-0680 • Jct US-501 & SR-129 (NW of town) take SR-129 E .4 mile
✪	1	✓		✓	South Hill • 315 Furr St, 23970 • 434-447-3610 • I-85 Exit 12A take US-58 E .1 mile
✪	1				Stafford • 217 Garrisonville Rd, 22554 • 540-720-0059 • I-95 Exit 143B take SR-610 W 1 mile
✪	1	✓			Staunton • 1028 Richmond Ave, 24401 • 540-886-8566 • I-81 Exit 222 take US-250 W 1 mile
✪		✓		✓	Sterling • 45415 Dulles Crossing Plz, 20166 • 571-434-9434 • I-66 Exit 53 go N 12.5 miles on SR-28, E .4 mile on Severn Way, N .2 mile on Atlantic Blvd
✪		✓			Stuart • 19265 Jeb Stuart Hwy, 24171 • 276-694-2520 • 2 miles east of town along US-58
✪		✓	◆		Suffolk • 1200 N Main St, 23434 • 757-925-0224 • I-664 Exit 13A take US-460 W 5.8 miles then follow US-460 BR 4 miles & N on Main St .7 mile

☆	🛡	🕐	⛽	🚫	Store Details
✪	1	✓		✓	Suffolk • 6259 College Dr, 23435 • 757-483-8860 • I-664 Exit 8B take SR-135 S .2 mile
✪		✓			Tappahannock • 1660 Tappahannock Blvd, 22560 • 804-443-1188 • Jct US-360 & US-17 (S of town) take US-360/US-17 N .8 mile
✪	2	✓		✓	Vienna • 1500B Cornerside Blvd, 22182 • 571-623-3300 • I-495 Exit 47A go W 2 miles on SR-7/Leesburg Pike
✪	1	✓			Virginia Beach • 657 Phoenix Dr, 23452 • 757-498-9633 • I-264 Exit 19A go S .7 mile on Lynnhaven Pkwy, W on Guardian Ln, and S .1 mile on Phoenix Dr
✪	8	✓		✓	Virginia Beach • 1149 Nimmo Pkwy, 23456 • 757-430-1836 • I-264 Exit 20 follow 1st Colonial Rd/SR-615 S 4.2 miles, continue on SR-615 S 2.4 miles & E at Nimmo Pkwy .5 mile
✪	6	✓			Virginia Beach • 2021 Lynnhaven Pkwy, 23456 • 757-416-3480 • I-264 Exit 19A follow SR-414 S 5.1 miles
✪	1	✓			Virginia Beach • 4821 Virginia Beach Blvd, 23462 • 757-278-2004 • I-264 Exit 17B go N .4 mile on Independence Blvd then W .2 mile on Columbus St
✪					Warrenton • 700 James Madison Hwy, 20186 • 540-341-3568 • 1.5 miles south of town center along James Madison Hwy
✪	1	✓			Waynesboro • 116 Lucy Ln, 22980 • 540-932-2500 • I-64 Exit 94 take US-340 N .4 mile
✪	2	✓		✓	Williamsburg • 731 E Rochambeau Dr, 23188 • 757-220-2772 • I-64 Exit 234 take SR-199 E .8 mile & Rochambeau Dr E .3 mile
✪	1	✓			Winchester • 2300 S Pleasant Valley Rd, 22601 • 540-667-9111 • I-81 Exit 313B take US-50 W .3 mile then Pleasant Valley Rd S .6 mile
✪	5	✓			Winchester • 201 Maranto Manor Dr, 22602 • 540-868-5076 • I-81 Exit 307 go E 1.2 miles on SR-277 then N 1.4 miles on Warrior Dr then E 1.7 miles on Tasker Rd
✪	5	✓			Winchester • 501 Walmart Dr, 22603 • 540-545-8730 • I-81 Exit 317 take SR-37 S 4 miles, US-50 W .3 mile & Echo Ln N
✪	2	✓		✓	Woodbridge • 14000 Worth Ave, 22192 • 703-497-2590 • I-95 Exit 158B follow Prince William Pkwy W 1 mile then go S at Worth Ave .3 mile
✪	1	✓			Woodstock • 461 W Reservoir Rd, 22664 • 540-459-9229 • I-81 Exit 283 take SR-42 E .3 mile

☆	🛡	🕐	⛽	🚫	Store Details
✪	1	✓			Wytheville • 345 Commonwealth Dr, 24382 • 276-228-2190 • I-81 Exit 70 take US-21 S .1 mile then W on Commonwealth Dr
✪	3	✓	◆		Yorktown • 2601 George Washington Mem Hwy, 23693 • 757-867-8004 • I-64 Exit 258B merge onto US-17 N 2.5 miles

WASHINGTON

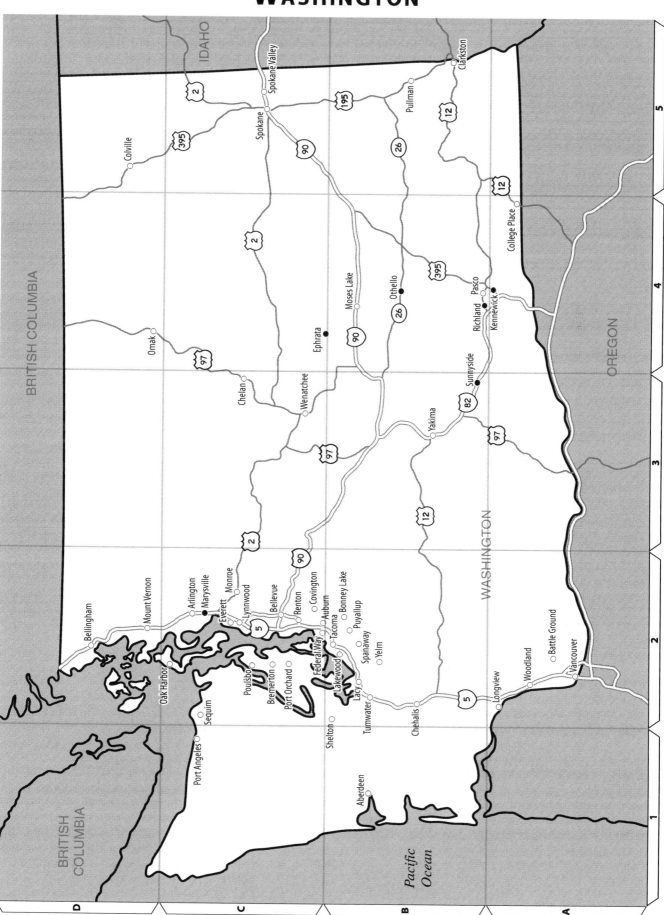

☆	🛡	🕐	⛽	🚫	Store Details
●		✓			Aberdeen • 909 E Wishkah St, 98520 • 360-532-7595 • About .5 mile east of town center along US-12
●	1	✓			Arlington • 4010 172nd St NE, 98223 • 360-386-4608 • I-5 Exit 206 go E .6 mile on SR-531
●	6	✓		✓	Auburn • 762 Supermall Way SW, 98001 • 253-735-1855 • I-5 Exit 142A follow SR-18 E for 3.8 miles then go S .5 mile on C St, W .4 mile on 15th St, and N .4 mile on Supermall Way
●	7	✓			Battle Ground • 1201 SW 13th Ave, 98604 • 360-723-9004 • I-5 Exit 11 go E 5.4 miles on SR-502 then S .7 mile on 20th Ave and E .5 mile on Scotton Way
☆	1			✓	Bellevue • 12620 SE 41st Pl, 98006 • 425-201-7543 • I-405 Exit 10 go E .3 mile on Coal Creek Pkwy then N .4 mile on 124th Ave
☆	2			✓	Bellingham • 4420 Meridian St, 98226 • 360-647-1400 • I-5 Exit 256, go N on SR-539 for 1.2 miles, then E on Stuart Rd .2 mile
●		✓			Bonney Lake • 19205 WA Hwy 410 E, 98391 • 253-826-9144 • I-5 Exit 127, go E 12 miles on SR-512, N .4 mile on SR-167, E 5.4 miles on SR-410
☆					Bremerton • 6797 WA Hwy 303 NE, 98311 • 360-698-2889 • 4.2 miles north of town center via SR-303
●	1	✓			Chehalis • 1601 NW Louisiana Ave, 98532 • 360-748-1240 • I-5 Exit 79, west of exit
●		✓		✓	Chelan • 108 Apple Blossom Dr, 98816 • 509-682-4291 • 1.3 miles east of town center via US-97-ALT
●					Clarkston • 306 5th St, 99403 • 509-758-8532 • In town .2 mile north of US-12 and 5th St intersection
●		✓			College Place • 1700 SE Meadowbrook Blvd, 99324 • 509-525-3468 • From Walla Walla, S on SR-125 (9th St) for 3.3 miles, then W on SE Meadowbrook
●		✓			Colville • 810 North Hwy, 99114 • 509-684-3209 • From Jct SR-20 & US-395 go S on US-395 for 9.6 miles
☆				✓	Covington • 17432 SE 270th Pl, 98042 • 253-630-7791 • I-5 Exit 142A follow SR-18 NE for 11.4 miles, 272nd St/SR-516 E .4 mile, N at 172nd Ave and E on 270th Pl
●		✓	◆		Ephrata • 1399 Southeast Blvd, 98823 • 509-754-8837 • I-90 Exit 151 take SR-283 NE for 14.8 miles, N on SR-28 for 4.5 miles, E on SR-282 for 1 mile
☆	2			✓	Everett • 11400 Highway 99, 98204 • 425-923-1740 • I-5 Exit 186 go W .8 mile on 128th St; continue .7 mile on Airport Rd; go N .4 mile on Evergreen Way

☆	🛡	🕐	⛽	🚫	Store Details
●	1	✓		✓	Everett • 1605 SE Everett Mall Way, 98208 • 425-789-3361 • Northbound travelers use I-5 Exit 189 and turn left onto SR-527 for .5 mile to Everett Mall Way and turn left; Southbound travelers use I-5 Exit 189 and follow signs for Everett Mall Way
☆	1			✓	Federal Way • 1900 S 314th St, 98003 • 253-941-9974 • I-5 Exit 143 go W on 320th St for .5 mile, N on 20th Ave for .4 mile, W at 314th St
●	1	✓		✓	Federal Way • 34520 16th Ave S, 98003 • 253-835-4965 • I-5 Exit 142B take SR-18 W for .3 mile then N at 16th Ave S
●	3	✓	❖	✓	Kennewick • 2720 S Quillan St, 99337 • 509-586-1554 • I-82 Exit 113 go N on US-395 for 2 miles, E on W 27th Ave for .1 mile, S at South Quillan St
●	1	✓			Lacey • 1401 Galaxy Dr NE, 98516 • 360-456-6550 • I-5 Exit 111 follow signs for Marvin Rd/SR-510 E for .5 mile then S at Galaxy Dr
●	3	✓		✓	Lakewood • 7001 Bridgeport Way W, 98499 • 253-513-0949 • I-5 Exit 129 go W on 74th St for 2.4 miles, W on 75th St .3 mile then N on Bridgeport Way .3 mile
●	3	✓			Longview • 540 7th Ave, 98632 • 360-414-9656 • I-5 Exit 36 go W 2.5 miles on SR-432 then S .3 mile on SR-411/3rd Ave
●	4				Longview • 3715 Ocean Beach Hwy 2, 98632 • 360-355-3016 • I-5 Exit 39 go W 3.4 miles on SR-4
☆	1			✓	Lynnwood • 1400 164th St SW, 98087 • 425-741-9445 • I-5 Exit 183 go E on 164th St SW for .5 mile
●	4	✓		✓	Marysville • 8713 64th St NE, 98270 • 360-386-3004 • I-5 Exit 199 go E 3.3 miles on SR-528
●	1	✓	◆	✓	Marysville • 8924 Quilceda Blvd, 98271 • 360-657-1192 • I-5 Exit 200, west of exit
●		✓			Monroe • 19191 N Kelsey St, 98272 • 360-365-4033 • About 1 mile north of town center and US-2 via Chain Lake Rd and Kelsey St
●	4	✓			Moses Lake • 1005 N Stratford Rd, 98837 • 509-765-8979 • I-90 Exit 179 go NW on SR-17 for 3.6 miles then S on Stratford Rd for .2 mile
●	1	✓		✓	Mount Vernon • 2301 Freeway Dr, 98273 • 360-428-7000 • I-5 Exit 227 go W .1 mile on College Way then N .4 mile on Freeway Dr
☆					Oak Harbor • 1250 SW Erie St, 98277 • 360-279-0665 • From town center go W .7 mile on Pioneer Way and SR-20 then go N .1 mile on Erie St

☆	🛡	🕐	⛽	🚫	Store Details
●		✓			Omak • 902 Engh Rd, 98841 • 509-826-6002 • From town travel NE on US-97 for 2 miles, E on Sandflat Rd for .3 mile, S on Vista Vu Dr for .5 mile, E on Engh Rd
●		✓	◆		Othello • 1860 E Main St, 99344 • 509-488-9295 • 1.2 miles east of town center on Main St/SR-24
●	1	✓			Pasco • 4820 N Rd 68, 99301 • 509-543-7934 • I-182 Exit 9 go N on Road 68 for .5 mile
●		✓			Port Angeles • 3411 E Kolonels Way, 98362 • 360-452-1244 • Off US-101 about 3.5 miles east of town center
●		✓			Port Orchard • 3497 Bethel Rd SE, 98366 • 360-874-9060 • From town center go E .5 mile on Bay St then S 1.8 miles on Bethel Ave
●		✓			Poulsbo • 21200 Olhava Way NW, 98370 • 360-697-3670 • From town center go N 1 mile on Front St, W .9 mile on Lindvig Way/Flinn Hill Rd, then N .3 mile on Olhava Way; near SR-3/SR-305 jct
●		✓			Pullman • 1690 SE Harvest Dr, 99163 • 509-334-2990 • From town center go S 1.2 miles on SR-27/Grand Ave then E .3 mile on Bishop Blvd
●	10	✓			Puyallup • 310 31st Ave SE, 98374 • 253-770-4399 • I-5 Exit 127 go E on SR-512 for 8.7 miles to SR-161 exit; E on 31st Ave; N on Meridian; and E on 31st Ave
●		✓			Puyallup • 16502 Meridian E, 98375 • 253-446-1741 • I-5 Exit 127 take SR-512 E for 8.7 miles then SR-161 (Meridian) S for 3.1 miles
☆	1			✓	Renton • 743 Rainier Ave S, 98057 • 425-227-0407 • I-405 Exit 2 go N on Rainier Ave for .5 mile
●	1	✓	❖		Richland • 2801 Duportail St, 99352 • 509-628-8420 • I-182 Exit 3B go N on Queensgate Dr for .2 mile then E on Duportail
●		✓			Sequim • 1110 W Washington St, 98382 • 360-683-9346 • 1.4 miles west of town center via Washington St
●		✓			Shelton • 100 E Wallace Kneeland Blvd, 98584 • 360-427-6226 • 2 miles northwest of town off US-101 at Wallace Kneeland Blvd
●	9	✓			Spanaway • 20307 Mountain Hwy E, 98387 • 253-846-6008 • I-5 Exit 127 take SR-512 E for 2.1 miles then SR-7 S for 6.1 miles
☆	6				Spokane • 2301 W Wellesley Ave, 99205 • 509-327-0404 • I-90 Exit 281 go N on US-2 for 3.2 miles then W on W Wellesley for 2.5 miles
●	7	✓		✓	Spokane • 9212 N Colton St, 99218 • 509-464-2173 • I-90 Exit 281 go N on US-2/US-395 for 5.8 miles, E at Magnesium Rd and N at Colton St for .4 mile
●	4	✓			Spokane • 1221 S Hayford Rd, 99224 • 509-459-0602 • I-90 Exit 277B go W 3.7 miles on US-2 then N .1 mile on Hayford Rd
●	1	✓			Spokane Valley • 15727 E Broadway Ave, 99037 • 509-922-8868 • I-90 Exit 291B go S .4 mile on Sullivan Rd then E .2 mile on Broadway Ave
●	1	✓			Spokane Valley • 5025 E Sprague Ave, 99212 • 509-795-3491 • I-90 Exit 283B go N .2 mile on Freya St then E .7 mile on Sprague Ave
●	1	✓	❖		Sunnyside • 2675 E Lincoln Ave, 98944 • 509-839-7339 • I-82 Exit 69 take SR-241 N for .4 mile then E at Yakima Valley Hospital for .4 mile, N on Lincoln
●	1			✓	Tacoma • 1965 S Union Ave, 98405 • 253-414-9526 • I-5 Exit 132 go W .7 mile on SR-16 then N .3 mile on Union Ave
●	1	✓		✓	Tumwater • 5900 Littlerock Rd SW, 98512 • 360-350-6019 • I-5 Exit 102 go W .3 mile on Trosper Rd then S .3 mile on Littlerock Rd
●	1	✓		✓	Vancouver • 221E NE 104th Ave, 98664 • 360-885-0734 • I-205 Exit 28 go W on Mill Plain Blvd for .8 mile then N on 104th Ave
☆	1			✓	Vancouver • 9000 NE Hwy 99, 98665 • 360-571-0300 • I-5 Exit 4 go NE on 78th St & N at SR-99 for .7 mile
●	3	✓	◆		Vancouver • 14505 NE Fourth Plain Blvd, 98682 • 360-258-2654 • I-205 Exit 30B go E 1.2 miles on SR-500 then continue E 1.4 miles on Fourth Plain Blvd
●	4	✓		✓	Vancouver • 430 SE 192nd Ave, 98683 • 360-256-0109 • I-205 Exit 28 go E on Mill Plain Blvd for 3 miles, E on Southeast 1st St for .9 mile then S on Southeast 192nd Ave
●		✓			Wenatchee • 2000 N Wenatchee Ave, 98801 • 509-664-2448 • 3.2 miles northwest of town center via SR-285
●	1			✓	Woodland • 1486 Dike Access Rd, 98674 • 360-841-9131 • I-5 Exit 22, west of exit
●	1	✓			Yakima • 1600 E Chestnut Ave, 98901 • 509-248-3448 • I-82 Exit 33 go E .3 mile on Yakima Ave/Terrace Heights Dr then S .1 mile on 17th St
●	7	✓			Yakima • 6600 W Nob Hill Blvd, 98908 • 509-966-0478 • I-82 Exit 34 go W 7 miles on Nob Hill Blvd
●		✓			Yelm • 17100 State Hwy 507 SE, 98597 • 360-400-8050 • 1.6 miles southeast of town center via SR-507

WEST VIRGINIA

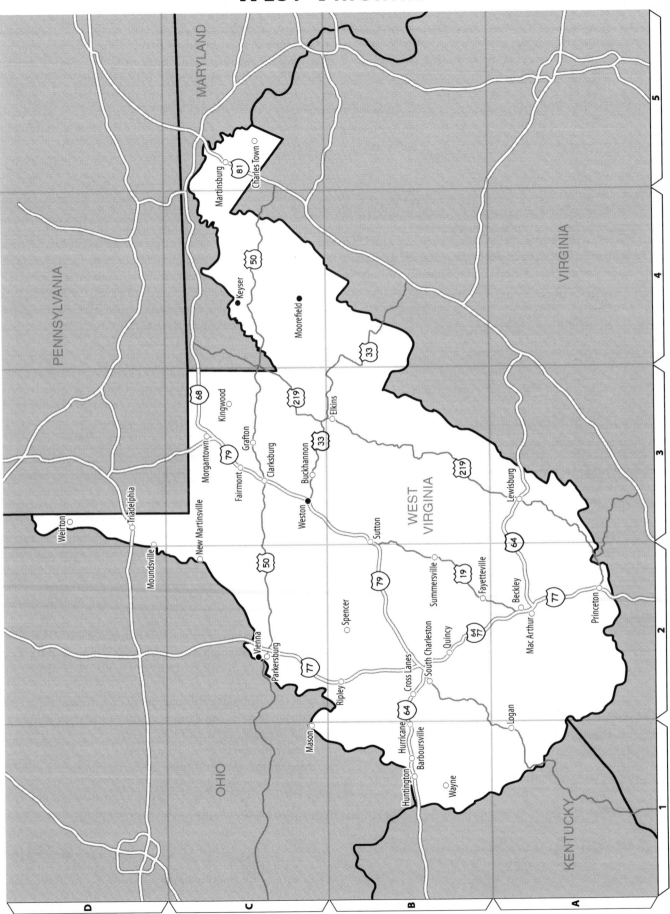

☆	◯	🕐	⛽	🚫	Store Details
✪	1	✓			Barboursville • 25 Nichols Dr, 25504 • 304-733-0789 • I-64 Exit 20 go N on E Mall Rd for .4 mile, then E on Melody Farms Rd
✪	4	✓			Beckley • 1330 N Eisenhower Dr, 25801 • 304-255-7800 • I-64 Exit 124 take US-19 N for 3.6 miles
✪		✓			Buckhannon • 100 Buckhannon Crossroads, 26201 • 304-472-2589 • I-79 Exit 99 take US-33 E for 12 miles
✪		✓			Charles Town • 96 Patrick Henry Way, 25414 • 304-728-2720 • I-81 Exit 5 go E on SR-51 for 12.4 miles, then N on US-340 BR for 1 mile
✪	1	✓			Clarksburg • 550 Emily Dr, 26301 • 304-622-1954 • I-79 Exit 119 go E on US-50 for .5 mile, S on Emily
✪	1	✓			Cross Lanes • 100 Nitro Market Pl, 25143 • 304-769-0100 • I-64 Exit 47A go S .2 mile on Golf Mountain Rd, W .4 mile on Lakeview Dr, S .2 mile on Nitro Blvd
✪		✓			Elkins • 721 Beverly Pike, 26241 • 304-636-2138 • 2.2 miles south of town center via US-219/US-250
✪	1	✓			Fairmont • 32 Tygart Mall Loop, 26554 • 304-366-0444 • I-79 Exit 132 go E on US-250 (Fairmont Ave) for .5 mile then left at the mall
✪		✓			Fayetteville • 204 Town Center Rd, 25840 • 304-574-1086 • 2.2 miles south of town via US-19
✪		✓			Grafton • 1 Walmart Ln, 26354 • 304-265-6294 • 2.7 miles northeast of town center via US-119
✪	1	✓			Huntington • 3333 US Hwy 60, 25705 • 304-525-8889 • I-64 Exit 15 go .5 mile W on US-60/Midland Trail
✪	1	✓			Hurricane • 167 Progress Way, 25526 • 304-562-0475 • I-64 Exit 34, north of exit
✪		✓	❖		Keyser • RR 4 Box 82, 26726 • 304-788-8160 • 3.4 miles southwest of town center via US-220
✪		✓			Kingwood • 100 Walmart Dr, 26537 • 304-329-4020 • 3 miles west of town center via SR-7
✪	1	✓			Lewisburg • 520 N Jefferson St, 24901 • 304-645-5280 • I-64 Exit 169, south of exit
✪		✓			Logan • 77 Norman Morgan Blvd, 25601 • 304-752-7391 • 4 miles west of town center along US-119
✪	1	✓			Mac Arthur • 1881 Robert C Byrd Dr, 25873 • 304-256-6480 • I-64/I-77 Exit 42, south of exit about .7 mile
✪	1	✓		✓	Martinsburg • 800 Foxcroft Ave, 25401 • 304-263-6061 • I-81 Exit 13 go .3 mile on CR-15 then S on Foxcroft
✪	1	✓			Martinsburg • 5680 Hammonds Mill Rd, 25404 • 304-274-5176 • I-81 Exit 20, east of exit
✪		✓			Mason • 320 Mallard Lane, 25260 • 304-773-9125 • .7 mile south of town center via SR-62
✪		✓	◆		Moorefield • 11 Harness Rd, 26836 • 304-538-3490 • 1.8 miles north of town center via US-220
✪	1	✓			Morgantown • 6051 University Town Centre Dr, 26501 • 304-598-3239 • I-79 Exit 155 go E .4 mile on Chaplin Hill Rd/Osage Rd then S 1 mile on University Town Centre Blvd
✪	2	✓			Morgantown • 215 Four H Camp Rd, 26508 • 304-292-4786 • I-68 Exit 1 go S on US-119 for .3 mile the W on CR-7 for 1.2 miles
✪	10	✓			Moundsville • 10 Walmart Dr, 26041 • 304-843-1580 • I-470 Exit 1 take SR-2 S for 9.5 miles
✪		✓			New Martinsville • 1142 S Bridge St, 26155 • 304-455-6522 • 1 mile north of town off SR-2 (3rd St) at Russell Ave
✪	4	✓			Parkersburg • 2900 Pike St, 26101 • 304-489-1905 • I-77 Exit 170 go NW on SR-14 for 3.4 miles
✪	1	✓		✓	Princeton • 201 Greasy Ridge Rd, 24740 • 304-431-2100 • I-77 Exit 9 take US-460 E for .3 mile, then S on Greasy Rideg Rd
✪	2	✓			Quincy • 1001 Warrior Way, 25015 • 304-220-3001 • I-77 Exit 85 go N .5 mile on Lopez Bridge/Quincy Dock Rd then W 1.1 miles on US-60 and S .3 mile on Warrior Way
✪	1	✓			Ripley • 200 Academy Dr, 25271 • 304-372-4482 • I-77 Exit 138 go E .2 mile on US-33 then N .5 mile on Accademy Dr
✪	4	✓			South Charleston • 2700 Mountaineer Blvd, 25309 • 304-746-1720 • I-64 Exit 54 follow SR-601 S 1.6 miles to US-119 and continue 1.8 mile S to Southridge Blvd and turn left
✪		✓			Spencer • 97 Williams Dr, 25276 • 304-927-6920 • .3 mile east of town center off Main St/US-33 at Williams Dr
✪		✓			Summersville • 200 Wal St, 26651 • 304-872-6734 • 3 miles northeast of town center along US-19
✪	1	✓		✓	Sutton • 369 Scotts Fork-Bonnie Rd, 26601 • 304-689-3004 • I-79 Exit 67, west of exit
✪	1	✓			Triadelphia • 450 Stewart Ln, 26059 • 304-547-1726 • I-70 Exit 10 go W .6 mile on Cabela Dr

☆	♡	🕐	⛽	🚭	Store Details
✪	4	✓	◆		Vienna • 701 Grand Central Ave, 26105 • 304-422-3522 • I-79 Exit 179 go W on SR-68 for 3.5 miles, N on Virginia Ave & NW at Murdock Ave
✪	8	✓			Wayne • 100 McGinnis Dr, 25570 • 304-272-3633 • I-64 Exit 8 go S on SR-152 for 7.2 miles, then W on Moore Rd
✪		✓			Weirton • 400 Three Springs Dr, 26062 • 304-723-3445 • 4 miles southeast of town, south of US-22 Exit 4
✪	1		◆		Weston • 110 Berlin Rd, 26452 • 304-269-1549 • I-79 Exit 99 go E on US-33 for .6 mile then N on Berlin Rd

WISCONSIN

☆	⬡	🕐	⛽	🚫⛽	Store Details
✪		✓			Antigo • 200 E State Hwy 64, 54409 • 715-627-1382 • From town center go N 1.6 miles on US-45 then E .2 mile on SR-64
✪		✓			Appleton • 955 Mutual Way, 54913 • 920-954-6300 • US-41 Exit 137 take College Ave W for .5 mile then S at Casaloma Dr
✪		✓			Appleton • 3701 E Calumet St, 54915 • 920-996-0573 • US-41 Exit 134 take SR-441 NE for 6.2 miles then E on Calumet
✪		✓			Ashland • 2500 Lake Shore Dr E, 54806 • 715-682-9699 • 2 miles northeast of town along US-2
✪	8	✓			Baraboo • 920 US Hwy 12, 53913 • 608-356-1765 • I-90/94 Exit 92 take US-12 SE for 7.4 miles
✪		✓		✓	Beaver Dam • 120 Frances Ln, 53916 • 920-887-8900 • 2.9 miles northeast of town center; from US-151 Exit 135 go E .3 mile on Gateway Dr then N .2 mile on Frances Ln
✪	1	✓		✓	Beloit • 2785 Milwaukee Rd, 53511 • 608-362-0057 • I-90 Exit 185A go W on Milwaukee Rd for .4 mile
✪		✓		✓	Berlin • 861 County Road F, 54923 • 920-361-1600 • 2 miles west of town center
✪	3	✓			Black River Falls • 611 WI Hwy 54, 54615 • 715-284-2434 • I-94 Exit 116 go SW on SR-54 for 2.6 miles
✪	4				Brown Deer • 6300 W Brown Deer Rd, 53223 • 414-410-2548 • I-43 Exit 82B go W 3.7 miles on SR-100/Brown Deer Rd
✪		✓		✓	Burlington • 1901 Milwaukee Ave, 53105 • 262-767-9520 • I-43 Exit 29 go E on SR-11 for 11.8 miles & N on Milwaukee Ave for 2 miles
✪		✓			Chilton • 810 S Irish Rd, 53014 • 920-849-9551 • 1.5 miles southeast of town center along US-151 at Irish Rd
✪		✓			Chippewa Falls • 2786 Commercial Blvd, 54729 • 715-738-2254 • I-94 Exit 70 go N on SR-53 for 9.1 miles, N on SR-53 BR for 1 mile & E at Commercial Blvd
✪		✓			De Pere • 1415 Lawrence Dr, 54115 • 920-336-3416 • US-41 Exit 161, go E on Scheiring Rd for .2 mile, then N on Lawrence Dr
✪	1				Delafield • 2863 Heritage Dr, 53018 • 262-646-8858 • I-94 Exit 287 go S on US-83 for .5 mile, then E on Heritage
✪	1	✓			Delavan • 1819 E Geneva St, 53115 • 262-740-1815 • I-43 Exit 21 go W on SR-50 for 1 mile

☆	⬡	🕐	⛽	🚫⛽	Store Details
✪					Dodgeville • 601 E Leffler St, 53533 • 608-935-2723 • From Governor Dodge State Park (north of town) go S on SR-23 for 3 miles, then E on Leffler St
✪	2	✓			Eau Claire • 3915 Gateway Dr, 54701 • 715-834-0733 • I-94 Exit 70 take US-53 N for 1.5 miles to Golf Rd E to Gateway Dr
✪		✓			Fond Du Lac • 377 N Rolling Meadows Dr, 54937 • 920-921-6311 • US-41 Exit 99 go W on SR-23 for .2 mile then N on Rolling Meadows Dr
✪	3	✓			Franklin • 6701 S 27th St, 53132 • 414-761-9560 • I-43 Exit 9 go S on 27th St for 2.6 miles
✪					Germantown • W190 N9855 Appleton Ave, 53022 • 262-255-1285 • US-41 Exit 54 go W on Lannon Rd for .8 mile, then S on Appleton for 1 mile
✪		✓			Green Bay • 2440 W Mason St, 54303 • 920-499-9897 • US-41 Exit 168 take SR-54 W for .6 mile
✪	2	✓			Green Bay • 2292 Main St, 54311 • 920-465-1333 • I-43 Exit 181 go W .6 mile on Manitowoc Rd/Verlin Rd then N .6 mile on Main St
✪	2			✓	Greendale • 5301 S 76th St, 53129 • 414-978-9016 • I-43/894 Exit 7 go S .2 mile on 60th St; W 1 mile on Layton Ave; S .8 mile on 76th St
☆	2	✓		✓	Greenfield • 10600 W Layton Ave, 53228 • 414-529-0455 • I-694 Exit 3 go W .5 mile on Beloit Rd then S 1 mile on 108th St
✪		✓			Hartford • 1220 Thiel St, 53027 • 262-670-5803 • US-41 Exit 64B take SR-60 W 8 miles
✪		✓			Hayward • 15594 State Hwy 77, 54843 • 715-634-8228 • .7 mile northeast of town center, east of US-63/SR-77 jct
☆	1				Hudson • 2222 Crest View Dr, 54016 • 715-386-1101 • I-94 Exit 2 go S on Carmichael for .1 mile, then W on Crest View
✪	1	✓		✓	Janesville • 3800 Deerfield Dr, 53546 • 608-754-7800 • I-39/I-90 Exit 171A, east of highway
✪	8	✓			Jefferson • 1520 S Main St, 53549 • 920-674-2258 • I-94 Exit 267 go S 7.6 miles on SR-26
✪	5	✓			Kenosha • 3500 Brumback Blvd, 53144 • 262-652-1039 • I-94 Exit 342 go E 3.6 miles on SR-158/52nd St then N 1.2 miles on SR-31/Green Bay Rd
✪	8	✓			La Crosse • 4622 Mormon Coulee Rd, 54601 • 608-788-1870 • I-90 Exit 3 go S on SR-35 for 7.8 miles

☆	◌	🕐	⛽	Ⓢ	Store Details
✪		✓			Ladysmith • 800 W 10th St S, 54848 • 715-532-2039 • From town center go W .5 mile on US-8, S .7 mile on SR-27, W .2 mile on College Ave
✪	9	✓			Lake Geneva • 201 S Edwards Blvd, 53147 • 262-248-2266 • I-43 Exit 27A take US-12 SE for 8.1 miles (to Exit 330A) then W on SR-50 for .4 mile
✪	1				Madison • 4198 Nakoosa Trl, 53714 • 608-241-8808 • I-39/I-90 Exit 138B go W about 1 mile on SR-30 then US-51 N .3 mile to Commercial Ave and turn right .2 mile to store
☆					Madison • 7202 Watts Rd, 53719 • 608-276-9393 • I-39/I-90 Exit 142A take US-12 W 11.6 miles to Exit 255, S on Gammon Rd .3 mile, W on Watts Rd .3 mile
✪	1	✓			Manitowoc • 4115 Calumet Ave, 54220 • 920-684-4214 • I-43 Exit 149 take US-151 NE for 1 mile
✪		✓			Marinette • 2900 Roosevelt Rd, 54143 • 715-735-5117 • 2.6 miles southwest of town, south of US-41 at Roosevelt Rd
✪		✓			Marshfield • 2001 N Central Ave, 54449 • 715-486-9440 • 1.6 miles northeast of town center via SR-97
✪		✓			Medford • 1010 N 8th St, 54451 • 715-748-9000 • From town center go E .6 mile on SR-64 (Broadway Ave) then go N .6 mile on SR-13 (8th St)
✪	1	✓			Menomonie • 180 Cedar Falls Rd, 54751 • 715-235-6565 • I-94 Exit 41, go N on Broadway .2 mile then E on Cedar Falls Rd
✪		✓			Merrill • 505 S Pine Ridge Ave, 54452 • 715-536-2414 • US-51 Exit 208 at SR-64, west of exit
✪	1			✓	Milwaukee • 401 E Capitol Dr, 53212 • 414-967-7804 • I-43 Exit 76A go E on Capitol Dr for .9 mile
✪	2				Milwaukee • 3355 S 27th St, 53215 • 414-383-1113 • I-43 Exit 9 go N on 27th St for 1.6 miles
✪	7				Milwaukee • 10330 W Silver Spring Dr, 53225 • 414-355-0892 • I-43 Exit 78 go W on Silver Spring Dr for 6.2 miles
✪		✓		✓	Minocqua • 8760 Northridge Way, 54548 • 715-356-1609 • From town center go N 1.3 miles on US-51 then W .8 mile on SR-70
✪	4	✓			Monona • 2151 Royal Ave, 53713 • 608-226-0913 • I-39/I-90 Exit 142A follow US-12/US-18 W 3.5 miles to Exit 264 then go S .1 mile on Towne Dr and left onto Royal Ave
✪					Monroe • 300 6th Ave W, 53566 • 608-325-7701 • 2 miles west of town center off SR-11 at 6th Ave

☆	◌	🕐	⛽	Ⓢ	Store Details
✪	1	✓			Mukwonago • 250 Wolf Run, 53149 • 262-363-7500 • I-43 Exit 43 go SE on SR-83 for .3 mile, then N on Wolf Run
✪	2	✓			Muskego • W159 S6530 Moorland Rd, 53150 • 414-209-0317 • I-43 Exit 57 go S 1.8 miles on Moorland Rd
✪		✓			Neenah • 1155 W Winneconne Ave, 54956 • 920-722-0782 • US-41 Exit 131 go E on Winneconne Ave .6 mile
✪	1			✓	New Berlin • 15205 W Greenfield Ave, 53151 • 262-796-1620 • I-94 Exit 301A go S .5 mile on Moorland Rd then E .2 mile on SR-59/Greenfield Ave
☆					New London • 1717 N Shawano St, 54961 • 920-982-7525 • 1.5 miles north of town via US-45-BR
✪		✓			New Richmond • 250 W Richmond Way, 54017 • 715-246-5509 • I-94 Exit 10 follow SR-65 N 10.8 miles then go W .1 mile on Richmond Way
✪	1	✓			Onalaska • 3107 Market Pl, 54650 • 608-781-8282 • I-90 Exit 5 take SR-16 NE for .5 mile
✪		✓			Oshkosh • 351 S Washburn St, 54904 • 920-231-1575 • US-41 Exit 117 take W 9th Ave for .2 mile then N at Washburn
☆	3			✓	Pewaukee • 411 Pewaukee Rd, 53072 • 262-695-1847 • I-94 Exit 294 go N on Pewaukee Rd 2.7 miles
✪		✓			Platteville • 1800 Progressive Pkwy, 53818 • 608-348-4888 • 2 miles east of town at US-151 Exit 21, west of exit
✪	1	✓			Plover • 250 Crossroads Dr, 54467 • 715-345-7855 • I-39 Exit 156 go E on CR-HH for .2 mile then S on Cross-roads Dr
✪	10	✓			Plymouth • 428 Walton Dr, 53073 • 920-892-7523 • I-43 Exit 126 take SR-23 W for 8.9 miles, SR-57 S for .4 mile
✪	1	✓			Portage • 2950 New Pinery Rd, 53901 • 608-742-1432 • I-39 Exit 92 take US-51 S for 1 mile
✪		✓			Prairie Du Chien • 38020 US Hwy 18, 53821 • 608-326-2408 • 3 miles south of town center along US-18
✪		✓			Rhinelander • 2121 Lincoln St, 54501 • 715-362-8550 • From Jct US-8 & SR-17 (W of town) take US-8 E for .7 mile & US-8 BR for 2.9 miles
✪		✓			Rice Lake • 2501 West Ave, 54868 • 715-234-6990 • US-53 Exit 143 take SR-48 W for .2 mile then S on West Ave
✪		✓			Richland Center • 2401 US Hwy 14 E, 53581 • 608-647-7141 • From Jct SR-60 & US-14 (in Gotham) take US-14 NE for 7.4 miles

☆	🛡	🕐	⛽	🚫	Store Details
✪		✓			Saint Croix Falls • 2212 Glacier Dr, 54024 • 715-483-1399 • 3 miles east of town via US-8
✪	1	✓			Saukville • 825 E Green Bay Ave, 53080 • 262-284-9616 • I-43 Exit 96, east of exit
✪		✓			Shawano • 1244 E Green Bay St, 54166 • 715-524-5980 • 1.4 miles east of town center; from SR-29 Exit 225 go N 2 miles on SR-22 then E 1.4 miles on Green Bay St
✪	1	✓			Sheboygan • 3711 S Taylor Dr, 53081 • 920-459-9300 • I-43 Exit 123 go E .2 mile then S at Taylor Rd
✪	1	✓		✓	Sheboygan • 4433 Vanguard Dr, 53083 • 920-459-9410 • I-43 Exit 128, west of exit
✪	4	✓		✓	South Milwaukee • 222 N Chicago Ave, 53172 • 414-501-1121 • I-94 Exit 319 go E 3.8 miles on College Ave then S .2 mile on Chicago Ave
✪	2	✓			Sparta • 1600 W Wisconsin St, 54656 • 608-269-7501 • I-90 Exit 25 take SR-27 N for 1.4 miles then W at SR-16 for .6 mile
☆	8				Stoughton • 1800 US Hwy 51, 53589 • 608-873-5453 • I-39/I-90 Exit 156 take US-51 W for 7.9 miles
✪					Sturgeon Bay • 1536 Egg Harbor Rd, 54235 • 920-746-0402 • 1.3 miles northeast of town center on Egg Harbor Rd
✪	5	✓			Sturtevant • 3049 S Oakes Rd, 53177 • 262-598-8702 • I-94 Exit 335 go E 4.4 miles on Durand Ave/SR-11
✪	4	✓			Sun Prairie • 1905 McCoy Rd, 53590 • 608-837-6339 • I-39/90 Exit 135 follow US-151 N 3.3 miles to Exit 101 then E .2 mile on Main St
✪	6	✓			Superior • 3705 Tower Ave, 54880 • 715-392-6060 • I-35 (in Minnesota) Exit 253A take US-2 E for 2.7 miles, N at Belknap St for .7 mile & E on Tower Ave for 1.8 miles
✪	1	✓			Tomah • 222 W McCoy Blvd, 54660 • 608-372-7900 • I-94 Exit 143, west of exit
✪		✓			Viroqua • 1133 N Main St, 54665 • 608-637-8511 • .8 mile north of town center on Main St (US-14/US-61)
✪	9	✓			Watertown • 1901 Market Way, 53094 • 920-261-7270 • I-94 Exit 267 take SR-26 N for 7.8 miles, E on SR-19 for .6 mile
✪	6	✓		✓	Waukesha • 2000 S West Ave, 53189 • 262-521-1815 • I-43 Exit 50 go N 4.7 miles on SR-164 then W .4 mile on SR-59
✪	1	✓			Wausau • 4300 Rib Mountain Dr, 54401 • 715-359-2282 • I-39 Exit 188 go E on Rib Mountain Dr for .6 mile

☆	🛡	🕐	⛽	🚫	Store Details
✪		✓		✓	West Bend • 1515 W Paradise Dr, 53095 • 262-334-5760 • From Jct US-41 & US-45 go N on US-45 for 9.7 miles then W on Paradise Dr for .4 mile
✪	2	✓		✓	West Milwaukee • 4140 W Greenfield Ave, 53215 • 414-978-2004 • I-94 Exit 308B go S 1 mile on Miller Park Way then E .1 mile on Greenfield Ave
✪					Whitewater • 1362 W Main St, 53190 • 262-473-7744 • 1.4 miles west of town center via Main St
✪	1	✓		✓	Wisconsin Dells • 130 Commerce St, 53965 • 608-253-3490 • I-90/I-94 Exit 89 take SR-23 W for .2 mile
✪		✓			Wisconsin Rapids • 4331 8th St S, 54494 • 715-423-1900 • 3 miles south of town center along SR-3

WYOMING

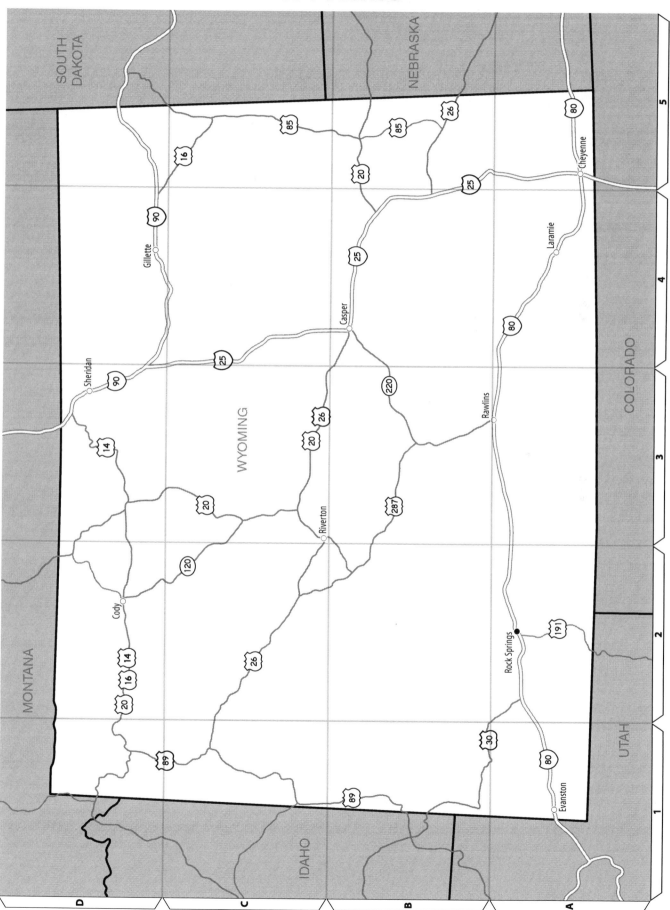

☆	◌	⏱	⛽	🚭	Store Details
✪	4	✓			Casper • 4255 Cy Ave, 82604 • 307-232-9593 • I-25 Exit 188B take SR-220 SW for 1.6 miles, S on Cy Ave 2.4 miles
✪	1	✓			Casper • 4400 E 2nd St, 82609 • 307-237-0991 • I-25 Exit 185 go S on SR-258 for .4 mile, E on 2nd St
✪	1	✓			Cheyenne • 580 Livingston Ave, 82007 • 307-823-6810 • I-80 Exit 364, north of exit
✪	5	✓		✓	Cheyenne • 2032 Dell Range Blvd, 82009 • 307-632-4330 • I-80 Exit 364 go N on SR-212 for 2.5 miles, W at Dell Range Rd for 1.6 miles
✪		✓			Cody • 321 Yellowstone Ave, 82414 • 307-527-4673 • 2.2 miles west of town center via Yellowstone Ave (US-14/US-16/US-20)
✪	1	✓			Evanston • 125 N 2nd St, 82930 • 307-789-0010 • I-80 Exit 5 go NW on Front St .3 mile, S on 2nd St
✪	1	✓			Gillette • 2300 S Douglas Hwy, 82718 • 307-686-4060 • I-90 Exit 126 take SR-59 S for .3 mile
✪	1	✓			Laramie • 4308 E Grand Ave, 82070 • 307-745-6100 • I-80 Exit 316 go N on Grand Ave for 1 mile
✪	1	✓			Rawlins • 2390 E Cedar St, 82301 • 307-417-3001 • I-80 Exit 215, north of exit
✪		✓			Riverton • 1733 N Federal Blvd, 82501 • 307-856-3261 • 1.3 miles north of town center on Federal Blvd (US-26)
✪	1	✓	◆		Rock Springs • 201 Gateway Blvd, 82901 • 307-362-1957 • I-80 Exit 102 go E on Dewar Dr for .5 mile, then N at Gateway Blvd
✪	1	✓			Sheridan • 1695 Coffeen Ave, 82801 • 307-674-6492 • I-90 Exit 25 take US-14 W for .3 mile then N on Coffeen for .5 mile

Made in the USA
San Bernardino, CA
19 October 2018